Understanding Economics

Leaving Certificate

Richard Delaney

Edco

Contents

Introduction

This book is a result of a detailed study and analysis of the requirements of the Leaving Certificate economics syllabus and of past examination papers for both Ordinary and Higher level students. It has a threefold aim, to introduce students to the essential concepts used in economics, to demystify the terminology used in the subject and to prepare students for the type of questions which they can expect to encounter in the Leaving Certificate examination.

Each topic is introduced in simple but precise language. All basic definitions are highlighted throughout the chapters and each chapter gives a summary of the essential points which the student should know. Graduated questions are given in each chapter, which are suitable for both the Ordinary and the Higher level papers. There is also a linked reference to a separate extensive chapter on past Leaving Certificate questions and suggested answers.

Included is a glossary covering a wide range of terms used in economics and which have appeared on Leaving Certificate examinations. This is of great benefit to the students for quick revision and for Section A questions.

Students are guided through many of the proofs of laws and theories which are required in the examination. These include very simple arithmetical proofs of the Principle of Equi-Marginal Utility (The Law of Equi-Marginal Returns) and The Law of Comparative Advantage.

All the latest macro-economic measures are included in the text. These include the modern terminology used in government finances and the latest method in the preparation and presentation of the government's budget.

Along with the traditional role of the government in the economy there is also detailed information on The National Development Plan, 2007–13; The National Spatial Strategy; and Transport 21.

The book includes the new format for the presentation of *The National Income Statistics* introduced by the CSO in August 2007, which brings Ireland in line with the European System of Accounts (ESA). An explanation of the phenomenon of 'sub-prime lending' is also included.

Chapters 1 and 2 serve as a general introduction to economics and economic systems. The microeconomics section of the course is covered in Chapters 3–16. The Factor Markets are dealt with in Chapters 26–30, and the remaining chapters cover the macroeconomics section of the course. Note: Chapter 14 and Chapter 16 may not be suitable for students sitting the Ordinary level paper.

Chapter 1
An Introduction to Economics

Economics

When it was coming close to your Junior Certificate examination people advised you to use your limited study time wisely, to set targets (aims) and decide how much time you should devote to each subject to get the best possible results.

That is what economics is all about!

There are many items we want to purchase, but the income available to us to purchase them is limited. Likewise, there are many items we want to produce, but the resources available to us are limited, e.g. raw materials. Therefore, we have to make choices in order to get the best value from our income when we buy items. We also have to make choices to get the best use of the limited resources available to us when we produce items.

Definition of economics

Economics is a **social science** which studies human behaviour in relation to people's **aims** and the **scarce resources** available to them to achieve these aims, knowing that the resources have alternative uses.

Let us now analyse this definition.

According to *The Chambers Dictionary* **science** is 'knowledge ascertained by observation and experiment, critically tested and brought under general principles'.

Economists acquire knowledge in many different ways and then by using deductive and inductive (see p. 6) reasoning they state various laws and principles. Thus economics is a science and because it deals with human behaviour it is a **social science**.

However, unlike other sciences such as physics and chemistry, the laws in economics are not constant as the conditions to which the laws apply are constantly changing. For example, people's incomes are constantly changing and new and better technology is always being developed. Thus the laws and principles in economics are dynamic.

The **aims** mentioned in the definition refer to those goods and services which people require from an economy. These aims are subdivided into **needs** and **wants**.

⁕Needs

Definition of needs

Needs are the essentials that are required for survival in life. These are basic food, basic clothing and basic shelter.

If we have these we can survive. In our economy we take these essential needs for granted. However, you must remember that Ireland, according to the International Monetary Fund figures, has the fifth highest purchasing power per head of population in the world. Elsewhere, a large proportion of the world's population has an income below the subsistence level.

Fig 1.1 The basic essentials

⁕Wants

Definition of wants

Wants are anything in excess of our needs. Examples of wants include items such as TVs, designer clothes, cars and holidays. The list is infinite.

Any given society determines its own needs and wants. Economists examine these needs and wants and then advise society how best to attain them. From this we say that economics is a neutral science. Economists deal with given facts and not what 'ought' to be.

The **scarce resources** mentioned in the definition refer to the **factors of production**.

The goods and services which we produce are referred to as **wealth**. Thus wealth is a stock of goods and services.

Fig 1.2 A holiday is an example of a want

The Factors of Production

Definition of the factors of production

The factors of production are those resources which we use to produce wealth.

Example

When a new production business is established the construction of a new factory will need land on which to build it. Bricks, cement and timbers are needed to create the structure. Labour is required to put all of these together. JCBs and cement mixers aid the labourers' activities and somebody must coordinate all the work, put up the money for all of this and bear the risk if the new business is not financially successful. All of these are examples of factors of production.

We require a tremendous amount of resources to produce any product. Try making a list of all the resources which had to be used to make your desk and the chair on which you are sitting!

For convenience purposes these factors of production are divided into four categories or groups called **land**, **labour**, **capital** and **enterprise**.

✳Land

Definition of land

Land is anything provided by nature which helps to create wealth.

In the example above, this is the land on which the factory is built, but it is also the timber used in the building, as this too is provided by nature. Other examples of land in the economic sense are the sea, oil, gas and even climate.

Land has two distinctive characteristics:

1. Land is fixed in supply, i.e. mankind cannot increase or decrease the supply of land. We can change the nature of it and its usefulness. Today, we generally acknowledge that while land is fixed in supply some of the items regarded as land are not renewable. When we use oil in our home-heating system we change its nature into ash and gas and these cannot be reconverted into oil.

2. Because it is provided by nature land has no cost of production, i.e. it does not cost mankind anything to bring it into existence.

✳Labour

Definition of labour

Labour is any human effort which helps to create wealth.

In the example above, labour includes the bricklayers, the electricians and the architects.

✳Capital

Definition of capital

Capital is anything made by man, which is then used to help create wealth.

In the example above, the JCBs used to dig the land and the cement mixers are all capital. In fact, the finished factory is also capital, because it is something man-made which is then used to produce some other product.

Other examples of capital include computers, roads and tractors, as these are all made by man and then used to produce other goods and services.

Another way of understanding capital is to define it as wealth used in the creation of more wealth.

✻Enterprise

Definition of enterprise

Enterprise (or organisation) is that special human activity which organises the other factors of production and bears the risk involved in production.

In the example on p. 2, the people who coordinate the building of the factory and put up the money to finance it are the entrepreneurs, i.e. the providers of enterprise.

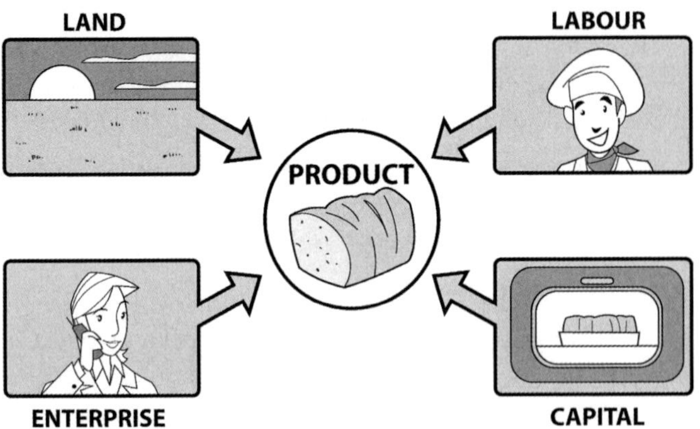

Fig 1.3 The factors of production used in producing bread

Factors of production can be used for many different purposes. For example, the piece of land on which your school was built could have been used as a farm, or it could have been used to provide a playground, or it could have been used as a site for houses. But it could have been used only for one of these purposes at a time. Thus **factors of production have alternative uses**.

There are not enough factors of production available to produce all of our needs and wants. This is why we say that they are **scarce**. Therefore, we must make choices when deciding which goods to produce.

Because we have to make choices there is an **opportunity cost** involved in the production and consumption of most goods.

✻Opportunity cost

Definition of opportunity cost

Opportunity cost is the item which you must do without when you have to make a choice between two items which you want to purchase or produce.

For example, if you have only €20 and you want to purchase two different items which cost €20 each, e.g. a DVD and a €20 Top-Up on your mobile phone, you must make a choice. The opportunity cost of the purchase is the item which **you do not purchase**. If you purchase the Top-Up then the DVD is the opportunity cost of the transaction. The €20 paid for the Top-Up is **the financial cost**. The same concept applies to a producer of goods.

✻Externalities

Definition of externalities

The decisions we make also create **externalities**. An externality is the unintended side effect of a calculated decision to do something.

For example, if a new major production factory is located in your area then it may cause air pollution and traffic congestion. On the other hand, the local county council may receive extra revenue in the form of rates, and so may be able to provide better local amenities for the people of the area.

Let us now distinguish between two commonly used terms: wealth and income.

Wealth and Income

Definition of wealth

Wealth is a stock of goods and services, i.e. goods which you have accumulated, e.g. a car, a house or a computer.

Definition of income

Income is a flow of goods and services, i.e. it is possible to have a very high standard of living and to spend all your earnings and have nothing left to show for that spending.

You could spend all your earnings on food, electricity, rent, and a good social life and have nothing left over. You have had the use (flow) of goods and services but you have no wealth.

Remember that wealth and income constitute only part of our overall welfare. It also comprises the state of our health, degree of happiness and the social conditions under which we live.

The Aims of Economics

1. **To achieve the efficient use of scarce resources** (i.e. the factors of production) which are available to society in order to satisfy as many of society's needs and wants as possible.

2. **To achieve an equitable distribution of wealth**. In modern economies, this means rewarding people in proportion to the contribution they make to the creation of wealth, while at the same time providing an income for those people who cannot provide one for themselves.

3. **To create stability in an economy**. This is an attempt to avoid the cycle of booms and slumps in the performance of an economy.

Microeconomics

Microeconomics deals with **individual units** in economics and the interaction between them, e.g. the individual consumer, the individual household and the individual firm. It deals with supply and demand, showing how many goods will be produced and consumed at given market prices at given times.

Macroeconomics

Macroeconomics is the study of the entire economy in broad total terms, e.g. the total income in the economy, the total level of employment, the total amount of production.

Deductive reasoning

Deductive reasoning means drawing conclusions from generally held principles, i.e. drawing conclusions from the general to the particular. For example, it is a widely held principle that countries import more goods when their national incomes increase. Therefore, we conclude that imports into Ireland will increase when its national income increases.

Inductive reasoning

Inductive reasoning means drawing conclusions from observing many particular situations, i.e. drawing conclusions from the particular to the general. For example, a study was undertaken of 1,000 retail shops and it was observed that when the prices of goods were increased in these shops the quantity of goods sold in these shops fell. Thus we conclude that demand falls when prices increase. This of course assumes that no other factor, which influences demand, changes at that time. Hence the term frequently used in economics, *ceteris paribus*, i.e. other things being equal.

LEARN THE KEY POINTS

1. Definition of economics
2. Definitions of needs and wants
3. Definitions of land, labour, capital and enterprise
4. Understand why the factors of production are regarded as scarce resources
5. Definition of opportunity cost
6. Definition of externalities
7. Definitions of wealth and income
8. Know the three basic aims of economics
9. Know the distinction between macroeconomics and microeconomics
10. Know the difference between inductive and deductive reasoning

Notes about the Exam

✳The importance of definitions

The Leaving Certificate examination paper in economics is divided into two sections. Section A is made up of nine short questions which require one or two sentence answers. These are, mostly, based on basic definitions and formulae which you learn throughout the course of your study of economics. You must answer six of these questions. They carry a total of 100 marks out of the entire 400 marks to be gained in the examination.

Section B is made up of eight 'full type' questions of which four must be answered. Most of these questions have subdivisions and included in many of these subdivisions are definition type questions. Thus very many more marks can be picked up for simple definitions. In a previous Higher Level paper (Section B), 65 marks were available for definitions if you answered questions 3, 4, 5 and 7. Thus if you scored 100 marks in Section A and also correctly answered only the definitions mentioned in questions 3, 4, 5 and 7 in Section B you would have obtained a total of 165 marks. You require 160 marks to pass the paper, i.e. a D3.

From this point of view the Leaving Certificate examination in economics is one of the fairest examinations. However, it must be emphasised that accuracy and clarity are required in these definitions.

At the conclusion of each chapter there is a list of key points which you need to know. Most of these should be treated as definition type questions.

The number of questions set at the end of each chapter reflects the depth of knowledge and understanding required of the particular topic and the frequency of their occurrence in the Leaving Certificate examination.

Chapter 33, Exam Questions and Answers, includes many past Leaving Certificate questions and sample answers. A reference is given on the Questions box at the conclusion of most chapters, starting at chapter 5, indicating which Leaving Certificate questions and sample answers are relevant to that chapter. The sample answers are a guideline to answering the questions. These answers are suggestions and are not the exclusively correct answers, i.e. there may be alternative answers which are also acceptable.

Copy questions 1–5 into your answer book and complete each of the sentences by filling in the blank spaces.

1 Economics is a __________ science as it deals with __________ behaviour.

2 Capital is anything __________ by man which helps in the production of __________.

3 Basic food is an example of __________.

4 Labour is regarded as a __________ as it is one of the items used in the production of wealth.

5 Macroeconomics is the study of __________ whereas microeconomics deals with __________.

6 Why is economics regarded as a science?

7 Why are the laws in economics regarded as being dynamic laws?

8 'Economics is a science of choice.' Justify this statement.

9 Why is economics regarded as a neutral science?

10 Michael O'Reilly won €250,000 in the Lotto. He decided to set up his own economics consultancy business and invest his winnings in the business. In order to do this he must rent an office, equip it with computers, hire computer program analysts, hire temporary cleaning staff, purchase reams of paper on which to print his reports and purchase a car to enable him to travel around the country to meet with his clients, all of whom run their own businesses. Identify a minimum of two of each of the factors of production which are involved in this operation. Justify each of your answers.

11 Before Michael O'Reilly set up this business he was employed by another firm and was earning a wage of €1,000 per week. Identify two opportunity costs to Michael of setting up his own business.

12 Michael's decision to set up his own business creates a number of externalities. Identify some of these.

13 Explain briefly why an individual who earns €700 per week may be wealthier than an individual who earns €2,000 per week.

14 Give your own examples to distinguish between inductive and deductive reasoning.

15 Distinguish between wealth and welfare.

Chapter 2
Economic Systems

Throughout history different tribes and societies organised their economic affairs in a manner suited to their own needs. However, as nations evolved and national governments were formed more official economic systems were developed. These systems vary from free enterprise economies at one extreme to centrally planned economies at the opposite extreme.

All of these systems must answer three questions:

1. What goods are to be produced?
2. How are these goods to be produced?
3. Who is to benefit from the production?

Free Enterprise System

Under the free enterprise system (sometimes referred to as capitalism) all resources are privately owned. This system is based on the theory advocated by Adam Smith (see p. 350) that an economy develops better when individuals are allowed to pursue their own self-interest. He called this 'the invisible hand' of free enterprise. Under this system the government plays no role in purely economic activities.

1. Under this system, producers produce goods which they perceive will be purchased in sufficient quantities to earn a profit from them. Thus they are reacting to consumers' needs and wants. The term 'consumer sovereignty' is often used in this context. This implies that it is the consumer who determines what goods will be created, as the producers will make only those goods which are demanded in sufficient quantities to make them profitable.
2. The producers will produce these goods using the minimum amount of the **factors of production**. This reduces their costs, makes them competitive and helps to improve profit margins.
3. Only those people who supply the factors of production benefit from the production and even then this is determined by their relative contribution to the production process.

Under the theory of this system, the people who could not contribute to production would not earn or receive any income, e.g. the infirm or old people. It is doubtful that a pure free enterprise system exists in any part of the world.

✳For free enterprise

People who are in favour of free enterprise claim that the competitive nature of this system leads to the efficient use of the scarce resources. It gives consumers freedom of choice, as firms will produce any goods which are demanded in sufficient quantities to make them profitable.

✳Against free enterprise

People who argue against free enterprise claim that it leads to an uneven distribution of wealth. The lack of government regulation of the economy leads to exploitation of labour and enormous social costs such as destruction of the landscape and air pollution.

Those who argue against free enterprise claim that it leads to an uneven distribution of wealth

Centrally Planned Systems or Command Systems

Under the centrally planned system, advocated by Karl Marx and Vladimir Lenin, all resources are publicly owned. This system claims public ownership of the means of production. Government control of all areas of economic activity is essential in order to eliminate the inequalities of the distribution of wealth. Therefore, a central authority, usually a government, controls all economic activity.

1. Central planners determine the assortment of goods to be produced.
2. The central planners allocate resources for the production of goods, fix the quantities of the goods to be produced and also set the price of these goods.
3. The benefits of production are allocated according to the social needs of individual units such as families, towns and so on.

People who are in favour of a centrally planned economy claim that economic development can be achieved at a much faster rate than in a free enterprise economy. The state (government) can begin building heavy industry in an underdeveloped economy without waiting years for capital to accumulate from profit earned in small industries and without the need for foreign investment.

Critics of the centrally planned economy argue that planners cannot predict consumers' needs and wants and sometimes create shortages of essential items. This was evident in the Soviet Union before the collapse of communism in that country. These critics also claim that the lack of incentive for the individual worker greatly reduces the workers' motivation and thus leads to a lower output per person.

A crowd of shoppers press against a butcher's counter during a food shortage before the collapse of communism in the Soviet Union

Mixed Economies

Somewhere between the two extremes of the purely free enterprise economy and the centrally planned economy is the mixed economy. This type of economy allows most of the major production and distribution decisions to be made by the private sector, but the government intervenes to ensure the supply of essential goods to everybody. From time to time the government is also involved in planning the organisation of the economy and its future development.

✳Indicative planning

The government's involvement is often done through a planning process known as **indicative planning**. Here, the government negotiates collectively with the trade unions, industry representatives, employer representatives, representatives of the unemployed, and farming representatives and comes up with strategies such as national wage agreements and plans for economic development. Examples of these include Towards 2016, The National Development Plan and Transport 21. The various bodies involved in these negotiations are collectively known as **the social partners**.

✳Fiscal policy

The government also influences the economy through its fiscal policy, which is its policy on taxation and government spending.

✳Monetary policy

The economy can also be influenced by monetary policy, i.e. policy on the supply of money, on interest rates and on borrowing. This is controlled by the European Central Bank but implemented in Ireland by our Central Bank.

LEARN THE KEY POINTS

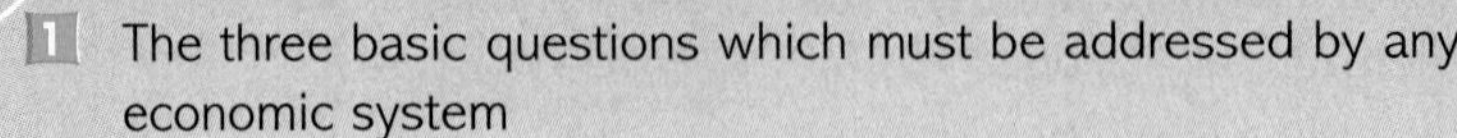

1. The three basic questions which must be addressed by any economic system
2. The distinction between free enterprise, centrally planned and mixed economic systems

Questions

Copy questions 1–5 into your answer book and complete each of the sentences by filling in the blank spaces.

1 In a centrally planned economy all economic decisions are taken by a ____________.

2 In a free enterprise economy producers will produce only those goods for which there is ____________ demand and which are ____________ for the producer.

3 In a mixed economy the government often engages in talks with the ____________ ____________ in order to plan the future ____________ of the economy.

4 The planning referred to in question 3 is known as ____________ planning.

5 Government fiscal policy is concerned with government ____________ and government ____________.

6 Can you identify any advantages which a centrally planned economy may have over a free enterprise economy? Justify your answer.

7 What are the major disadvantages of a centrally planned economy?

8 What is meant by monetary policy? Which body decides our monetary policy and which body is responsible for implementing it in Ireland?

9 Is the Irish economy a free enterprise, a centrally planned or a mixed economy? Give reasons for your answer.

10 What do you understand by the term 'consumer sovereignty'?

11 Do you think consumer sovereignty is an adequate explanation of the goods which are produced in the free market economies? Give reasons for your answer.

Chapter 3
The Market Mechanism

The Market Price

Definition of market price

The **market price** of a product is the price at which that product is currently selling.

Many people assume that the selling price of a product is determined by adding the cost of producing that product to a mark up for profit for the producer. If this were the case then no new businesses would fail! On the other hand, it cost the artist, Picasso, very little to produce his paintings, but today you may have to pay millions of euros for one of them!

Before going any further let us clarify two terms: supply and demand.

Supply and demand

Definition of supply

When we speak of the **supply of a product** we mean the number of units of that product which producers are willing to make available for sale at any given price at any given time.

Definition of demand

When we speak of **the demand for a product** we mean the number of units of that product which people are willing to purchase at any given price at any given time.

In a free enterprise economy the price of any product is ultimately determined by the market mechanism. This is the interaction between the supply of and the demand for that product. It is the price which brings about an equal supply of and demand for a product. It is often called the 'market price' or 'the equilibrium price'.

1 The market price (or simply the price) of a product will **go up if the demand for it is greater than its supply**.

The demand for a good is greater than the supply of a good when people want to buy more units of it than there are available for sale at the current market price.

In this situation, people will compete with each other to get the limited number available thus driving up its price. Think of an auction.

Fig 3.1 An auction

2 The market price of a product will **go down if the supply of it is greater than its demand**.

The supply of a good is greater than the demand for it when people want to buy less units of it than there are available for sale at the current market price.

In this case, the seller will reduce the price to dispose of all the surplus goods. Think of 'Sales' in a clothes shop at the end of a season.

3 People (consumers) tend to buy more units of a product at a low price than at a high price, as the product gives them better value for money at the low price.

Therefore, as the price of a product goes down consumers tend to buy more units of it and vice versa.

This is normally shown on a demand curve (D) which is a graph showing the number of units of a good which people are willing to purchase at any given market price at any given time.

Fig 3.2 Demand (D) for the product falls from 7 units to 3 units when the price of it is increased from €5 to €10

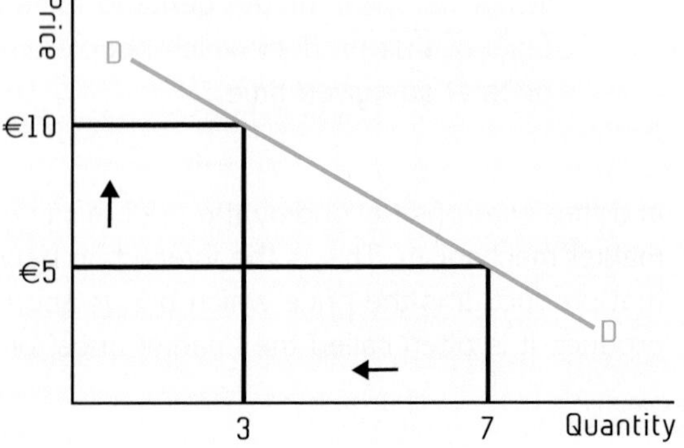

4 As the price of a product goes up producers tend to increase the supply of it as it becomes more profitable to do so.

Therefore, as the price of a product goes up producers tend to supply more units of it and vice versa.

This is normally shown on a supply curve (S) which is a simple graph showing the number of units of a good made available for sale at any given market price at any given time.

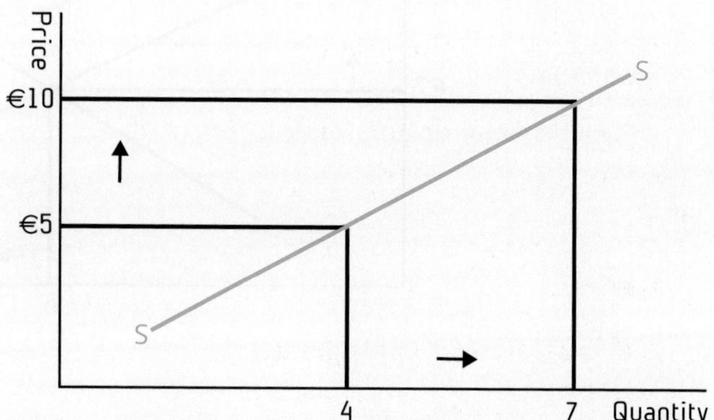

Fig 3.3 The supply (S) of the product went up from 4 to 7 units when the price of it increased from €5 to €10

5 Therefore, when the number of units of a product available for sale (i.e. the supply of it) is equal to the number of units which people want to purchase (i.e. the demand for it), the price will stabilise. This price is the market price.

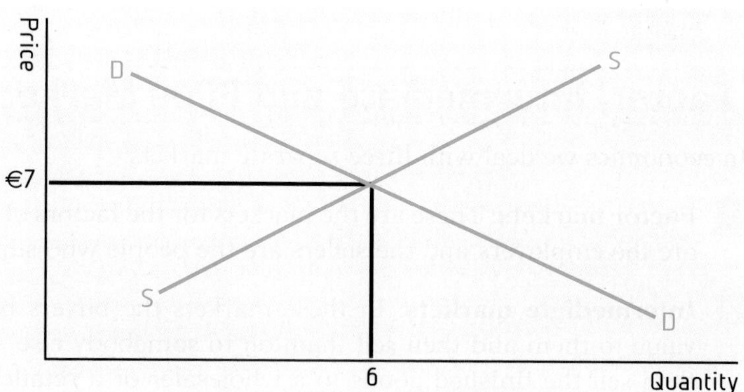

Fig 3.4 When demand is at the level represented by D the demand for and the supply (S) of the product are equal at a quantity of 6 units giving a market price of €7

Effect of a change in demand

However, if the demand increased, i.e. if consumers were willing to buy more of the good at any given price, to the level represented by D2 on Fig 3.5, and supply remained at the same level, then the demand for and the supply of the product would now be equal at a quantity of seven units causing the price to go up to €8.

Fig 3.5 When demand increased and supply remained unchanged the market price increased from €7 to €8

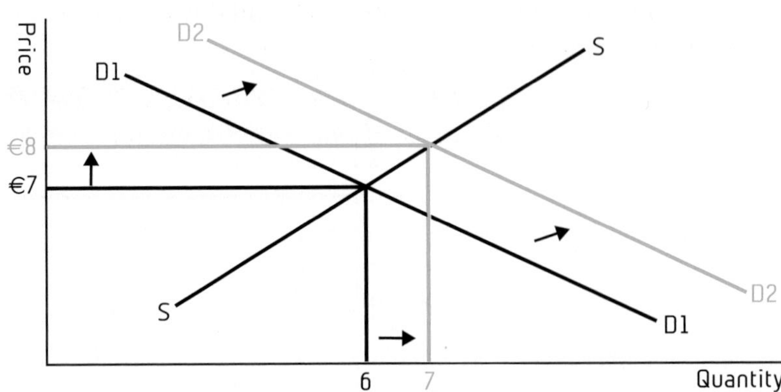

⁕Consumer surplus

If you assume that the market price of a product is €8 but an individual consumer would willingly pay €12 for it, then that consumer has a **consumer surplus** of €4.

Thus **consumer surplus** is the **difference** between the market price of a product and the **higher price** which the consumer would be willing to pay for that product rather than do without it.

Factor, Intermediate and Final Markets

In economics we deal with three separate markets.

1. **Factor markets:** These are the markets for the factors of production. The buyers are the employers and the sellers are the people who supply these factors.
2. **Intermediate markets:** In these markets the buyers buy goods to either add value to them and then sell them on to somebody else, or to process them and then sell the finished goods to a wholesaler or a retailer. For example, when a firm buys raw materials it is buying on the intermediate market.
3. **Final markets:** Here the goods are sold to the final users of them, i.e. the consumers of the goods. This is the market in which we do our daily shopping.

LEARN THE KEY POINTS

1. Definitions of supply and demand
2. Know what is meant by 'the market price'
3. Know how 'the market price' is determined
4. Explain the market mechanism
5. Understand the meaning of consumer surplus
6. Distinguish between factor, intermediate and final markets

Questions

Copy questions 1–5 into your answer book and complete each of the sentences by filling in the blank spaces.

1. In a free enterprise economy the price of any product is determined by the ____________ mechanism.
2. The market mechanism is the interaction of the ____________ of and the ____________ for a product.
3. The equilibrium price of a product is arrived at when the ____________ of and the ____________ for that product are ____________.
4. The supply of a product tends to ____________ when the market price increases because ____________ ____________.
5. Consumer surplus is the ____________ between the ____________ price of a product and the ____________ price which a consumer is willing to pay for it rather than ____________ it.
6. Draw a clearly labelled diagram showing the demand for and supply of a good. Use the label 'P' to show the market price for this good and the label 'Q' to show the quantity demanded and supplied.
7. Repeat the diagram from question 6 and show on it the effect of a decrease in supply, i.e. the supply curve moves to the left of its original position. Now show the new market price (P2), and the new quantity (Q2).
8. Would you expect the price of a product on the intermediate market to be greater than or less than the price of that same product on the final market? Explain your answer.
9. Explain clearly what we mean when we say that 'the supply of a good is greater than the demand for a good'.
10. What is meant by the term 'the equilibrium price'?
11. Under what circumstances could you justify the government intervening in the market mechanism?

Chapter 4
Introduction to Demand

Demand

In everyday language we use the word **demand** to mean that we insist on something.

In economics the word **demand** has a very restricted meaning.

Definition of demand

Demand means the number of units of a good which consumers are willing to purchase at any given market price at any given time.

Demand can be established through market research. Like all statistics this can be presented or displayed in many different forms. The two forms most commonly used in economics to display demand are **demand schedules** and **demand curves**.

Definition of demand schedule

A **demand schedule** is a table showing the demand for a good at any given market price at any given time.

The overall or market demand schedule for a product is the aggregate demand of all the schedules of individual consumers. Thus we could have an individual's demand schedule and a market demand schedule. Assume that there are only two consumers of product X, i.e. Joe and Mary. Their combined demand schedules make up the market demand schedule, see Table 4.1.

Table 4.1 *The market demand schedule for product X*

Price	Joe's demand	Mary's demand	Market demand
€1	20	30	50
€2	18	25	43
€3	16	18	34
€4	14	12	26
€5	12	10	22

Definition of a demand curve

A demand curve is a **graph** showing the demand for a good at any given market price at any given time, see Fig 4.1.

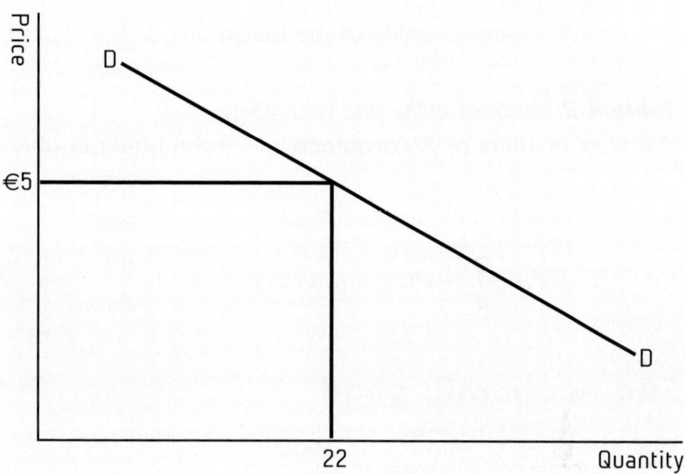

Fig 4.1 The demand curve for product X

Jargon

Every science or profession has its own terminology called jargon. These are words that have a specific meaning within a particular subject. Now let us introduce you to some jargon used in economics.

✳Utility

Definition of utility

Utility is the amount of benefit or satisfaction derived from the consumption of a good.

Two completely separate concepts were used in the defining of utility. If you go to a restaurant for a meal and order a big juicy steak with chips, fried onions and mushrooms you will probably really enjoy eating this meal. Thus you get **satisfaction** from its consumption.

On the other hand, when you visit your doctor he may decide that the most efficient treatment for your ailment is the injection of an antibiotic by means of a large hypodermic needle. You will get **benefit** from the injection, but you will not get any satisfaction from it.

While it is difficult to measure utility we assume that it can be measured by using 'units of utility', more commonly called **utils.**

Definition of marginal utility (MU)

Marginal utility (MU) is the addition to **total utility (TU)** caused by the consumption of one extra unit of a good. Thus if you get a total utility of 53 utils from the consumption of 3 units of a good and your total utility goes up to 64 utils when you consume the fourth unit of that good, then your marginal utility of the fourth unit is 11.

Table 4.2 *Marginal utility and total utility*

Number of units of X consumed	Total utility in utils	Marginal utility in utils
1	20	—
2	38	18
3	53	15
4	64	11

An economic good

Definition of an economic good

An **economic good** is one which commands a price, i.e. a product which people are willing to pay for.

In order for a product to be classified as an economic good it must have **all three** of the following characteristics.

1. **It must give utility:** The consumer must get some benefit or satisfaction from its consumption.
2. **It must be transferable:** The ownership or the benefit of it must be transferable from the seller to the buyer.
3. **It must be scarce in relation to the demand for it:** Would you pay for sand at a sandy beach to make sandcastles?

Assumptions Made about Consumers

When economists give advice, make laws or state theories that concern consumers, then the economists make certain assumptions about the consumers. Economists assert that their laws or theories are based on their belief that these assumptions hold good. There are four basic assumptions made about consumers and their behaviour.

1. **It is assumed that consumers act rationally.**
   For example, if there are two identical products selling at different prices then the consumer will buy the cheaper of the two. Economic theories or laws have to assume this because if people are not acting rationally then there is no point giving them advice and guidance.

2 It is assumed that consumers have limited incomes.
This means that consumers do not have sufficient income to be able to purchase **all** of their wants. Hence the concept of opportunity cost mentioned in Chapter 1.

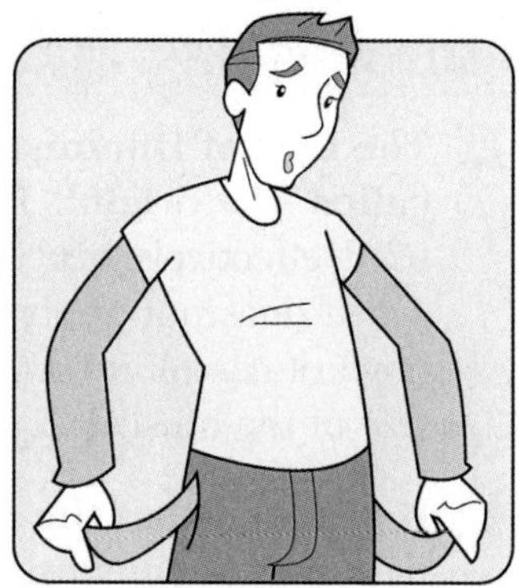

Fig 4.2 *This man has a very limited income!*

3 It is assumed that consumers aim to get the maximum utility from the way they spend their incomes.
As we assume that consumers act rationally it is rational to assume that they will spend their incomes on those goods and services which give them the highest possible utility. In this way, they are getting the best value from their limited incomes.

4 It is assumed that consumers are subject to the Law of Diminishing Marginal Utility.

Definition of the Law of Diminishing Marginal Utility

The law states that as a consumer consumes extra units of a good, then at some stage the **marginal utility** derived from the consumption of that good will decrease.

Let us refer back to the meal in the restaurant. If you went back there again three hours later and ordered the same meal it is highly unlikely that you would get the same satisfaction from it the second time.

The following table highlights this law.

Table 4.3 *An individual's utilities derived from the daily consumption of bars of chocolate*

Quantity	1	2	3	4	5	6	7
Total utility	200	480	770	1,000	1,200	1,380	1,540
Marginal utility		280	290	230	200	180	160

In this example the Law of Diminishing Marginal Utility sets in when the fourth bar is consumed.

Note: By definition MU is the addition to total utility got from the consumption of an **extra** unit of a good. Therefore, the MU of the first item is not **normally** shown as there was no consumption of the good before the first one.

Assumptions Underlying the Law of Diminishing Marginal Utility

1. **The Law of Diminishing Marginal Utility only applies after a certain point called 'the origin'.** The origin is the minimum quantity of a good that can be used effectively and MU does not decrease until this quantity is consumed, e.g. it does not apply after the first spoonful of cornflakes from your morning bowl of cereal; it only applies after the first bowl. (It obviously depends on the size of the bowl!)

2. **It assumes that the total utility of a good is not totally used up before the next unit is consumed.** If you eat a Mars bar today and do not eat another one until a week later then the MU will not decrease as the total utility from the first one is fully used up.

3. **The law assumes that income does not change.** As income rises then MU may not fall as consumption increases.

4. **This law does not apply to addictive goods or to medicines.** With these goods MU may actually increase as consumption increases. For example, if you get a prescription from a doctor for ten tablets you may not get the benefit of that prescription until the tenth tablet is taken.

✳Equilibrium

Definition of equilibrium

In economics the word **equilibrium** means the ideal situation to be in under any given set of circumstances. This is the situation to which consumers and producers aspire.

When consumers are in equilibrium it means that they are getting the maximum possible utility from their income.

The Principle of Equi-Marginal Utility

The Principle of Equi-Marginal Utility is also known as the **Law of Equi-Marginal Returns**. It states that a consumer will be in equilibrium when his/her income is spent in such a way that the ratio of marginal utility (MU) to price (P) is the same for all goods which he/she consumes.

$$\frac{\text{MU of good A}}{\text{P of good A}} = \frac{\text{MU of good B}}{\text{P of good B}} = \frac{\text{MU of good C}}{\text{P of good C}}$$

and so on for all goods consumed.

Proof

Assume that a consumer has an income of €80 per week which he/she spends on two products X and Y which are priced at €20 and €10 respectively.

The utilities derived from each of these goods are seen in Table 4.4. Note that the MU figures for the first items are not normally shown as there was no total utility when consuming a zero quantity.

Note that the maximum number of units of X which this consumer could purchase is 4, i.e. 4 × €20 = €80. Likewise, the maximum number of Y which can be purchased is 8 units, i.e. 8 × €10 = €80

Table 4.4 *Utilities derived from the products X and Y*

Product X			Product Y		
Qty	TU	MU	Qty	TU	MU
1	1,000		1	2,000	
2	1,800	800	2	2,600	600
3	2,500	700	3	3,100	500
4	3,100	600	4	3,500	400
			5	3,800	300
			6	4,000	200
			7	4,100	100
			8	4,150	50

Now let us look at all the possible combinations that the consumer could purchase with the income of €80 and also show the utilities derived from each combination.

Table 4.5 *Combinations*

Possible combinations	Utilities from each product	Combined total utility
4X + 0Y	3,100 + 0	3,100
3X + 2Y	2,500 + 2,600	5,100
2X + 4Y	**1,800 + 3,500**	**5,300**
1X + 6Y	1,000 + 4,000	5,000
0X + 8Y	0 + 4,150	4,150

The combination of 2X + 4Y gives the highest total utility.

The ratio of MU:P of 2X is 800:20 or 40:1
The ratio of MU:P of 4Y is 400:10 or 40:1

This means that each last euro spent on **both** X and Y adds the same extra utility to the consumer's total utility.

Or

The consumer is getting the same value from each last euro spent on this combination.

In an examination situation if you are asked to use your own figures to prove this principle proceed as follows:

Assume that the consumer has a relatively small income, e.g. €80 which is spent on two products, namely X and Y. Ensure that the price of X is twice the price of Y and that both prices are evenly divisible into the income.

(a) **You** pre-decide what combination will give the highest total utility, e.g. 2X + 4Y.

(b) Make up **any** utility figures for X (ensure total utility figures are increasing and MU figures are decreasing).

(c) From the MU figures for product X get the MU of 2X, divide by 2 and put this in as the MU figure for 4Y. Remember that Y is half the price of X.

(d) Next make out utility figures for Y by **starting** with the **MU for 4Y**. Then start working backwards filling in the figures for 3Y, 2Y and 1Y ensuring that the **MU is increasing** as you move backwards.

(e) Then start working forwards from 4Y ensuring that **MU is decreasing** as you move forwards.

LEARN THE KEY POINTS

1. Definitions of demand, a demand schedule and a demand curve
2. Definitions of utility and marginal utility
3. Definition of an economic good and know its characteristics
4. Know the assumptions made about consumers
5. Learn the definition and give the assumptions of the Law of Diminishing Marginal Utility
6. Definition of the Principle of Equi-Marginal Utility (Higher level students should know its proof)

Copy questions 1–9 into your answer book and complete each of the sentences by filling in the blank spaces.

1 Demand is the number __________ a good __________ service that __________ are __________ to purchase at __________ given __________ at __________ time.

2 A demand schedule is a __________ while a demand curve is a __________ showing the demand for a good.

3 Utility is the __________ or __________ which a consumer gets from the __________ of a __________ or service.

4 Marginal utility is the __________ utility got from the __________ of an extra __________ of a good.

5 An economic good is one which consumers are willing __________.

6 The Law of Diminishing Marginal Utility states that as a consumer consumes __________ of a good the __________ derived from the __________ of that good will __________ decrease.

7 The number of units of utility which a consumer receives from the consumption of a good is measured in __________.

8 In economics the word 'equilibrium' refers to the __________ situation to be in under any given __________.

9 A consumer is in equilibrium when he/she spends his/her income in such a way the __________ of Marginal __________ to __________ is the __________ for all goods consumed by the consumer.

10 Explain fully the three characteristics of an economic good.

11 There are three consumers of a given product. Each consumer has his/her own individual demand schedule. Show the three different individual demand schedules at prices €1, €2, €3 and €4. Show how these individual demand schedules are used to compile the market demand schedule for this product.

12 Graph the market demand curve for the figures mentioned in question 11.

13 The table below shows the total utility (TU) and the marginal utility (MU) which a consumer receives as extra units of a good are consumed by that consumer.

Table 4.6

Units consumed	1	2	3	4	5	6	7
TU in units	100	250	550	800	1,020	1,220	1,370
MU in units	100	150	?	?	?	?	?

(a) Fill in the missing figures.

(b) How many units of the good are consumed **before** diminishing marginal utility sets in? Explain your answer. Note: Be careful when answering this type of question as sometimes you may be asked to state the quantity **at** which the law sets in.

14 Explain fully the assumptions governing the Law of Diminishing Marginal Utility.

15 Explain fully the assumptions made in economics concerning consumer behaviour.

16 Explain fully why the total utility that a consumer receives from the increased consumption of a product increases while the marginal utility decreases.

17 A consumer who is in equilibrium purchases 5 units of product X and 10 units of product Y. The price of each unit of X is €10 and the price of each unit of Y is €30. The marginal utility of the fifth unit of X is 30 units. What is the marginal utility of the tenth unit of Y? Explain your answer.

18 A consumer who is in equilibrium purchases 10 units of product X and 10 units of product Y. The price of each unit of X is €10. The marginal utility of the tenth unit of X is 50 units and the marginal utility of the tenth unit of Y is 200 units. What is the price of each unit of Y? Explain your answer.

19 A consumer is in equilibrium and spends his income on two products namely X and Y. The MU of X is 20 units and its price is €5 while the MU of Y is 40 units and its price is €10. Assume that the price of Y decreases to €8. The consumer continues to spend all of his/her income on the two products. This consumer has no desire to change his/her consumption of X. Would you expect the consumer to increase or decrease his/her consumption of Y? Explain your choice. What will be the MU of Y after the changed consumption?

20 A consumer who has an income of €100 per week spends it all on two products, namely product X priced at €20 per unit and product Y which is priced at €10 per unit. Make out your own utility figures for both products to prove that the Principle of Equi-Marginal Utility applies when the consumer purchases 3 units of X and 2 units of Y.

Chapter 5
The Factors Influencing a Consumer's Demand for a Good

We stated in Chapter 3, The Market Mechanism, that consumers tend to buy more of a good when its price goes down and less of it when its price goes up. However, there are many factors that determine the number of units of a good that a consumer buys. These factors are listed below and will be examined in some detail. Note we use the capital letter D to indicate demand.

Factors Governing a Consumer's Demand for a Good

1. The price of the good (P1)
2. The person's income (Y)
3. The price of other goods (Pog)
4. The person's taste (T)

These determine demand for most products on a day-to-day basis.

plus to a lesser degree

5. The price and availability of credit (Cr.)
6. The consumer's expectations about the future (E)
7. Government regulations (G)
8. Unforeseen circumstances (U)

These determine our demand only for some products some of the time.

To summarise it can be said that:

D = f (P1, Y, Pog, T, Cr., E, G, U)

✳ 1 The price of the good (P1)

An increase in the price of a good causes less of that good to be purchased because the consumer is getting less value per euro spent on it.

A decrease in its price causes more of it to be purchased because the consumer is getting more value per euro spent on it.

Note: The statements above assume that no other factors that affect demand have changed at the same time. Remember the term *ceteris paribus*.

When more of a good is purchased as a direct result of a decrease in price, this is called an **extension** in demand.

When less of a good is purchased as a direct result of an increase in price, this is called a **contraction** in demand.

When demand changes as a direct result of a change in the price of the good itself it is called **the substitution effect**. It is always positive in the sense that it will always react in the same way, i.e. P goes up then D goes down and vice versa.

It is often referred to as **a movement along the D curve**.

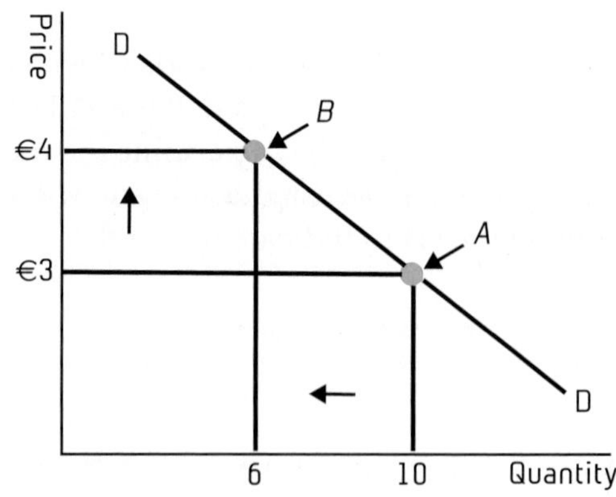

Fig 5.1 *A contraction in D or a movement along a demand curve as D changes from point A to point B on the same D curve*

(Higher level students should see Note 1 at the end of the chapter.)

✳2 The person's income (Y)

When referring to income economists always mean real income, i.e. the purchasing power of money income. This can change when there is any change in the relationship between money income and prices.

Real income will **increase** in any of the following circumstances:

1. Money income remains unchanged and prices decrease.
2. Money income increases and prices remain unchanged.
3. Money income increases at a faster rate than the rate of increase in prices.
4. Money income decreases at a slower rate than the rate of decrease in prices.

Reverse the above to get decreases in real income.

A positive income effect

A positive income effect means that a change in income will cause demand to change in the same direction as the change in income. Thus if income increases demand also increases and if income decreases demand also decreases. This applies to the vast majority of goods in the economy. They are called **normal goods**.

Definition of a normal good

A **normal good** is one which has a positive income effect.

Example

A young person who has just taken up employment for the first time and is on a relatively low income may have to settle for one foreign holiday a year. However, as that person's income increases he or she can now afford to take extra foreign trips abroad each year.

When demand goes up as a result of a change in income it is called an **increase in demand** or **an upward shift in demand**.

When demand goes down as a result of a change in income it is called a **decrease in demand** or **a downward shift in demand**.

A negative income effect

A negative income effect means that a change in income will cause demand to change in the opposite direction to the change in income. Thus when income goes up then demand goes down. This happens with **inferior goods**.

Definition of an inferior good

An **inferior good** is one which has a negative income effect.

Example

A family on a very low income may be forced to eat a lot of cheap staple foods such as bread and rice. However, as the family income increases they can now afford other more luxurious foods and so their demand for bread will decrease as it is sometimes replaced with these other food items. Thus you can see that as the income went up the demand for bread decreased.

It is important to know the difference between an increase in demand and an extension in demand. An increase in demand happens when more of a good is purchased without any change in price, whereas an extension in demand happens when more of a good is purchased as a direct result of a decrease in price. The same distinction is made between a decrease in demand and a contraction in demand.

An increase in demand and a decrease in D are sometimes called a **movement of the D curve**.

Fig 5.2 The diagram represents an increase in demand (or an upward shift in demand) as the demand curve has moved to the right of its original position showing that more units of it will be demanded at any given market price

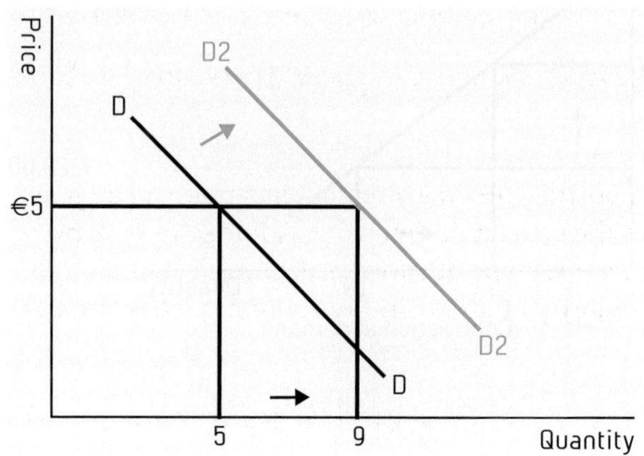

Normal Goods, Inferior Goods and Giffen Goods

1 **Normal goods** have the ordinary reaction to a change in price, i.e. when P goes up D goes down and vice versa. They also have the normal reaction to a change in income, i.e. when income goes up, D also goes up and vice versa.

2 **Inferior goods** have an unusual reaction to a change in income, i.e. when income goes up D goes down and vice versa. (Remember: I for Inferior and I for Income.)

3 **Giffen goods** are very unusual goods that have an unusual reaction to a change in price, i.e. when the price goes up D goes up and vice versa. These apply in situations where necessary expenditure on them takes up a very large percentage of a person's or a family's income. If the price of these products increases then these people may have to forego spending on some other products and spend more on these goods, thus increasing their demand for these goods. The situation normally only applies to people who are on a very low real income. Bread and rice are examples of Giffen goods.

(Higher level students should see Note 2 at the end of the chapter.)

✳3 The price of other goods (Pog)

Substitute goods

Substitute goods are two or more different goods which can be substituted for each other to satisfy any one given need or want, e.g. a Ford car and a similar sized Opel car, tea and coffee, a bus and a train service on the same route.

When the price of a good increases it causes a contraction in the D for that good and an increase in the D for its substitute and vice versa for a price decrease. The D for the two goods changes in the opposite direction.

If we assume that Ford and Opel make two very similar cars then these are substitutes for each other. If the price of the Ford increases it will cause an increase in the demand for the Opel car as it has now become **relatively** cheaper.

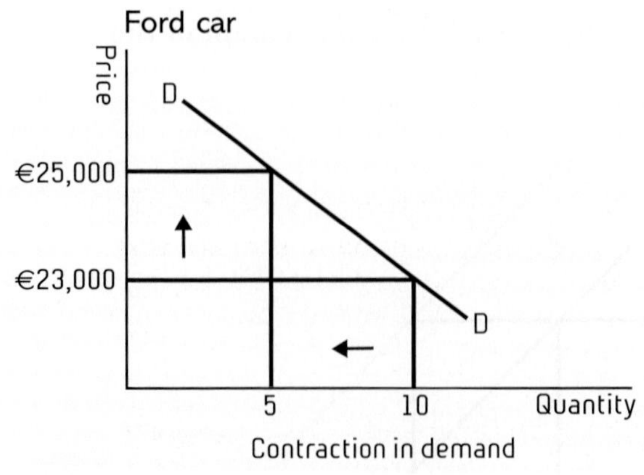

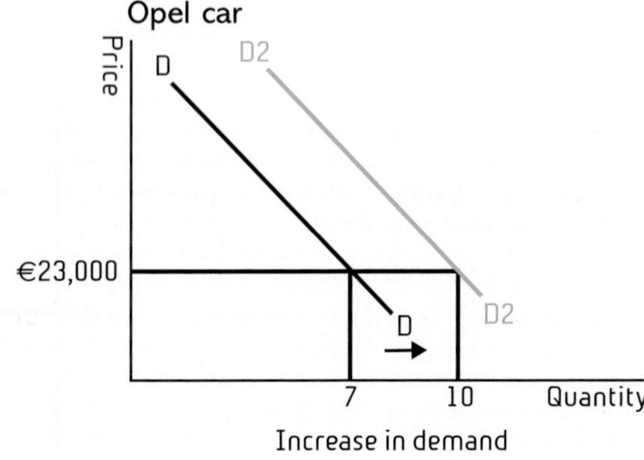

Fig 5.3 Contraction and increase in demand (D)

Complementary goods

Complementary goods are two or more different goods that **must** be purchased together to satisfy any given need or want, e.g. knives and forks. The purchase of two complementary goods is normally regarded as one transaction. Thus if the price of one of the goods changes, it changes the cost or price of the transaction. Therefore, when the price of one of the goods increases it causes a contraction in D for that good and a decrease in the D for its complement. The D for the two goods changes in the same direction.

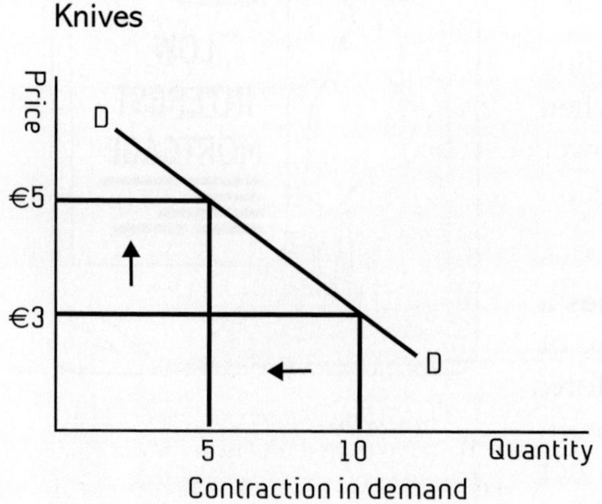

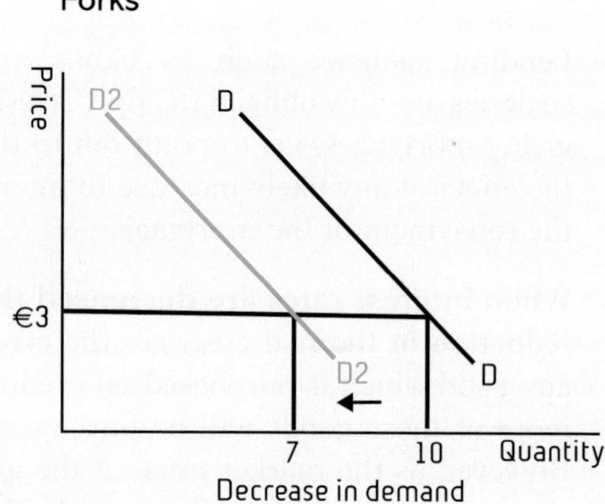

Fig 5.4 Contraction in D and decrease in D

Goods in derived demand

A good is in derived D when it is not demanded for its own direct utility but for the additional utility which it gives to another good, e.g. the D for blocks is derived from the D for buildings.

This works in the same way as complementary goods. If the price of houses decreased this would cause an extension in the D for houses and an increase in the D for blocks.

✻4 The person's taste (T)

Taste reflects the amount of marginal utility derived from the consumption of a good. Thus if we say that a person's taste has changed **in favour of a good** this means that he/she is now getting a greater amount of marginal utility from the consumption of that good. When MU increases and there is no change in price this **causes an increase in D** (remember the Principle of Equi-Marginal Utility).

Conversely a change in taste against a good causes a decrease in the D for that good.

✳5 The price and availability of credit (Cr.)

Some people argue that the availability of loans and changes in interest rates should not be taken as a separate influence on demand. They believe that interest is 'the price of another product', i.e. money. However, the demand for houses and cars in Ireland increased very substantially when interest rates went down in the late 1990s and early 2000s. Thus the increase in the demand cannot be solely credited to a rise in incomes. Also the demand for houses began to decrease towards the end of 2006 and into 2007 as interest rates increased.

Fig 5.5 *Low interest rates cause an increase in demand for expensive consumer durable goods and private capital goods*

Lending agencies such as banks and building societies are now obliged to apply stress tests when giving mortgages, i.e. to point out to the borrower the effect of any likely increase in interest rates on the repayment of the mortgage.

When interest rates are decreased this causes a reduction in the real cost, i.e. the credit price, of any good which is purchased on credit. Therefore, more of these goods will be purchased on credit. However, as the market price of the good has not changed the result is **an increase in D**.

Example

- Cash price of car = €20,000
- Flat rate of interest 10% p.a. over 3 years
- Interest = €6,000
- **Credit price = €26,000**
- New rate of interest = 5% p.a. over 3 years
- Interest = €3,000
- **Credit price = €23,000**

This is normally only associated with expensive consumer durable goods.

Likewise, if credit is not available many people could not afford to purchase certain expensive goods. If monetary policy was changed and more credit was made available in the economy the D for these types of goods would increase.

✳6 The consumers' expectations about the future (E)

Consumers' expectations about the price, or the availability, of a good can cause an increase or a decrease in demand for that good.

If consumers believe that the price of a good, which they consume on a regular basis, may increase in the near future they may increase their purchase of this good before the price increase occurs. In this way, they will be saving money by paying the cheaper price now, rather than the dearer price later.

Example

People may know that next year's coffee harvest is going to be a poor one resulting in a decrease in supply on the world market. This would indicate to them that the price of coffee will increase in the not too distant future. Therefore, they will stock up on the coffee before the price goes up. Thus their **individual** demand for coffee would increase.

Note: Only consumers who have a relatively large income can do this. A person or family requiring all its income for day-to-day expenditure cannot afford to do it. Also the product being stockpiled must be reasonably durable.

Likewise, if people believe that a price increase is the first of many more increases they will also increase their demand for the good. This happens on the stock exchange on a regular basis. Speculators (bulls), will buy up shares when they see the price beginning to increase, in order to sell the shares at a higher price later. Thus as price increases demand also increases, temporarily, leading to a **perverse demand curve** (see p. 35).

Fig 5.6 An example of a perverse D curve

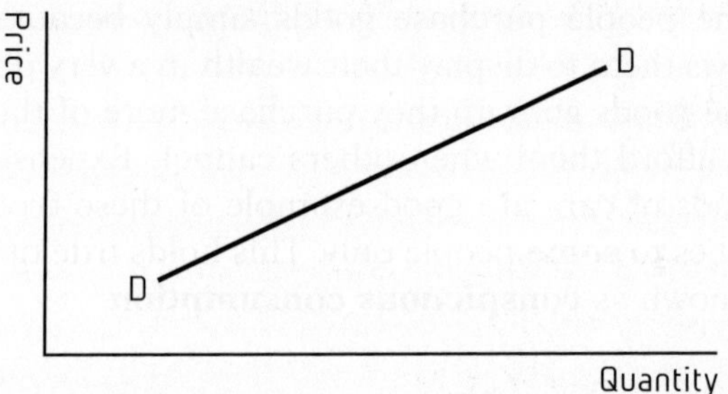

✳ 7 Government regulations (G)

The government can bring in legislation or lay down regulations which can influence the demand for some goods or services. At the time of writing this chapter the government is proposing that all houses will have to be graded based on the quality of insulation in them. This will increase the demand for all insulation materials.

Fig 5.7 An example of a government regulation

Likewise, the government has also introduced regulations banning the sale of cigarettes in packets of ten. This is aimed at reducing the demand for cigarettes as the government believes that young people will not have sufficient funds to purchase the packets of twenty and so will not start to smoke.

✻8 Unforeseen circumstances (U)

Occasionally, circumstances occur which nobody could reasonably be expected to forecast which may cause an increase or a decrease in the demand for a good. For example, if Ireland experienced an unusually long and hot summer this may cause an increase in the demand for sunglasses and a decrease in the demand for home-heating oil.

Note: Remember that an increase in demand is often called an upward shift in demand, while a decrease in demand is often called a downward shift in demand. This arises from the fact that an increase in demand causes the demand curve to shift upwards from its original position. Likewise, a decrease in demand causes the demand curve to shift downwards.

Exceptions to the Law of Demand

From your study so far you can understand that the basic law of demand would state that the demand for a good would go down when its price went up and vice versa. However, there are some exceptions.

1. **Giffen goods**
   These have already been explained, see p. 30.

2. **Goods of ostentatious consumption (snob goods)**
   Some people purchase goods simply because the goods are expensive. This allows them to display their wealth in a very obvious manner. When the price of these goods goes up they purchase more of them to highlight the fact that they can afford them when others cannot. Expensive designer clothing and certain brands of cars are good example of these types of goods. Remember that this applies to **some** people only. This holds true up to a certain price level only. This is known as **conspicuous consumption**.

Fig 5.8 Conspicuous consumption

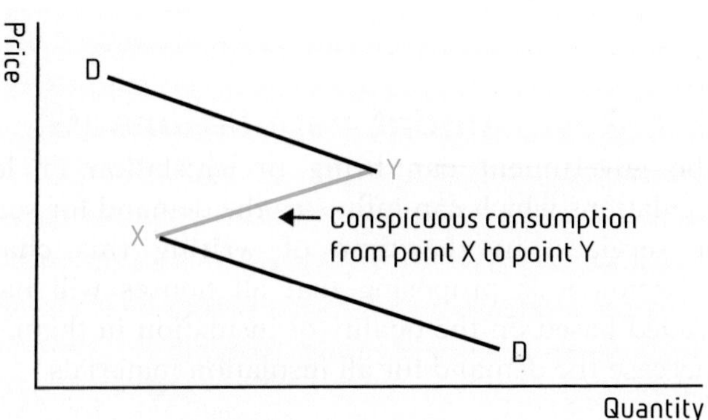

3. **Goods affected by consumers' expectations**
   Sometimes an increase in the price of a product will cause people to increase their purchase of this good as they fear that this price increase is only the first

of many more and they want to purchase as much of the good as possible before it becomes too expensive. These goods have a **perverse D curve**, i.e. the curve slopes upwards from left to right.

✻The paradox of value

Some products have a **high value in use** and **low value in exchange**, whereas other products have a low value in use but a high value in exchange. For example, water has a very high value in use (it is vital), but a low value in exchange, whereas it is the opposite with diamonds. This occurs because while the total utility of water is greater than the total utility of diamonds the marginal utility of water, in normal circumstances, is less than the marginal utility of diamonds.

Table 5.1 *Utilities of water*

Qty (pints of water)	TU	MU
20	5,000	
21	5,100	100
22	5,150	50

Table 5.2 *Utilities of diamonds*

Qty (number of diamonds)	TU	MU
1	1,000	
2	1,900	900
3	2,700	800

Note 1

Proof that demand goes down when price goes up

Refer back to the utility figures for X and Y on p. 23. At a price of €20 for X and a price of €10 for Y and an income of €80 the combination of **2X and 4Y** gave the highest possible total utility. Now assume that the price of Y increases to €20. The new possible combinations of purchase are shown in Table 5.3.

Table 5.3 *New possible combinations of purchases*

Possible combinations	Utilities from each product	Combined total utility
0X + 4Y	0 + 3,500	3,500
1X + 3Y	1,000 + 3,100	4,100
2X + 2Y	1,800 + 2,600	4,400
3X + 1Y	**2,500 + 2,000**	**4,500**
4X + 0Y	3,100 + 0	3,100

It can be seen that the combination which now gives the highest total utility is that of **3X and 1Y**. Before the price increase 4 units of Y were purchased now only 1 unit of Y is purchased. Therefore, the D for Y has gone down (**contracted**) as a direct result of its price increase. This is the only conclusion **to be drawn from this change in the price of Y**.

The reverse could be shown for a price decrease.

Note 2

The full effect of a price change

When we looked at the effect on demand of a change in the price of a product we saw that it caused a **substitution effect** which was always positive, i.e. when price goes up it causes a contraction in D and vice versa. This assumed that no other factor which affects D had changed at the same time.

However, when we looked at the effect on D of a change in income we saw that one of the ways real income could change was when price changed and money income remained unchanged, thus causing an **income effect** which could be either positive or negative.

Therefore, when a price change occurs, which results in a change in real income, then both the substitution effect and the income effect happen simultaneously.

Remember that the substitution effect is always positive, while the income effect can be either positive or negative.

Therefore, there are different possible results when the two effects combine.

Possible combined effects

1. The positive substitution effect could combine with a positive income effect causing more of the good to be purchased when the price goes down and vice versa when the price goes up. This happens for **normal goods**.

2. The positive substitution effect could combine with a weaker negative income effect still resulting in more of the good being purchased when the price goes down and vice versa when the price goes up. This happens for **inferior goods**.

3. The positive substitution effect could combine with a stronger negative income effect resulting in less of the good being purchased when the price goes down and vice versa when the price goes up. This happens for **Giffen goods**. Therefore, when the price of Giffen goods goes up the D for them also goes up, and when their price goes down the demand for them also goes down.

Therefore, it can be said that in the vast majority of cases that when the price of a good goes up the D for it goes down, and that when the price of a product goes down the D for it goes up. This is known as the **normal laws of demand** and these goods have a normal downward sloping D curve.

LEARN THE KEY POINTS

1. Learn and explain the factors which influence a consumer's demand for a good
2. Know the difference between a movement along a demand curve and a movement of a demand curve
3. Know the meaning of real income and how it can change
4. Know how to distinguish between a positive and a negative income effect
5. Learn the exceptions to the Law of Demand
6. Know what a perverse demand curve is
7. Explain the paradox of value
8. Learn the difference between a normal good, an inferior good and a Giffen good

Exam Q&A: See p. 362

Copy questions 1–6 into your answer book and complete each of the sentences by filling in the blank spaces.

1. When the price of a good decreases it causes an ____________ in the demand for that good.
2. A contraction in the demand for a good happens when ____________ units of a good are demanded because the price of the good ____________.
3. An increase in demand means ____________ units of the good are demanded at any ____________ price.
4. A downward shift in demand means ____________ units of the good are demanded at any ____________ price.
5. A positive income effect means that ____________ and ____________ will change in the ____________ direction.
6. When demand goes down as a result of an increase in income this is known as a ____________ income effect.
7. Draw two clearly labelled diagrams to distinguish between an extension in demand and an increase in demand.

8 The diagram below represents a consumer's demand for a normal good.

Fig 5.9

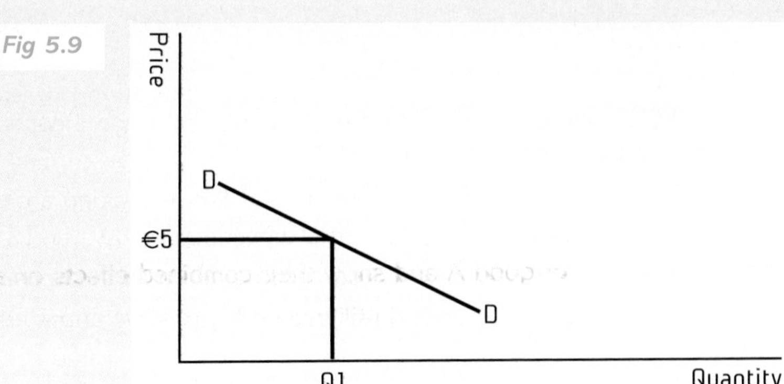

State and show the effect on the demand for this good in each of the following circumstances. Use separate diagrams for each answer.

(a) The price of the good decreases
(b) The price of a substitute good decreases
(c) The price of a complementary good decreases
(d) The consumer's taste changes against the product
(e) The consumer's income increases

9 'The prices of many normal goods have increased over the last five years but the demand for them has not changed.'

Does this contradict the Law of Demand which states that demand goes down when price goes up? Explain your answer.

10 Explain why the demand curve for a normal good slopes downwards from left to right.

11 Explain clearly four different circumstances which would cause a consumer's real income to decrease.

12 The weather forecasters state that next summer will be an unusually cold and wet one. Assuming this forecast is accurate state four goods or services whose demand will decrease from their normal annual level next summer. Explain your answer.

13 'All Giffen goods are inferior goods but not all inferior goods are Giffen goods.' Explain this statement.

14 What is meant by the term 'conspicuous consumption'? Show on a diagram and explain the effect which this form of consumption has on the shape of a demand curve.

15 Distinguish between the value in use and the value in exchange of a product.

16 Discuss, in detail, four factors which influence consumers' demand for goods on a day-to-day basis.

17 Show how the Principle of Equi-Marginal Utility (the Law of Equi-Marginal Returns) can be used to prove that the demand for a good increases when its price decreases.

18 A consumer spends all income on two goods: good A and good B. Both goods are normal goods but they are not complementary goods. The price of good A is increased and the price of good B remains unchanged. The consumer continues to spend all income on the two goods. Distinguish between the substitution effect and the income effect of the price increase on the demand for good A and show their combined effects on a diagram.

19 How is the concept of marginal utility used to explain the paradox of value?

20 Explain why a decrease in the interest rate charged on loans could cause an increase in the demand for new cars.

Chapter 6 Elasticity of Demand

So far we have stated that if the price of a good went up or if the consumer's income went down then the demand for a good would go down.

However, if you are the seller of a good you need more specific information. For example, you want to know the effect on your revenue (income) if the price of the good you are selling is increased or decreased. That is, you want to know the relationship between the change in the price of the good you are selling and the change in your total revenue.

The concept of elasticity of demand is used to show the sensitivity of demand to: (i) a change in the price of the good itself, (ii) a change in consumers' income and (iii) a change in the price of another good.

Price Elasticity of Demand (PED)

Definition of price elasticity of demand (PED)

Price elasticity of demand (PED) measures the relationship between a change in the price of a good and the resulting change in the demand for that good.

Or

It measures the sensitivity of the demand for a product to a change in the price of the product.

There are two methods of measuring price elasticity of demand.

1. **Point elasticity of demand** measures the PED between two specific prices only. The formula for this is:

$$\frac{\text{Proportionate change in quantity demanded}}{\text{Proportionate change in price}}$$

This measurement of PED is not widely used as it gives two different answers depending on whether you are increasing or decreasing the price of a good.

Example

Assume there are 100 units of a good purchased when its price is €1 and 75 units purchased when the price went up to €1.50.

Using this formula the PED is:

– 25% divided by + 50% = – 0.5

However, if we reverse the above and had the price going down from €1.50 to €1, and assuming the same demand figures, then using this formula the PED is:

+ 33.33% divided by – 33.33% = –1.00

Thus this formula can be misleading as it is too specific.

2 A more useful measurement of price elasticity of demand is one known as **arc elasticity of demand**. This gives the same answer regardless of price increasing or decreasing. It takes the average change in demand for any price change between two stated prices and is the most commonly used form. The formula used is:

$$\frac{P1 + P2}{Q1 + Q2} \times \frac{\Delta Q}{\Delta P}$$

Where:

P1 = original price: P2 = new price: Q1 = original quantity: Q2 = new quantity. Delta Q = the change in quantity: Delta P = the change in price.

(Apply the prices and quantities given in the example above and you will see that the answer is – 0.71429 no matter which price is taken as P1.)

Price elasticity of demand can be:

(a) **Elastic:** A change in the price of the good causes a more than proportionate change in the demand for it.

Or

The percentage change in demand is greater than the percentage change in price.

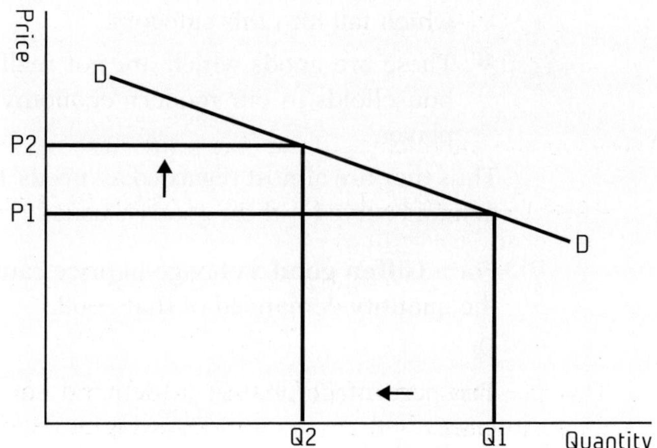

Fig 6.1 *An elastic demand curve for holiday cruises*

This normally applies to luxury goods as we can quite easily cut back our expenditure on these goods as they are not essentials. The demand curve for these goods has a degree of slope of > 45 degrees.

(b) **Inelastic:** A change in the price of the good causes a less than proportionate change in the demand for it.

Or

The percentage change in demand is less than the percentage change in price.

This normally applies to necessities as it is difficult to cut back our expenditure on these goods. The demand curve for these goods has a degree of slope of < 45 degrees.

Fig 6.2 *An inelastic demand curve for the domestic use of electricity*

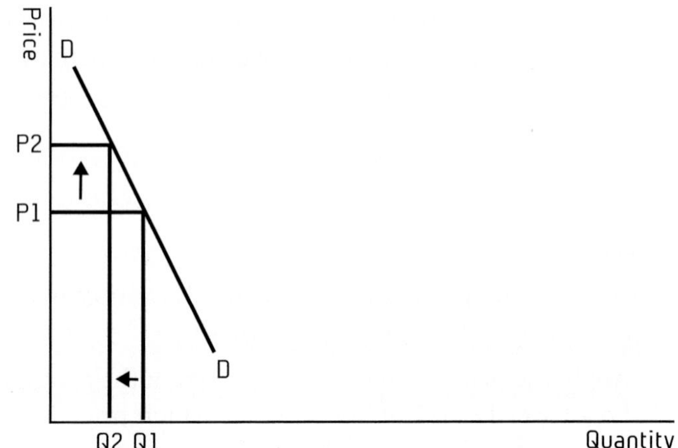

(c) **Equal to unity:**

(i) For a normal good a change in price causes the demand to change in such a way that the total revenue from the sale of the good does not change.

- The term 'luxury-necessities' has been coined to describe goods which fall into this category.
- These are goods which are not really necessities but which most households in our modern economy take for granted, e.g. a DVD player.

Thus they are almost regarded as 'needs' but really they are 'wants'. The demand curve for these goods is usually represented by a 45 degree line.

(ii) For a **Giffen good** a change in price causes a proportionate change in the quantity demanded of that good.

Or

The percentage change in demand equals the percentage change in price.

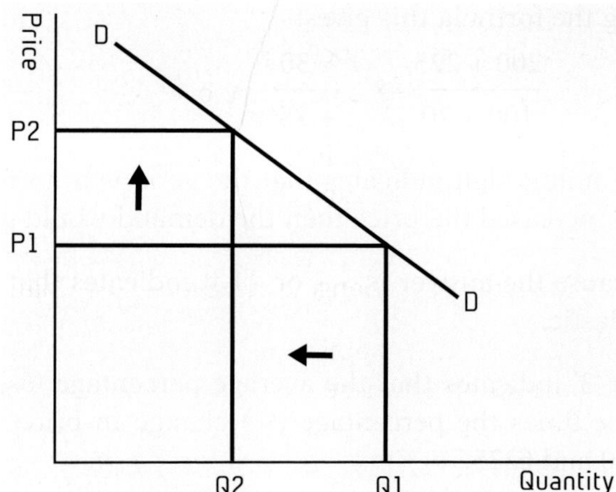

Fig 6.3 This curve represents the demand for DVD players

Application of formula

(a) If the answer is a negative number then the good is a normal good, e.g. when P goes up demand goes down. Thus when you apply the formula you have:

$$\frac{P1 + P2}{Q1 + Q2} \times \frac{-\Delta Q}{+\Delta P} \quad \text{equals a negative number}$$

Remember N for negative and N for normal.

(b) If the answer is a positive number then the good is a Giffen good, because when the price of a Giffen good increases its demand also increases. Thus when you apply the formula you have:

$$\frac{P1 + P2}{Q1 + Q2} \times \frac{+\Delta Q}{+\Delta P} \quad \text{equals a positive number}$$

(c) If the answer is > + or – 1 then the price elasticity of demand is elastic.

(d) If the answer is < + or – 1 then the price elasticity of demand is inelastic.

(e) If the answer is = to + or – 1 then the price elasticity of demand is equal to unity.

(f) The actual number itself in the answer (ignoring the + or – signs) is the number by which you multiply the percentage (%) change in price to get the percentage (%) change in demand.

An example of the application of the formula

When the original price of a product (P1) was €200 the quantity demanded (Q1) was 100.

When the price of the good increased (P2) to €225 the demand for the good (Q2) fell to 70.

Applying the formula this gives:

$$\frac{200 + 225}{100 + 70} \times \frac{-30}{+25} = -3$$

1 The minus sign indicates that the good is a normal good. This tells you that if you increased the price then the demand would go down.

2 Because the answer is > + or – 1 it indicates that the price elasticity of demand is elastic.

3 The '3' indicates that the average percentage (%) change in demand would be three times the percentage (%) change in price for any price change between €200 and €225.

PED and Changes in Total Revenue for Normal Goods

1 When price elasticity of demand (PED) is **elastic** then price and total revenue change in **opposite directions**. Therefore, if you want to increase revenue from the sale of a good whose PED is elastic you would decrease price.

Example

Assume the PED for a product is – 2 and its initial price is €2 and 100 units of the good are demanded. This gives a total revenue of **€200**.

Assume the price is decreased to €1.50 i.e. by 25%. The good is a normal good (the – sign), so demand will go up by (25% × 2) 50% to 150 units.

The new total revenue is 150 × €1.50 = **€225**.

2 When price elasticity of demand is **inelastic** then price and total revenue change in the **same direction**. Therefore, if you want to increase revenue from the sale of a good whose PED is inelastic you would increase price.

Example

Assume the PED for a product is – 0.5: its price is €2 and 100 units of the good are demanded. This gives total revenue of **€200**.

Assume the price increases to €2.50, i.e. by 25%. The good is a normal good (the – sign), so demand will go down by (25% × 0.5) 12.5% to 87.5 units.

The new total revenue is 87.5 × €2.50 = **€218.75**.

3 When price elasticity is **equal** to **unity** then by definition the total revenue will **remain unchanged** after any price change.

Example
P1 = €8 and Q1 = 400 units. TR = €3,200
P2 = €4 and Q2 = 800 units. TR = €3,200

Now apply the formula:

$$\frac{P1 + P2}{Q1 + Q2} \times \frac{\Delta Q}{\Delta P}$$

$$= \frac{12}{1{,}200} \times \frac{400}{-4} = \frac{+4{,}800}{-4{,}800} = -1$$

Note: The above statements only apply to normal goods.

Total revenue and price always change in the same direction for Giffen goods regardless of the degree of elasticity. Just think of the logic of it. If the price of a Giffen good is increased then the demand for it will increase. Thus more goods are sold at a higher price.

Exceptional Degrees of PED

1 Price elasticity of demand (PED) can be perfectly inelastic. This means that there will be no change in the demand for the product over a given price range. The PED in this case is equal to zero.

Fig 6.4 Perfectly inelastic demand curve

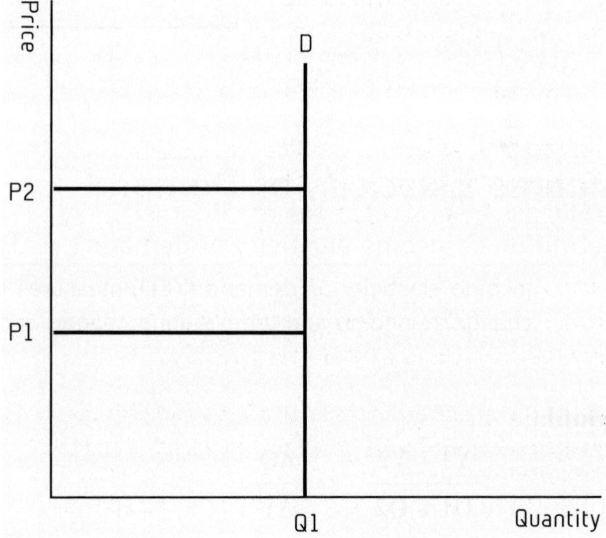

This form of PED applies to essential goods. If an individual has to take vital medication on a regular basis then the increase in price does not affect this individual's demand for this good, provided of course that the price does not increase to the point where the individual could not afford to purchase the good.

Irish society recognises this point and through the government implements schemes where the individual only has to pay a maximum price for prescriptions. Any cost above that maximum is paid for through social welfare or Department of Health schemes.

It also applies to very cheap household goods which only account for a minute percentage of the household income, e.g. salt.

2 Price elasticity of demand can be perfectly elastic. This means that any change in price causes demand to change to zero. The PED in this case works out to be equal to infinity. (We deal with this in more detail in Chapter 12, Perfect Competition.) The demand curve for this type of product is in Fig 6.5.

Fig 6.5 Perfectly elastic demand curve

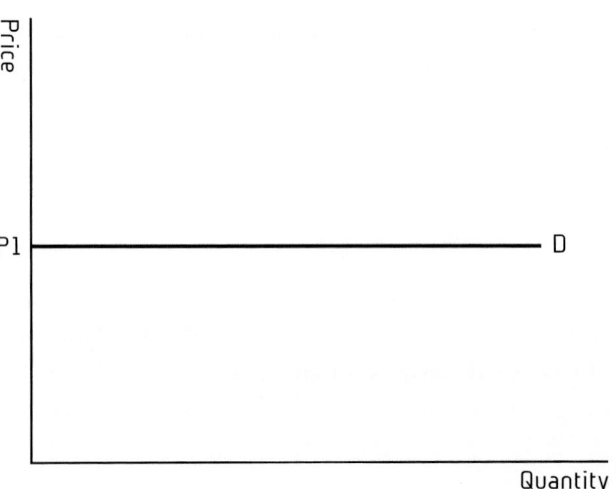

Income Elasticity of Demand

Definition of income elasticity of demand (YED)

Income elasticity of demand (YED) measures the relationship between a change in income and the resulting change in demand.

Formula:

$$\frac{Y1 + Y2}{Q1 + Q2} \times \frac{\Delta Q}{\Delta Y}$$

Where:

Y1 = original income: Y2 = new income: Q1 = original quantity: Q2 = new quantity.
ΔQ = the change in quantity: ΔY = the change in income.

Income elasticity of demand can be:

(a) **Elastic:** A change in income will cause a more than proportionate change in demand.

(b) **Inelastic:** A change in income will cause a less than proportionate change in demand.

(c) **Equal to unity:** A change in income will cause a proportionate change in demand.

Application of formula:

(a) If the answer is a positive number then the good is a normal good.

If income increases then demand for normal goods also increases so when applying the formula you get:

$$\frac{Y1 + Y2}{Q1 + Q2} \times \frac{+\Delta Q}{+\Delta Y} \quad \text{equals a positive number}$$

(b) If the answer is a negative number the good is an inferior good.

If income increases then demand for inferior goods decreases so when applying the formula you get:

$$\frac{Y1 + Y2}{Q1 + Q2} \times \frac{-\Delta Q}{+\Delta Y} \quad \text{equals a negative number}$$

(c) If the answer is > + or –1 then the income elasticity of demand is elastic.

(d) If the answer is < + or –1 then the income elasticity of demand is inelastic.

(e) If the answer = + or –1 then the income elasticity is equal to unity.

(f) The actual number itself in the answer (ignoring the + or – sign) is the number by which you multiply the percentage (%) change in income to get the percentage (%) change in demand.

Cross Elasticity of Demand

Definition of cross elasticity of demand (CED)

Cross elasticity of demand (CED) measures the relationship between the change in price of one good (A) and the resulting change in demand for another specific good (B).

Formula:

$$\frac{P(A)1 + P(A)2}{Q(B)1 + Q(B)2} \times \frac{\Delta Q(B)}{\Delta P(A)}$$

Where:

P(A)1 = the original price of (A): P(A)2 = the new price of (A)
Q(B)1 = the original quantity of (B): Q(B)2 = the new quantity of (B)
ΔP(A) = the change in price of (A): ΔQ (B) = the change in quantity of (B)

Cross elasticity of demand can be:

(a) **Elastic:** A change in the price of (A) will cause a more than proportionate change in the demand for (B).

(b) **Inelastic:** A change in the price of (A) will cause a less than proportionate change in the demand for (B).

(c) **Equal to unity:** A change in the price of (A) will cause a proportionate change in the demand for (B).

Significance of answer to applied formula

1. If the answer to the applied formula is a positive (+) number then the two goods are substitutes for each other.

Proof

If (B) is a substitute for (A) then its demand will go up, i.e. + change in Q(B), when the price of (A) goes up, i.e. + change in P(A).

Therefore, when applying the formula you have:

$$\frac{P(A)1 + P(A)2}{Q(B)1 + Q(B)2} \times \frac{+\Delta Q(B)}{+\Delta P(A)} \quad \text{equals a positive number}$$

2. If the answer to the applied formula is a negative (–) number the two goods are complementary goods **or** the demand for one is derived from the demand for the other.

Proof

If (B) is a complement of (A) then when the price of (A) goes up the demand for both goods will go down.

Therefore, when applying the formula you have:

$$\frac{P(A)1 + P(A)2}{Q(B)1 + Q(B)2} \times \frac{-\Delta Q(B)}{+\Delta P(A)} \quad \text{equals a negative number}$$

1. If the answer is > + or –1 then the cross elasticity of demand for (B) in relation to a change in the price of (A) is elastic.

2. If the answer is < + or –1 then the cross elasticity of demand for (B) in relation to a change in the price of (A) is inelastic.

3. If the answer = + or –1 then the cross elasticity of demand for (B) in relation to a change in the price of (A) is equal to unity.

4. The actual number itself in the answer (ignoring the + or – sign) is the number by which you multiply the percentage (%) change in price of (A) to get the percentage (%) change in demand for (B).

Factors Governing the Degree of Elasticity of Demand

1 **The degree of necessity of the product:** If a product is a vital one people must buy it, therefore its demand tends to be inelastic. On the other hand, people can do without luxury goods, and therefore their demand tends to be elastic.

2 **The availability of close substitutes:** If there are close substitutes available for a good then the demand for these goods tends to be elastic, as people will switch to the substitutes when prices rise and vice versa.

3 **The fraction of income spent on the product:** When consumers spend only a small fraction of their incomes on a product then the demand for this product tends to be inelastic, as any increase in price will account only for a small fraction of income and vice versa.

4 **The durability of the product:** If a product is durable (i.e. has a potentially long lifespan) people can delay replacing the product. Thus the demand for these goods tends to be elastic as an increase in price usually leads to a more than proportionate fall in demand.

5 **The effectiveness of advertising – habits of purchase – brand loyalty:** A successful advertising campaign can result in improved loyalty to a product, thus decreasing its degree of elasticity.

6 **The degree of elasticity of its more expensive complement:** The degree of elasticity of demand for a good which is a complementary good tends to be determined by the degree of elasticity of demand of the more expensive of the complements.

7 **The number of uses that the product has:** Sugar has very many different markets, e.g. it is used as a sweetener in drinks and in the confectionery industry. This point often raises heated debate. Some people argue that the more uses a product has the more elastic its demand will be, as all sectors of its market will

Fig 6.6 Sugar has many different uses

be hit when there is a price rise. Others argue that the more uses a product has the less vulnerable it is to changes in price, as demand may remain high in some of these markets and so be less elastic. In reality, it has to be the average of the combined elasticities of demand in all of the markets.

8 **The time factor:** The more time people have to adjust to the change in the price of a good, the more elastic the demand for the good tends to be. For example, if the price of oil increases substantially, initially people would still have to purchase it as there is no ready substitute available. Thus in the short term the PED would be inelastic.

However, in time other cheaper products would be developed as substitutes for oil, and the demand for it would then fall dramatically. Thus in the long term the PED would be elastic.

A knowledge of price elasticity of demand is important to:

- A seller of a good who is contemplating changing the price of his product.
- The Minister for Finance when contemplating changes in indirect taxes.

A knowledge of income elasticity of demand is important to:

- Production planners when contemplating what products to produce in the foreseeable future.

A knowledge of cross elasticity of demand is important to:

- Producers of substitute goods when contemplating price changes.
- Producers of goods which are in joint demand, so that they know the effect on the demand for their product arising from a change in the price of a complementary product.
- Producers of a good whose demand is derived from the demand for another product, so that they know the effect on the demand for their product arising from a change in the price of the good from which the demand is derived.

LEARN THE KEY POINTS

1. Definitions and formulae for price, income and cross elasticities of demand
2. Understand the meanings of elastic, inelastic and equal to unity for each type of elasticity
3. Interpret the answer to any of the applied formulae
4. Know the factors which influence the degree of elasticity
5. Know how the degree of price elasticity of demand influences the change in total revenue after a price change
6. Know who needs to be aware of all forms of elasticity

Exam Q&A: See p. 366

1. Define price elasticity of demand and give the formula for measuring it, stating what each symbol in the formula stands for.
2. When the above formula is applied explain the difference between the meaning of a negative and a positive number in the answer.
3. What is meant by the statement 'the price elasticity of demand for a good is elastic'?
4. What is meant by the statement 'the price elasticity of demand for a good is inelastic'?
5. Draw a demand curve for a product in such a way that it will show that the price elasticity of demand for that product is inelastic. State one product whose price elasticity of demand may be inelastic.
6. The PED for a good is –1.5 and the present demand for this good is 100 units. Calculate the new level of demand if the price of this product were decreased by 10 per cent. Show your calculations.
7. A consumer buys 80 units of a good when its price is €1.50. The price is increased to €1.75 and the consumer now buys 70 units of it.
   (a) Calculate the consumer's price elasticity of demand. Show all your workings.
   (b) Is demand for this good elastic, inelastic or equal to unity (unitary elastic)?
   (c) The seller of the above good wishes to earn maximum revenue from the sale of his good. What changes, if any, should the seller make in the selling price of the good to earn maximum revenue? Explain your answer.
8. A producer produces four products and the PED of these is as shown below. The producer wishes to increase the total income from the sale of each of these goods. State in each case what change, if any, he should make to the selling price of the good. Justify your answer.

   Product A = +1   Product C = – 0.5
   Product B = – 2.5   Product D = –1
9. Why should the Minister for Finance be aware of the PED of products in general?
10. Does the minister's knowledge of the general level of PED pose any dilemmas for him or her? Explain your answer.
11. Define income elasticity of demand and give the formula for measuring it, stating what each symbol in the formula stands for.

12 Is the YED for normal goods negative or positive? Explain your answer.

13 A person's income doubled from €500 per week to €1,000. However, there was no change in his demand for this product. It was 10 units before and after the income increase. Calculate his YED for this product.

14 Can you identify any product which may have the YED which you calculated in question 13? Give an explanation for your choice.

15 Define cross elasticity of demand and give the formula for measuring it, stating what each symbol in the formula stands for.

16 The cross elasticity of demand for bricks is elastic. Why is this statement meaningless?

17 When the CED for product B is negative in relation to a change in the price of product A then B is a substitute for A. Is this statement true or false? Explain your answer.

18 You are given the following information:

- The cross elasticity of demand between good A and good B = + 4.5
- The cross elasticity of demand between good A and good C = – 0.5
- The cross elasticity of demand between good A and good D = – 2.5
- The cross elasticity of demand between good A and good E = + 0.5

(a) Which of these goods are complements to good A? Explain your answer.

(b) Which of these goods is the closest substitute for good A? Explain your answer.

19 The demand for product X is derived from the demand for product Y. The price of product Y decreases from €1 to €0.75. The cross elasticity of demand for product X in relation to a change in the price of product Y is – 0.5. What is the percentage change in demand for product X? Show your calculations.

20 Explain fully five factors that influence the degree of elasticity of demand for a product.

Chapter 7
Supply and Elasticity of Supply

Definition of supply (S)

Supply (S) is the number of units of a good made available for sale at any given market price at any given time.

Just as we saw in the chapter on demand, supply can also be displayed on either a supply schedule or a supply curve.

⁂A supply schedule

Definition of a supply schedule

A **supply schedule** is a table showing the number of units of a good made available for sale at any given market price at any given time.

Table 7.1 *Example of a supply schedule*

Price	€1	€2	€3	€4	€5
Quantity	6	7	8	9	10

The market supply schedule of a product is the aggregate supply schedules of all firms in that market. Thus we could have an individual firm's supply schedule and a market supply schedule. Assume that there are only two suppliers of product X, i.e. Half-Mad Ltd and Fully-Mad Ltd. Their combined supply schedules make up the market supply schedule.

Table 7.2 *Composition of market supply*

Price	Half-Mad Ltd's supply schedule	Fully-Mad Ltd's supply schedule	Market supply schedule
€1	20	30	50
€2	28	40	68
€3	36	55	91
€4	50	72	122

Note: Supply increases as price increases, whereas demand decreased as price increased.

✳A supply curve

Definition of a supply curve

A **supply curve** is a graph showing the number of units of a good made available for sale at any given market price at any given time.

Fig 7.1 Example of a supply curve

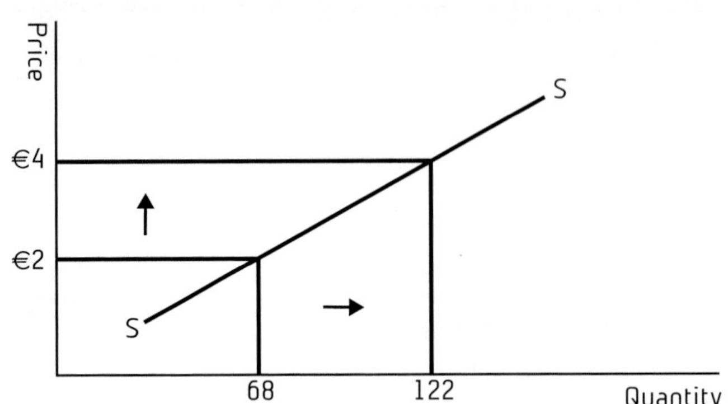

Entrepreneurs, who set up businesses, are attracted into business by the prospect of making a profit. We must assume that these people act rationally and will be attracted into the most profitable industries suited to their interests and talents. Thus as an industry becomes more profitable more entrepreneurs will be attracted into that industry, thereby making more of that industry's goods available for sale. Look at the definition of supply.

Likewise, as an industry becomes less profitable some of the less efficient firms will be forced out of the industry resulting in less goods being available for sale. It cannot always be assumed that the firms remaining in that industry will make up the shortfall, as they may already be producing to their maximum capacity.

Factors Governing the Supply of a Good

1. The market price of the good (P1)
2. The price of other goods (Pog), sometimes written as P2-N
3. The cost of production (C)
4. The state of technology (Tch)
5. The level of taxation (Tx)
6. Other unforeseen circumstances, e.g. strikes or shortages of raw materials (U)
7. The role of the government (G)
8. The number of suppliers in the market (N)

Thus S = f (P1, Pog, C, Tch, Tx, U, G, N)

A change in the price of the product (P1) causes either an extension or a contraction in supply, or a movement along the supply curve.

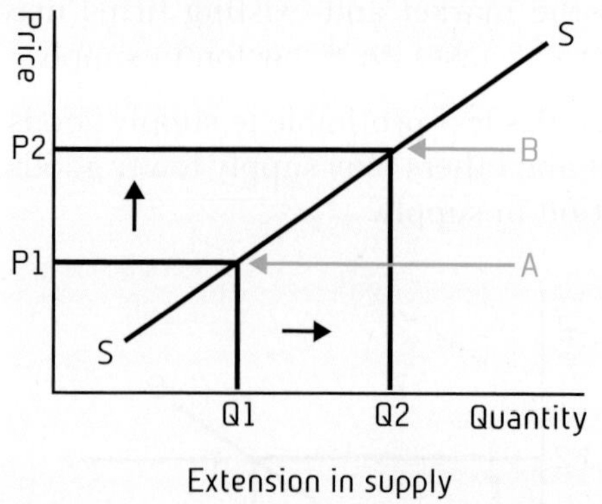

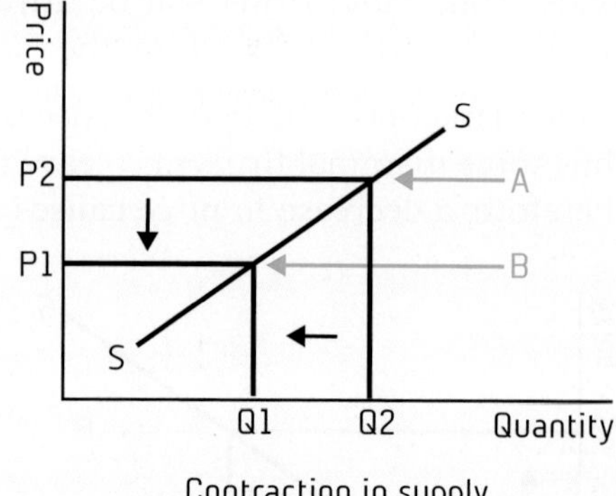

Fig 7.2 Extension and contraction in supply

In each of these diagrams the supply changed (after the price changed) from point A to point B along the same supply curve.

Therefore, extensions and contractions in supply are shown as movements along a supply curve.

A change in any of the other factors governing supply causes either an increase or a decrease in supply, or a movement of the supply curve.

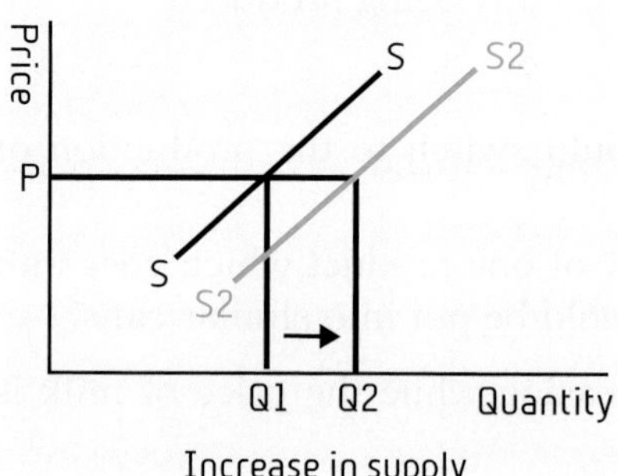

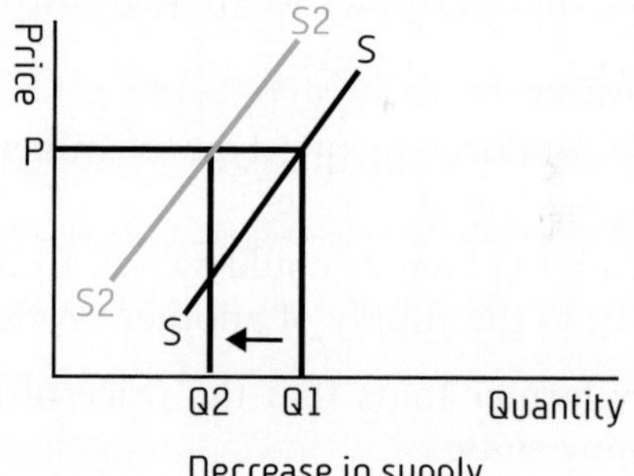

Fig 7.3 Increase and decrease in supply

An increase in supply is shown by moving the supply curve to the right of its original position. A decrease in supply is shown by moving the supply curve to the left of its original position.

When you analyse the factors which affect supply remember that supply is motivated by profit.

Note: In the following explanations a marginal firm is one which is just surviving in an industry at the existing market prices and the existing cost structures. It could be put out of business if there is any fall in its income or any increase in its costs.

✳1 The market price of the good (P1)

As the market price of a product increases it becomes more profitable to supply goods. Thus more firms will be attracted into the market and existing firms may supply more goods. Therefore, the increase in price causes an extension in supply.

As the market price of a product decreases it becomes less profitable to supply goods. Thus some marginal firms may leave the market and others may supply fewer goods. Therefore, a decrease in price causes a contraction in supply.

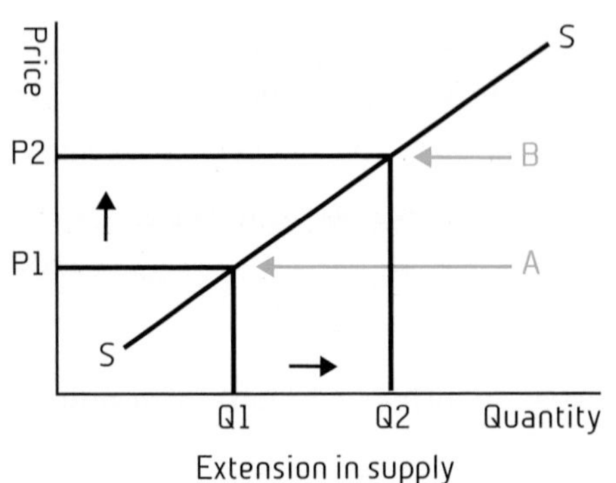

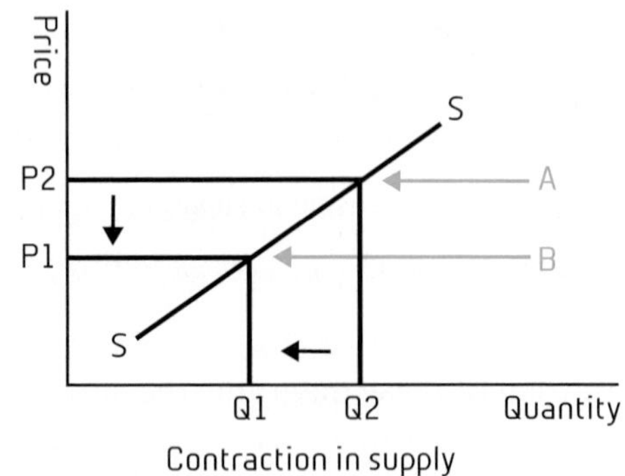

Fig 7.4 Extension and contraction in supply

✳2 The price of other goods (Pog)

In the context of supply, the price of other goods (Pog) refers to other goods that the supplier could produce as an alternative to those presently being produced.

Examples

- The producer of one type of mineral water could switch to the production of another mineral water.
- A canning factory could switch from the supply of one product which goes into cans, to the supply of another product which could be put into similar cans.

A dairy farmer finds that the price of beef is increasing while the price of milk is remaining static.

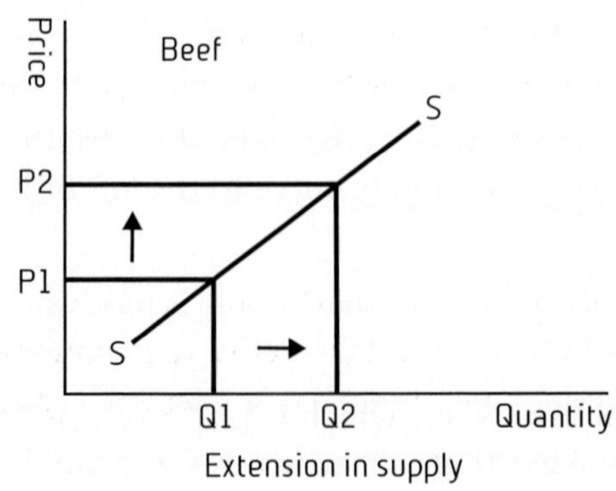

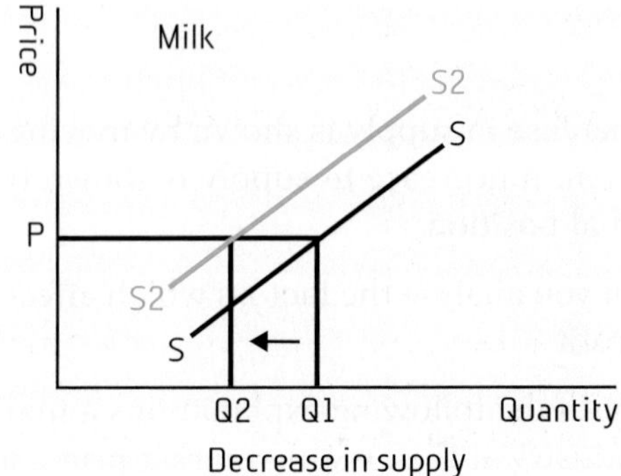

Fig 7.5 Extension and decrease in supply

Assume that the increase in the price of beef now makes it more profitable than milk and that the farmer can switch to beef production. If he is acting rationally he will do so. Hence the total supply (S) of milk is decreased as a result of the increase in the price of beef. See Fig 7.5.

The reverse would happen if there was a decrease in the price of beef while the price of milk remained static, i.e. there would be an increase in the S of milk and a contraction in the S of beef.

✳ 3 The cost of production (C)

As the cost of production increases it becomes less profitable to supply goods. Thus some marginal firms will cease production resulting in a decrease in supply.

Therefore, an increase in the cost of production causes a decrease in supply. A decrease in the cost of production makes it more profitable to supply goods and attracts more firms into the industry causing an increase in supply.

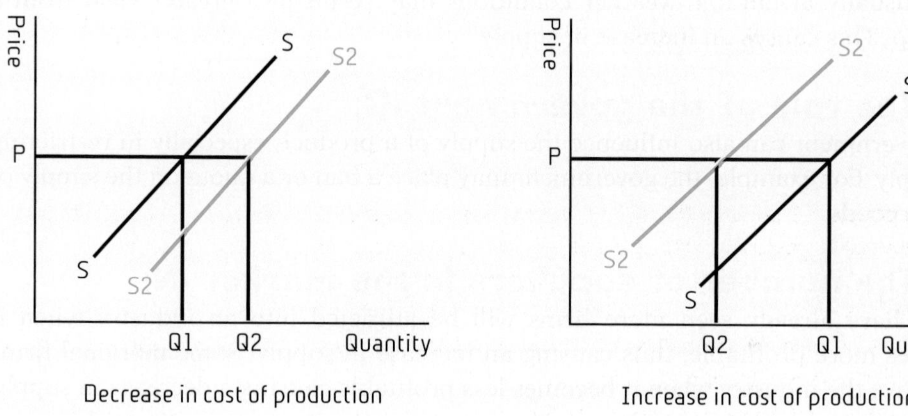

Fig 7.6 Decrease and increase in the cost of production

✳ 4 The state of technology (Tch)

As technology improves more goods can be produced for the same or even a lower total cost, thus reducing the average cost of each item produced. This increases the profitability of the industry resulting in a greater supply.

Therefore, as technology improves supply increases.

✳ 5 The level of taxation (Tx)

As the level of taxes on profits (corporation profit taxes) increases, entrepreneurs are left with less profit, thus reducing their profit. This may force some marginal firms out of production resulting in a decrease in supply.

Likewise, an increase in indirect taxes may result in an increase in the cost of production. This may reduce profit levels and force some marginal firms out of the industry. This assumes that the firm cannot pass on the taxation increase to the consumer.

A decrease in these taxes will have the opposite result.

Therefore, an increase in taxation causes a decrease in supply and a decrease in tax will cause an increase in supply.

✳6 Unforeseen circumstances (U)

Many events occur which cannot be forecast, but they can influence supply. These can result in either an increase or a decrease in supply, i.e. they can have a negative or a positive influence on supply.

Examples

- Workers go on strike. This causes a decrease in supply.
- Unusually favourable weather conditions may result in a greater yield from a crop. This causes an increase in supply.

✳7 The role of the government (G)

The government can also influence the supply of a product, especially in restricting its supply. For example, the government may place a ban or a quota on the supply of certain goods.

✳8 The number of suppliers in the market (N)

As we have already seen more firms will be attracted into an industry when it becomes more profitable, thus causing an increase in supply. Some marginal firms may leave the industry when it becomes less profitable causing a decrease in supply.

Remember that the reaction of supply to each of the factors stated above assumes that it is the only factor which has changed at a given time.

Other Aspects of Supply

✳Joint supply

Joint supply is when the supply of one product automatically creates a supply of another product. The classic example of this in Ireland is the rearing of cattle in order to create a supply of beef, which then automatically creates a supply of hides which can be used in the leather industry. Also think of sheep in relation to the supply of mutton and wool.

✳ Fixed supply

Fixed supply is when the supply of a product cannot be changed in the short run regardless of any change in the market price. The best examples of these are perishable goods brought to a market on a given day. Their supply would be represented by the supply curve shown below.

Fig 7.7 Fixed supply

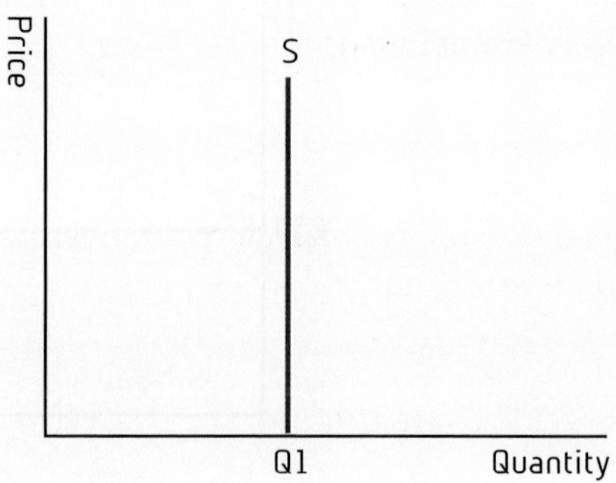

✳ Supply restricted by limited capacity

An industry's capacity to supply a good may temporarily be restricted, e.g. by a shortage of specialised labour or raw materials. Thus when the industry reaches its maximum capacity it is unable to increase the supply even if the market price continues to increase. This is represented by the supply curve shown in Fig 7.8. You can see that the supply continues to increase in line with the increase in the market price up to a price of €10.

However, once the maximum capacity is reached, Q1, then supply cannot be increased beyond that point even though the market price continues to increase.

Fig 7.8 Supply restricted by limited capacity

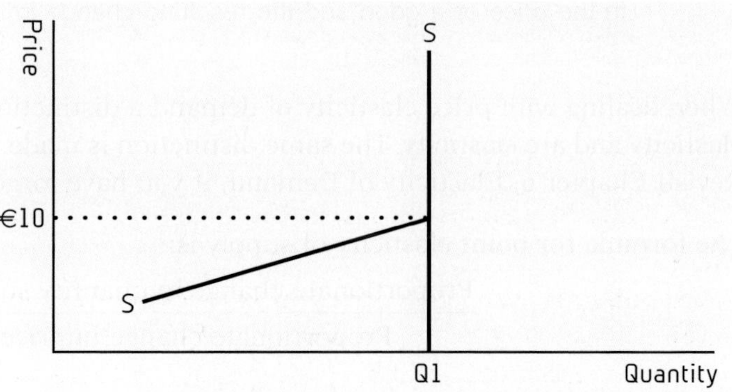

✳Supply restricted by a minimum market price

Remember that firms have to cover their costs in order to stay in production in the long term. Thus many goods or services will not be supplied if the market price is below a minimum price. Therefore, no producers will come into the market until that price is reached. This is represented in Fig 7.9.

Fig 7.9 Supply restricted by a minimum market price

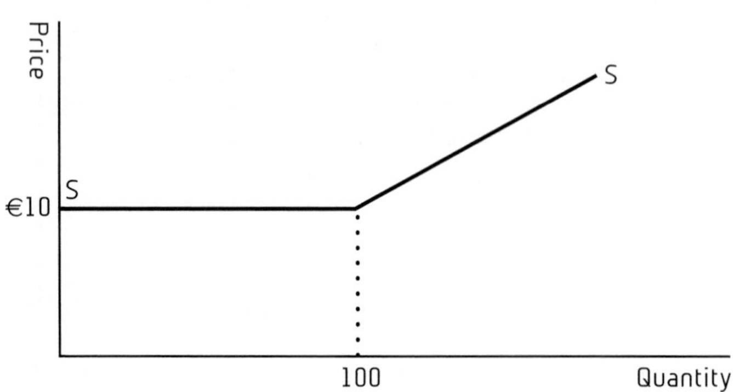

Here, suppliers are not willing to enter the market until the market price is €10. At this price, they are willing to supply 100 units. If the market price increases above €10 then they are willing to increase their supply.

Note: This supply curve would also apply to the supply of labour if a minimum wage rate was enforced.

Price Elasticity of Supply (PES)

Definition of price elasticity of supply (PES)

Price elasticity of supply (PES) measures the relationship between a change in the price of a good and the resulting change in the supply of that good.

When dealing with price elasticity of demand a distinction was made between point elasticity and arc elasticity. The same distinction is made in price elasticity of supply. Revisit Chapter 6, Elasticity of Demand, if you have forgotten this distinction.

The formula for point elasticity of supply is:

$$\frac{\text{Proportionate change in quantity supplied}}{\text{Proportionate change in price}}$$

The formula for arc elasticity of supply is:

$$\frac{P1 + P2}{Q1 + Q2} \times \frac{\Delta Q}{\Delta P}$$

The symbols in this formula are the same as in price elasticity of demand with the exception that Q refers to the quantity supplied.

In most situations supply increases when price increases, therefore the PES is normally a positive figure.

Example

The market price of a product increased from €10 to €12 and the supply of the product increased from 100 units to 150 units.

Applying the formula above we get:

$$\frac{10 + 12}{100 + 150} \times \frac{+ 50}{+ 2} = + 2.2$$

The significance of the answer to the formula

1. If the PES is > 1 then it is elastic, i.e. a change in price will cause a more than proportionate change in supply.
2. If PES is < 1 then it is inelastic, i.e. a change in price will cause a less than proportionate change in supply.
3. If PES = 1 then it is equal to unity, i.e. a change in price will cause a proportionate change in supply.
4. If PES = 0 then the supply is perfectly inelastic. This happens when a good is fixed in supply.

Fig 7.10 Perfectly inelastic supply

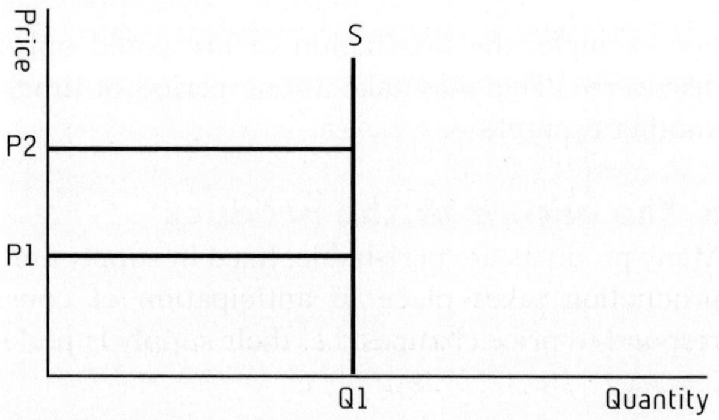

5. The absolute value of the PES is the number by which you multiply the percentage change in the price to get the average percentage change in supply over that price range.

Factors Governing Elasticity of Supply

1 The degree of specialised labour or capital used in production

The production of some goods needs the employment of highly specialised labour or specialised capital. If extra units of these forms of labour and capital are not immediately available then it is very difficult for a firm to react to a change in the market price. In this situation the elasticity of supply would be inelastic.

2 Is the firm operating at full capacity?

If a firm is capable of producing more goods with its present resources, the elasticity of supply will be elastic, as the firm can easily increase its production if it becomes more profitable to do so, as a result of an increase in the market price.

However, if a firm was producing to its full capacity it could not react quickly to any increase in the market price, as it may have to build or purchase a larger factory to do so. In this case, the elasticity of supply will tend to be inelastic.

3 The mobility of the factors of production

Firms allocate their resources to the most profitable use. Thus if factors are mobile the elasticity of supply will be elastic for goods whose prices have increased, as the firm can switch its resources to the production of these goods.

4 The time period under consideration

The shorter the time period available to the producer to change production levels, the more inelastic the supply will be and vice versa.

For example, the production of ore could only be increased if a new mine was discovered. This may take a long period of time, perhaps years. Housing would be another example.

5 The nature of the product

Many products are perishable, fixed in supply and take a long time to produce. Their production takes place in anticipation of consumption. These products cannot respond to price changes, i.e. their supply is perfectly inelastic, e.g. crops.

LEARN THE KEY POINTS

1. Definition of supply
2. Understand the supply schedule
3. Understand the supply curve
4. Explain the movement along a supply curve
5. Explain the movement of a supply curve
6. The factors which influence supply
7. Understand joint supply
8. Understand fixed supply
9. Supply restricted by limited capacity
10. Supply restricted by a minimum market price
11. Definition of and formula for price elasticity of supply
12. The significance of the answer to the applied formula
13. The factors governing price elasticity of supply

Exam Q&A: See p. 368

Copy questions 1–6 into your answer book and complete the sentences filling in the blank spaces.

1 Supply refers to the amount of goods suppliers are ____________ to make available for ____________ at any ____________ at any ____________.

2 A supply curve normally slopes ____________ from left to right.

3 A supply curve is a ____________ which shows the relationship between the market price of a good and the number of units of it which suppliers are willing to ____________.

4 A product is fixed in supply when ____________.

5 Price elasticity of supply is elastic when the percentage change in ____________ is greater than the percentage change ____________.

6 A marginal firm is one ____________.

7 What is 'joint supply'? Give examples other than the ones mentioned in this chapter.

8 Draw two clearly labelled diagrams to distinguish between a movement of a supply curve and a movement along a supply curve.

9 The diagram below represents a change in the supply of a product. This change may have been caused by one or more of the following factors:

(a) An increase in the cost of production
(b) An improvement in the technology used to produce the good
(c) A decrease in the market price of the good
(d) An increase in the price of another good
(e) An increase in the taxes on profits

Select which factor(s) mentioned may have caused the change and explain your answer.

Fig 7.11

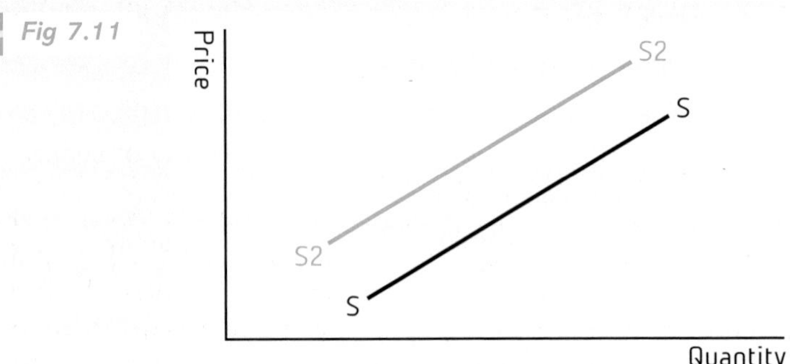

10 Including a change in the price of the good state and explain four factors which would result in a reduction in the supply of a good. Use diagrams to highlight your answer.

11 When the market price of a product changed from €20 to €30 a firm increased its supply of that good from 100 units to 180 units. Calculate this firm's price elasticity of supply for this good. Show your workings.

12 What degree of price elasticity of supply would you expect to be applicable to the supply of Irish potatoes on the Irish market in any given year? Explain your answer.

13 Explain fully any four factors which influence the degree of price elasticity of supply.

14 State the difference between supply restricted by limited capacity and supply restricted by a minimum market price. Use diagrams to highlight your answer.

15 Ireland has a very low level of corporation profit taxation. Suggest a reason why our government adopts this taxation policy.

Chapter 8
An Introduction to Costs of Production

When examining the factors which influence supply we stated that cost of production was one of these influences. This chapter is an introduction to the various costs involved in running a business. Let us analyse these costs of production.

A Cost of Production

A cost of production is any payment which must be paid, or any income which must be given up, in order to stay in production. A firm would have to close down if it did not pay employees their wages (they would not go to work). If it did not pay its suppliers for raw materials it would not receive any more materials. If it did not pay its electricity bill its power would be cut off. These are all payments for the factors of production which are essential to stay in production.

*An explicit cost

An explicit cost is any cost which has actually been paid or is due for payment. For example, if you are running a business you must pay wages, insurance and so on. These costs are shown in the accounts of the business, i.e. in the trading account, profit and loss account and the balance sheet.

*An implied cost

An implied cost is any income which you forego in order to run your business. For example, you are employed and earning €200 per week, but you get lucky and win €1m on the Lotto. You decide to leave your job and invest the €1m in a business. There are now two implied costs to you to run your business. They are (a) the €200 per week wages and (b) the interest which you could have earned on the €1m.

Because of the nature of production we must look at these costs in two different time periods: the short run (SR) and the long run (LR).

The short run (SR)

Definition of the short run (SR)

The **short run (SR)** is a period of time sufficiently short so that at least one of the factors of production being used is fixed in quantity. For example, if you lease a factory for six months you are committed to paying the lease on this for the six months, i.e. there is at least one fixed cost in the short run.

To identify or define the actual time period associated with the short run is like defining the length of a piece of string. In the example above the short run is six months because the size of the factory and the cost of the lease are fixed for that six-month period.

However, to a person operating a painting and decorating business the short run may be a matter of days until the employer can employ another person in the business. On the other hand, the short run could be a matter of years for a mining industry, i.e. the time period needed to locate another mine and get it into operation.

The long run (LR)

Definition of the long run (LR)

The **long run (LR)** is a period of time sufficiently long to allow the firm to change the quantity of all of the factors of production being used.

At the end of the six-month lease on the factory you can lease or build a bigger or smaller factory according to your needs, i.e. in the long run all costs are variable costs.

A fixed cost (FC)

A fixed cost (FC) does not change in the short run, as the volume of production changes, e.g. bank loan repayments, rates on buildings and payments to employees who are on a contracted wage for an agreed period of time.

A variable cost (VC)

A variable cost (VC) changes as the volume of production changes, e.g. cost of raw materials, power and transport.

Definitions of other costs

- **Average fixed cost (AFC)** = FC divided by the quantity produced
- **Average variable cost (AVC)** = VC divided by the quantity produced
- **Total cost (TC)** = FC + VC
- **Average (Total) cost (AC)** = TC divided by the quantity produced
- **Marginal cost (MC)** = the addition to total cost brought about by the production of an extra unit of the product

Table 8.1 *Costs of production*

QTY	FC	VC	TC	MC	AFC	AVC	A(T)C
1	50.00	40.00	90.00	—	50.00	40.00	90.00
2	50.00	60.00	110.00	20.00	25.00	30.00	55.00
3	50.00	100.00	150.00	40.00	16.67	33.33	50.00
4	50.00	150.00	200.00	50.00	12.50	37.50	50.00

Revenue or Income

Revenue is the income which a firm gets from selling its goods or services. Thus total revenue is the price received per item multiplied by the number of items sold.

Average revenue is the total revenue divided by the quantity sold.

Normal Profit

Normal profit is the minimum level of profit required to keep an entrepreneur in production in the long run.

Example

Assume the situation of the Lotto winner mentioned earlier and assume an interest rate of 5 per cent. When he subtracts all his annual explicit costs from his annual total revenue from the business he may be left with an accounting profit of €40,000.

However, if he had remained in employment and deposited the €1m in a bank he would have earned €60,400 (52 weeks @ €200 + €50,000 interest).

Thus if he is acting rationally he will not stay in production in the long run. The minimum profit which the business must pay him is this €60,400. Notice that these figures do not even factor in any compensation for the risk which the entrepreneur undertook.

As already stated a cost of production is any payment which must be paid to keep production going.

Therefore, normal profit is a cost of production in the long run because if the business does not earn this amount for the entrepreneur the business will close.

Thus when a firm's **total revenue** (the total income) = its **total cost** (inclusive of implied costs), then it is said to be earning **normal profit**.

Or

Dividing both totals by quantity, a firm is earning normal profit when:

Average Revenue (AR) = Average Cost (AC)

Supernormal profit

Supernormal profit (SNP) is any profit greater than or above normal profit and is earned when AR > AC.

Note: The word 'super', as used in this context, is the Latin word meaning 'above'. It does not have the common usage of 'great'.

Subnormal profit

Subnormal profit is any profit less than normal profit and happens when AR < AC.

LEARN THE KEY POINTS

1. Define cost of production
2. Define an explicit cost of production
3. Define an implied cost of production
4. Explain the short run
5. Explain the long run
6. Understand fixed costs
7. Understand variable costs
8. Understand average fixed costs
9. Understand average variable costs
10. Understand total cost
11. Define average (total) cost
12. Define marginal cost
13. Define total revenue
14. Define average revenue
15. Define normal profit
16. Explain why normal profit is a cost of production in the long run
17. Explain what two factors must equal each other for normal profit to be earned
18. Explain supernormal profit
19. Explain subnormal profit

Copy questions 1–7 into your answer book and complete the sentences filling in the blank spaces.

1 The short run is a ____________ of time sufficiently short so that at least ____________ factor of production being used is ____________ in quantity.

2 The long run is a ____________ of time sufficiently long so that ____________ of the factors of production being used are ____________ in quantity.

3 A cost of production is any ____________ which must be paid or any ____________ which must be ____________ to stay in business.

4 A fixed cost is one which does ____________ change in the ____________ as the quantity produced ____________.

5 A variable cost is one which ____________ as the volume of production increases.

6 An implied cost is any ____________ which the owner of a business must ____________.

7 Marginal cost is the ____________ to ____________ cost caused by the production of an ____________ unit of a good.

8 Complete the table below.

Table 8.2

QTY	FC (€)	VC (€)	TC (€)	MC (€)	AFC (€)	AVC (€)	ATC (€)
1	100	150					
2	100	280					
3	100	430					
4	100	600					

9 From the figures below make out a table for quantities 1 to 4 showing: Qty, FC, VC, TC, MC, AFC, AVC and ATC.
The fixed cost of producing a product is €1,000. The variable cost for the first item is €200.
The marginal costs of the second, third and fourth items are €500, €700 and €1,000 respectively.

10 Explain why an implied cost is the equivalent to an opportunity cost.

11 Explain clearly why normal profit is regarded as a cost of production in the long run.

12 Distinguish between subnormal profit and supernormal profit.

13 A manufacturer of toys has the following costs of production:
(a) The lease on a factory
(b) Electricity costs
(c) Raw materials
(d) Monthly repayments on a three-year bank loan
(e) Annual insurance on the factory
(f) A six-month lease on a delivery van
(g) Petrol costs associated with the use of the delivery van
(h) Wages for casual labour hired on a daily basis when the firm is very busy
(i) The PRSI and pension contributions paid by the firm for two full-time employees

Identify the fixed costs and the variable costs in this list and explain why you have identified each as either a fixed or a variable cost.

14 Would you expect average fixed cost to increase or decrease as the level of production increases in the short run? Explain your answer.

15 For what period of time does the short run exist? Explain your answer.

16 Normal profit is earned when the total revenue received by a firm is equal to all the costs which it must pay for. Is this a true or a false statement? Explain your answer.

Chapter 9
Costs of Production in the Short Run

In Chapter 8, An Introduction to Costs of Production, we stated that the short run (SR) is a period of time sufficiently short so that at least one of the factors of production being used is fixed in quantity.

Fixed Costs (FC)

Assume a firm starts up a business and enters into a contract to rent a factory for six months. The company **must** pay the rent on the factory for that period. This is a **fixed cost**, as the rent must be paid regardless of the level of production. The factory's owner is only interested in the rent being paid and not in the company's volume of production.

Therefore, in the short run the firm has no control over its fixed costs.

Variable Costs (VC)

When the firm starts to produce goods it must buy in raw materials, pay its electricity bill, pay its employees and meet all other costs associated with increasing its production. All of these costs are variable costs, as they increase when production levels increase and decrease when production levels decrease.

Therefore, the firm has control over these costs in the short run by being able to alter its level of production. Thus in the short run a firm has control over its variable costs.

Therefore, in the short run the business has to concern itself only with the control of its variable costs.

The Long Run (LR)

The definition of the long run stated that it was a period of time sufficiently long to enable the firm to change the quantity of all of the factors of production which it uses. Thus in the long run all costs are regarded as variable costs and the firm has control over all of its costs.

Therefore, in the long run the business has to concern itself with the control of all of its costs because they are all regarded as variable costs.

For these reasons we examine the short run and long run costs of production separately. In this chapter we examine the short run costs.

Most people are familiar with the apparently contradictory sayings, 'Many hands make light work' and 'Too many cooks spoil the broth'. At the early stages of production, in the short run, the firm's average cost tends to decrease as it benefits from the spread of its fixed costs over a greater number of units produced. Thus 'many hands make light work'!

***Table 9.1** Decreasing average costs*

QTY	FC	VC	TC	AFC	AVC	SR ATC
1	50	40	90	50.00	40.00	90.00
2	50	60	110	25.00	30.00	55.00
3	50	100	150	16.67	33.33	50.00

(See Chapter 8, p. 66, for an explanation of the abbreviated terms.)

However, as more and more people (variable factors) are employed in the fixed sized factory they will, eventually, tend to get in each other's way and the production per person will begin to slow down, thus increasing the average cost of production. Thus 'too many cooks spoil the broth'!

***Table 9.2** Increasing average costs*

QTY	FC	VC	TC	AFC	AVC	SR ATC
4	50	150	200	12.50	37.50	50.00
5	50	225	275	10.00	45.00	55.00
6	50	305	355	8.33	50.83	59.17
7	50	395	445	7.14	56.43	63.57
8	50	505	555	6.25	63.13	69.38
9	50	645	695	5.56	71.67	77.22
10	50	835	885	5.00	83.50	88.50

The Law of Diminishing (Marginal) Returns

'Many hands make light work' and 'Too many cooks spoil the broth' are sayings highlighted in economics by the Law of Diminishing Returns, or as it is alternatively known, the Law of Diminishing Marginal Returns.

Definition of the Law of Diminishing Marginal Returns

The **Law of Diminishing Marginal Returns** states that as extra units of a variable factor of production are added to a fixed factor then eventually the average output per variable factor employed will decrease.

In the example below we are assuming that the fixed factor of production is a small workshop being used to produce toys and that the variable factors are the people employed in that workshop.

Table 9.3 Fixed factors of production

Variable factors	Total output	Average output per factor employed
1	500	500
2	1,200	600
3	**1,950**	**650**
4	2,400	600
5	2,800	560
6	3,000	500
7	3,100	442.86

There are increasing returns up to the point where the third person is employed, and then diminishing returns set in as the average output per factor employed decreases as the fourth, fifth, sixth and seventh variable factors are employed.

This could also be shown on a diagram as follows:

Fig 9.1 A representation of the Law of Diminishing Returns

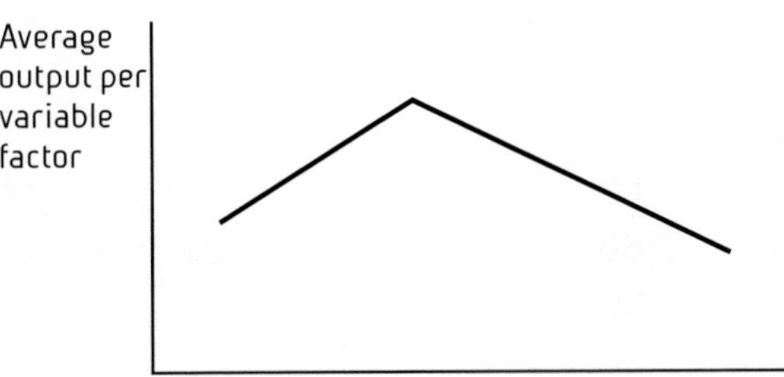

An alternative way of looking at this is to state that as extra variable factors of production are added to a fixed factor then eventually the **marginal output** per variable factor begins to decline.

Table 9.4 Marginal output per variable factor

Variable factors	1	2	3	4	5	6	7
Total output	500	1,200	1,950	2,400	2,800	3,000	3,100
Marginal output	—	700	750	450	400	200	100

✻Assumptions governing the Law of Diminishing Returns

1. The law applies to the short run (SR) only. There is at least one fixed factor of production being used.
2. It assumes that the same production methods are used when extra variable factors are employed.

3 It assumes that the quality of each of the extra variable factors employed is constant.

The shapes of the average costs curves in the SR

Let us assume that the fixed cost of producing a product is €50. In Table 9.5 below we show the costs associated with the production of this product.

Table 9.5 *Production costs*

QTY	FC	VC	TC	AFC	AVC	SR ATC	MC
1	50	40	90	50.00	40.00	90.00	
2	50	60	110	25.00	30.00	55.00	20.00
3	50	100	150	16.67	33.33	50.00	40.00
4	50	150	200	12.50	37.50	50.00	50.00
5	50	225	275	10.00	45.00	55.00	75.00
6	50	305	355	8.33	50.83	59.17	80.00
7	50	395	445	7.14	56.43	63.57	90.00
8	50	505	555	6.25	63.13	69.38	110.00
9	50	645	695	5.56	71.67	77.22	140.00
10	50	835	885	5.00	83.50	88.50	190.00

Let us now plot these average variable costs (AVC) onto a graph.

You can see from the figures in Table 9.5 and the graph in Fig 9.2 that at the third item of production the average variable costs (AVC) begin to increase. This happens because the Law of Diminishing Returns has now set in.

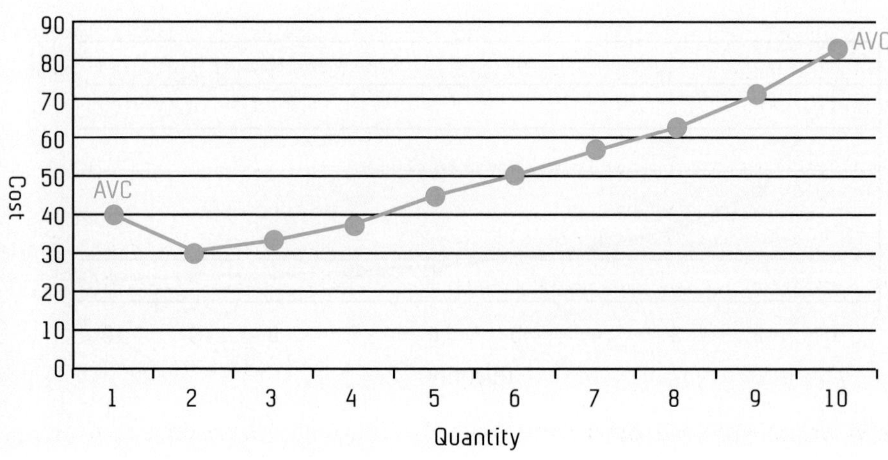

Fig 9.2 The average variable cost curve (AVC)

You will also notice that the short run (SR) average (total) cost curve (ATC) stops decreasing at this point and if you look at the graph in Fig 9.3 for the SR ATC you will notice that it is almost U-shaped.

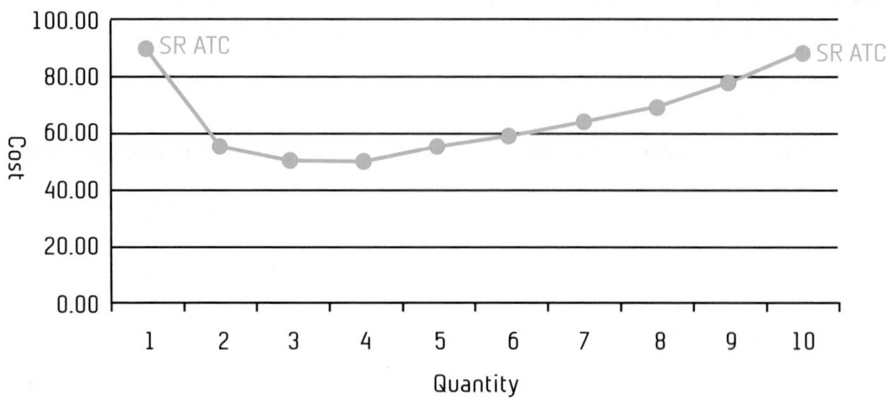

Fig 9.3 The short run (SR) average total cost curve (ATC)

This happens because the benefit of the spread of the fixed costs becomes insignificant after the production of three units. Then the Law of Diminishing Returns sets in driving up the SR ATC.

From the figures you will also notice that the average fixed cost (AFC) decreases very rapidly over the early levels of production and that the decrease slows down and is almost insignificant at the higher levels of production. This is a simple matter of arithmetic, as the same value is progressively being divided by bigger numbers.

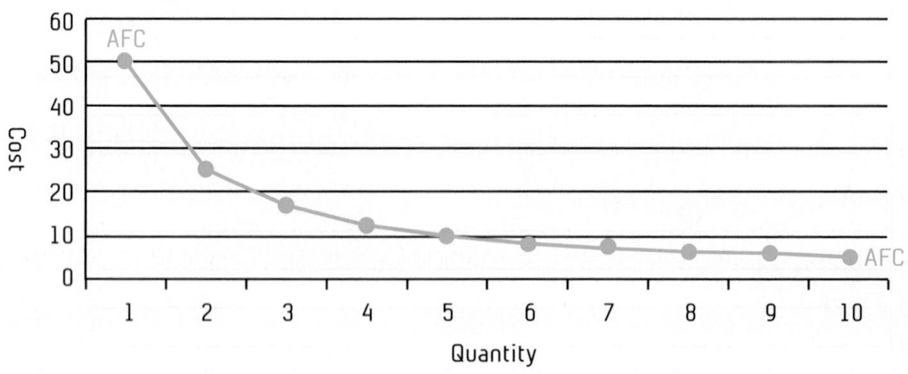

Fig 9.4 The average fixed cost (AFC)

The Relationship between Marginal Cost and SR Average Cost

The relationship between marginal cost and short run (SR) average cost (AC) is a straight arithmetical one. If we look at Table 9.6 you will see this relationship.

Table 9.6 *Cost table*

QTY	FC	VC	TC	AFC	AVC	SR ATC	MC
1	50	40	90	50.00	40.00	90.00	
2	50	60	110	25.00	30.00	55.00	20.00
3	50	100	150	16.67	33.33	50.00	40.00
4	50	150	200	12.50	37.50	50.00	50.00
5	50	225	275	10.00	45.00	55.00	75.00
6	50	305	355	8.33	50.83	59.17	80.00
7	50	395	445	7.14	56.43	63.57	90.00
8	50	505	555	6.25	63.13	69.38	110.00
9	50	645	695	5.56	71.67	77.22	140.00
10	50	835	885	5.00	83.50	88.50	190.00

Up to quantity 3 the marginal cost (MC) is less than the previous average cost (ATC), thus the average must decrease.

Therefore, when the marginal is less than the previous average the average must fall.

At quantity 4 the marginal cost is equal to the previous average cost, thus the average cost will not change.

Therefore, when the marginal is equal to the previous average the average will not change.

After quantity 4 the marginal cost is greater than the previous average cost, thus the average cost must increase.

Therefore, when the marginal is greater than the previous average the average cost must increase.

Finally, notice that marginal cost and average cost are equal to each other at average cost's lowest point.

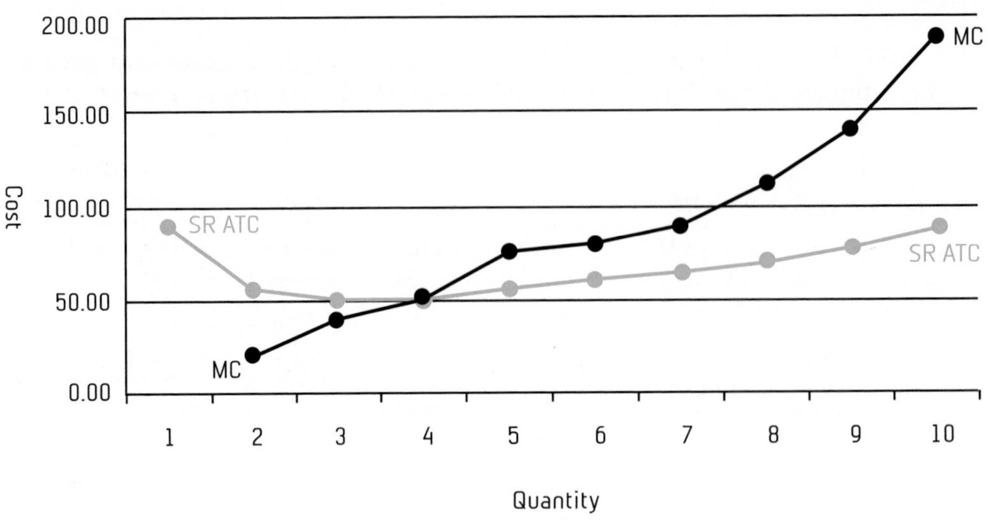

Fig 9.5 Graph of marginal cost (MC) and short run average total cost (SR ATC)

Summary

Whether MC is increasing or decreasing the following always applies:

1. If MC < the previous AC then AC will decrease.
2. If MC = the previous AC then AC will not change.
3. If MC > the previous AC then AC will increase.

The simplest way to understand this is as follows:

- Assume that there are three people in a room all aged 20. Thus the average age is 20.
- Now assume a fourth person (the marginal person) comes into the room whose age is 40, the average age increases to 25. Here the marginal > than the previous average, so the average increased.
- If, however, the fourth person was 16 years of age the average would fall to 19. Here the marginal < than the previous average.
- Finally, if the fourth person was also 20 years of age then the average would remain at 20. Here the marginal equalled the previous average.

From now on any time you draw diagrams with average and marginal cost curves intersecting each other always ensure that the MC curve cuts the AC curve at AC's lowest point.

LEARN THE KEY POINTS

1. Explain why a firm has no control over its fixed costs in the SR
2. Explain why a firm has control over its variable costs
3. State and use figures to demonstrate the Law of Diminishing Returns
4. Apply this law to an explanation of the shape of the SR average variable cost curve
5. Explain the shape of the SR average cost curve
6. Demonstrate the relationship between marginal cost and average cost

Exam Q&A: See p. 371

1 Explain clearly why we distinguish between production in the short run and production in the long run.

2 State the Law of Diminishing Returns and use your own figures to demonstrate it.

3 Complete the table below.

Table 9.7

Variable factors	1	2	3	4	5	6
Total output	800	1,500	2,300	3,000		
Marginal output					600	500

4 What are the assumptions governing the Law of Diminishing Returns?

5 Why does the Law of Diminishing Returns apply to the short run only?

6 Explain the effect of the Law of Diminishing Returns on the shape of the short run average variable cost curve.

7 'When marginal cost is increasing, average cost must also increase.' Is this a true or a false statement? Explain your answer.

8 Draw a diagram showing the relationship between marginal cost and the short run average cost curve.

9 'Why does the marginal cost curve cut the average cost curve at average cost's lowest point?

10 'As output increases the average fixed cost per item produced always decreases, but the total fixed cost remains unchanged.' Explain this statement with the aid of a diagram.

Chapter 10
Costs in the Long Run

The Short Run (SR)

You will recall from previous chapters that the short run (SR) is a period of time sufficiently short so that at least one of the factors of production being used by a firm is fixed in quantity.

A product can be produced by using different combinations of the factors of production. Once a combination is decided on, the firm is stuck with this combination in the short run. Each different possible combination of the factors of production will have its own short run average cost curve (SRAC curve).

Note: For demonstration purposes we are using L-shaped short run average cost (SRAC) curves. Most SRAC curves tend to be U-shaped due to the law of diminishing returns. We will also show these later in the chapter.

Assume that there are four possible combinations of the factors of production which could be used to produce a product. Each of these would have its own SRAC curve, i.e. SRAC1, SRAC2, SRAC3 and SRAC4 as shown in Fig 10.1.

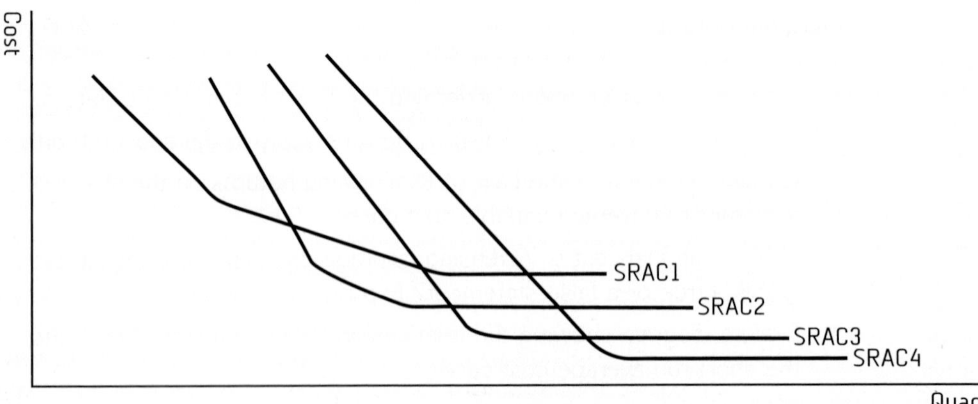

Fig 10.1 Possible short run average cost curves (SRAC)

Each of these combinations will give a different average cost curve (AC) for the production of any given quantity (see quantity 1 on Fig 10.2).

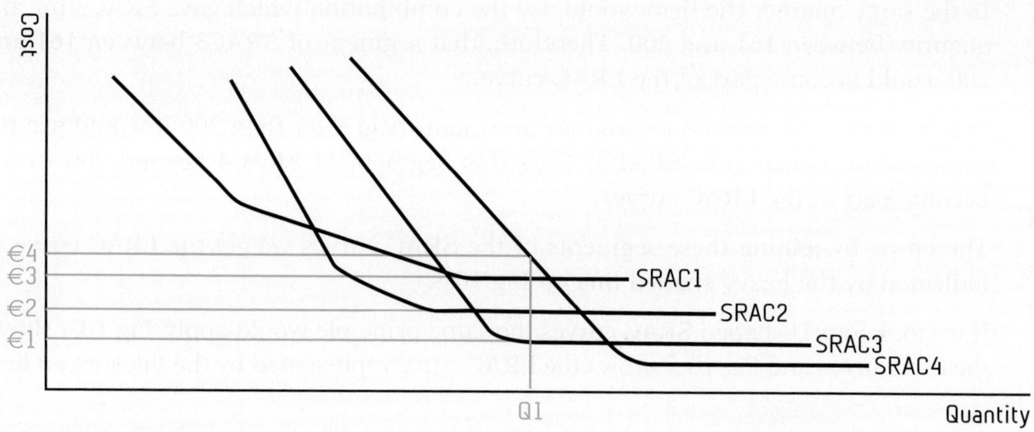

Fig 10.2 Each SRAC curve gives a different AC for any given quantity

The Long Run (LR)

The long run (LR) is a period of time sufficiently long to allow a firm to change the combination of all of the factors of production which it is using. Therefore, when the firm knows what quantity it will be producing in the LR it will opt for the combination of the factors of production which gives the lowest AC for that quantity.

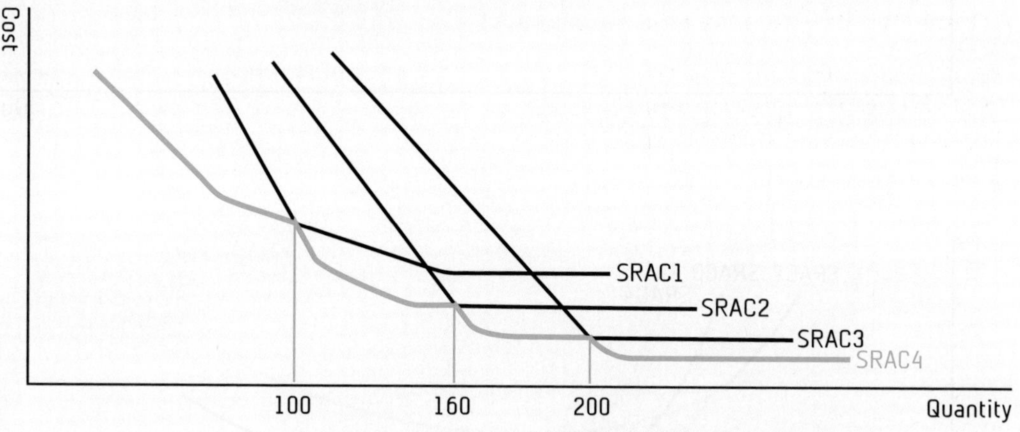

Fig 10.3 Long run average cost curve (LRAC)

If in the LR the firm wants to produce any quantity between 1 and 100 it will opt for the combination of the factors of production which gave SRAC1. Therefore, that segment of SRAC1 between 1 and 100 will become part of the long run average cost (LRAC) curve, see Fig 10.3.

Likewise, if the firm wanted to produce any quantity between 101 and 160 it would use the combination which gave SRAC2. Therefore, that segment of SRAC2 between 101 and 160 will become part of the LRAC curve, see Fig 10.3.

In the same manner the firm would use the combination which gave SRAC3 for any quantity between 161 and 200. Therefore, that segment of SRAC3 between 161 and 200 would become part of the LRAC curve.

Finally, if the firm wanted to produce any quantity greater than 200 it would use the combination which gave SRAC4. Thus that segment of SRAC4 beyond 200 would become part of the LRAC curve.

Therefore, by joining these segments of the SRAC curves we get the LRAC curve as indicated by the heavy shaded line on Fig 10.3.

If we took four U-shaped SRAC curves the same principle would apply. Fig 10.4 shows the four curves and Fig 10.5 shows the LRAC curve represented by the thick green line.

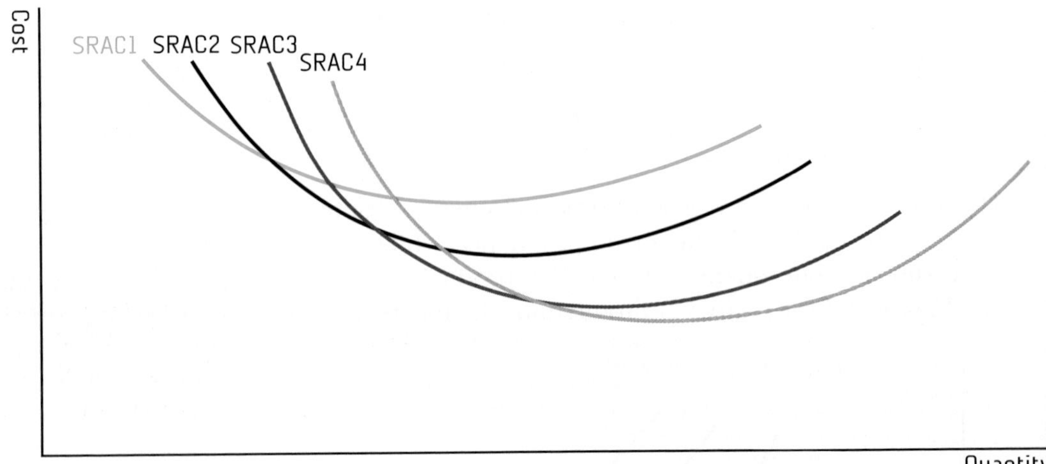

Fig 10.4 U-shaped SRAC curves

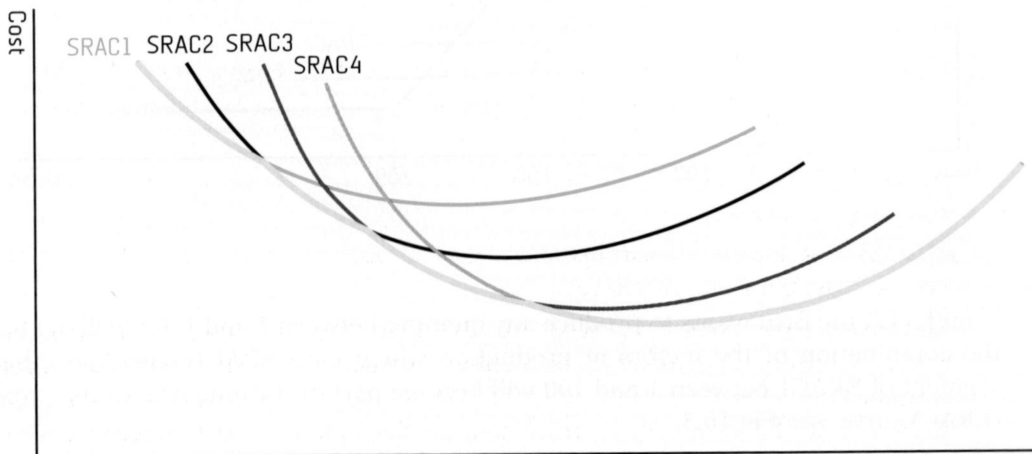

Fig 10.5 U-shaped LRAC curve

The Shape of the LRAC Curve

The shape of the LRAC curve is determined by the interaction of the economies and diseconomies of scale, i.e. the cost advantages and disadvantages of increasing production. If the economies of scale outweigh the diseconomies of scale then the AC will decrease. If the diseconomies of scale outweigh the economies of scale then the AC will increase, and if they counter-balance each other then the AC will remain constant.

Economies and diseconomies of scale are sub-divided into internal and external economies and diseconomies of scale.

Definition of internal economies of scale

Internal economies of scale are those forces **within** the firm which **decrease** AC as the size of the firm increases.

Definition of internal diseconomies of scale

Internal diseconomies of scale are those forces **within** the firm which **increase** AC as the size of the firm increases.

*Internal economies of scale

- **Financial economies:** As a firm grows in size it usually has more sources of finance, e.g. more shareholders and a better opportunity of raising debentures. Debentures are loans secured against the assets of the firm on which only the annual interest has to be paid until the end of the term of the loan. If the firm is a long established one with a good credit rating it can usually borrow money at lower interest charges.
- **Economies of construction:** It is cheaper, per cubic metre, to build a large building than a small one.
- **Specialisation of machinery:** Large firms can justify and benefit from the purchase of specialised machinery. Look at the following example.
  The cost of machine = €1m
  If production = 1m units, AC of the machine per unit produced would be €1.
  However, if the production was only 0.1m units, AC of the machine per unit produced would be €10.
- **Specialisation of labour:** The same principle applies as applies to machinery.
- **Purchasing economies:** As a firm increases in size and is buying larger quantities of supplies it can usually negotiate bulk discounts, thus reducing the average cost per item purchased.
- **Marketing economies:** The cost of advertising per unit sold is cheaper. For example, if the cost of an advertisement is €100,000 and the number of units sold is 2,000,000 then the average cost of advertising per unit sold is €0.05 cents. However, if the number of units sold is 500,000 then the average cost of advertising per unit sold is €0.20 cents.
- **Distribution economies:** It is cheaper per item delivered to deliver large quantities than small quantities.

Internal diseconomies of scale

- **Managerial diseconomies:** Large firms, by their very nature, tend to have complex structures for both the upward and downward flow of information leading to misinformation which can cause many problems.
- **Lack of morale of employees:** Many employees in big firms often regard themselves as small cogs on a big wheel and feel that their input is insignificant. This can lead to boredom and discontent among the employees. A discontented workforce tends to be less productive than a contented one. Thus average output per employee tends to decrease.
- **Non-productive employees:** Large firms tend to have a high proportion of 'non-productive' employees, e.g. supervisors, clerical staff, canteen staff and human resource officers. These people are not directly involved in the production of goods and this often results in an increase in fixed costs, thus increasing the average cost of production.

External economies of scale

Definition of external economies of scale

External economies of scale are those forces **outside** the firm which **decrease** AC as the size of the industry increases.

- **Specialisation of production of components:** As an industry expands it becomes profitable for different firms to specialise in the manufacturing of the component parts needed for a finished product. For example, in the car manufacturing industry one firm makes plugs, another makes tyres, another makes windows and so on. Each of these firms benefits from the economies of scale and so can supply the components at a lower price to the different car manufacturers. If the individual car manufacturers had to make these components themselves they would be doing so on a much smaller scale and thus would not benefit from the economies of scale.
- **Service industries:** As an industry expands more service industries spring up around it, which reduces the costs of the main industry. For example, as more firms enter an industry there are a greater number of firms faced with the same insurable risks. This will encourage insurance companies to offer lower insurance rates to these firms. This reduces the overhead costs of running the firms in the industry.
- **Education and training:** As an industry expands educational and training institutions are established to provide the skilled workers required by the industry. This provides the firms with a more productive workforce and reduces training costs. These institutions may be provided by the government or by the private sector.
- **Research and development:** Many firms may not have the long-term capital needed to invest in full-time research and development (R and D). However, if these firms come together they can employ an outside agency to undertake this R and D for them. Thus specialised full-time R and D agencies will be established to service this particular industry. Thus the individual firms will benefit from this specialisation while they concentrate on their main work.

- **Infrastructure:** As an industry begins to expand and shows the potential of making a significant contribution to the entire economy, the government may be encouraged to improve the national infrastructure, thus lowering the industry's delivery, communications and waste disposal costs.

⁂External diseconomies of scale

Definition of external diseconomies of scale

External diseconomies of scale are those forces **outside** the firm which **increase** AC as the size of the industry increases.

- **Raw materials:** As an industry expands it may encounter a scarcity of the raw materials needed. At this stage, you should now appreciate that a growing scarcity of these materials in relation to the demand for them will drive up their cost.
- **Skilled labour:** Likewise, a scarcity of the skilled or specialised labour required by the industry may occur, thus driving up wages in the industry. However, this tends to be a short-term diseconomy, as the high wages will encourage others to acquire the required skills in the long run.
- **Infrastructure:** The expansion of the infrastructure may not keep pace with the expansion of the industry. This could result in an increase in the industry's delivery, communications and waste disposal costs.

Applying the economies and diseconomies of scale to the average cost curve we see that the AC will go down if the economies outweigh the diseconomies. This usually happens at the earlier stages of production.

If the diseconomies of scale counter-balance the economies of scale the AC will remain constant.

Finally, if the diseconomies outweigh the economies the AC will increase. This usually happens at the higher levels of production. Thus the AC curve tends to be U-shaped.

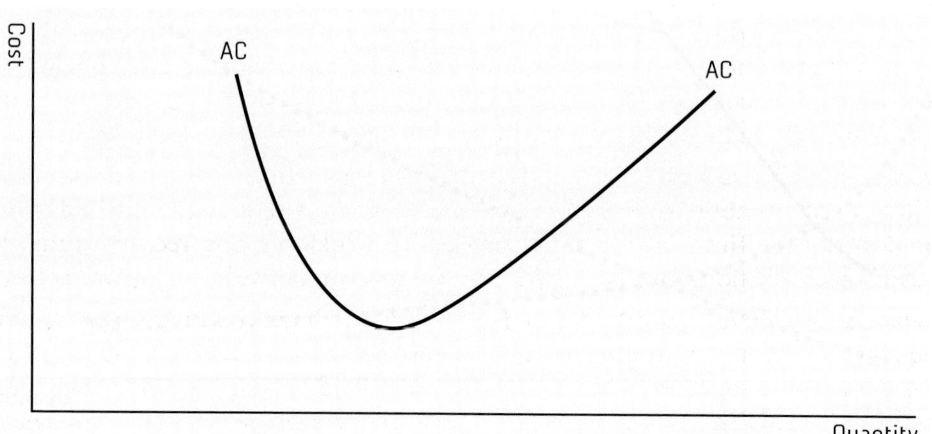

Fig 10.6 U-shaped AC curve

Returns to Scale

Returns to scale express the relationship between the change in the number of inputs (factors of production) being used to produce a good and the resulting change in production.

✳ Examples of returns to scale

For the examples of returns to scale let us assume that a firm doubles all the inputs which it uses.

1. If output exactly doubles then there are constant returns to scale.
2. If output more than doubles then there are increasing returns to scale.
3. Decreasing returns to scale will occur if the resulting output was less than doubled.

Review of Costs

✳ Identification of cost curves

Fig 10.7 shows the general trend in costs of production.

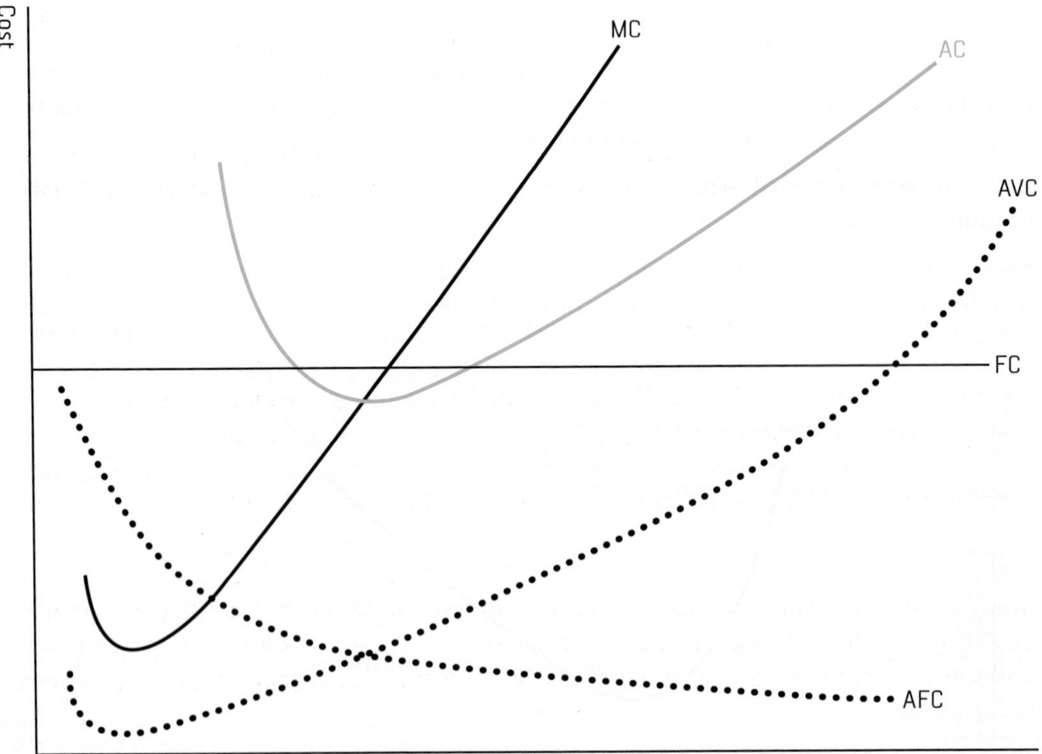

Fig 10.7 Trends in production costs

- **Fixed costs (FC)** remain unchanged as the volume of production changes, therefore it is a straight line parallel to the quantity axis.
- **Average fixed cost (AFC)** must decrease as the volume of production changes as you are dividing a fixed number (FC) by a bigger number as the quantity of production increases.
- **Average variable costs (AVC)** will begin to increase when the Law of Diminishing Returns sets in.
- **Average cost (AC)** will decrease so long as marginal cost is less than the previous average cost and average cost will increase when marginal cost is greater than the previous average cost. Therefore, marginal cost must cut average cost at average cost's lowest point.
- **Marginal cost (MC)** will decrease if the economies of scale outweigh the diseconomies of scale and it will increase if the diseconomies outweigh the economies of scale.

✳Small firms in the Irish economy

We have examined the economies of scale and have seen the enormous cost advantages which accrue to firms who produce goods on a very large scale. However, the majority of businesses in Ireland operate on a small or medium scale. Why is it that these firms do not expand and why is it that they can survive? There are many answers to these questions and the following are the most common.

1 Limited size of a market

The limited size of the Irish market may not be suitable for large-scale business as there are no economies of scale. In this situation, a small firm may survive, as it will not have to compete against any large firms.

2 Personal service

Many consumers who only purchase small quantities of a product on a regular basis often feel that their custom is not appreciated by large firms and that they are not getting the service which they think they deserve. These consumers often turn to smaller businesses where they know the local owner and feel that this business gives them a better service. Thus these smaller businesses can survive by offering this personal service. Think of the number of small butcher shops which are still surviving!

3 Consumer loyalty

Many small firms have established a very good reputation for the quality of the goods and services which they provide to their customers. These customers come to rely on and trust these firms and stay loyal to them even when bigger firms try to enter the market.

4 The desire for a viable community

The residents of small communities frequently support 'the local man' to ensure continuity of supply in their area. These residents want to have a community where most goods are available locally. This ensures the local small trader is supported. Thus if the small trader makes a good living then the business will survive. Think of the protests that take place when a local post office or a small regional hospital is threatened with closure.

5 Nature of the commodity

Heavy finished goods, which are made from local raw materials and which are costly to transport over long distances, may be manufactured locally on a small scale to supply local markets. This may be cheaper than bringing these goods to the local market from a bigger firm located far from it.

6 Membership of voluntary groups

Some firms producing on a small scale may offset the disadvantage they have in competition with large producers by adopting a joint marketing strategy with other small suppliers, e.g. hotel groups and individually owned grocery shops trading under a shared name.

7 Financial restraints

Some firms cannot expand due to lack of finance. Many firms have already borrowed to their maximum limit and cannot get access to other funding and thus cannot expand.

8 Desire to retain control

Some small or medium sized profitable firms which are family owned, or owned by a small number of people may be reluctant to expand if it means that other people would have to be brought in to provide finance or management expertise. The original owners would prefer to retain overall control of the business as they feel it is their 'baby'.

Location of Firms

The actual location of a firm can have a significant effect on the efficiency or profitability of that firm. This next section takes a look at the factors which influence an entrepreneur's decision to locate his/her business in any given area or region.

The nature of the industry in which the firm operates will have a significant bearing on its location.

Traditionally, industries have been classified as **supply-oriented**, **market-oriented** or **footloose**.

Supply-oriented industries

Supply-oriented industries are those industries, everything else being equal, which benefit more from being located nearer to the source of their raw materials than being located near the market for their output. These are bulk-decreasing industries. In these industries, the raw materials are heavier or more bulky than the finished product. Thus transport costs are greatly reduced by locating near the source of the raw materials. The meat-processing industry is an example of this type of industry.

✻Market-oriented industries

Market-oriented industries are those industries, everything else being equal, which benefit more from being located nearer the market for their product rather than being located near the source of their raw materials. These are bulk-increasing industries. In these industries, the finished product is heavier or more bulky than the raw materials. Thus transport costs are greatly reduced by locating near the market for the finished goods. The furniture-making industry is a good example. Retail industries also have to be located as near as possible to their markets.

✻Footloose industries

Footloose industries are those industries which have no particular advantage being located either near the source of their raw materials, or being located near the market for their products. Thus the cost of transporting the goods is not given the same priority as is given by the two above. The firms in these industries have a greater choice of location. Therefore, they weigh up many factors before deciding on any given location.

Many multinational companies fall into this category and can cause competition between countries or regions to attract them to that country or region. They consider the following factors.

- **The cost of land:** Land close to towns and cities is very expensive. Thus if the firm required a lot of land cost is a very important factor.
- **The availability of labour:** If the business is a labour intensive one it will have to examine regions with a plentiful supply of suitable labour and eliminate areas where the labour is unavailable.
- **The cost of labour:** Many potentially suitable areas may have a plentiful supply of the required labour, but the wage rates may vary in these locations. Here, everything else being equal, the firm would opt for the area with the lower wage rate. Think of the number of manufacturing firms which are leaving Ireland to locate in lower-wage countries.
- **The availability of a reliable power and water supply:** While we may take these resources for granted in Ireland, our supply of these is often overstretched, particularly for production purposes. This is one of the important factors which stops companies moving to Third World countries.
- **The availability of a good transport infrastructure:** This is essential to reduce the cost and time involved getting the goods to and from the business. It is also a factor to ensure ease of access for the labour force. Remember, too, that many firms, whether in the export or the import sectors, may require good sea and air transport.
- **The availability of a good communications system:** The speed and reliability of a communications system is becoming increasingly important. As trade

becomes more global it is essential for some firms to be able to communicate with other firms in different locations and in different time zones. Hence the importance of a broadband communications system.

- **Government inducements:** The government may offer grants to businesses to locate in some of the less developed regions of the country. This reduces the set-up costs for firms and hopefully creates a bigger return on the money which they themselves invest in the business. Some regions can also offer tax concessions to locate there.
- **The social capital available in the area:** If a company has to attract a labour force to an area then the geographical mobility of the labour will be greatly influenced by the social, housing and educational facilities of the area.
- **Environmental issues:** The location of some firms or industries may be restricted by the potential risks, arising from the production of the goods, to the health and safety of the people in the region. Production may also be detrimental to the environment of some regions. Think of the number of objections that are heard when it is proposed to locate an incinerator in an area.

LEARN THE KEY POINTS

1. How to construct the LRAC curve and know the relationship between the LRAC curve and the SRAC curve
2. Define and list the internal and external economies and diseconomies of scale
3. Show the effect which they have on the shape of the LRAC curve
4. Explain the reasons why small and medium sized firms can still exist
5. Explain (a) constant returns to scale, (b) increasing returns to scale and (c) decreasing returns to scale
6. Know and explain the factors which determine the location of a business

Exam Q&A: See p. 373

Copy questions 1–8 into your answer book and complete each of the sentences by filling in the blank spaces.

1. The LRAC curve is constructed by joining together the segments of the various ____________ cost ____________ which give the lowest ____________ for any given quantity.
2. The shape of the LRAC curve is determined by the interaction of the ____________ and ____________ of scale.
3. The LRAC curve will slope downwards when the economies of scale ____________ the ____________ of scale.
4. The LRAC curve will slope ____________ when the economies of scale are ____________ by the diseconomies of scale.
5. The internal economies of scale are the forces ____________ the firm which cause the AC to ____________ as the firm's production level ____________.
6. The internal diseconomies of scale are the forces within the firm which cause the AC to ____________ as the firm's production level ____________.
7. The external economies of scale are the forces ____________ of the firm which cause the AC to ____________ as the size of the ____________ grows.
8. The ____________ diseconomies of ____________ are the forces ____________ of the firm which increase AC as the size of the ____________ grows.
9. Describe fully how the long run AC curve is constructed.
10. Explain fully why the long run AC curve tends to be U-shaped.
11. Many medium sized firms have an L-shaped AC curve. Explain how this could arise.
12. The majority of businesses in Ireland are small or medium-sized enterprises. How can these survive against competition from very large enterprises that benefit from the economies of scale?
13. Distinguish clearly the difference between market-oriented industries and supply-oriented industries.
14. How do footloose industries differ from the two industries mentioned in question 13?
15. State and explain any five factors which a footloose firm would consider when deciding on the location of its operation.

Chapter 11
Production Levels in the Short Run and the Long Run

Revision of Essential Terms

- **Supply (S)** means the number of units of a good made available for sale at any given market price at any given time.
- **The short run (SR)** is a period of time sufficiently short so that at least one factor of production used is fixed in quantity.
- **The long run (LR)** is a period of time sufficiently long so that all of the factors of production used are variable in quantity.
- **Fixed costs (FC)** are costs which do not change as the quantity of goods produced changes in the SR, e.g. lease on a factory and repayments on a term loan.
- **Variable costs (VC)** are costs which change as the quantity of goods produced changes, e.g. raw materials and electricity.
- **Marginal cost (MC)** is the addition to **total cost** (TC) brought about by the production of an extra unit of a product.
- **Average revenue (AR)** is the total income received divided by the quantity sold. If you rationalise this you will see that it is the price at which the product is sold.
- **Marginal revenue (MR)** is the addition to total revenue (TR) brought about by the sale of an extra unit of a product.
- **Equilibrium for a producer** occurs when the firm earns the maximum possible profit or, in the SR, keeps its losses to the minimum possible level.
- **Normal profit (NP)** is the minimum level of profit which an entrepreneur must earn to stay in production in the long run.
- **Supernormal profit (SNP)** is any profit above normal profit.

In the short run there is always at least one fixed factor of production used. Therefore, there is at least one fixed cost. This has to be paid even if no production takes place.

Production in the Short Run

Remember that in the short run a firm has no control over its fixed costs but it can control its variable costs.

✳Point 1

A producer will stay in production in the SR so long as its total revenue (TR) is at least equal to its variable costs (VC).

Or

Its average revenue (AR) is at least equal to its average variable costs (AVC). (This is simply dividing TR and VC by the quantity produced.)

Example 1

Table 11.1 *AR > AVC*

Qty	FC	VC	AVC	TC	AR	TR	Loss
5	€3,000	€1,000	€200	€4,000	€250	€1,250	– €2,750

Here the firm is losing €2,750. But if it closed down in the SR it would have to pay out its FC of €3,000. By staying in production it is saving €250. It can be seen that its AR > AVC.

Example 2

Table 11.2 *AR < AVC*

Qty	FC	VC	AVC	TC	AR	TR	Loss
5	€3,000	€1,000	€200	€4,000	€150	€750	– €3,250

Here the firm is losing €3,250. But if it closed down in the SR it would only have to pay out its FC of €3,000. By staying in production it is adding €250 to its losses. It can be seen that its AR < AVC.

Note: Therefore, to stay in production in the short run AR must at least equal AVC.

✳Point 2

A producer, in equilibrium, will always produce the output or quantity which gives the maximum profit or the minimum loss in the SR. This happens at the output where MR = MC, provided MC > MR at all production levels after that.

Think of the logic of this. If you add more to your income (MR) than you add to your cost (MC), the profit must go up or the losses will go down. On the other hand, if you add more to the cost (MC) than to your income (MR), the profit will go down or the losses will increase.

Example

Table 11.3 *A firm's costs and revenue in the SR*

€ Qty	€ FC	€ VC	€ AVC	€ TC	€ MC	€ AR	€ TR	€ MR	€ Loss
1	5,000	200	200.00	5,200	—	500	500	—	4,700
2	5,000	400	200.00	5,400	200	500	1,000	500	4,400
3	5,000	700	233.33	5,700	300	500	1,500	500	4,200
4	5,000	1,100	275.00	6,100	400	500	2,000	500	4,100
5	**5,000**	**1,600**	**320.00**	**6,600**	**500**	**500**	**2,500**	**500**	**4,100**
6	5,000	2,200	366.67	7,200	600	500	3,000	500	4,200
7	5,000	2,900	414.29	7,900	700	500	3,500	500	4,400

Here it can be seen that the firm's minimum loss (i.e. €4,100) is incurred when it produces 5 units and at that output MR = MC and at all outputs after that MC > MR.

It should also be noted that the firm's AR of €500 > its AVC of €320. Therefore, this is its equilibrium production level in the SR.

Therefore, equilibrium in the SR is where:

(i) AR is at least = AVC

And

(ii) MR = MC provided MC > MR after that.

The same condition applies in the SR even if the firm is making a profit.

Production in the Long Run

✳Point 1

To stay in production in the long run a firm must earn a minimum of normal profit (see notes on Costs of Production on p. 67).

Therefore, the first requirement for long run production is that:
AR must at least = AC

✳Point 2

To be in equilibrium in the LR the firm must earn maximum profit, therefore it will produce the quantity where:
MR = MC provided MC > MR after that.

Table 11.4 *A firm's costs and revenue in the LR*

Qty	€ FC	€ VC	€ AVC	€ TC	€ MC	€ AC	€ AR	€ TR	€ MR	€ Profit
1	7,000	1,000	1,000	8,000	–	8,000	6,000	6,000	6,000	–2,000
2	7,000	4,000	2,000	11,000	3,000	5,500	6,000	12,000	6,000	1,000
3	7,000	8,000	2,666.66	15,000	4,000	5,000	6,000	18,000	6,000	3,000
4	7,000	13,000	3,250	20,000	5,000	5,000	6,000	24,000	6,000	4,000
5	**7,000**	**19,000**	**3,800**	**26,000**	**6,000**	**5,200**	**6,000**	**30,000**	**6,000**	**4,000**
6	7,000	26,000	4,333.33	33,000	7,000	5,500	6,000	36,000	6,000	3,000
7	7,000	34,000	4,857.14	41,000	8,000	5,857.14	6,000	42,000	6000	1,000

Here again it can be seen that the firm's equilibrium output is 5 units earning it the maximum profit of €4,000 and at this output MR = MC (with MC > MR after that) and AR > AC.

Therefore, equilibrium in the LR is where:

(i) AR is at least = AC

(ii) MR = MC provided MC > MR after that.

LEARN THE KEY POINTS

1. Equilibrium in the short run is where:
   (a) AR is at least equal to AVC
   And
   (b) MC = MR provided MC > MR for all production levels after that

2. Equilibrium in the long run is where:
   (a) AR is at least equal to AC
   And
   (b) MC = MR provided MC > MR for all production levels after that

Copy questions 1–5 into your answer book and complete each of the sentences by filling in the blank spaces.

1 A firm will stay in production in the short run if its average ____________ is at least equal to its average ____________.

2 A firm will stay in production in the long run if its ____________ is at least equal to its ____________.

3 If a firm's MR is greater than its MC the firm's losses will ____________.

4 If a firm's MC is greater than its MR the firm's profits will ____________.

5 A firm will earn maximum profit when its ____________ is equal to its ____________ provided its MC is greater than its ____________ for all quantities after that.

6 Why would a firm, in the short run, be more concerned about its variable costs than its fixed costs?

7 Under what circumstances would you advise a firm to stay in production even though it is losing money?

8 A firm has fixed costs of €1,000. The variable cost of producing the first item is €20. The total cost of producing the second item is €1,040. After that the marginal cost increases by €20 when each extra unit is produced. The firm receives a fixed price of €60 per item sold. What level of output would this firm produce in the short run? Justify your answer.

9 If the figures in question 8 held true in the long run and the total market demand for the product was only 10 units, what quantity, if any, would the firm produce in the long run? Justify your answer.

10 Make out your own table of figures to show that a firm is in equilibrium when

(a) Its AR is at least equal to its AC

(b) Its MR is equal to its MC

(c) Its MC is greater than its MR for all quantities after the equilibrium quantity

Chapter 12
Perfect Competition

In Chapter 12 and the four following chapters we will examine the diverse conditions under which firms in different industries operate and look at their **equilibrium position**. You may recall that the term equilibrium refers to the ideal situation under any given set of circumstances. As different firms work under diverse conditions the equilibrium positions of the firms are different.

These different conditions are referred to as **the forms of competition** or **market structures**. All of these forms of competition operate under conditions which have specific characteristics.

When we examine the **equilibrium** of a firm we lay emphasis on three essential points:

1. The **quantity** the firm will produce.
2. The **price** it will receive for each unit sold.
3. The **profit level** it earns.

We will also comment on its average cost of production.

The first of these forms of competition is known as **perfect competition**, so called because no one firm operating in this type of industry has any competitive advantage over the other firms in the industry.

Assumptions for the Existence of Perfect Competition

1. There are many small firms in the industry. Each firm produces such a tiny fraction of the total supply of the industry that no one firm, by its own actions, can influence the market price.
2. There are very many buyers or consumers in the industry. Each consumer consumes such a tiny fraction of the total consumption of the industry that no one buyer's consumption is big enough to affect the market price.
3. All firms aim to make maximum profits, therefore the firm will produce the quantity where MC = MR provided MC > MR at all quantities after that.

4 There is freedom of entry into and exit from the industry. This means that anybody who has the knowledge and the money can set up in the industry. There are no social or political pressures forcing a firm to stay in production.

5 There is widespread knowledge of the profit level being earned in the industry. This means it is widely known whether the firms are earning normal, supernormal or subnormal profit. It does not imply that the absolute profit being made by each firm is known.

As a result of the assumptions 4 and 5, only normal profit (NP) can be earned in the long run. If the market price were big enough so that supernormal profits (SNPs) were being earned this would attract more firms into the industry, increasing total supply and thereby reducing the market price. This would continue to happen until only normal profits were being earned. Likewise, if the market price were so small that the firms were earning subnormal profit then some firms would begin to leave the industry. This would decrease supply and increase the market price. This would continue until the remaining firms were earning normal profit (see 'SNPs in the SR in Perfect Competition', p. 99).

6 The products produced by all firms are homogeneous, i.e. they are identical and consumers have no preference for the product of one firm over that of another firm. As a result, it would be pointless for an individual producer to advertise his/her product. When you (or your parents) go shopping for cabbage you do not look for Farmer Smith's cabbage in preference to Farmer Murphy's cabbage. Thus the only form of advertising in perfect competition would be generic or industrial advertising, which promotes the product of an industry rather than the product of an individual firm (see Chapter 15, Forms of Advertising, p. 128).

7 Each firm has a perfectly elastic supply of the factors of production, i.e. the unit cost of each of the factors of production is the same for all firms.

8 All firms produce at the lowest possible average cost.

The LR Equilibrium of a Firm in Perfect Competition

✳Price

Because of assumptions 1 and 2 (see p. 95) each firm is a **price taker**, i.e. it must charge the price which is determined by the interaction of the total supply of and total demand for the product in the industry.

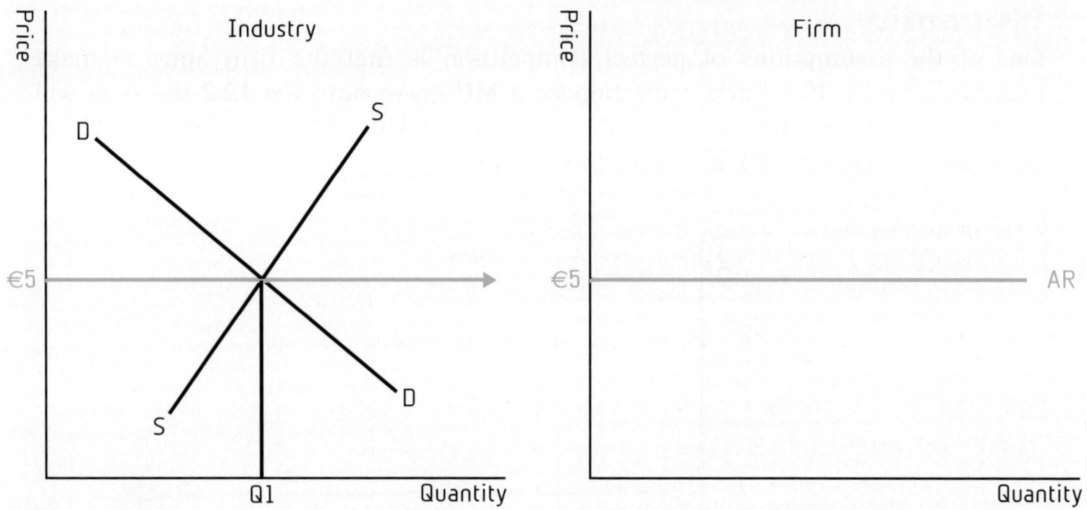

Fig 12.1 *These diagrams show that the price of €5 is determined by the interaction of total S and total D in the industry and that the firm must sell each unit of its product at that price, i.e. the AR for the firm is €5*

When AR is constant for all quantities sold then MR is also constant and equal to AR.

Table 12.1 *AR = MR in perfect competition*

Quantity	AR	TR	MR
1	€5	€5	–
2	€5	€10	€5
3	€5	€15	€5
4	€5	€20	€5
5	€5	€25	€5

Therefore, both AR and MR are represented by the same line, as shown in Fig 12.2.

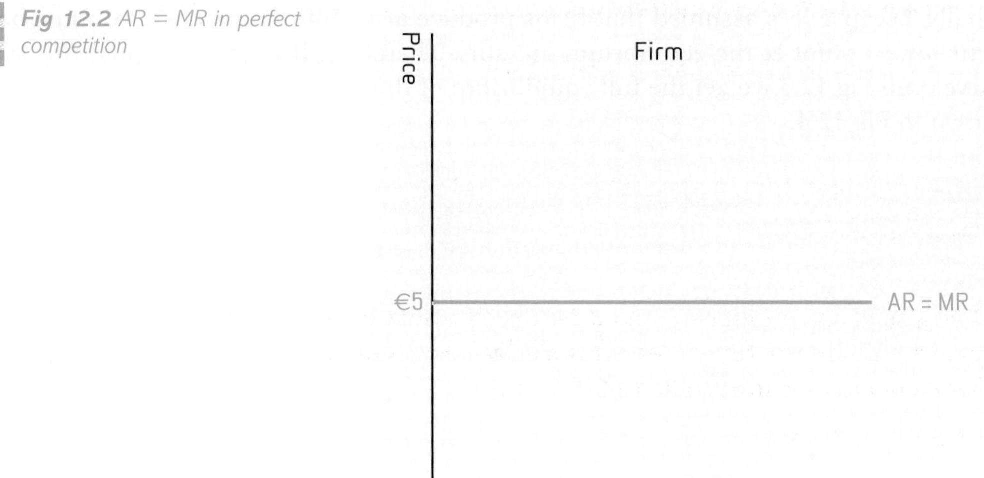

Fig 12.2 *AR = MR in perfect competition*

✳Quantity

One of the assumptions of perfect competition is that the firm aims to make maximum profit. If we now superimpose a MC curve onto Fig 12.2 the firm will produce the quantity where MR = MC provided that MC > MR after that. Therefore, the firm will produce 100, as shown in Fig 12.3.

Fig 12.3 This quantity is known as the equilibrium quantity

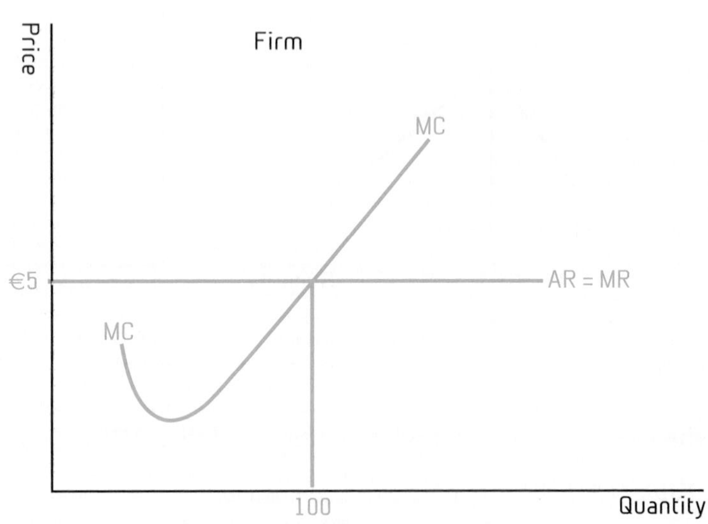

✳Profit level

Firms can only earn normal profit in the long run. This is because it is assumed that there is full knowledge of the profit levels being earned and that there is freedom of entry into and exit from the industry. Therefore, **AC must equal AR** at the equilibrium output.

Finally, because it is assumed that firms produce at the minimum cost, AC must be at its lowest point at the equilibrium quantity. Therefore, if we superimpose the AC curve onto Fig 12.3 we get the full equilibrium of the firm in perfect competition, as shown in Fig 12.4.

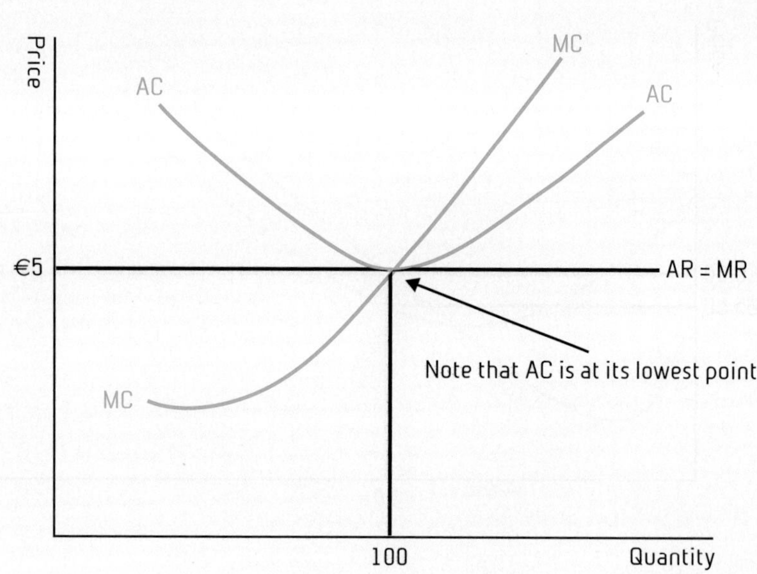

Fig 12.4
Long run equilibrium in perfect competition

Summary

AR = MR (because price is constant)
MR = MC (because of profit maximisation)
AR = AC (because of normal profit)
AC is at its lowest point.

Therefore, AR = MR = MC = AC, at AC's lowest point.

SNPs in the SR in Perfect Competition

You will recall that all firms in perfect competition are price takers. Thus it is possible that the price or AR could be greater than the AC in the short run. If this happens then the short run equilibrium will be as shown in Fig 12.5.

Here the firm is earning maximum profit producing 50 units as MR = MC and MC > MR after that. You will also notice that AR (€6) > ATC (€5.50) so the firm is earning SNPs of 50c per item.

Logically if the average total cost (ATC) is covered by the average revenue (AR) then the average variable cost (AVC) must also be covered as ATC = AVC + AFC.

Remember that this situation could not prevail in the long run. We assume that there is widespread knowledge of the profit level being earned in the industry and that there is freedom of entry into the industry. The existence of the SNPs will attract

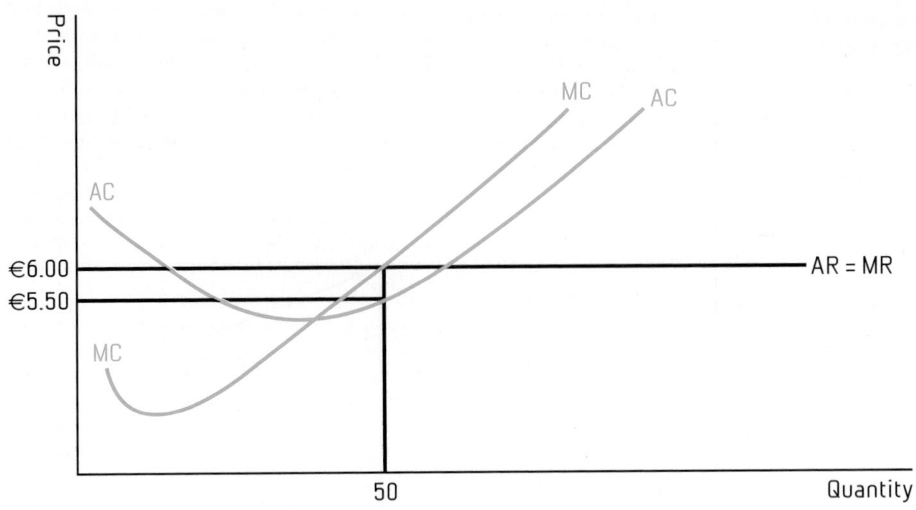

Fig 12.5 Short run equilibrium in perfect competition

more firms into the industry. The resulting increase in supply will drive down the market price and this will continue until the firms are only earning normal profit. This new market price, €5, is shown on Fig 12.6 and the firm will decrease its production to 45 units at the lower price of €5.

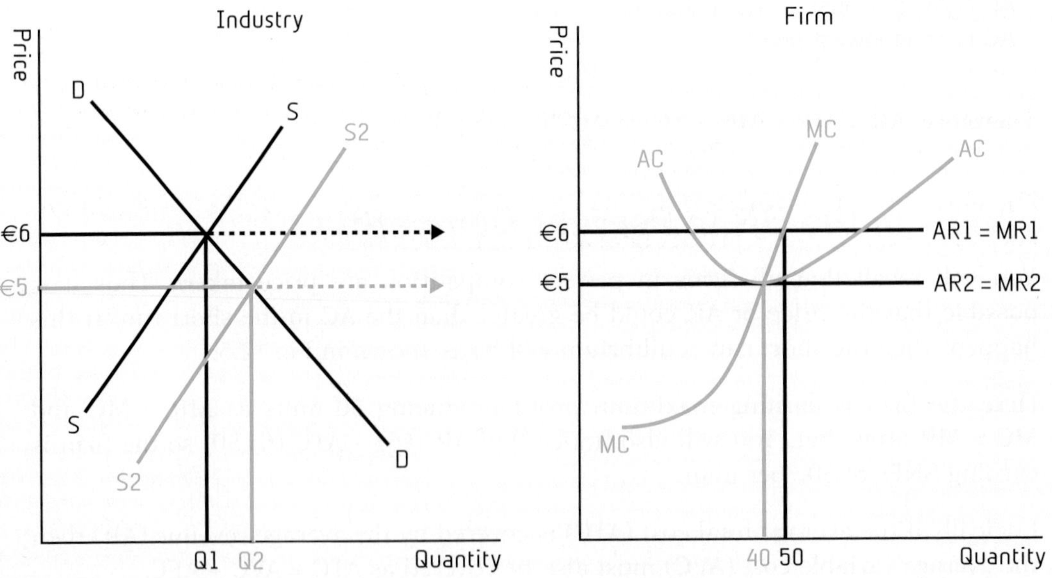

Fig 12.6 In the long run the increase in supply causes a decrease in market price ensuring the firm only earns normal profit

Advantages of perfect competition

1. The product is produced and sold at the lowest point on the AC curve ensuring that it is sold to the consumer at the lowest possible price.
2. Because the product is produced at the lowest point of the AC curve it means that there is no wastage of resources.
3. Only normal profits are earned in the long run, therefore there is no exploitation of consumers.
4. The consumer is guaranteed to get the same quality product at the same price no matter where it is purchased. This is because the products of all firms are homogeneous (the same kind) and the firms are price takers.
5. Perfect competition encourages efficiency as only those firms which can produce and sell at the lowest AC will survive.

Disadvantages of perfect competition

1. There is no choice to the consumer as all the products sold are homogeneous.
2. All the firms in the industry are relatively small. Thus they may not benefit from the economies of scale. Therefore, their lowest possible AC may be relatively high, resulting in high prices to the consumers.

It should be noted that the concept of perfect competition is highly theoretical. It is extremely unlikely that there could be a perfectly elastic supply of the factors of production and that all firms would produce at the same low average cost.

The closest examples to perfect competition in Ireland would be the production of potatoes and carrots for private household consumption.

The Construction of the SR and LR Supply Curves of a Firm in Perfect Competition

A supply curve is a graph which shows the relationship between the market price of a good and the number of units of the good made available for sale at any given time.

In perfect competition the firm always produces the output that gives either maximum profit or minimum loss.

This happens when MC = MR, provided that MC > MR for all quantities produced after that.

In perfect competition firms are price takers. Thus price (AR) is the same no matter how many units are supplied. Thus AR = MR in perfect competition.

Table 12.2 *AR = MR in perfect competition*

Quantity	AR	TR	MR
1	€5	€5	–
2	€5	€10	€5
3	€5	€15	€5
4	€5	€20	€5

Thus in perfect competition AR and MR are represented by the same line, as shown in Fig 12.7.

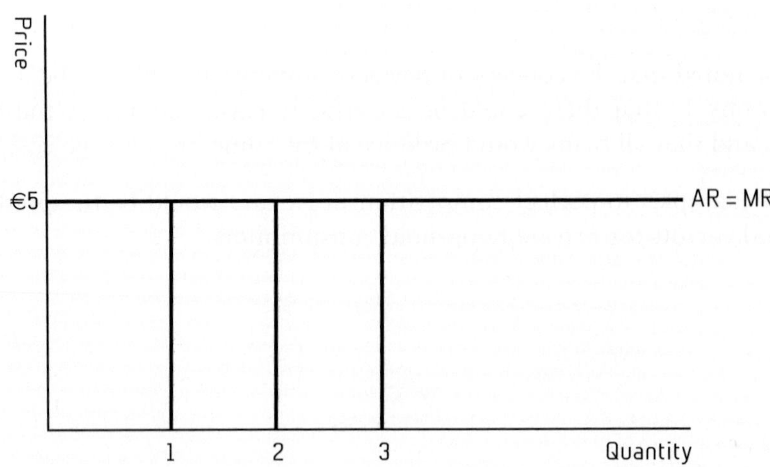

Fig 12.7 *AR = MR in perfect competition*

Now look at the different quantities which would be produced by a firm at four different possible market prices, namely €1, €2, €3 and €4, as shown in Fig 12.8.

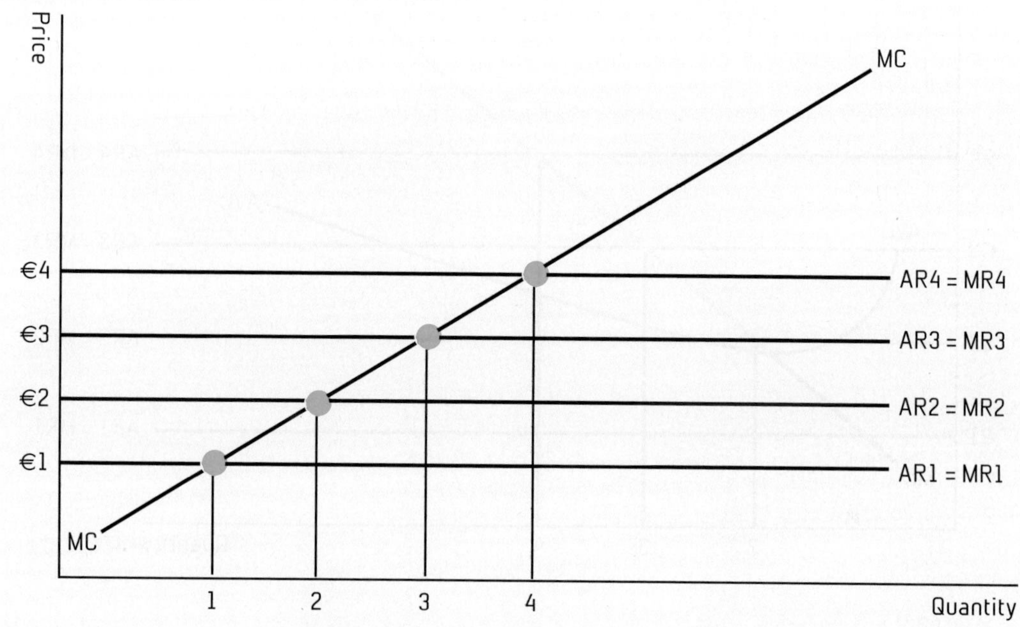

Fig 12.8 Production quantities at €1, €2, €3 and €4

- At €1 one unit will be supplied as here MR1 = MC and MC > MR1 after that. This gives one point on the supply curve.
- At €2 two units will be supplied as here MR2 = MC and MC > MR2 after that. This gives another point on the supply curve.
- At €3 three units will be supplied as here MR3 = MC and MC > MR3 after that. This gives another point on the supply curve.
- At €4 four units will be supplied as here MR4 = MC and MC > MR4 after that. This gives another point on the supply curve.

Note: Each of these points is a point on the MC curve. No matter what market price is taken it will still give a point on the MC curve.

Thus the MC curve shows the relationship between the market price of a product and the number of units of a good made available for sale at any given time. Therefore, by definition, the MC curve is the supply curve.

However, production will only take place in the short run if AR is at least equal to AVC, i.e. AR = or > AVC.

If AR < AVC then the firm should cease production and only pay its fixed costs. Therefore, only that part of the MC curve that is above the AVC curve will constitute the SR supply curve.

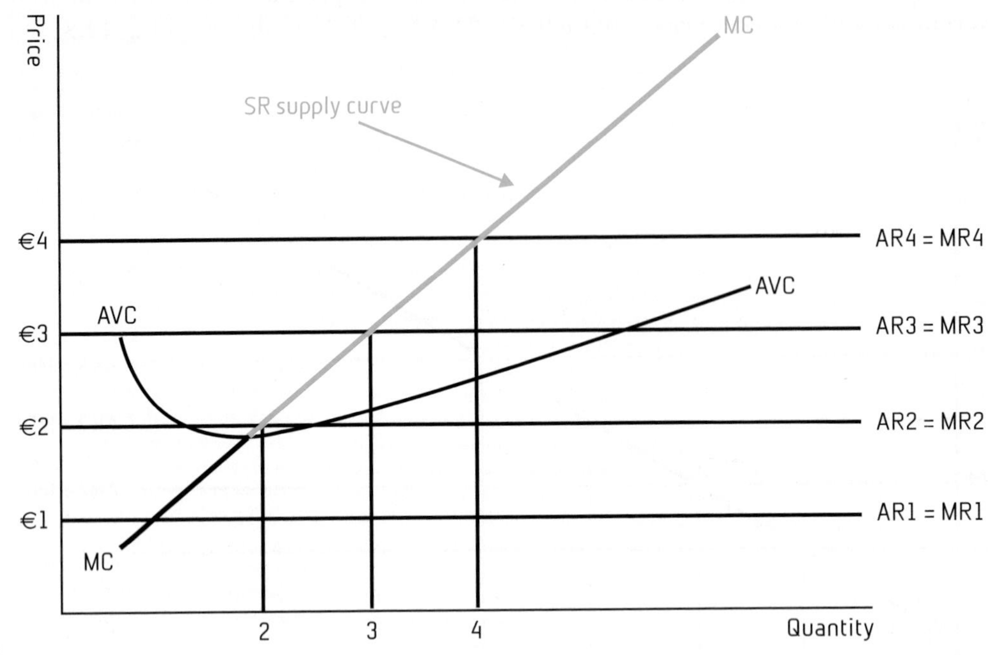

Fig 12.9 Short run (SR) supply curve

Production will take place only in the long run if AR is at least equal to AC, i.e. the firm must earn a minimum of normal profit to stay in production in the long run.

Therefore, only that part of the MC curve that is above the AC curve will constitute the LR supply curve.

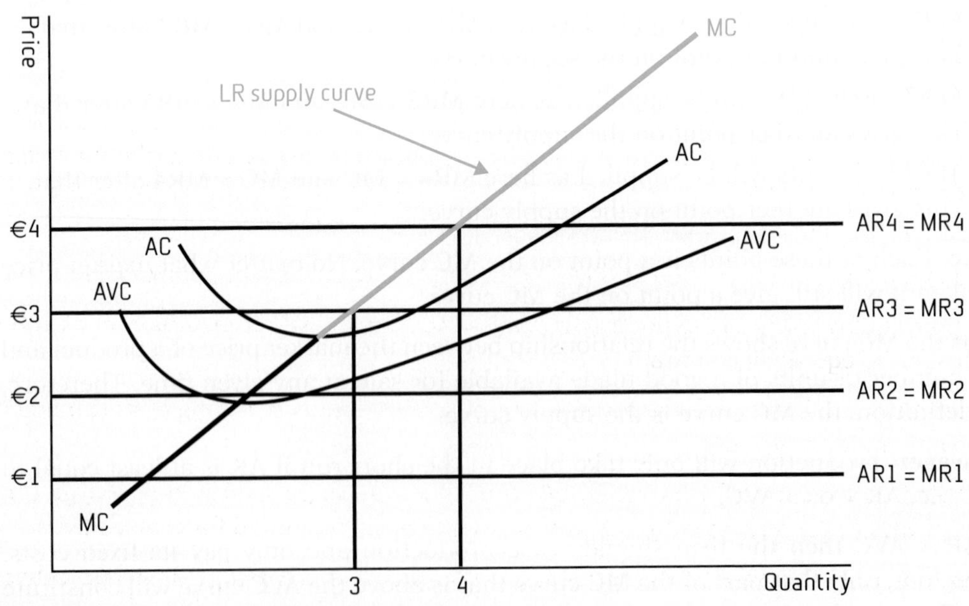

Fig 12.10 Long run (LR) supply curve

The Relationship between MPP and MRP in Perfect Competition

Marginal physical product (MPP) is the addition to total production caused by the employment of an extra unit of a factor of production.

Marginal revenue product (MRP) is the addition to total revenue caused by the employment of an extra unit of a factor of production.

In perfect competition the firm is a price taker. Therefore, it receives the same price (AR) per unit sold, no matter how many units it sells.

Therefore, in perfect competition MPP × AR is always equal to MRP.

Table 12.3 *MPP x AR = MRP*

Qty of labour	Total production	MPP	AR	Total revenue	MRP
1	100	–	€10	€1,000	–
2	120	20	€10	€1,200	€200
3	135	15	€10	€1,350	€150

Here it can be seen that when the second unit of labour is employed its MPP of 20 × AR of €10 (i.e. €200) = the MRP of €200.

Also when the third unit of labour is employed its MPP of 15 × AR of €10 (i.e. €150) = the MRP of €150.

This does not happen in any other form of competition. This will be illustrated in Chapter 13, Monopoly.

Perfectly Elastic Demand

In Chapter 6, Elasticity of Demand, we stated price elasticity of demand (PED) can be perfectly elastic. This means that any change in price will cause demand to change to zero. The PED in this case works out to be equal to infinity.

Let us take a point on the demand (AR) curve of a firm in perfect competition.

The point being taken is the point where AR = AC = MR = MC at the quantity of 100, as this is the equilibrium output.

Remember that there is a large number of firms in the industry selling homogeneous (the same kind of) goods.

In perfect competition firms are price takers, i.e. the price which they charge for their product is determined by the overall supply of and demand for the product.

Thus if a firm increased its price all its customers would switch to some other supplier to get the identical product at a cheaper price. It is assumed that consumers

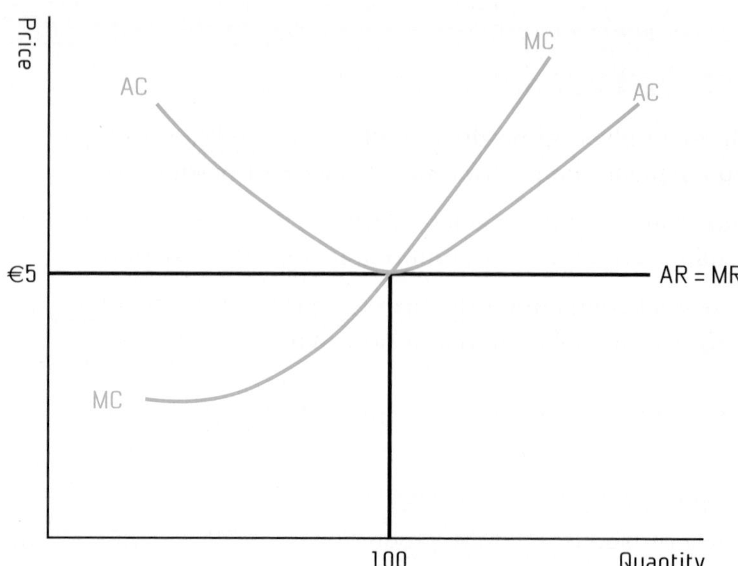

Fig 12.11 PED is perfectly elastic at any quantity in perfect competition

act rationally. Thus the firm's sales would fall to zero. When a change in price causes demand to change to zero the PED is said to be perfectly elastic.

If the firm decreased its price then its AR would be less than its AC resulting in subnormal profits. This would result in the firm ceasing production. Therefore, the sales would drop to zero. This again indicates that the PED is perfectly elastic for this firm.

LEARN THE KEY POINTS

1. The assumptions of or the conditions for the existence of perfect competition
2. Understand the term 'homogeneous goods'
3. Explain, with the aid of diagrams, the concept of 'a price taker'
4. Explain why AR = MR in perfect competition
5. Explain, with the aid of diagrams, the SR and the LR equilibrium of a firm in perfect competition
6. Explain why firms in perfect competition can earn only normal profit in the long run
7. Explain the advantages and disadvantages of perfect competition
8. Understand why the price elasticity of demand for a firm's product, in perfect competition, is perfectly elastic
9. Explain the relationship between marginal physical productivity and marginal revenue productivity in perfect competition
10. Understand the construction of the short run and long run curve of a firm in perfect competition

Exam Q&A: See p. 374

Copy questions 1–6 into your answer book and complete each of the sentences by filling in the blank spaces.

1 The term 'homogeneous goods', as used in perfect competition, means that the goods produced by ____________ of the firms in the industry are ____________.

2 Firms who must sell their products at a certain price are known as ____________.

3 The market for goods produced by firms in perfect competition tends to be a large market as there is a very ________________________ producers and a very ____________ of consumers.

4 When firms have a perfectly elastic supply of the factors of production then the ____________ cost of each of the factors is ____________ for all firms.

5 In perfect competition AR, MR, AC and MC are all equal to each other at ____________.

6 In perfect competition the firm's short run supply curve is that part of the ____________ curve that is above the ____________ curve.

7 State and explain the assumptions governing perfect competition.

8 Describe, with the aid of a diagram, the long run equilibrium of a firm in perfect competition.

9 Describe the short run equilibrium of a firm in perfect competition earning supernormal profit. Why could this situation not continue in the long run? Use a diagram to illustrate your answer.

10 What are the advantages and disadvantages of perfect competition to the consumer?

11 Explain fully the relationship between the marginal physical product and the marginal revenue product of a firm in perfect competition. Use a diagram to illustrate your answer.

12 Draw the demand (AR) curve for a firm in perfect competition. Mark any point on this curve. Explain the price elasticity of demand for the product at that point.

13 Explain fully the construction, or derivation, of a perfectly competitive firm's long run supply curve.

Chapter 13 Monopoly

In this chapter we will examine the production of goods under conditions of monopoly. As implied by the prefix 'mono' there is only one firm in this type of industry. Thus it is the extreme opposite to perfect competition where there are many firms.

Iarnród Éireann is a monopolist

Assumptions for the Existence of a Monopoly

1. There is only one firm in the industry.
2. The firm aims to make maximum profits.
3. There are barriers to entry to the industry.
4. The monopolist can control either the price charged or the quantity sold, but not both.

How Monopolies Arise

1. **Through legislation:** In this situation the government passes legislation granting one firm the sole right to produce a product or to supply a service. Iarnród Éireann is a good example of this type of monopoly in Ireland.
2. **Through mergers and take-overs:** All the existing firms in the industry are taken over by one firm, or all the firms in the industry merge together to form one new firm.
3. **One firm has sole ownership of an essential factor of production:** If a firm had exclusive ownership of an essential raw material it could keep it for its own use only, thus preventing any other firm entering the market.
4. **Economies of scale:** This is a situation where, in some established industries, the cost of the fixed assets is regarded as a sunken cost as far as the existing supplier is concerned. If competitors attempt to enter the market the existing firm will lower its price to such a low level that no new firm could compete with this low price. Therefore, it would not be economical to set up a new firm in opposition to the established one.
5. **Cartels:** Sometimes the competing firms in an industry agree with each other to cooperate on pricing and market segmentation, i.e. not to compete with each other in certain geographical areas. This gives each of the firms a virtual monopoly in each of these regions.
6. **Product differentiation and advertising:** An existing firm may have created such a degree of brand loyalty that consumers would never switch to any new brand which may be launched.

Points 1, 2, 3, 4 and 6 act as **barriers preventing any new firms from entering the industry**.

LR Equilibrium of a Monopolist

In monopoly there is no distinction between the firm and the industry as there is only one firm in the industry. Therefore, the firm will have a normal downward sloping D or AR curve, i.e. in order to sell more of its products it will have to decrease its AR.

When AR is decreasing then, from a purely arithmetical point of view, MR is also decreasing. MR decreases at a faster rate than AR and it is less than AR.

Example

Table 13.1 *The relationship between AR and MR in monopoly*

Quantity	AR	TR	MR
1	€10	€10	–
2	€9	€18	€8
3	€8	€24	€6
4	€7	€28	€4
5	€6	€30	€2

This is represented on Fig 13.1 as follows:

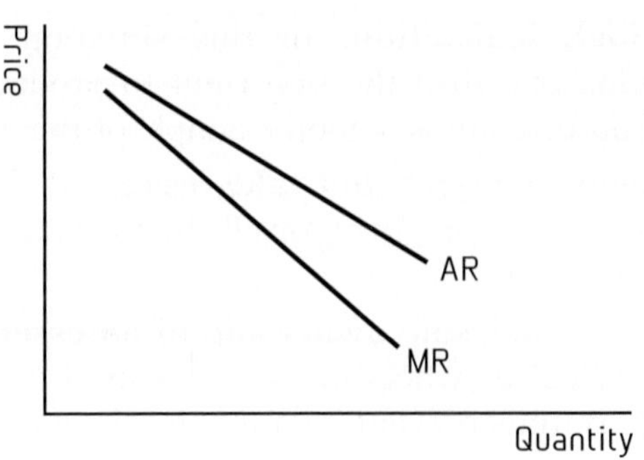

Fig 13.1 The relationship between AR and MR in monopoly

Superimpose any typical AC and MC curves onto these revenue curves and this will give the equilibrium of the monopolist.

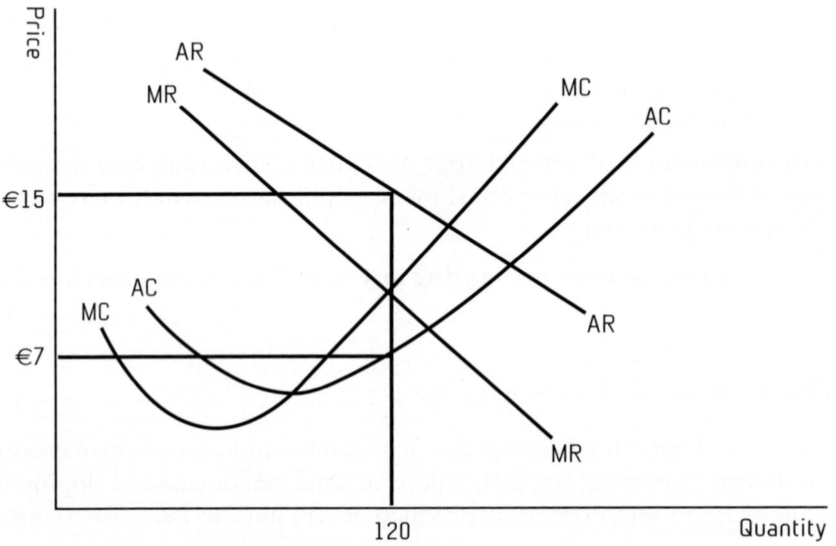

Fig 13.2 Long run equilibrium in monopoly

✳ 1 Output or quantity produced

It is assumed that the firm aims to make maximum profit, therefore it will produce the quantity where MR = MC, provided MC > MR after that, i.e. 120 on Fig 13.2.

✳ 2 Price

To get the market price for this quantity draw a line from 120 on the quantity axis up to the AR curve and then across to the price axis. This gives a price (AR) of €15.

✻3 Profit level

The AC for 120 is €7. This is less than the AR of €15. When AR > AC the firm is earning SNPs. In this situation, the firm is earning €8 supernormal profit per unit. This can continue in the long run in monopoly, as no other firm can enter the industry to increase the supply and bring down the AR.

Due to the lack of competition the average cost of a monopolist is seldom if ever at its lowest point at the equilibrium output.

Summary of the equilibrium of a monopolist

(i) AR > MR (ii) MR = MC (iii) AR > AC

✻Relationship between MPP and MRP in monopoly

You may recall that in perfect competition MPP × AR = MRP. This relationship does not hold true in any other form of competition.

In monopoly the firm must decrease its price if it is to increase its sales. The firm will be getting a smaller price for every unit it sells. Thus in monopoly, imperfect competition and oligopoly MPP × AR does not equal MRP.

Table 13.2 *MPP x AR > MRP*

Qty of labour	Total production	MPP	AR	Total revenue	MRP
1	100	–	€10.00	€1,000	–
2	120	20	€9.50	€1,140	€140
3	135	15	€9.00	€1,215	€75

Here it can be seen that when the second unit of labour is employed its MPP of 20 × AR of €9.50 = €190 and this is > MRP of €140.

Also when the third unit of labour is employed its MPP of 15 × AR of €9 = €135 and this is > the MRP of €75.

Thus in every form of competition except perfect competition, MPP × AR > MRP.

Advantages of monopoly

1. Monopolists can sometimes benefit from the economies of scale and can sometimes sell the product at a lower price than other forms of competition.
2. Production under conditions of monopoly can avoid wasteful duplication of resources. For example, in other forms of competition each firm may have specialised machinery that is under-used; with large-scale production in monopoly only one specialised machine is needed and it is fully utilised.
3. A monopolist may be less vulnerable to changes in the level of demand in the market, as it is earning SNPs. It may be able to afford to decrease P to maintain the same level of sales. A smaller firm earning only NPs may not be able to afford to do so. Therefore, employment may be more secure in monopoly.

Disadvantages of monopoly

1. A monopolist seldom, if ever, produces at the lowest point on the AC curve. This is due to lack of competition. This causes a waste of economic resources.
2. A monopolist earns SNPs, which indicates that the consumer is exploited. The consumer is being exploited as the monopolist is earning a bigger profit than is required to stay in production in the long run.
3. Consumers do not have a choice of products, as there is no other producer of the product.
4. There is no incentive to be innovative as there is no competition.
5. A monopolist may be able to practise price discrimination and thus further exploit the consumer.
6. Monopolists can control either the price of the product or the quantity supplied. However, the monopolist usually cuts its production level to increase the price of the good, thus under-utilising its resources.

Control of Monopolies

Monopolists are in a very strong position to exploit consumers and waste economic resources. This is fairly obvious from the disadvantages of monopoly which we have just seen. The Irish government is reluctant to allow monopolies to be created unless they are in the interest of the general public or in the interest of the consumers. To this end, the government has put into place legislation which makes it difficult for monopolies to be formed.

✳The Restrictive Practices Act (1972)

Under this Act:

'The Minister, if he thinks that the exigencies of the common good so warrant may,

(a) **Prohibit restrictive practices** including arrangements, agreements or understandings which prevent or restrict competition or restrain trade or the provision of any service or which involve resale price maintenance;

(b) **Prohibit unfair practices or unfair methods of competition** (whether or not relating to price);

(c) Make such provision as the Minister thinks necessary to **ensure the equitable treatment of all persons in regard to the supply or distribution of goods or the provision of services;**

(d) Make such other provision in regard to restrictive practices or unfair practices or unfair methods of competition (whether or not relating to price) affecting the supply and distribution of goods or the provision of services as he thinks fit.'

✳ Mergers and Takeovers (Control) Acts, 1978 to 1996

Under this Act:

'The (Competition) Authority was obliged to investigate every proposal referred to it and to report to the Minister on its investigation. The report of the Authority had to state its opinion as to whether or not the proposed merger or takeover concerned was likely to prevent or restrict competition or restrain trade in any goods or services and was likely to operate against the common good. The report had also to give the views of the Authority on the likely effect of the proposed merger or take-over on the common good in respect of the criteria attached at Appendix 1 to this report. The Minister, having considered the report of the Authority could, had she thought that the exigencies of the common good so warranted, by order prohibit a proposed merger or take-over either absolutely or subject to conditions. The Minister was required to publish any such report by the Authority, with due regard to commercial confidentiality, within two months of it being furnished to her by the Authority.'

✳ The Competition Act (1991) and Subsequent Amendments

This Act states:

'Subject to the provisions of this section, all agreements between undertakings, decisions by associations of undertakings and concerted practices which have as their object or effect the prevention, restriction or distortion of competition in trade in any goods or services in the State or in any part of the State are prohibited and void, including in particular, without prejudice to the generality of this subsection, those which

(a) Directly or indirectly fix purchase or selling prices or any other trading conditions;
(b) Limit or control production, markets, technical development or investment;
(c) Share markets or sources of supply;
(d) Apply dissimilar conditions to equivalent transactions with other trading parties thereby placing them at a competitive disadvantage;
(e) Make the conclusion of contracts subject to acceptance by the other parties of supplementary obligations which by their nature or according to commercial usage have no connection with the subject of such contracts.'

The creation of monopolies is also governed by EU directives, which have to be enforced in Ireland. Most of these directives eventually become part of Irish law.

Monopoly versus Perfect Competition

Let us compare the production of a good under conditions of monopoly with the production of that same good under conditions of perfect competition under two headings: (a) from the point of view of the employee and (b) from the point of view of the consumer.

It is important to point out that any valid comparisons should always show advantages and disadvantages under the given heading.

(a) **Are employees better off working in a perfectly competitive industry or in a monopolistic industry?**

1. Because there is a greater number of firms in a perfectly competitive industry there is usually a greater number of jobs in this industry, as each firm would require its own specialised form of labour. For example, each firm would need its own accountant, supervisor, marketing manager and production manager. In monopoly, the firm may have to employ only one person in each of these positions.
2. If one firm closes down in perfect competition it is still possible for the redundant staff to get employment in the same type of industry, as vacancies will always arise in some of the other firms in that industry. If the industry is a monopoly and it closes down then there is no hope of future employment in that industry.
3. Because there is a large number of firms in perfect competition employees have more bargaining power when negotiating their wages. In monopoly, there is only one employer, thus reducing the bargaining power of the employees.
4. Because the monopolist tends to be a large firm there may be more opportunities for promotion in this type of firm compared to the small firms in perfect competition.
5. Because monopolists earn supernormal profits it is more likely that employees could earn economic rent, whereas perfectly competitive firms earn only normal profit. Thus it is unlikely that they would pay any economic rent to their employees.
6. A monopolist may be less vulnerable to changes in the level of demand in the market. As it is earning SNPs it may be able to afford to decrease P to maintain the same level of sales. A smaller firm earning only NPs may not be able to afford to do so. Therefore, employment may be more secure in monopoly.

(b) **Do consumers fare better if a product is produced under conditions of monopoly or conditions of perfect competition?**

1. In perfect competition, firms earn only normal profit, whereas in monopoly the firm earns supernormal profit. Thus the consumer is not exploited in perfect competition, but is exploited in monopoly. From this point of view, the consumer fares better under perfect competition.

2 In perfect competition, all the firms are price takers. Thus the firm cannot manipulate its production to earn a higher price. In monopoly, the firm can restrict supply to drive up the price, thus exploiting the consumer. This would be particularly true if the PED was inelastic. Again from this point of view, the consumer fares better under perfect competition.

3 In perfect competition, the firm always produces the product at the lowest possible average cost ensuring that the consumer gets the good at the lowest possible price. Due to lack of competition the monopolist seldom, if ever, produces the good at the lowest possible average cost. This indicates that the consumer fares better under conditions of perfect competition.

4 In monopoly, there is only one supplier for the entire industry. This may enable the monopolist to benefit from the economies of scale. Thus AR may be greater than AC simply because the average cost is very low. If you look at Fig 13.3 you will see that the monopolist's AC cost is only €5, while the AC for the perfectly competitive firm is €12. Thus the monopolist may be able to sell the good at a relatively low price.

5 However, there are so many firms supplying the product in perfect competition it is unlikely that the firm will benefit from the economies of scale. Thus while its AR may equal its AC, its AC may be high resulting in a high price to the consumer. In this situation the consumer may fare better under monopoly. This is shown in Fig 13.3.

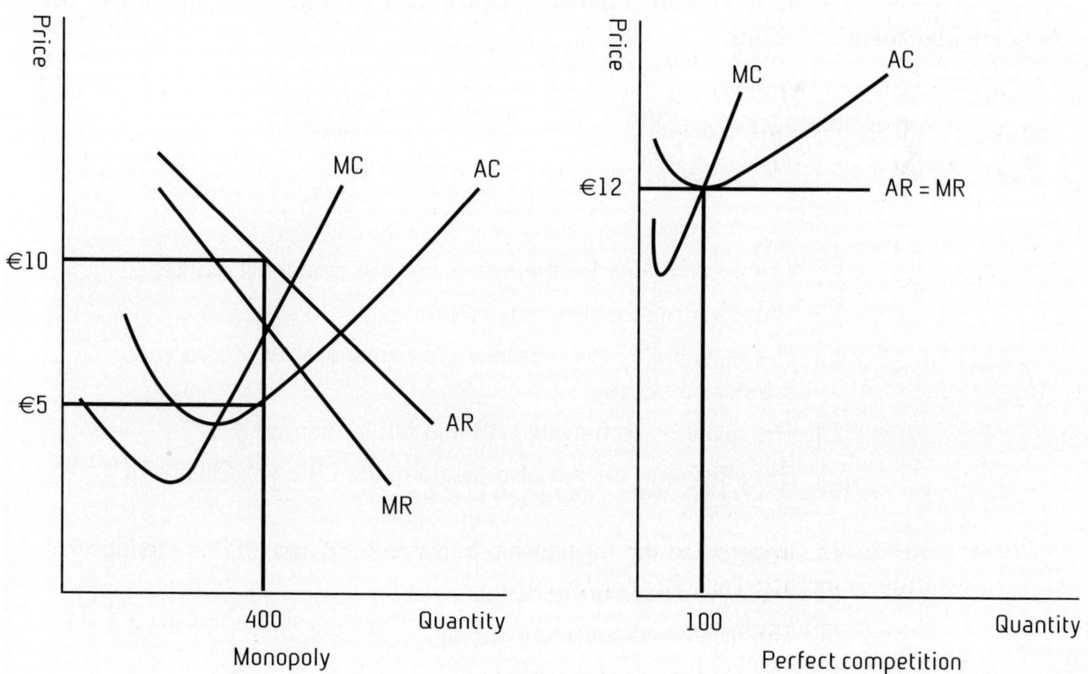

Fig 13.3 Monopoly and perfect competition

For historical reasons Ireland has a large, though decreasing, number of semi-state monopoly enterprises. These are often accused of being cost ineffective. However, there are a number of ways of making these bodies more cost effective.

1. Appoint experienced entrepreneurs and highly qualified people as members of the board of directors. These could replace people who are appointed simply because of their allegiance to a particular political party and who may not have any business acumen or experience. The new directors would be more cost conscious and be able to identify and eliminate inefficiencies.
2. Introduce the profit motive for the management team. Profit is the difference between income and cost. Thus in order to increase profit, management may concentrate more on decreasing costs rather than increasing price, particularly if the PED is inelastic.
3. Introduce competition in that particular industry by introducing deregulation. Competition normally encourages cost efficiency, as decreasing cost often gives a firm an advantage over its competitors.
4. Avoid any government interference in the day-to-day running of the company. Government intervention in the running of these bodies is often done for political gain only, and it is done regardless of the cost consequences to the firm.

Note: The term 'monopsony' indicates a market where there is only one buyer of the product. The only buyer for bomber planes in Ireland is the Irish Army, hopefully! It can also arise in a situation where a particular producer would be the only buyer for a particular form of labour.

LEARN THE KEY POINTS

1. The assumptions for the existence of a monopoly market
2. The ways monopolies may arise
3. The reason why the monopolist's demand or AR curve is downward sloping
4. The relationship between AR and MR in monopoly
5. Describe, with the aid of a diagram, the LR equilibrium of a monopolist
6. Understand the relationship between MPP and MRP in monopoly
7. The advantages of monopoly
8. The disadvantages of monopoly
9. The controls over monopolies
10. The means of making semi-state companies more cost effective

Exam Q&A: See p. 379

Copy questions 1–5 into your answer book and complete each of the sentences by filling in the blank spaces.

1 A monopolist can control either the ____________ at which the good is sold or the ____________ of the good ____________, but not ____________.

2 A monopolist's demand or AR curve is downward sloping because it is the ____________ demand curve.

3 Because the monopolist's AR is decreasing as sales increase its MR will be ____________ than the AR and the gap between AR and MR will get ____________ as the level of sales increases.

4 In the LR equilibrium of a monopolist AR > ____________ enabling the monopolist to earn ____________ profit.

5 The three acts which control monopolies are ________________________ ________________________ ________________________.

6 State and explain the assumptions governing monopoly.

7 State and explain the barriers which prevent new firms entering into competition with a monopolist.

8 Describe, with the aid of a diagram, the LR equilibrium of a monopolist.

9 Outline the relationship between MPP and MRP in monopoly.

10 Do consumers fare better if a product is produced under conditions of monopoly or under conditions of perfect competition?

11 Are employees better off working in a perfectly competitive industry or in a monopolistic industry?

12 How does monopoly lead to an inefficient use of resources?

13 Describe, with the aid of a diagram, the effect on the equilibrium of a monopolist of the imposition by the government of a lump sum tax. When answering this question remember that the tax will not vary with the level of production.

14 Describe, with the aid of a diagram, the effect on the equilibrium of a monopolist, if the government imposes a tax per unit of production. When answering this question remember that the tax will vary with the level of production.

15 Make suggestions as to how semi-state companies which are monopolists can be made more cost effective.

Chapter 14
Price Discrimination

This chapter explains the concept of price discrimination and how it affects consumers.

Definition of price discrimination

Price discrimination takes place when a producer sells the same product to two or more different markets at different prices and the difference in price is not related to any difference in costs in these markets.

Or

Price discrimination takes place when a producer sells the same product to two or more different markets at different ratios of marginal cost to price.

Both of these definitions mean the same thing!

This practice can be seen in operation on a daily basis. If you travel to school by public transport you will notice that students are charged a lower fare for a given journey than an adult making exactly the same journey to work.

Three Categories of Price Discrimination

Traditionally, price discrimination is divided into three categories.

1. **First degree price discrimination** occurs when the seller tries to eliminate consumer surplus. This works only if the seller has a relatively small number of buyers and knows what each is willing to pay rather than do without the product. It is aimed at getting the maximum possible revenue from each individual customer. A solicitor who knows the income of his/her clients and the importance of the service being provided could practise this.
2. **Second degree price discrimination** occurs when price concessions are given for bulk purchases. This is aimed at selling as much of the good as possible. Many manufacturers offer extra discounts to retailers when the retailers place large orders with the manufacturer. This is one of the reasons why very large chain stores can offer goods to consumers at lower prices than small, individually owned retail outlets.
3. **Third degree price discrimination** occurs when the producer divides his/her market into different categories based on their different price elasticities of demand, e.g. price of student airfares versus airfare price of executive travellers.

This is aimed at broadening the market for the product and selling it to as many people as possible. Many cinemas offer reduced prices to pensioners and students for the afternoon showings.

Conditions necessary for the practice of price discrimination

1. The firm must have some degree of **monopoly power** otherwise other firms could come into the market and supply the product to dearer segments of the market at a lower price.
2. The markets must be **separate** from each other, i.e. consumers in one market (the lower priced one) must not be able to transfer the product to consumers in the other market.
3. Consumers must have **different price elasticities of demand** and the seller must be able to distinguish these. Those with a higher price elasticity of demand would be charged the lower price.

   The following conditions make it easier to practise price discrimination.
4. **Consumer ignorance:** Consumers may not be aware that the product is available at a lower price in another market.
5. **Consumer inertia (indifference):** If the price difference in two markets is very small consumers may not be too concerned about the price difference. Therefore, they may not bother to find the lower priced goods.

Model 1

This model deals with a firm selling the same product to two markets and where it is the sole supplier (a monopolist) of the product in both markets.

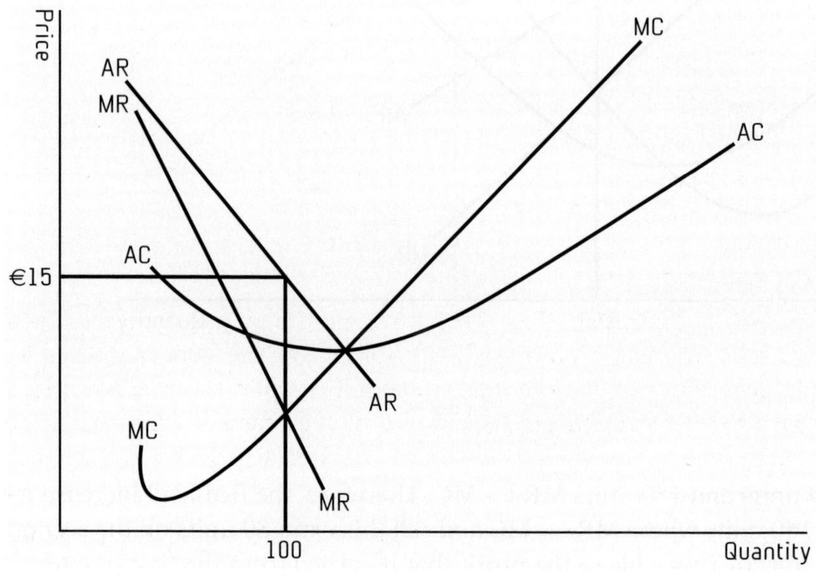

Fig 14.1 A monopolist selling to a single market

Fig 14.1 shows a monopolist selling to a single market. Because the monopolist aims to make maximum profit it will produce the quantity where MR = MC provided MC is greater than MR at all quantities after that. Here the firm will sell 100 units at a price of €15.

If the firm sold any more goods on this market its profits would decrease as MC > MR for all quantities after 100.

However, if the firm can find a new, separate market for its product and charge this market a higher price for every quantity over and above the original quantity of 100, then it can afford to increase its production. This is done in a situation where the producer identifies that some consumers will benefit from a consumer surplus if the product is sold to them at the lower price.

Remember that we assume that the markets are separate from each other and that the consumer who purchases the product at the lower price cannot transfer the product to the other segment of the market.

Because the firm now has a second market with a higher price for every quantity, it will also have a new set of revenue curves for this market. These are shown on Fig 14.2 as AR2 and MR2.

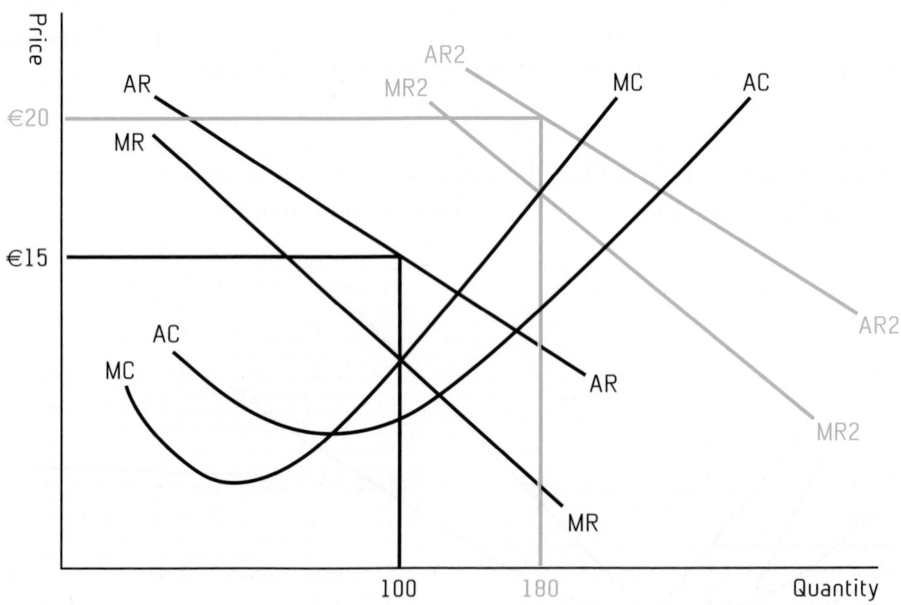

Fig 14.2 Equilibrium of the price discriminating monopolist

Now between 100 units and 180 units MR2 > MC. Therefore, the firm will increase its production up to 180 units where MR2 = MC and sell this extra 80 units on the second market at a price of €20. This adds to the profit that it earned from the first market.

The full equilibrium is:

Total quantity produced is 180

Of this:

100 units are sold on the first market at €15 each

80 units are sold on the second market at €20 each

✻Model 2

In this model the firm is selling the same product on two different markets, (i) on its own domestic market where the firm is a monopolist and (ii) on an export market where perfect competition exists.

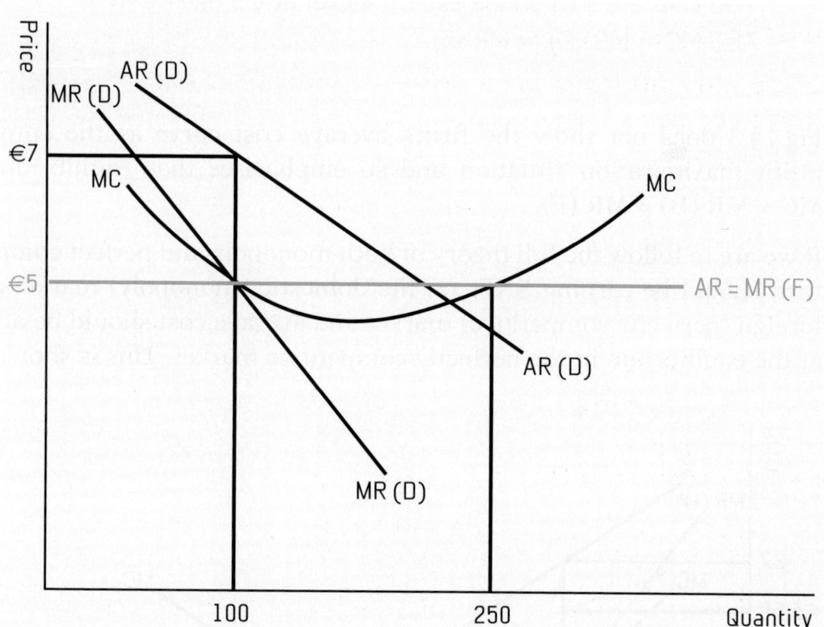

Fig 14.3 Long run equilibrium when selling on both the domestic market and the foreign market

Because the firm is selling on two different markets it will have separate sets of revenue curves for each of these markets.

- The domestic monopoly market is represented by the normal downward sloping monopoly revenue curves, i.e. **AR (D)** and **MR (D)**.
- The export market, where perfect competition exists, is represented by the normal perfectly competitive horizontal revenue curves, i.e. **AR** = **MR (F)**.
- Up to quantity 100 the MR (D) > MR (F), therefore, the firm would add more to its income (and thus profit) by selling these 100 units at €7 each on the domestic market.
- At the quantity of 100 the MR (D) is equal to MC and after that MC > MR (D).

From this it can be seen that the firm is earning the maximum possible profit from this domestic market.

- Between the quantity 100 and the quantity 250 MR (F) > MC, therefore the firm can add to its profit by selling the extra 150 units on the foreign market at €5 each.
- At the quantity of 250 the MR (F) is equal to MC and after that MC > MR (F).

The firm is earning the maximum possible profit from this export market.

The full equilibrium is:
Total quantity produced is 250

Of this:
100 units are sold on the domestic market at €7 each
150 units are sold on the export market at €5 each
Also MC = MR (D) = MR (F)

Fig 14.3 does not show the firm's average cost curve as the emphasis is on the profit maximisation situation and so emphasises that equilibrium occurs where MC = MR (D) = MR (F).

If we are to follow the full theory of both monopoly and perfect competition then the firm should be earning SNPs on the domestic (monopoly) market and NPs on the foreign (perfectly competitive) market and average cost should be at its lowest point at the equilibrium in the perfectly competitive market. This is shown in Fig 14.4.

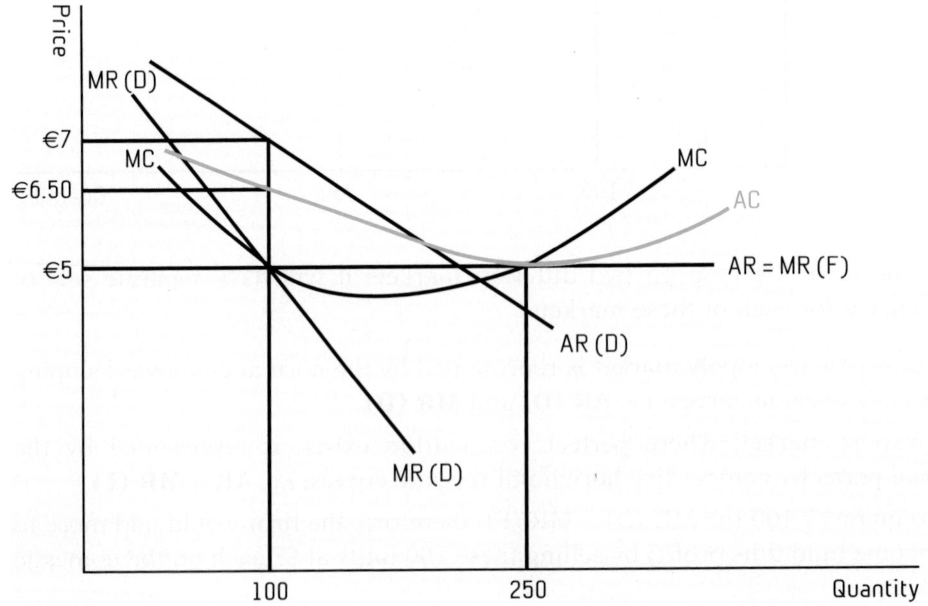

Fig 14.4 Normal profit on the foreign market and supernormal profit on the domestic market

You can see from Fig 14.4 that the AC on the domestic market is €6.50 while the AR is €7. Therefore, the firm (monopolist) is earning SNPs on this market.

However, the AC on the foreign market is €5 which is equal to its AR of €5. Therefore, the firm (perfectly competitive) is earning NP.

You should also note that AC is at its lowest point on the foreign market in keeping with the theory of perfect competition.

LEARN THE KEY POINTS

1. Definition of price discrimination
2. The three degrees of price discrimination
3. The condition necessary to practise price discrimination
4. The full description of the two models of price discrimination

Questions

Copy questions 1–5 into your answer book and complete each of the sentences by filling in the blank spaces.

1. A price discriminating monopolist charges ____________ prices for the ____________ product on two or more ____________ markets and the difference in price is not related to any difference in the ____________ of producing the product.
2. A doctor who charges a wealthy patient €60 per consultation and a poorer person €30 per consultation is practising ____________ degree price discrimination.
3. A price discriminating monopolist is in equilibrium when its MC is equal to the ____________ in ____________ market.
4. 'Consumer inertia' means that consumers are ____________ to the small difference in the ____________ being charged in different segments of the ____________ for the product.
5. A consumer whose price elasticity of demand for a product is highly inelastic is more likely to be charged a ____________ price for the product than the consumer whose price elasticity of demand is highly ____________.

6 Explain fully why a firm, which operates a price discrimination policy, faces at least two sets of revenue curves but only one set of cost curves.

7 Explain fully the three degrees of price discrimination.

8 Assume you are a supporter of Arsenal football club and reside in Ireland. You want to see the team playing on their home ground in London. You browse the web and find that you can get a flight to London in three months' time at a cost of €10. When you arrive at the airport you meet your neighbour who is also travelling on the same flight to London to attend the funeral of a close relative. However, he booked the flight only an hour before check-in time and had to pay €300 for the flight. What degree of price discrimination is being practised by the airline? Explain your answer.

9 'Dumping' – the selling of surplus goods on the export market at a price below the cost of production – is a form of price discrimination as consumers in the domestic market are charged a price well in excess of the cost of production. What factor enables the exporter to do this successfully? Explain you answer.

10 A firm is a monopolist on the home market and exports to a perfectly competitive market abroad. It seeks to maximise profits. Explain, with the aid of a clearly labelled diagram, the LR equilibrium of this price discriminating monopolist.

Chapter 15
Imperfect Competition

When you reflect back on perfect competition and monopoly you should realise that neither of these conditions for the production of goods offers the consumer any choice of product. All the goods produced by all the firms in perfect competition are homogeneous and there is only one supplier of the good in monopoly. You should also realise that perfect competition is really an idealistic form of production and that, in reality, firms set out to distinguish their products from those of their competitors.

Finally, from your study of the factors influencing the demand for a good you will have realised that the demand for any one good can be influenced by a change in the price of a substitute good. There are substitute goods available for most goods. These goods are produced under conditions known as **imperfect competition**.

Assumptions for the Existence of Imperfect Competition

1. There are many firms in the industry all producing products, which are **unique**, but are close substitutes for each other. This is the reason imperfect competition is sometimes referred to as **monopolistic competition**.
2. There are many buyers in the industry.
3. All the firms engage in product differentiation. This involves each firm endeavouring to persuade the consumers that its product is superior to those of the other firms. It is done through competitive advertising.
4. All firms aim to make maximum profits.
5. There is full knowledge of the profit levels being earned in the industry.
6. There is freedom of entry into and exit from the industry.
7. There can be competition between the firms for the factors of production, i.e. they do not have a perfectly elastic supply of the factors of production.

Short Run Equilibrium

When an industry starts up there is usually just one firm in that industry. Therefore, that firm is a monopolist in the short run (SR) and its equilibrium is the same as that of the long run (LR) equilibrium of a monopolist.

Fig 15.1 shows that the firm is earning SNPs as its AR of €15 > its AC of €7.

It also shows that its revenue curves are the normal downward sloping curves, so that to increase sales the firm must decrease price. You should recall that when AR is decreasing then MR is also decreasing, it is less than AR and it decreases at a faster rate than AR. This can be seen from the figures shown in Table 15.1.

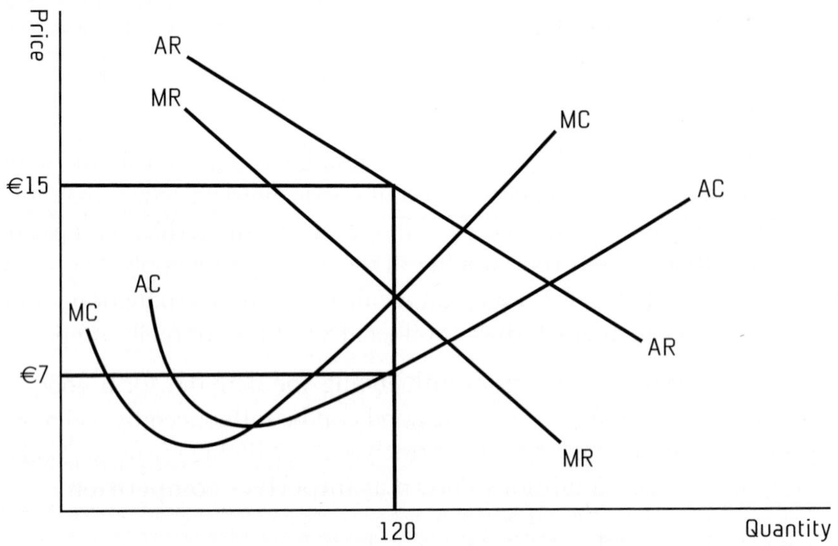

Fig 15.1 Short run equilibrium in imperfect competition

***Table 15.1** The relationship between AR and MR in imperfect competition*

Quantity	AR	TR	MR
1	€1.00	€1.00	–
2	€0.90	€1.80	€0.80
3	€0.80	€2.40	€0.60
4	€0.70	€2.80	€0.40

Long Run Equilibrium

Because of assumptions 5 and 6 (see p. 125) other firms will be attracted into the industry by the SNPs that are being earned. This has the effect of increasing the total supply of that type of product on the market, thus causing AR to decrease. Therefore, the position of the revenue curves begins to shift downwards.

At the same time, there is an increase in the demand for the factors of production being used, causing an increase in their costs. Also firms become involved in competitive advertising to increase or maintain their share of the market. This causes another increase in cost. These cost increases cause the position of the cost curves to move upwards.

With the increase in average cost (AC) and the decrease in average revenue (AR) the SNPs being earned will decrease. New firms will continue to come into the industry until all firms in it are earning only NPs.

The firm now produces the output where MR = MC (to earn maximum profit), i.e. a quantity of 100. The AR for this quantity is €8 and the AC is €8, thus AC = AR. Therefore, the firm is earning only NPs, see Fig 15.2.

Note that the AR curve is at a tangent to the AC curve and never cuts it ensuring that SNPs cannot be earned at any quantity whatsoever.

Note also that the AC is not at its lowest point at the equilibrium output. This is because:

- The firm is involved in competitive advertising, which is an extra 'non-production' cost.
- The AR curve is at a tangent to the AC curve.

  Therefore, mathematically, the degree of slope of both curves is identical at the point where they touch. (When two curves touch each other, without cutting each other, the degree of slope of the two curves is identical.) The AR curve (D) is a normal downward sloping D curve. Therefore, AC must also be downward sloping at that point; hence it cannot be at its lowest point.

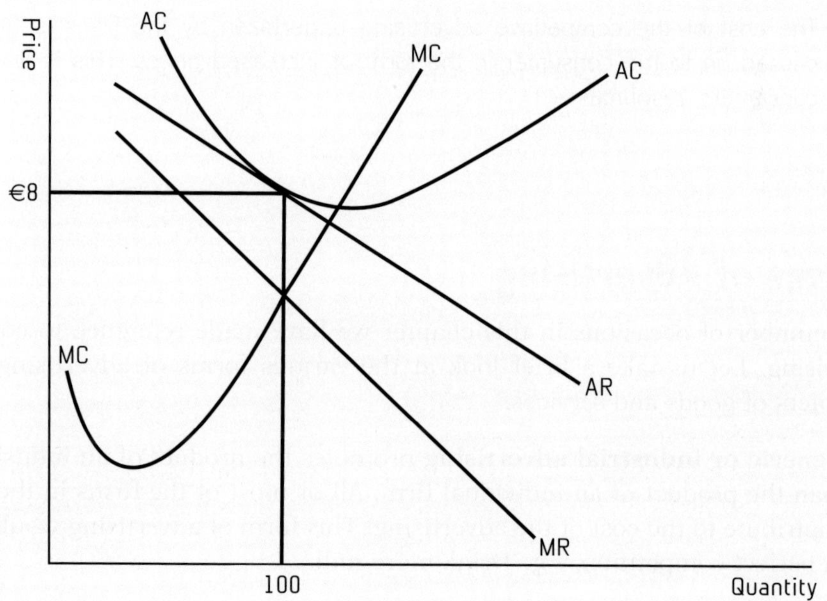

Fig 15.2 Long run equilibrium in imperfect competition

Advantages of imperfect competition

1. It offers the consumer a choice of goods. This does not happen in either perfect competition or monopoly.
2. The competitive advertising undertaken by the industry creates employment in the advertising industry.
3. If extra sales are generated by the advertising this may also create extra employment.
4. The money spent on advertising often reduces the price of newspapers, magazines, etc., to the consumer. This same logic applies to sponsorship by companies of sporting, cultural and social activities.
5. Consumers are not exploited (as they are in monopoly and oligopoly), as the firms earn only normal profits.

Disadvantages of imperfect competition

1. The firm does not produce at the lowest point on the AC curve. This indicates a waste of economic resources.
2. Excess capacity: This means that each firm is not producing to the full extent of its capacity. This happens because there are so many firms in the industry competing with each other that none of the firms can fully gain the advantages of the economies of scale. Again this indicates a waste of resources.
3. The cost of the competitive advertising undertaken by the firms is frequently passed on to the consumer in the form of increased prices. This is a waste of consumers' resources.

Forms of Advertising

On a number of occasions in this chapter we have made reference to competitive advertising. Let us take a brief look at the various forms of advertising used by promoters of goods and services.

1. **Generic or industrial advertising** promotes the product of an industry rather than the product of an individual firm. All or most of the firms in the industry contribute to the cost of the advertising. This form of advertising would be used in perfect competition, e.g. 'Drink more milk'.

2. **Competitive advertising** attempts to convince the consumer that Brand X is better than any of the substitute brands, e.g. 'Would you swap your one packet of Daz for two packets of Brand X?'

3 **Persuasive advertising** is a more subtle form of competitive advertising. No reference is made to competitors, but you are told that you really need, or deserve, this product, e.g. L'Oréal's motto 'Because you're worth it'. It is often used by the more expensive brands in an industry.

4 **Informative advertising** simply tells consumers about the existence of a product or service, or warns them of the dangers of consuming certain products, e.g. 'Every cigarette you smoke shortens your life'. This form of advertising is used by government departments to alert the public to their entitlements.

LEARN THE KEY POINTS

1. The assumptions of imperfect competition
2. Know why the AR and MR curves are downward sloping
3. The SR equilibrium of a firm in imperfect competition
4. The LR equilibrium of a firm in imperfect competition
5. Know and explain why average cost cannot be at its lowest point at the equilibrium output in imperfect competition
6. Know what competitive advertising means
7. Know the advantages and disadvantages of production under conditions of imperfect competition

Exam Q&A: See p. 384

Copy questions 1–6 into your answer book and complete each of the sentences by filling in the blank spaces.

1 In imperfect competition there is a large ____________ each of whom produces a ____________ product but all the products are ____________ for each other.

2 Product differentiation means that each firm attempts to persuade ____.

3 An alternative name for imperfect competition is ____________________.

4 Because the cost of the competitive advertising is frequently passed on to the consumer in the form of increased prices it results in a ____________ consumers' resources.

5 Consumers are not exploited in imperfect competition because ____.

6 Firms in perfect competition would engage in ____________ advertising, whereas firms in imperfect competition would engage in ____________ advertising.

7 Which cost and revenue figures are equal to each other at long run equilibrium in perfect competition, imperfect competition and monopoly? Explain the reason for this.

8 Explain fully the reasons average cost cannot be at its lowest point at long run equilibrium in imperfect competition.

9 Outline fully the advantages of production under conditions of imperfect competition.

10 Outline fully the disadvantages of production under conditions of imperfect competition.

11 List and explain the assumptions governing imperfect competition.

12 Firms in imperfect competition can earn supernormal profit in the short run but only normal profit in the long run. Explain this statement. Use diagrams to assist your explanation.

Chapter 16
Oligopoly

Many products which are mass-produced for a worldwide or nationwide market are made and supplied by a few very large firms. If you examine the worldwide manufacturing of cars you will see that the industry is controlled by a small number of multinational companies.

In Europe, Proctor & Gamble, and Unilever dominate the detergent industry. In Ireland, petrol distribution is controlled by a small number of firms. A few banks also run the Irish retail banking industry, as you will learn in Chapter 17, Money and Banking. These are all examples of **oligopolies** or **oligopolistic markets**.

Assumptions of Oligopolies

1. The industry is dominated by a few very large firms. All the firms produce goods which are very close substitutes for each other.
2. New firms may find it difficult to enter the industry. See below, 'Barriers to entry into the industry'.
3. The firms interact with each other. If one firm adopts a marketing strategy, which may give it an advantage over the other firms in the industry, then the others will automatically counteract it. For example, if one firm started to give out free gifts with its products then the other firms would do something similar.
4. In most cases, the firms aim to make maximum profits.
5. The firms may collude with each other. See 'Forms of collusion' on p. 132.
6. Product differentiation takes place. While the firms are selling similar products they tend to engage in a substantial amount of competitive advertising and brand marketing. Each firm is attempting to convince consumers that its product is better suited to their requirements.

✻Barriers to entry into the industry

1. **Economies of scale:** The existing firms may have the advantages of the economies of scale (see Chapter 13, Monopoly, for a detailed explanation).
2. **Limit pricing:** This is an agreement between firms in an oligopolistic market to set a relatively low price for their product which would make it unprofitable for

new firms to enter the market. This can be done because the existing firms in the industry would already be benefiting from economies of scale.

3. **Channels of distribution:** Existing firms may control these channels, and may refuse to supply retailers who carry the products of new firms.
4. **Brand proliferation:** Existing firms produce several brands of the same type of product, thus leaving very little room for new firms. This is very noticeable in the shaving market where both Gillette and Wilkinson Sword already sell a vast range of blades.

*Forms of collusion

1. **Price fixing:** An agreement between firms not to compete with each other on a price basis. Without this form of agreement firms could end up in a vicious price war where some of them could be put out of business and the remaining firms could have substantial short-term losses.
2. **Limit pricing:** See point 2 on p. 131.
3. **Agreement to avoid competition in given sales areas:** Because the firms in oligopoly tend to be very big, they also have high overhead costs. Therefore, they are each given a segment of the market in which they can act as a monopolist. This allows them to recoup their overheads in these sectors and then the firms compete in all other sectors. While this is an anti-competitive practice and illegal, it is normally done on a tacit (unspoken) basis.
4. **Agreeing to a quota system:** This is a system of limiting production levels to keep down supply and thus keep up price. This was practised extensively by the Organisation of Petroleum Exporting Countries (OPEC).
5. **Exclusivity:** A refusal by firms to supply retailers who do not exclusively stock their goods.

Forms of non-price competition

- Special offers
- Free gifts
- Sponsorship: local and national
- Money-off coupons
- Competitions
- '20% Extra' for the same price
- Free promotional samples
- Club points and loyalty card systems as operated by Superquinn, Dunnes and Tesco

Rigid prices or **sticky prices** are the terms used to describe a situation when oligopolists are unwilling to enter into price competition.

Equilibrium – Sweezy Model

1 It is assumed that firms interact with each other so that no one firm can gain an advantage by its actions. Therefore, if one firm decreases its price in order to gain a bigger share of the market, then the other firms will also decrease their prices. As a result, there is no significant gain to any of the firms. Thus for decreasing prices the firms face an inelastic D or AR curve.

Fig 16.1 The inelastic AR curve plus its associated MR curve

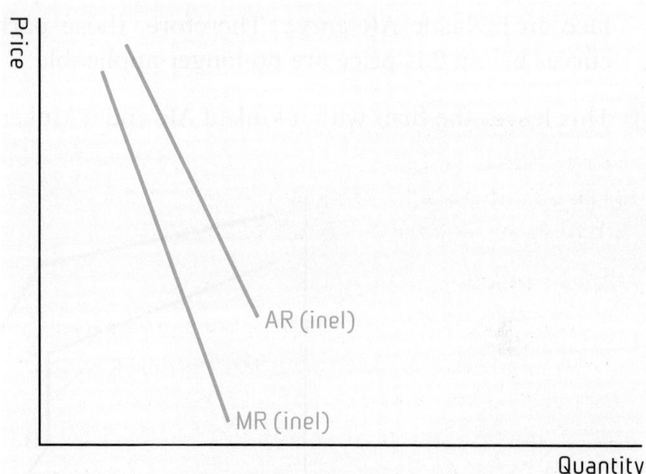

2 Likewise, if a firm increases its price, then the other firms now have the advantage of selling a similar product at a cheaper price. Therefore, this firm will lose a lot of its customers to the other firms. Thus for increasing prices the firms face an elastic D or AR curve. Therefore, the firms really face two different D or AR curves, one for decreasing prices and one for increasing prices as shown in Fig 16.2.

Fig 16.2 The elastic and inelastic AR curves and their associated MR curves

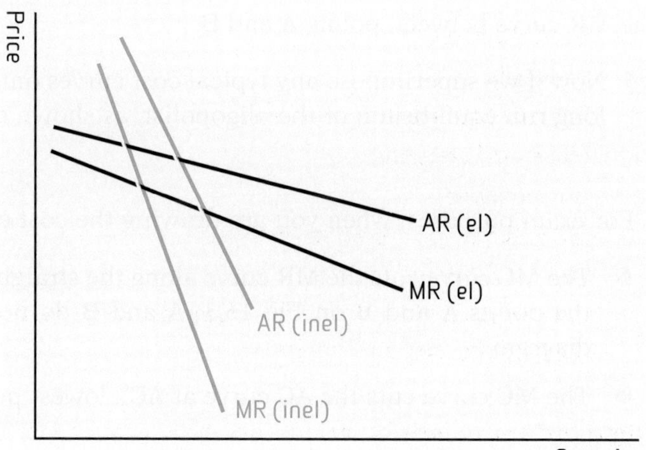

3 Therefore, all firms are reluctant to change their prices, as there is no gain to them to do so. Thus the firms will settle for the price where the two AR curves intersect.

4 The firm now knows that if it increases its price above this price that it will face an elastic AR curve. Therefore, those parts of the inelastic AR and MR curves above this price are no longer applicable to the firm.

5 Likewise, the firm knows that if it decreases its price above this price that it will face an inelastic AR curve. Therefore, those parts of the elastic AR and MR curves below this price are no longer applicable.

6 This leaves the firm with a kinked AR and a kinked MR curve as shown below.

Fig 16.3 Kinked AR and MR curves

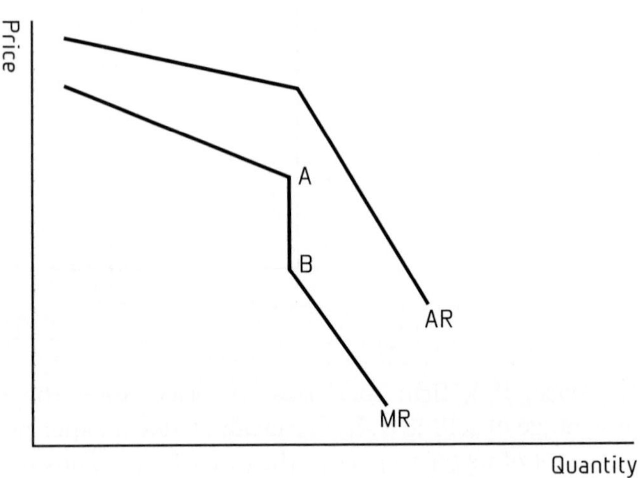

This diagram shows the revenue curves of the oligopolist.

Note: Because there are really two AR curves there will be a break or vertical line on the MR curve between points A and B.

7 Now if we superimpose any typical cost curves onto Fig 16.3 we can read off the long run equilibrium of the oligopolist, as shown on Fig 16.4 on p. 135.

For exam purposes, when you are drawing the cost curves ensure that:

- The MC curve cuts the MR curve along the straight-line part of it, i.e. between the points A and B on Fig 16.3. A and B do not have to be shown on the diagram.
- The MC curve cuts the AC curve at AC's lowest point.

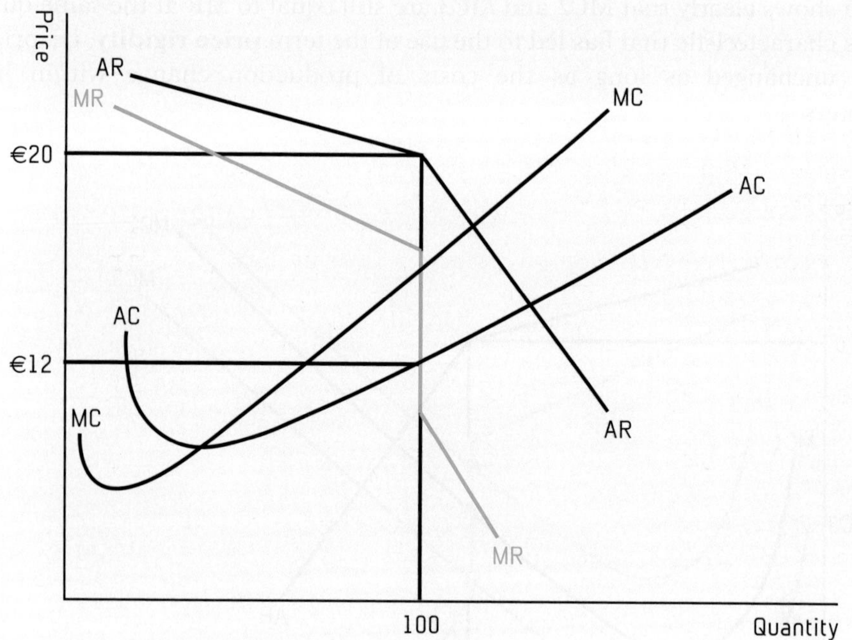

Fig 16.4 The long run equilibrium of an oligopolist

The Full Equilibrium of an Oligopolist

✳Quantity

It is assumed that the firm aims to earn maximum profits. Thus it will produce the quantity where MR = MC, in this case 100 units.

✳Price or AR

To get the price for 100 units draw a line from 100 on the quantity axis up to the AR curve and then across to the price axis, this gives a price of €20. Note that this is the price at the kink on the AR curve.

✳Profit level

The AC for 100 units is €12, therefore because the AR of €20 > AC of €12 the firm is earning SNPs. This can continue in the long run as it is very difficult for other firms to enter the industry, increase the supply and thus decrease the price.

Note: The quantity produced will not change if the position of the marginal cost curve changes to any point between the original points A and B on the MR curve.

Fig 16.5 shows clearly that MC2 and MC3 are still equal to MR at the same quantity. It is this characteristic that has led to the use of the term **price rigidity**, i.e. price will remain unchanged as long as the costs of production change within limited parameters.

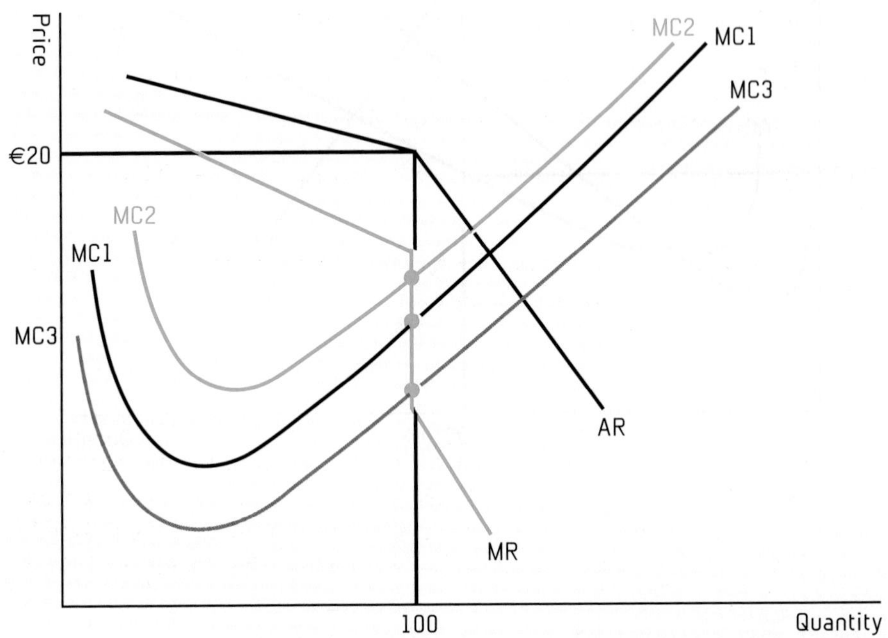

Fig 16.5 The price does not change if MC remains within the straight segment of the MR curve

Reasons Why Consumers Prefer Price Competition

1. Price competition leads to cheaper prices for the consumer.
2. The 'extras' offered under non-price competition cause the price of the good to go up, thus decreasing the consumer's real income.
3. Quite frequently the consumers do not need or want the offers under non-price competition.
4. Consumers frequently do not cash in their vouchers; therefore they are paying for something that they never receive.
5. Non-price competition reduces consumers' ability to choose what products they wish to buy.

Benefits of Non-Price Competition to Consumers

1. **Stability in prices:** Non-price competition means unchanging prices for consumers which leads to easier budgeting for them.
2. **Better quality:** Firms tend to compete with each other on the quality of their products and their after-sales services which benefit the consumer.
3. **Benefits of advertising:** Consumers get the benefits of advertising, e.g. sponsorship, reduced cost of papers and magazines.
4. **Consumers are more informed about the products:** This arises from extensive advertising.
5. **Consumer loyalty is rewarded:** This is in the form of free gift tokens and loyalty cards based on volume purchased.

The Baumol Model or Sales Maximisation Model

The Baumol model states that firms do not always aim to produce the quantity which maximises profit, but instead will produce the quantity which will generate the greatest income for the firm, assuming that the profit earned reaches a stated target level. In the example in Fig 16.6, on p. 138, assume the minimum profit is normal profit.

A firm may try to maximise revenue for a number of reasons:

1. To enhance the careers of the management team, i.e. they want to be seen as people capable of developing more market for a product.
2. To leave less market share for their competitors.
3. To protect the firm's market in the event of a future decrease in demand.
4. By increasing sales the firm can increase production to a level where it gains maximum benefit from the economies of scale and produces the product at the minimum average cost.
5. Firms may be afraid of government intervention if their maximum profits seem excessive. If excessive profits were being earned there may be pressure put on the government to place a large lump sum tax on these profits. Thus firms may be willing to accept a lower profit than the maximum profit. In this way, firms may retain a greater profit than that which would be left after the lump sum tax.

In this situation the firm will continue to increase its sales so long as each extra unit sold adds to the total revenue of the firm, i.e. so long as marginal revenue is positive. In Fig 16.6 this is 12,000 units being sold at an average revenue of €4.60, giving total revenue of €55,200.

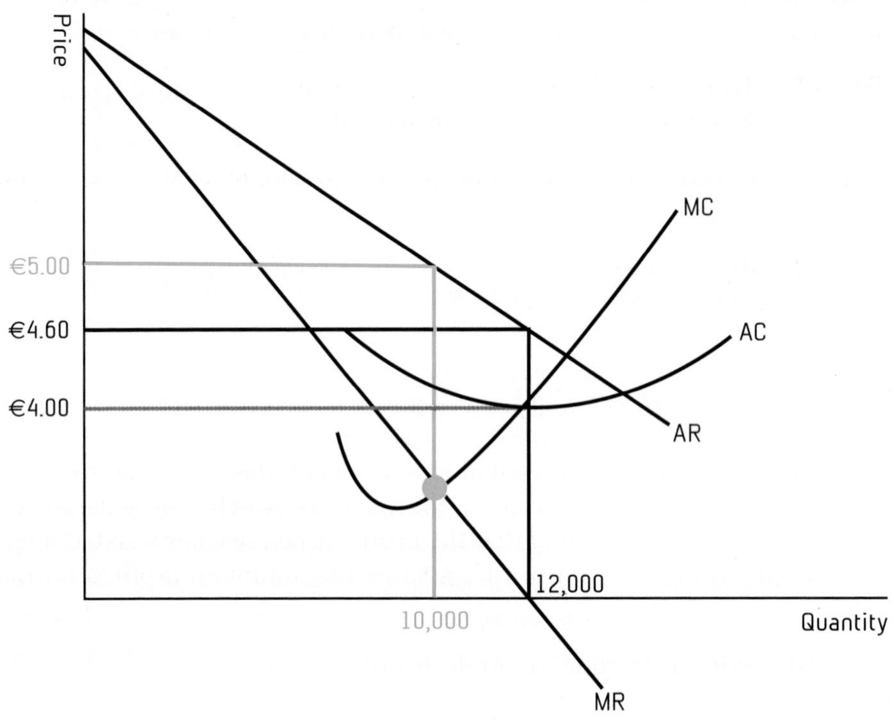

Fig 16.6 Baumol model of revenue maximisation

Notice four points at this quantity of production.

1. Any further increase in sales would lead to a decrease in total revenue, as marginal revenue becomes negative after that quantity.
2. Average cost is at its lowest point for this quantity.
3. The firm is not maximising its profit, as the marginal cost for 12,000 units is greater than the marginal revenue. However, it is earning supernormal profit because AR > AC for this quantity.
4. If the firm produced the quantity of 10,000 which enables them to earn maximum profit, i.e. where MR = MC, then its total revenue would be only €50,000 (10,000 × €5).

An Alternative Method of Displaying the Baumol Model

An alternative way of displaying the Baumol model is shown in Fig 16.7. On this diagram you can see that at point **M** sales revenues are at the maximum and so the firm produces Q2. However, the quantity that gives maximum profit is Q1. By producing Q2 the firm is earning less than the maximum profit. This can be seen clearly by comparing the green lines, representing the maximum profit, with the dotted lines, representing the actual and targeted profit level.

Finally point **M** on the total revenue curve is the point where marginal revenue becomes negative hence total revenue begins to decrease.

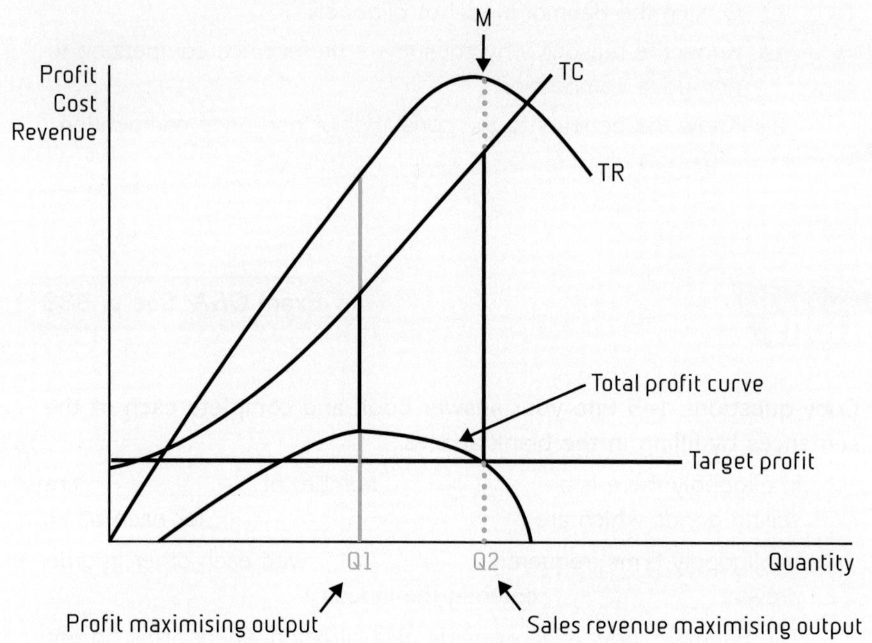

Fig 16.7 The Baumol model showing revenue maximising output

LEARN THE KEY POINTS

1. The assumptions and features of oligopoly
2. The barriers to entry to oligopoly
3. The forms of collusion
4. The forms of non-price competition
5. The construction of the revenue curves in the Sweezy model
6. The full explanation of the equilibrium in the Sweezy model
7. Know why some firms prefer to maximise revenue rather than to maximise profit
8. Outline the Baumol model of oligopoly
9. Know the reasons why consumers prefer price competition to non-price competition
10. Know the benefits to the consumer of non-price competition

Questions

Exam Q&A: See p. 389

Copy questions 1–5 into your answer book and complete each of the sentences by filling in the blank spaces.

1. In oligopoly there is a ____________ number of ____________ firms selling goods which are ______________________ for each other.
2. In oligopoly firms frequently ____________ with each other in order to prevent ____________ entering the industry.
3. The Baumol model is an example of a situation where firms do not aim to produce the ____________ which earns ____________ profit.
4. Oligopolistic firms face an ____________ demand curve for increasing prices and an ____________ demand curve for ______________________.
5. Price rigidity refers to a situation where firms are reluctant to ________________.
6. State and explain the assumptions for the existence of oligopoly.
7. State and explain barriers which make it difficult for new firms to enter an oligopolistic market.
8. State and explain the forms of collusion commonly practised by oligopolists.

9 Why do producers prefer non-price competition?

10 Consumers may benefit from non-price competition. State and explain any four of these benefits.

11 State and explain the reasons why some firms prefer to maximise revenue rather than to maximise profit.

12 Explain, with the aid of diagrams, the shape of the revenue curves in oligopoly.

13 Explain, with the aid of a diagram, the long run equilibrium of an oligopolist under the Sweezy model.

Chapter 17
Money and Banking

This chapter examines the function and history of money. It also looks at banking, in particular banks in the Eurozone and financial institutions in the Irish market. It also discusses the roles of the International Monetary Fund (IMF) and the World Bank.

Money

Definition of money

Money is anything that is generally accepted by the majority of people in exchange for goods and services.

Functions of Money

1. **A means of exchange:** Money enables people to freely exchange the goods and services that they produce. This overcomes the greatest drawback of the barter system, 'the double coincidence of needs and wants'. Under the pre-money barter system, you had to find somebody who had what you wanted and who wanted what you had. With money, a person has only to find somebody who has what he/she wants, give this person money in exchange and then that person can exchange the money for anything he/she wants.

2. **A measure of value:** The amount of money given for a product is a reflection of the value of that product. If you pay €10 for product A and €5 for product B this indicates that A is twice as valuable as B. This function is also often referred to as 'a unit of account'. When keeping a record of credit transactions it is simpler to write down that you are owed €500, rather than note that you are owed 1 suit, 2 pairs of shoes, 6 pairs of socks.

3. **A means of deferred payments:** This enables the operation of an efficient credit system that would not be possible under the barter system. Under the barter system, people giving the credit had to know what they needed in the future, which was not always possible. Therefore, under the barter system people were reluctant to give credit. The existence of money overcomes this difficulty.

Credit is an essential feature of our modern economy. Just think of buying a house. The vast majority of people could not buy one if they could not borrow money. Almost all businesses depend on credit.

4 **A store of wealth**: Saving is simplified by exchanging the goods which we produce for money and simply storing (saving) the money. The saved money can be exchanged for goods or services (wealth) in the future.

Characteristics of a Good Money Form

In our definition of money we stated that it is anything which is accepted by the majority of people in exchange for goods and services. However, from a practical and a value point of view, the items being used as money must have certain characteristics.

1 **It must be instantly recognisable:** If some people have a doubt about the authenticity of the item being used as money then they will not accept it. Therefore, it is no longer, by definition, money.

2 **It must be portable:** Whatever is being used as money must be capable of being carried about, discreetly and safely, in large value.

3 **It must be reasonably durable:** This is a practical characteristic to cut down the cost of having to replace it on a frequent basis.

4 **It must be divisible into units of small value:** This is to enable the purchase of goods of low value and to enable people to give change after a transaction.

5 **It must be scarce in relation to the demand for it:** This is a characteristic of any good which has a value.

A Brief History of Money

✳Coinage

Earlier we identified 'the double coincidence of needs and wants' (see p. 142) as the major disadvantage of the barter system. In order to overcome this disadvantage people began to exchange acceptable commodities as 'money'. These were objects which were useful for their own intrinsic value, as well as acting as a means of exchange. These objects are often referred to as 'commodity money'. Many early examples included cattle, pigs, seashells, iron nails, salt and pepper.

The discovery of the touchstone led the way for metal-based commodity money and coinage. Any soft metal can be tested for purity on a touchstone. This enabled people to calculate the total content of a particular metal in a coin. Gold is a soft metal, it is scarce and it is storable and therefore was ideal as a money form. As a result, the use of monetary gold spread very quickly. Metal-based coins had the advantage of having their own intrinsic value within the coins themselves. However, many people abused these coins by the clipping and sweating of the coins to extract some of the precious metal.

This led to the dual circulation of 'good money' and 'bad money'. Good money was coinage, which still contained the true amount of precious metal, while bad money was coinage from which some of the precious metal had been removed. This led to the famous law known as Gresham's Law, which stated that bad money drives out good money. Eventually, standardised flat coins were introduced. These coins are accepted purely for their exchange value, rather than for any intrinsic value. They are now part of our legal tender system.

Banknotes

While there were banks of various descriptions in existence even in pre-Christian times, our modern banking system evolved only from the seventeenth century onwards. People who had accumulated large amounts of precious metals, such as gold, deposited this gold with goldsmiths who had the strong safes, which were needed to store the gold. The goldsmith issued receipts for these deposits and when the depositor needed to pay a debt he/she presented the receipt for the gold, melted it down and converted it to coinage. The coins were then used to pay the debt.

Fig 17.1 Goldsmiths were the original bankers

Gradually it became obvious that it would be more convenient to simply pass on the goldsmith's receipt as a means of payment. To make this easier for their clients the goldsmiths issued receipts for small values. For example, if you had deposited €500 worth of gold, the goldsmith would have given you 500 receipts of €1.

Because the goldsmiths were trusted, their receipts were gradually passed from one person to another and very few were actually presented for payment of gold. These receipts were the forerunners of our modern banknotes and were fully backed by gold. This was the beginning of the Gold Standard, which lasted into the early twentieth century, and meant that all receipts would be honoured in gold.

Goldsmiths soon realised that few of the receipts were actually presented for payment and began to issue receipts for amounts in excess of the lodgements they held. This system could continue so long as there was not 'a rush on the bank', i.e. too many people wanting to convert their receipts to gold at the same time. Thus began the modern system of credit creation, which we will examine later in this chapter.

Irish currency

The first tentative steps towards an Irish currency began with coinage. Under the *Coinage Act, 1926*, the Minister for Finance was authorised to issue token coins of silver, nickel and bronze.

The Currency Act, 1927, provided for a new unit of value, to be known as the *Saorstát* pound, which would be maintained at parity with the pound sterling. Convertibility to sterling would be ensured by a full backing by British government securities, liquid sterling balances and gold, under the control of the Currency Commission, and was underpinned by a guarantee that Irish banknotes would be paid at par in sterling (without fee, margin or commission) at the Bank of England.

This link to sterling was maintained until March 1979. At this time, Ireland was preparing for membership of the EMS (European Monetary System) and had agreed to keep its exchange rate with other potential members within stated limits.

Towards the end of March 1979, sterling gained support from rising oil prices and appreciated strongly against all EMS currencies. By 30 March, sterling breached the upper fluctuation limit against the Belgian franc. As an EMS member, the Irish pound could not follow. Just over fifty years after its formal adoption, the link between the Irish pound and sterling was broken, and the Irish punt was introduced. It remained in circulation until 2002 when the euro was introduced.

(This history is based on extracts from an article in the *Central Bank's Quarterly Bulletin*, Spring, 2003, entitled 'The Irish Pound: From Origins to EMU' by John Kelly.)

Forms of Money

In settling our day-to-day transactions we tend to use two different forms of money.

1. **Cash**, i.e. notes and coins.
2. **Claims on banks:** Claims on a bank are obtained by (a) lodging money to a bank, (b) obtaining a loan from a bank and (c) using a credit card. We pass our claim on a bank by writing cheques or using our credit and debit cards, or by arranging with the bank to transfer money from our account to someone else's account.

Note: Legal tender is any money form which must be accepted in settlement of a debt. All our euro notes are legal tender and our coins are also legal tender up to varying amounts for each type of coin. Cheques are not legal tender.

The Money Supply

Traditionally, the supply of money was divided into two simple categories based on the ease of access to the money.

- **M1 The narrow money supply** is the notes and coins outstanding (in circulation) plus all balances in current accounts in all licensed banks in the state.
- **M3 The broad money supply** is M1 plus balances in deposit accounts in all licensed banks plus borrowings from other credit institutions, less inter-bank balances.

Today we identify the three categories of money supply.

***Table 17.1** The European Central Bank and the Irish Central Bank identify three categories of money*

Narrow money supply or M1	Broad money supply or M3 = M2 +
Currency outstanding and overnight deposits	Repurchase agreements[1]
Intermediate money supply or M2 = M1 +	Debt securities up to 2 years' maturity[2]
Deposits with an agreed maturity up to 2 years	Money market funds/units[3]
Deposits redeemable at notice up to 3 months	
Post office savings, bank deposits	

Source: *The Central Bank*

Notes

1 **Repurchase agreements** (RPs or Repos) are financial instruments used in the money markets and capital markets. The full name for them is Sale and Repurchase Agreements and under the agreements one person sells securities to another for cash and agrees to repurchase the security from the cash provider for a greater sum of cash at some later date.

2 **Debt securities** cover bonds, debentures and notes that usually give the holder the unconditional right to a fixed money income or contractually determined variable money income. They include bonds such as treasury bonds, equity-related bonds (e.g. convertible bonds) and Eurobonds.

3 **Money market funds** are securities that can be purchased through most stockbrokers or directly from banks. They are mostly used by people who sell a stock and then put the proceeds in a money market fund account until they decide where they want to reinvest the money. The funds can also be used to build cash.

The figures given in Table 17.2, on p. 147, for the money supply are for illustrative purposes only to give you some concept of the money supply in Ireland. You can find updated values for this on the Central Bank's website and the CSO website.

Table 17.2 *Money supply at 28 September 2007*

Currency outstanding	€67,106m
Overnight deposits	€84,294m
Narrow money supply or M1	**€91,400m**
Deposits with an agreed maturity up to 2 years	€91,673m
Deposits redeemable at notice up to 3 months	€13,125m
Post office savings, bank deposits	€1,302m
Intermediate money supply or M2	**€197,501m**
Repurchase agreements	€273m
Debt securities up to 2 years maturity	– €25,626m
Money market funds/units	€56,647m
Broad money supply or M3	**€2228,795m**

Source: *The Central Bank*

Note: The figure for debt securities with up to 2 years' maturity is a negative sum as the incomes due on these bonds leave the Eurozone.

Banking

✳Banking ratios

- **The primary liquidity ratio** (PLR) is the ratio of cash which the banks must hold to claims on the banks.
- **The secondary liquidity ratio** (SLP) is the ratio of liquid assets held by the banks to claims on the banks. (This was a safeguard used by the banks to enable them to access cash quickly.)

The Creation of Credit by the Bank

Banks can create credit (money) by lending a multiple of their cash holdings.

Fig 17.2 Banks rely on cash deposits

Example

- Mr A lodges €1,000 cash in a bank.
- Assuming a PLR of 10% (1:10) the bank must keep €100 of this in cash. This is 10% of Mr A's claim.
- This leaves the bank with €900 cash.
- This €900 cash represents 10% of a loan which the bank could give to another customer, Mrs B.
- The value of the loan would be €9,000.
- Thus the bank has created €9,000 which was not in existence before the €1,000 cash deposit, i.e. 9 times the original deposit.
- The bank now has €100 in cash for the PLR for Mr A's deposit and it has €900 cash for the PLR for Mrs B's loan thus satisfying the PLR requirement.

Note: To test the validity of your answer to a question about the amount of money which a bank can create from a cash deposit subtract the numbers in the PLR (e.g. if the PLR is 1:10, subtract the one from the ten to give you nine) and multiply the answer by the cash deposit. Remember, that this is not an explanation, it is simply a test of your answer.

✳ Limitations on the powers of the banks to create credit

1. From the above example it can be seen that a bank can lend out a multiple of its cash deposits. Thus the size of its cash deposits is the first restriction on a bank's ability to create credit.
2. Banks are in existence to make a profit. If banks give loans then these loans must be repaid. Thus the banks can only lend to customers who are capable of repaying the loans. Therefore, there has to be a certain level of wealth within the economy to back up these loans.
3. Any changing of the PLR automatically alters the banks' ability to grant loans. If the PLR used in the example above was changed from 1:10 to 1:5 then a bank could create a loan of only €4,000. Follow the logic displayed in the example and prove this for yourself.
4. The banks are also restricted by the credit guidelines set by the European Central Bank and the Central Bank.

Banks always attempt to reconcile the conflict between the need for liquidity to meet their customers' requirements and their desire to maximise profits for their shareholders.

Banks have to contend with the conflict that exists in their business. On the one hand, banks must always ensure that they have sufficient cash to meet their customers' demands. This is known as their **liquidity requirement** since cash means liquidity. On the other hand, banks are owned by shareholders who require dividends and this requirement puts pressure on the banks to be as profitable as possible. This is the fundamental conflict between liquidity and profitability.

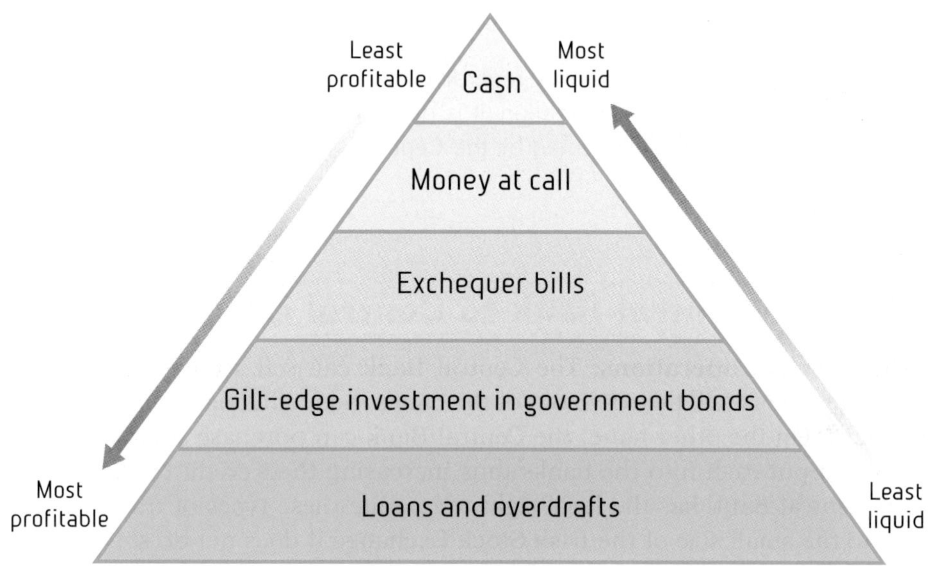

Fig 17.3 *Loans and overdrafts represent approximately 50%*
Gilt-edge investments in government bonds represent approximately 20%
Exchequer bills represent approximately 12%
Money at call represents approximately 8%
Cash represents approximately 10%

Fig 17.3 illustrates the strategy banks will adopt in their efforts to reconcile the conflict between liquidity and profitability. A small proportion of a bank's assets will be held in liquid form in the form of cash and money at call. As can be seen from the diagram, the largest segment is profit-making assets with approximately 50 per cent of their assets in the form of loans and overdrafts. The most successful portfolio of assets would be one that would enable the bank to earn maximum profits while maintaining the required degree of liquidity.

Notes

1. **Exchequer bill**s are, in effect, 91-day loans given to the government at a fixed rate of interest. In practice the government invites the banks to tender for these bills and then it issues a contract to repay the sum in total, along with the interest, by a given date.

2 When bank current account holders are allowed to withdraw more money from their accounts than they actually have in their accounts they are receiving **overdrafts**. The amount overdrawn must be repaid within an agreed period of time, but does not have to be repaid in fixed instalments. Interest is, of course, charged on the overdrafts.

Definition of monetary policy

Monetary policy is the policy regarding the amount of money in circulation, interest rates and credit creation. It is determined by the European Central Bank (ECB) and implemented by the Central Bank.

Powers of Central Bank to Control Credit Creation

1 **Open market operations:** The Central Bank can sell securities on the Stock Exchange. This will take cash out of the banks thus reducing their credit creating capacity. On the other hand, the Central Bank can purchase securities for cash. This will put cash into the banks thus increasing their credit creating capacity. Our Central Bank has the legal right to operate these types of transactions, but due to the small size of the Irish Stock Exchange it does not do so.

2 **Supplementary deposits** (formerly called special deposits)**:** The Central Bank can call in cash deposits from the banks, thus reducing their cash holdings, leading to a reduction in lending capacity.

3 **Manipulation of the rediscount rate and the short-term facility rate (STF):** Effectively this is the rate of interest which the Central Bank charges the commercial banks when they borrow cash from it. Any change in the STF causes the banks to change their rates accordingly. If the STF was increased, then the banks would have to increase their rates to their customers causing a contraction in demand for loans.

4 **Foreign exchange swaps:** Banks are permitted to hold foreign currencies for their customers' requirements. If the banks are running low on cash they can temporarily swap some of their foreign currency for Irish currency. This improves their credit creating capacity.

5 **Altering of the PLR by the Central Bank:** This could mean that the banks would have to hold more cash for their customers' requirements thus reducing their credit creating capacity and vice versa.

6 **Advice and directives:** Here the Central Bank lays down guidelines on credit policy which the banks normally adhere to, as it is in their own long-term interest to do so. There is also the danger of not having their licences renewed if they do not follow these guidelines.

The Central Bank and Financial Services Authority of Ireland Act, 2003

The Central Bank of Ireland, established in 1943, has been restructured and renamed as the Central Bank and Financial Services Authority of Ireland.

The Central Bank and Financial Services Authority of Ireland Act, 2003 established the Irish Financial Services Regulatory Authority (IFSRA), to manage the supervision of all financial institutions in Ireland.

The Central Bank of Ireland

The Irish Financial Services Regulatory Authority operates within the legal structure of the Central Bank but has its own chief executive, chairman and board of directors. However, some of these directors also sit on the board of the Central Bank and Financial Services Authority of Ireland. Thus while the Central Bank and the IFSRA have separate roles they cooperate closely.

The Role of the European Central Bank

The (Irish) Central bank is a member of the European System of Central Banks (ESCB), which is made up of the European Central Bank (ECB) and the national central banks of the EU member states.

The main objective of the ESCB is the maintenance of price stability (the control of inflation) in the Eurozone in order to protect the purchasing power of its citizens.

The ECB is responsible for formulating and implementing monetary policy for the Eurozone. It is comprised of:

- **The Executive Board:** This is a full-time executive board made up of a president, a vice president and four other nominees.
- **The General Council:** This is the Executive Board plus the governors of all of the Central Banks in the EU.
- **The Governing Council:** This is the Executive Board plus the governors of the Central Banks of the Eurozone countries.

The Governing Council formulates monetary policy and the Executive Board implements it in conjunction with the national Central Banks.

Monetary Policy Instruments of ECB

1. **Main refinancing operations (MROs):** These are open market operations with the credit institutions (banks) to provide liquidity, cash, for them.
2. **The marginal lending facility:** This allows banks to borrow cash on an overnight basis and the interest charged is the basis for the STF.
3. **The deposit facility:** This allows banks to make overnight deposits and the interest received becomes the basis for all deposit rates, sometimes known as the base rate or ECB rate of interest
4. **Minimum reserve requirements:** This lays down the minimum deposit which all banks must have with their national Central Bank.

The Irish Central Bank's main responsibilities

The Central Bank's EU responsibilities include:

1. **Contributing to the maintenance of price stability (low inflation) and a stable financial system.** This responsibility is achieved through cooperation with the ECB and other national Central Banks in producing economic forecasts for use in determining monetary policy, and by implementing ESCB monetary policy and exchange rate policy decisions efficiently. It works in close cooperation with the Financial Regulator to ensure that financial stability is maintained in Ireland.
2. **Ensuring safe and reliable payment and settlement systems** to enable firms and individuals to make payments to each other. Eurozone monetary policy operations are implemented through the inter-central-bank system known as TARGET[4]. Nearly every EU credit institution is linked to TARGET and although the system was primarily developed to meet the needs of the single monetary policy, it can also be used for transmitting both inter-bank and customer payments.
3. **Producing and distributing euro banknotes and coins and ensuring the security and integrity of the euro currency.** The ECB has the sole right to issue euro banknotes and approves the volume of euro coins to be issued in euro area countries. With the approval of the ESCB, the Central Bank issues euro banknotes and coins in Ireland and is responsible for ensuring the quality and authenticity of euro banknotes.
4. **Managing foreign exchange assets, on behalf of the European Central Bank.** At the start of the European Monetary Union (EMU), the euro area national Central Banks transferred a part of their foreign reserves to the ECB. In the case of Ireland, this amounted to €451 million. The remaining reserves continue to be managed by the Central Bank on behalf of the ECB, in accordance with the investment policy of the ECB.

[4] TARGET is an acronym for Trans-European Automated Real-time Gross settlement Express Transfer system.

The Central Bank's domestic responsibilities include:

5 **Providing advice and guidance on Irish economic policies.**
The Central Bank is responsible for the provision of economic analysis for the government with a view to promoting policies that are consistent with price stability and long-term growth in Ireland.

6 **Serving the public interest.**
It is accountable to the public through having transparent and active systems of public accountability and external reporting. It also assists the government in the drafting of relevant legislation both domestically and at EU level.

7 **Acting as banker to the government.**
All government income is lodged with the Central Bank and all payments made by the government are drawn on Central Bank cheques.

The Rate of Exchange of a Currency

There are six factors that determine the rate of exchange of a currency.

1 The purchasing power parity theory

The purchasing power parity theory states that, in a free market, the rate of exchange of a currency will settle at the point where its internal purchasing power is equal to its external purchasing power. This means that the rate of exchange will settle at the point where a given quantity of a country's currency will buy the same quantity of goods whether it is spent on the domestic market or on the foreign market.

What is the value of €185 in US dollars?

For example, if the average price of products is €10 in Ireland and the average price of products is $30 in the USA then the rate of exchange of the euro against the dollar would be €1 = $3.

Weaknesses of this theory

- It does not take into account the additional cost of transporting the goods between the countries.
- It does not take into account that many economic goods are not, realistically, tradable, e.g. health services, housing and transport.
- The assumption that there is free trade between countries is unrealistic. Many countries operate forms of protectionism.

*2 The balance of payments

The rate of exchange is the price of one currency in terms of another currency. Like all prices it is therefore determined by the interaction of supply and demand.

The demand for a country's currency on the international market is mostly derived from its exports, as foreign importers must purchase the country's currency to pay for the goods.

The supply of a country's currency on the international market is mostly determined by the country's imports, as importers must buy foreign currency to pay for the imports.

Thus if the value of a country's exports is greater than the value of its imports, then the price (exchange rate) of the currency will increase and vice versa.

*3 The role of speculators

Currencies are regarded as commodities which can be bought and sold on the international market. This attracts speculators into the market. If these people feel that a currency will increase in value then they will buy up this currency, thus increasing the demand for it and automatically increasing its price (rate of exchange).

Likewise, if speculators feel that a currency may decrease in value they will sell it, thus creating a supply of it and decreasing its price (rate of exchange).

*4 The role of multinational companies

Like all other companies, multinationals aim to maximise the use of their assets. Thus if a branch of a multinational company in one country has spare cash and another branch in a different country is in need of cash, then the multinational will transfer the spare cash to the branch in need of it to save interest charges on overdrafts.

Assuming that the two countries in question use different currencies this will automatically create (a) a supply of one currency, thus bringing down its value, and (b) a demand for the other currency, thus increasing its value.

✳5 Intervention by Central Banks

(In the Eurozone intervention is done by the ECB.)

If a Central Bank feels that the rate of exchange of its currency on the international market is either too high or too low in relation to the performance of its economy, then it can use its own resources to either buy or sell its currency on the international market. If a Central Bank feels that the rate of exchange for its currency is too high, thus making it difficult to export, then it will sell (increase the supply of) its currency on the international market, thus bringing down its rate of exchange.

✳6 International agreements

Sometimes countries that are members of a trading group will agree to accept each other's currency at fixed rates of exchange in order to eliminate the exchange rate risks involved in international trade. This was done in the EU prior to the single currency. However, these agreements do not tend to last in the long run as certain restraints are placed on each of the economies in order to maintain these rates of exchange.

Fixed and Floating Rates of Exchange

✳Fixed rates of exchange

A fixed rate of exchange system is one where the values of currencies are agreed on and each country undertakes to exchange its currency at the agreed value. The governments agree to undertake whatever action is necessary to maintain these rates of exchange.

Advantages of fixed rates of exchange

1. They eliminate the exchange risk involved in importing on credit. For example, an Irish importer ordered goods on credit from the USA for $100,000 when the rate of exchange was €1 = $1.20. Thus he expected to pay €83,333.33 for the goods. He then sold the goods in Ireland for €93,333.33 and assumed that he had made a profit of €10,000. However, before he paid for the goods the rate of exchange had changed to €1 = $1. Thus he has to pay €100,000 for them and lost money on the transaction.
2. They eliminate the risk involved in international borrowing. The same principle applies as in 1 above.
3. Fixed rates of exchange make speculation in currencies futile. Speculation often distorts the true value of a currency.

Disadvantages of fixed rates of exchange

1. Countries may have to use up large amounts of their foreign reserves to intervene on the international markets to maintain the value of the currency at the fixed rate.
2. Governments may have to implement policies which are detrimental to the requirements of their own economy. For example, if the country increases its interest rates to curb imports this may also have a detrimental effect on the demand for domestically produced goods.

✳Floating rates of exchange

Under the floating rates of exchange system currencies are allowed to find their own value on the international market through the interaction of the supply of and demand for the currencies.

Advantages of floating rates of exchange

1. The currency will automatically reach its real value on the international market, which reflects the state of the economy.
2. Countries do not have to use their foreign reserves to intervene on the international markets.
3. In the long run, the balance on the current account in the balance of payments will be brought into equilibrium, because if a country's exports are less than its imports then the value of its currency will go down on the international market, thus making their exports cheaper and their imports more expensive.

Disadvantages of floating rates of exchange

1. The element of uncertainty in importing on credit could result in a reduction in international trade. (See Advantages of fixed rates of exchange, p. 155.)
2. Likewise, borrowing on the international market could be discouraged which could be detrimental to economic development.
3. Floating rates of exchange encourage speculation in currencies, which can undermine the real value of a currency.

Economic and Monetary Union (EMU)

In this chapter we will deal only with the monetary aspects of the EMU. See Chapter 23, The European Union, for the economic aspects of it.

Three elements of the EMU

1. The establishment of a single currency among participating members.
2. The creation of a single monetary policy implemented by the European Central Bank (ECB) as outlined above.
3. Co-ordination of economic and budgetary policies. (This should lead, eventually, to a common fiscal policy and to tax harmonisation.)

✳ The evolution of the euro

The Treaty of Maastricht

The Treaty on European Union and Economic and Monetary Union (EMU) was agreed in Maastricht and signed in February 1992. It came into force in November 1993. Under this treaty it was agreed that national currencies would be replaced by a single European currency – provided the countries concerned met a number of economic conditions. The most important of the 'Maastricht criteria' were: (i) that the country's budget deficit cannot exceed 3 per cent of its gross domestic product (GDP) for more than a short period; (ii) public borrowing must not exceed 60 per cent of GDP; (iii) prices and (iv) interest rates must also remain stable over a long period, as must (v) exchange rates between the currencies concerned.

January 1994: The establishment of the European Monetary Institute

The European Monetary Institute (EMI) was set up and new procedures were introduced to monitor EU countries' economies and encourage convergence between them.

June 1997: The Stability and Growth Pact

The Amsterdam European Council agreed the Stability and Growth Pact. A new exchange rate mechanism was designed to ensure stable exchange rates between the euro and the currencies of EU countries that remain outside the Eurozone. This meeting also agreed on a design for the 'European' side of the euro coins.

May 1998: Eleven countries qualified for the euro

At a meeting in Brussels, from 1–3 May 1998, the EU's political leaders decided that eleven EU countries met the requirements for membership of the euro area. These were Austria, Belgium, Finland, France, Germany, Ireland, Italy, Luxembourg, the Netherlands Portugal and Spain. (Greece joined them on 1 January 2001.)

1 January 1999: Birth of the euro

This is the start of the transitional period that was to last until 31 December 2001. Each of the eleven countries had a fixed rate of exchange against the euro and thus a fixed rate against each other. From this point onwards, the European Central Bank took over from the EMI and became responsible for monetary policy, which is now defined and implemented in euro. International trading in the euro began on 4 January 1999.

1 January 2002: Euro coins and notes were introduced

Fig 17.4

On 1 January 2002 euro-denominated notes and coins were put into circulation. This was the start of the period during which national currency notes and coins were withdrawn from circulation. The period ended on 28 February 2002.

Thereafter, only the euro was legal tender in the Eurozone countries. As of 1 January 2008, fifteen countries use the euro. They are: Austria, Belgium, Cyprus, Finland, France, Germany, Greece, Ireland, Italy, Luxembourg, Malta, the Netherlands, Portugal, Slovenia and Spain.

Effects of the introduction of the euro on the Irish economy

On the consumer

1. **Foreign travel:** The introduction of the euro has decreased the cost of travelling within the Eurozone. There is no need to acquire a different currency thus eliminating the banking charges involved. The growing use of debit cards with the Cirrus facility also ensures better management of money for the prudent traveller while abroad in the Eurozone. This allows travellers to withdraw money from their own bank accounts only as they need it. And the traveller does not come home with pockets full of useless change and small value banknotes.

   Travelling outside the Eurozone is also easier since the euro is an international currency and therefore widely accepted in many places outside the Eurozone, particularly in tourist destinations.

2 **Inflation:** Initially the introduction of the euro led to inflation within Ireland. Ironically some of this inflation was due to the lower rates of interest available as a result of entry to the EMU.

3 **Price comparisons** can now be made within all Eurozone countries, allowing for greater transparency.

4 **Greater choice of financial products:** Irish consumers can now choose where to save, borrow, invest and seek insurance, thereby facilitating increased competition. This is further evidenced by the increased competition in the retail-banking sector in the Irish economy. Bank charges are being reduced and the arrival of many non-national banks on the Irish market has resulted in better interest rates being offered to savers.

5 **Greater awareness and competition:** The euro has resulted in greater awareness as regards prices and Irish consumers can now seek better value for their euro.

6 **Prudent management of the economy:** Membership of the Eurozone constrains the government in relation to economic policy and ensures prudent management occurs. For example, the country's budget deficit cannot exceed 3 per cent of its gross domestic product (GDP) for more than a short period and public borrowing must not exceed 60 per cent of GDP.

7 **Low interest rates on loans:** The lower interest rates instigated since the introduction of the euro have benefited consumers, resulting in increased borrowings and a higher standard of living. However, the Central Bank has issued a number of warnings that the level of debt in the private sector of the economy is rising at an alarming rate.

8 **Savers** benefit from a wider and more diversified offer of investment and saving opportunities. Investors can spread their risks more easily and have given some an appetite for riskier ventures!

In the commercial sector

1 **Exchange risk eliminated:** No devaluation or revaluation has taken place, resulting in increased certainty in international trade.

2 **Easier payment for trading:** As no conversion charges apply to trade within the Eurozone this facilitates speedier payment, which is very beneficial to an open economy such as Ireland's. An open economy is one which trades with other economies.

3 **Lower interest rates:** One of the major benefits of the euro has been access to lower competitive interest rates for firms. This greatly reduces the set up costs and the cost of working capital for Irish industries.

4 **Cost of imported raw materials and capital goods:** These should now be more competitive due to open competition, the absence of currency fluctuations and more transparency in international pricing.

5. **Pressure for domestic competitiveness:** Employees are becoming increasingly aware that success as an economy depends on being competitive and this has ensured moderation in wage increases.

6. **Increased trade opportunities:** Access to EU markets is easier and leads to greater opportunities. As the size of the EU market increases greater opportunities for Irish exporters are created.

7. **Fluctuating value of the euro:** Companies dealing with customers outside the Eurozone will still face the risks associated with floating rates of exchange.

On the government

1. **The loss of the ability to manipulate exchange rates to manage the balance of trade:** When Ireland had its own independent punt it was possible for the government to correct a deficit on the balance of trade by devaluing the currency. This made Ireland's exports cheaper and its imports more expensive.

2. **The loss of some degree of sovereignty:** As more directives are issued from the European Parliament and from the European Central Bank, Ireland's capacity to pass legislation which may be beneficial to the nation is being eroded.

3. **Loss of direct control over national monetary policy:** This is now determined by the European Central Bank. Theoretically, we have an input into the monetary policy. The absolute size of the Irish economy is small, therefore greater emphasis will be placed on the needs of the larger economies.

4. **Budgetary policy:** There will, eventually, be some loss of control over our budgetary policy as we move closer and closer to tax harmonisation.

If sterling remains outside the euro

The UK is very important to the Irish economy as 33 per cent of our imports are from the UK and 25 per cent of our exports go to the UK.

1. Fluctuating sterling will affect imports and exports depending on the relative change in exchange rates.

2. The planning and management of any sterling debt becomes more difficult.

Financial Institutions in the Irish Market

✻Commercial or associated banks

Allied Irish Banks plc, The Governor and Company of the Bank of Ireland, National Irish Bank Ltd, Ulster Bank Ltd, Permanent TSB and the Central Bank of Ireland are members of the DBCC (Dublin Bankers' Clearing Committee), an unincorporated association which overseas the operation of the clearing system.

The first four banks are known as the associated banks. They are essentially clearing banks, which provide a broad range of retail and wholesale banking services. They were traditionally responsible for the money transmission system.

These associated banks accept deposits, give loans to the general public and operate such services as night safes, money transfers, foreign exchange, purchase and sale of shares and operate a 24-hour on-line banking system.

AIB and the Bank of Ireland are Irish owned institutions. Ulster Bank is a subsidiary of the UK National Westminster Bank group. National Irish Bank is a member of Danske Bank Group, a Danish banking organisation. The Ulster Bank and National Irish Bank are much smaller in terms of size than the Bank of Ireland and the AIB.

The Permanent TSB emerged as a result of a series of amalgamations of the various trustee savings banks. These merged with the Irish Permanent Building Society and Irish Life Assurance.

A recent arrival on the Irish commercial banking scene is Halifax, which took over the retail section of the Royal Bank of Scotland in Ireland.

✳Merchant banks

Merchant, or wholesale, banks deal only with the business sector of the community. These banks offer a variety of services to the business sector of the community. These include:

1. **The issuing of irrevocable letters of credit or bills of exchange.** These are essential in international trade. These two are slightly different but serve the same function for an exporter or an importer.

   ### Example

   For example, assume you wish to import €250,000 worth of goods from a Japanese exporter. You would be unwilling to send the money in advance of receiving the goods as you would find it very difficult to get your money back in the event of a non-delivery. On the other hand, the Japanese exporter would be unwilling to supply the goods without payment. This dilemma can be solved by the use of an irrevocable letter of credit from a merchant bank. You lodge, or arrange to lodge, the €250,000 with a merchant banker in Ireland. This bank then sends a letter to the Japanese exporter's bank undertaking to pay the money at a certain date in the future. In this way, you know that the money will not be paid until you receive the goods and the exporter is guaranteed to receive his/her money. The exporter may, if he/she so wishes, discount this before it is due for payment, i.e. sell it on to somebody else at a discount usually to another merchant bank.

2. **Organising the issue of new shares** by companies and also underwriting the issue. The issue is usually done through Initial Public Offers (IPOs), when the merchant bank tries to place a certain percentage of the new shares with interested parties before the shares go on general offer to the public. When the merchant banks act as underwriters they are guaranteeing that they will purchase any shares not purchased.

3 **Organising mergers and takeovers:** The merchant banks have experienced corporate solicitors working for them who can handle all the legal work involved in these transactions. They can also provide the money needed to finance the transactions.

4 **Loans and deposits** which are usually for substantial sums of money.

5 **Offering a range of solutions** for the business customer wishing to accept debit or credit cards as a form of payment, such as point-of-sale terminals and internet facilities, which enables the processing of credit and debit card transactions in real time over a secure link.

6 **Provide factoring facilities:** A business can sell/discount their debtors to these banks and the banks then collect the full amount when payment becomes due.

Industrial banks

Industrial banks are the main providers of instalment loans for the purchase of cars, furniture and expensive consumer durable goods. They tend to work in conjunction with shops and garages, which receive a fee or a commission from the banks. These forms of loans tend to carry high interest rates.

Fig 17.5 Industrial banks provide loans for car purchases

Sub-prime lenders

Sub-prime lending is the practice of granting loans (mortgages, car loans, credit cards etc.) to borrowers with a poor or no credit rating. You may recall from p. 148 that the normal banking practice is to grant loans only to those borrowers who show ability to repay the loans. Thus the mainstream banks would not normally give loans to customers with a poor credit record.

In recent times (in banking terms), many financial institutions have sprung up who are willing to grant loans to people with a poor credit rating. These are known as sub-prime lenders. The term **sub-prime**, in this context, means 'below the best or ideal' and refers to the status of the borrowers.

The loans are given at an interest rate well in excess of the normal interest rates charged by the mainstream lenders. Many borrowers are willing to pay these rates in order to secure loans. Homeowners who find themselves in financial difficulties turn to these lenders. Thus it can be a very profitable practice. However, the risk of the borrowers defaulting on the loans is very high.

Sub-prime lenders rely heavily on securitising, or parcelling up, their loans and selling them on to investors (frequently these are mainstream banks) as a way of funding their operations. If there is a high default rate on the repayment of the loans the mainstream banks could face a serious liquidity crisis.

Many sub-prime lenders in the US have acted in an irresponsible manner and have granted loans to people with little or no collateral. Hundreds of thousands of these have defaulted on the loans. These borrowers have become known as NINJAs, i.e. 'no income, no job or assets'. There is a fear that a similar situation could arise in the Irish market.

Other financial institutions

As well as those listed above, there are also very many building societies, post offices and credit unions all around the country.

Note: The Inter-Bank-Market is where a bank with a temporary surplus of cash can lend this surplus to another bank which is experiencing a temporary shortage of cash. These loans are usually for extremely short periods of time. The rate of interest charged on this market is one of the contributory factors influencing the rate of interest charged by banks to their customers.

International Financial Institutions

✻The International Monetary Fund (IMF)

What is the IMF?

The IMF is the world's central organisation for international monetary cooperation. It was established in the 1940s at Bretton Woods, New Hampshire, USA to agree international economic policies. These policies were aimed at avoiding any repetition of the events that led to the Great Depression of the 1930s. It is governed by a board of governors, which is drawn from all member countries.

The IMF performs three main activities:

1. It monitors national, global and regional economic and financial developments. It advises member countries on their economic policies. This is known as its 'surveillance' role.
2. It lends members hard currencies to assist them to design programmes to correct any balance of payments problems.
3. It offers technical assistance in its areas of expertise, such as training for government and central bank officials.

Where does the IMF get its money?

The IMF's finances come mainly from levies or quotas that each member country must contribute. Quotas are assessed on the value of the country's economy and trading activity. For example, the United States, the world's largest economy, has the largest quota in the IMF. The quotas are reviewed from time to time and can be changed in line with changes in each country's economy.

Countries must deposit 25 per cent of their quota in any of the major currencies, such as US dollars or Japanese yen. The balance is payable in the member's own currency when and as needed.

Most common use of IMF funds

Under its Poverty Reduction and Growth Facility, the IMF provides concessional loans, i.e. loans with an annual interest rate of 0.5 per cent and a maturity of 10 years, to its poorest member countries. The majority of the IMF's loans now fall into this category.

In 2005, it set up the Exogenous Shocks Facility. Using this facility it can give concessional loans to low-income countries that are suffering a balance of payments problem that is beyond their own control, provided they are not already receiving funds under the Poverty Reduction and Growth Facility.

The IMF also provides emergency assistance to countries coping with balance of payments problems caused by natural disasters or military conflicts. The interest rates are subsidised for low-income countries.

Source: *IMF*

A Sri Lankan girl in a refugee camp after the tsunami in 2005 – Sri Lanka is one of the countries that received financial assistance from the IMF in the wake of a natural disaster

✳The World Bank

The World Bank is a vital source of financial and technical assistance to developing countries around the world.

It is not a bank in the common sense. It is made up of two unique development institutions owned by 185 member countries:

- The International Bank for Reconstruction and Development (IBRD) aims to reduce poverty in middle-income and creditworthy poorer countries by promoting sustainable development through loans, guarantees, risk management products, and analytical and advisory services. (Source: *IBRD* website)
- The International Development Association (IDA) aims to reduce poverty by providing interest-free loans and grants for programmes that boost economic growth, reduce inequalities and improve people's living conditions.

The IDA is one of the largest sources of assistance for the world's eighty-two poorest countries, thirty-nine of which are in Africa. It is the single largest source of donor funds for basic social services in the poorest countries.

The IDA lends money on concessional terms. This means that IDA loans have no interest charge and repayments are stretched over 35 to 40 years, including a 10-year grace period.

From the time it was set up in 1960, the IDA has given loans and grants totalling US$161 billion. In recent times, the average value of the loans, on a yearly basis, is US$8 billion and about 50 per cent of this goes to Africa. (Source: *IDA* website)

Sources of finance

IBRD lending to developing countries is primarily financed by selling AAA-rated bonds in the world's financial markets. The IBRD earns a small margin on this lending.

The greater proportion of its income comes from lending out its own capital. This capital consists of reserves built up over the years and money paid in from the bank's 185 member country shareholders. These funds are replenished every three years by forty donor countries.

Additional funds are regenerated through repayments of loans, which are then available for relending.

Roughly 40 per cent of the IBRD's income goes on funding IDA loans and the IBRD also pays for World Bank operating expenses and has contributed to the IDA and debt relief.

The following three organisations are also part of the World Bank Group.

The International Finance Corporation (IFC)

The main aim of the IFC is to assist the development of the private sector in developing countries. Its particular aim is the development of productive enterprises and efficient capital markets.

The Multilateral Investment Guarantee Agency (MIGA)

The main aim of MIGA is to encourage foreign direct investment (FDI) into developing countries. Many companies are unwilling to invest in developing countries due to their concerns about the investment environment and political instability. The MIGA attempts to assist investors by offering political risk insurance, technical assistance and a dispute mediation service. (Source: *MIGA* website)

The International Centre for Settlement of Investment Disputes (ICSID)

The main aim of the ICSID is to facilitate the settlement of investment disputes between governments and foreign direct investors by providing conciliation and arbitration services to governments of member countries of the World Bank and investors who originate from other countries who are also members of the World Bank.

Agreement to enter these dispute resolution procedures is voluntary, but once the consent is given then neither side can withdraw from the procedures and are bound by the findings of the ICSID. (Source: *ICSID* website)

*The European Investment Bank (EIB)

The role of the European Investment Bank is to contribute towards the integration, balanced development and economic and social cohesion of the EU member countries. To do this it raises funds on the markets, which it then directs towards financing capital projects according with the objectives of the EU.

The six main objectives of the bank's funding

1 Cohesion and convergence

This policy is aimed at supporting developments in the less favoured regions and in particular to meet the challenges of enlargement of the EU. In 2004, €28 billion was devoted to projects located in these regions.

2 Support for small and medium sized enterprises

Supporting investment by small and medium sized enterprises (SMEs) is a key factor in the EIB's activities. The SME sector accounts for over 75 million jobs and 99 per cent of all European enterprises.

3 Environmental stability

The EIB promotes the environmental policy of the EU. The protection and improvement of the environment is a priority objective of the bank as outlined in the bank's Corporate Operational Plan (COP) 2005–2007 and mentioned in the EIB's Environmental Statement 2004.

4 Implementation of the Innovation 2010 Initiative

In 2000, the EU set itself a target of establishing a competitive, innovative and knowledge-based European economy, capable of sustaining economic growth with more and better jobs and greater social cohesion by 2010.

5 Development of Trans-European Networks of transport and energy

The Trans-European Networks (TENs) are large infrastructure networks of transport, energy and telecommunications essential to the developmental and integration goals of the EU.

6 Sustainable, competitive and secure energy

This is the aim of achieving a secure source of energy which is both sustainable and cost effective.

Source: *Europa.eu*

LEARN THE KEY POINTS

1. Definition of money
2. Functions of money
3. Characteristics of a good money form
4. The different forms of money
5. The primary liquidity ratio
6. The secondary liquidity ratio
7. How banks create money and credit
8. The limitations on the powers of the banks to create money and credit
9. The powers of the Central Bank to control the amount of money and credit that it creates
10. The functions of the Central Bank
11. The monetary policy of the ECB and how it is implemented
12. Know the three elements of the EMU
13. Know the effects on the Irish economy of the introduction of the euro
14. Know the roles of the IMF, The World Bank and the European Investment Bank

Exam Q&A: See p. 392

Copy questions 1–5 into your answer book and complete each of the sentences by filling in the blank spaces.

1 Money is anything ____________ by the majority of people in exchange for ____________ and ____________.

2 The double coincidence of needs and wants meant that under the barter system a person wishing to obtain a product must be able to find someone who ____________ and who ____________.

3 Gresham's Law states that ____________ drives out ____________.

4 The Purchasing Power Parity Theory states that, in a free market, the rate of exchange of a currency will settle at the point where its ____________ power is equal to its ____________.

5 The Primary Liquidity Ratio is the ratio between the amount of ____________ which the banks ____________ hold and ____________ on the banks.

6 State and explain the functions of money.

7 State and explain the characteristics of a good money form.

8 The rate of exchange between the € and the $ changed from €1 = $1.20 in year 1 to €1 = $1.00 in year 2. State whether the euro went up or down in value in relation to the dollar. Give a brief explanation of your answer.

9 Assume that there are floating rates of exchange. Explain fully how a country's international trading situation, i.e. value of exports in relation to value of imports, could affect the value of its currency on the international market.

10 Assume an individual lodges €50,000 cash into his bank account and the Primary Liquidity Ratio is 1:20.
   (a) What is the maximum loan which the bank can grant on the basis of this lodgement? Explain your answer in detail.
   (b) Explain the total value of all claims on the bank after the loan has been granted and show how the bank has complied with the requirements of the Primary Liquidity Ratio.

11 Explain the restrictions within the banking industry itself which restrict the banks' ability to create money.

12 State and explain the methods available to the Central Bank to control the amount of money (credit) which the banks can create.

13 State and explain the functions of the (Irish) Central Bank.

14 Outline any two economic effects on the Irish economy of a decision by the UK to become a member the Eurozone.

15 Monetary policy is determined by the ECB. State and explain the means by which it implements its monetary policy within the Eurozone countries.

16 On the one hand, banks have a responsibility to their shareholders to maximise their profits. On the other hand, they have a responsibility to their customers to meet their liquidity requirements and to comply with the PLR as specified by the ECB and our own Central Bank. Explain how the banks attempt to reconcile these dual responsibilities.

17 Explain any three effects which the introduction of the euro has had on each of the following sectors of the Irish economy: (a) consumers, (b) the commercial sector and (c) the government.

18 Name the five institutions which make up the World Bank Group. Give a brief explanation of the functions of each of these institutions.

19 Give a brief outline of the six main objectives of the funding activities of the European Investment Bank.

20 (a) What was the original idea behind the foundation of the International Monetary Fund?
   (b) Outline the most common uses of IMF funds.

Chapter 18
Measuring the National Income

This chapter looks at how national income is measured. It examines the different methods that can be used to calculate the level and rate of growth of national income.

Definition of national income

> **National income** is the total of all incomes earned by residents of a country who supply the factors of production in any given period of time. It is normally measured annually.
>
> The symbol used to indicate national income is Y.

Methods of Measuring National Income

1. The expenditure method
2. The production method
3. The incomes method

All three of these methods should equal each other as all money spent (**expenditure**) is spent on goods and services, which are produced (**production**), and all **incomes** are earned from the production of goods and services.

Households earn their income by producing goods and then spend that income on goods that were produced, thus returning the money to the producer. This is known as the circular flow of income and is displayed as follows.

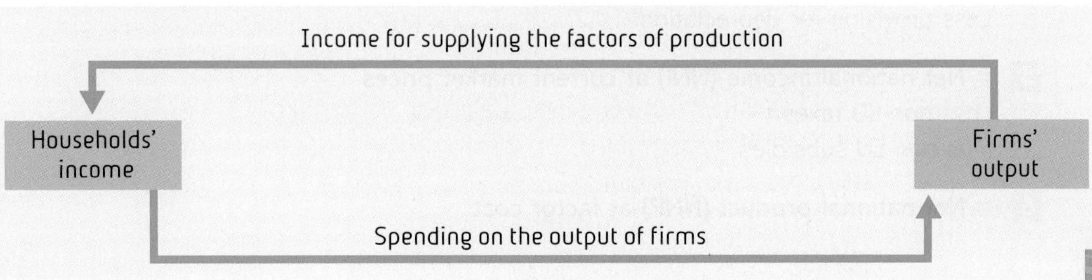

Fig 18.1 The circular flow of income

At any given time the circular flow of income can be increased or decreased by any extra inputs of funds (called injections) into it, or any withdrawal or leakage of funds from it. We will return to this in more detail in Chapter 19, Factors Determining the Size of the National Income.

Calculating the National Income

The National Income and Expenditure Report published in August 2007 by the CSO outlined updated methods of calculating the national income, which are in line with the European System of Accounts known as ESA95.

Note: The CSO in Ireland uses only the expenditure and the incomes methods.

The two methods used, i.e. the income and expenditure methods, should theoretically give the same answer. However, because the two methods use different data sources there will always be some difference in the final figures calculated by each method. The official level of GDP is taken to be an average of the expenditure and income estimates and a balancing item (statistical discrepancy) is displayed, which is half of the difference between the two estimates. If the income-based estimate is higher than the expenditure-based estimate, the discrepancy will have a negative sign in the income tables and a positive sign in the expenditure tables and vice versa.

✳The expenditure method

1. **Calculate total expenditure, allowing for statistical discrepancy**[1]
   Plus value of exports (these bring in more money, i.e. income)
   Less value of imports (these cause money to leave the country)

2. **= Gross domestic product (GDP) at current market prices**
   Plus or minus net factor income with the rest of the world[2]

3. **= Gross national product (GNP) at current market prices**
   Plus EU subsidies
   Less EU taxes

4. **= Gross national income (GNI) at current market prices**
   Less provision for depreciation[3]

5. **= Net national income (NNI) at current market prices**
   Less non-EU taxes
   Plus non-EU subsidies

6. **= Net national product (NNP) at factor cost**

Example

As per the method used by the CSO for national income statistics published in August 2007. (Figures used are the provisional figures for the year 2006 as per the CSO.)

Table 18.1 *Expenditure method*

	€m	€m
Total expenditure[1]		154,935
+ Statistical discrepancy	1,001	155,936
Plus exports	139,766	
Less imports	– 120,997	18,769
Gross domestic product (GDP) at current market prices	—	**174,705**
+ or – Net factor income with the rest of the world[2]	—	– 25,575
Gross national product (GNP) at current market prices	—	**149,130**
Plus EU subsidies	1,778	—
Less EU taxes	– 421	1,357
Gross national income (GNI) at current market prices	—	**150,487**
Less provision for depreciation[3]	—	– 18,436
Net national income (NNI) at current market prices	—	**132,051**
Less non EU taxes	– 24,607	—
Plus non EU subsidies	+ 912	– 23,695
Net national product (NNP) at factor cost	—	**108,356**
Gross national disposable income (GNDI) at current market prices[4]	—	148,665

Notes

[1] This includes **all** expenditure whether it is public or private, capital or current.

[2] This is mostly the difference between profits repatriated out of the country by foreign multinationals located in Ireland and profits repatriated back to Ireland by Irish companies located abroad. It is normally a negative figure in Ireland's case.

[3] This is the loss in value of capital goods (assets).

[4] Gross national disposable income at current market prices represents the income available for consumption expenditure and savings and is calculated by adding **net receipts of current international transfers, excluding EU subsidies and taxes** (see below), to gross national income at current market prices.

Net receipts of current international transfers excluding EU subsidies and taxes refer to payments under Third World aid programmes operated by non-governmental organisations (NGOs) and transfers related to non-life insurance business. In the above example for 2006 this was – €1,822.

Source: *CSO*

✳Incomes method

The main points to be noted in the updated incomes method are:

- The terms GDP and GNP are now reserved for valuation at market prices while **value added** is used for other valuations.
- Three valuations are now shown, i.e. **market prices**, **factor cost** and **basic prices**.
- The third one, GVA at basic prices, equals GDP at market prices minus product taxes plus product subsidies.
- Product taxes are taxes that are payable per unit of some good or service produced or transacted. Excise duties on drink and tobacco are examples of product taxes.
- Product subsidies are subsidies that are payable per unit of good or service produced or imported. They mostly relate to agricultural subsidies such as aid to farmers in less favoured areas.
- Non-product taxes are taxes on production excluding the product taxes mentioned above. Rates on commercial property and motor vehicle duties paid by businesses are examples of non-product taxes.
- Non-product subsidies are subsidies on production excluding the product subsidies mentioned above. Grants for employment creation are examples of non-product subsidies.

1 Calculate the total value of all incomes (including profits) earned in the country, ensuring that income or benefit-in-kind is included and that transfer payments are not included. (See notes below.)
Subtract stock appreciation as no factor of production was supplied for this extra value.

2 = **Net value added at factor cost**
Add depreciation

3 = **Gross value added (GVA) at factor cost**
Add non-product taxes
Subtract non-product subsidies

4 = **Gross value added (GVA) at basic prices**
Add product taxes
Subtract product subsidies

5 **= Gross domestic product (GDP) at current market prices**
Subtract net factor income with the rest of the world

6 This equals **gross national product (GNP) at current market prices**
Add EU subsidies
Subtract EU taxes

7 = **Gross national income (GNI) at current market prices**
Proceed as per expenditure method to arrive at net national product (NNP) at factor cost
Less provision for depreciation

8 = **Net national income (NNI) at current market prices**
Less non-EU taxes
Plus non-EU subsidies

9 **Equals net national product (NNP) at factor cost**

Example

As per the method used by the CSO for national income statistics published in August 2007. (Figures used are the provisional figures for the year 2006 as per the CSO.)

***Table 18.2** Incomes method*

	€m	€m
Agriculture, forestry and fishing net value added		3,206
Industry net value added		34,695
Building and construction net value added		14,811
Distribution, transport and communication net value added		20,546
Public administration and defence		5,485
Other services (including rent) net value added		56,528
Sub total		**135,271**
Less stock appreciation	– 329	
Less statistical discrepancy	– 1,011	– 1,340
Net value added at factor cost		**133,931**
Plus provision for depreciation		18,436
Gross value added at factor cost		**152,367**
Plus non-product taxes	1,678	
Less non-product subsidies	– 1,471	207
Gross value added at basic prices		**152,574**
Plus product taxes	23,351	
Less product subsidies	– 1,220	22,130
Gross domestic product (GDP) at current market prices		**174,705**
Net factor income with the rest of the world		– 25,575
Gross national product (GNP) at current market prices		**149,130**
Plus EU subsidies	1,778	
Less EU taxes	– 421	1,357
Gross national income (GNI) at current market prices		**150,487**
Less provision for depreciation		– 18,436
Net national income (NNI) at current market prices		**132,051**
Less non-EU taxes	– 24,607	
Plus non-EU subsidies	+ 912	– 23,695
Net national product at factor cost		**108,356**

Source: *CSO*

Notes

- **Benefit-in-kind** is any non-money income earned. Your employer may provide you with a car that you can also use in your private life, as distinct from work purposes only. This is, therefore, providing you with something of value. It is given to you instead of an increase in your wages. Remember that other people have to pay for their cars out of their net wages.

- A **transfer payment** occurs when the taxes levied on the income earned by one person are given as income to another person, e.g. social welfare payments. If transfer payments were included it would be the equivalent to double counting.
- **Statistical discrepancy** arises from the fact that GDP is calculated in two independent ways, i.e. the incomes and the expenditure methods. The two methods produce different estimates. The official level of GDP is taken to be the average of the two independent estimates and the statistical discrepancy is the amount by which each estimate has to be adjusted to bring it in line with the official estimate. If the income-based estimate is higher than the expenditure-based estimate, the discrepancy will have a negative sign in the income tables, as seen on p. 173.

✳Production method

This method of measuring the national income is not used by the CSO in Ireland. However, the following is an outline of the procedure that could be used.

- **Calculate the value of total production** in the economy (avoid double counting, see below).
- **Adjust for financial services**, i.e. the difference between interest earned by and paid by the financial institutions as this is not regarded as a factor income. This is a negative figure.
- **Adjust for changes in value of stocks of goods** (minus if stock appreciates as no factor of production was supplied, plus if stock depreciates as it is an expense).

  = Net domestic product at factor cost
- Adjust for **+ or – net factor income** with the rest of the world.

  = Net national product at factor cost

Double counting

If a manufacturer buys in raw materials for €1,000, processes them and then sells the processed goods for €1,500, the value of the manufacturer's production is €500, not €1,500. If we counted the value of his production at €1,500 we would be double counting as we would be including the value of the output produced by the provider of the raw materials. Remember that the total value of all production is €1,500 and that is made up of:

- Value of goods produced by the provider of the raw materials = €1,000
- Value added by the processor of the raw materials = €500
- Total value of all goods produced = €1,500

Distinction between GNP and GDP

The distinction between GNP and GDP is very important in Ireland. The GDP is the total value of all goods and services produced in this country. Hence it represents all the incomes generated here. It has already been shown that GNP is GDP + or – net factor income with the rest of the world. Profits that are repatriated by foreign owned companies located in Ireland are greater than the profits repatriated into Ireland by Irish companies based in other countries. Thus GNP is always less than GDP, i.e. the income remaining in the country is less than the income generated here.

Therefore, GDP is a better guide to the level of economic activity in the country, while GNP is a better guide to the standard of living in the country.

Tables 18.3 and 18.4 give summaries of the Irish national income 2002–2005 in both absolute values and average income per person.

Note the major difference between GDP and GNP.

Table 18.3 *National income in absolute terms*

	€m	€m	€m	€m
Gross product	2002	2003	2004	2005
GDP – value	129,947	138,941	147,569	161,163
GNP – value	106,248	117,218	124,354	135,914

Source: *CSO*

Table 18.4 *National income per person*

	€m	€m	€m	€m
GDP – per capita	33,175	34,919	36,493	39,016
GNP – per capita	27,125	29,459	30,752	32,903

Source: *CSO*

✳Use of national income statistics

1. National income statistics are used to measure the level of economic growth from year to year. For example, has our national income increased or decreased?
2. These statistics are used to compare the standard of living in one country with that of other countries. Because the statistics are developed using international standards, they can be used to compare Ireland's national income with that of other countries.
3. These statistics are used to evaluate the economic climate. Policymakers, analysts and researchers use them to examine the performance of the economy.
4. The statistics help government planning by identifying the regions and sectors of the Irish economy which are generating the most and the least income.
5. They can be used to justify the demand for wage increases. Trade unions may

argue that because the national income has grown by 10 per cent they are entitled to a share of that growth in the form of increased wages.

6 Another important use in recent years is for administrative purposes within the EU. For example, Ireland's contribution to the EU budget is partly based on GNP levels.

7 The GDP figures were also used in determining eligibility for EMU as the basis for the measurement of government deficit, and debt as percentages of GDP, which are criteria for membership.

Limitations as to use of national income statistics

1 National income statistics measure growth not welfare. Remember that our welfare includes more than the economic goods which we purchase. It also includes our health, friendships, intelligence and life expectancy (see Human Development Index on p. 179).

2 These statistics may be affected by population growth. If the value of the national income increases by a smaller percentage than the increase in the population, then there is a decrease in average income per head.

3 Non-market economic activities are not included. As economies progress over time, people grow less of their own food requirements or make fewer of their own clothes. Therefore, when comparing the national income over a period of time allowance should be made for these goods.

4 Changes in the quality of goods are not taken into account. If the size of the standard bar of chocolate gets smaller over a period of time, without its price changing, then your standard of living is decreasing.

5 'Bads' as well as 'goods' are counted. If there is a natural disaster, such as storm damage to houses, money must be spent to repair the damage. Because this money is now part of total expenditure it automatically increases the figure for national income. However, there is no increase in the standard of living. The extra money spent only restores what was already there.

6 The problem of inflation measured at current prices rather than constant prices is not taken into account. (See explanation on pp 177–178.)

7 The balance between the production of capital and consumer goods is not highlighted. When money is spent on capital it is counted as part of total expenditure and, as already mentioned, increases the national income. However, this expenditure may not increase the standard of living. Ask any person who has lost money on an investment.

8 Leisure has not been taken into account in the statistics. People may be working longer hours for the same income.

9 Distribution of any increase in national income is not highlighted. It is possible for 5 per cent of the population to acquire 90 per cent of any substantial increase in the national income. If these people do not spend very much of their increase, then the average income per person will not increase by any significant amount.

10 It is difficult to account for the black economy. In some economies, there is a very large amount of activity in the black economy. By its very nature this is not included in the national accounts, yet it does increase the standard of living of those who supply the goods and services in this type of market.

11 The statistics do not count externalities. These are costs that are externalised (passed on) to someone else, e.g. pollution to the environment.

Limitations in international comparisons of national income statistics

1 The statistics must be converted into a common currency. This can cause a very misleading comparison as the rates of exchange are based only on the common value of tradable goods.

2 Some countries are more market oriented than others. This is similar to point 3 in the previous list. As economies develop, labour tends to become more specialised. The people in these economies then go out and buy all of their other needs and wants. This expenditure is counted as part of total expenditure, thus increasing the national income in money terms. In other economies, people may be more self-sufficient and may grow a lot of their own vegetables, make more of their own clothes and paint and decorate their homes themselves. The people in these economies have the same goods and services, but they have not bought them. Total expenditure in these economies will be lower, thus giving the impression of a lower standard of living.

3 The nature of expenditure may differ greatly from country to country. One country may spend large sums of money building up an arsenal of defence weapons. This expenditure does not produce consumer goods. At the same time, a different country may spend a similar sum on social welfare benefits, which do increase the standard of living.

4 The distribution of the national income may not be the same in each country. Two countries, A and B may have similar size national incomes and similar size populations. If 90 per cent of the wealth in country A is owned by 10 per cent of the population, while at the same time there is an even distribution of the wealth in country B, then the average standard of living in both countries will be drastically different. Remember that the average is only a mathematical concept.

5 The size of the population in each country should be known. Remember, to find the average income the total income is divided by the number of people in the economy.

National Income at Current and Constant Prices

When comparing the national income statistics from one year to the next no allowance is made for the rate of inflation between these years, as all goods produced are measured statistically at current prices.

Look at the following examples:

Example 1

Year 1

Number of goods produced = 100,000

Average price = €10 each

GDP = €1,000,000

Year 2

Number of goods produced = 110,000

Average price = €10 each

GDP = €1,100,000

In Example 1, economic growth has occurred as the quantity of goods produced in year 2 has increased.

Example 2

Year 1

Number of goods produced = 100,000

Average price = €10 each

GDP = €1,000,000

Year 2

Number of goods produced = 100,000

Average price = €11 each

GDP = €1,100,000

In Example 2, no economic growth has taken place, as the quantity of goods produced has not increased in year 2. The increase in the GDP figure was caused by inflation.

✳Constant price

A methodology used to overcome this difficulty is to measure each year's figures at a constant price. This is done by choosing a base year and taking all the prices of all the products to be produced at a value of 100. Then the change in prices in subsequent or previous years are expressed as a percentage of the prices prevailing in the base year. Thus we succeed in comparing like with like.

The following figures, compiled by the IMF, show the differences when using each method.

Table 18.5 *Base year 2004*

			2003	2004	2005	2006 (Est)	2007 (Est)
Ireland	GDP constant prices	€Bs	141.472	147.569	155.723	164.794	174.095
Ireland	GDP current prices	€Bs	138.941	147.569	161.163	174.613	188.736

Source: *IMF*

Human Development Index

The Human Development Index (HDI) is a comparative measure of life expectancy, literacy, education and standard of living for countries worldwide. It is a standard means of measuring human wellbeing, especially child welfare.

The index was developed in 1990 by Pakistani economist, Mahbub ul Haq. It has been used since 1993 by the United Nations Development Programme in its annual Human Development Report.

Some people incorrectly refer to the HDI as the Happiness Index. GDP, on the other hand, only measures the economic standard of living not wellbeing. So an interesting exercise is to compare the HDI of a country with its GDP. You draw your own conclusions.

The + or – sign indicates the change in ranking since 2001. Hasn't Ireland done well!

Table 18.6 *Human Development Index*

Rank	Country		HDI
1		Norway	▲ 0.965 (+2)
2		Iceland	▲ 0.960 (+4)
3		Australia	▲ 0.957 (+2)
4		Ireland	▲ 0.956 (+10)
5		Sweden	▲ 0.951 (+2)
6		Canada	▲ 0.950 (+1)
7		Japan	▲ 0.949 (+6)
8		United States	▲ 0.948 (+4)
9		Switzerland	➤ 0.947 (=)
10		Netherlands	▲ 0.947 (+4)

Source: *United Nations Human Development Report 2006* (based on 2005 figures)

Table 18.7 Purchasing power parity per capita

Rank	Country	GDP (PPP) $ per capita
1	Luxembourg	69,800
2	Norway	42,364
3	United States	41,399
4	Ireland	40,610
5	Iceland	35,115
6	Denmark	34,740
7	Canada	34,273
8	Hong Kong	33,479
9	Austria	33,432
10	Switzerland	32,571

Source: *IMF 2005*

Note: GDP at PPP means at purchasing power parity. This assumes that goods have the same prices in all countries. Thus, from the above example, a person living in Luxembourg would be able to purchase roughly twice the amount of goods with his or her average income than a person living in Denmark.

Now note the difference between these same countries when we measure national income at GNP (GNI) rather than GDP.

Table 18.8 Contrast of national incomes at GDP and GNI

Rank	Country	GDP (PPP) $ per capita	Rank	Country	GNI (PPP) $ per capita
1	Luxembourg	69,800	1	Luxembourg	65,340
2	Norway	42,364	3	Norway	40,420
3	United States	41,399	2	United States	41,950
4	Ireland	40,610	8	Ireland	34,720
5	Iceland	35,115	7	Iceland	34,760
6	Denmark	34,740	10	Denmark	33,570
7	Canada	34,273	15	Canada	32,220
8	Hong Kong	33,479	9	Hong Kong	34,670
9	Austria	33,432	11	Austria	33,140
10	Switzerland	32,571	5	Switzerland	37,080

Source: *IMF 2005*

Trade Cycles

Most economies experience an ongoing succession of booms and slumps, i.e. inflationary periods followed by deflationary periods followed by inflationary periods and so on. These successions of changes in the economic welfare of an economy are called **trade cycles**.

Trade cycles are divided into four distinct phases.

1 The recovery phase

In the recovery phase unemployment is high, incomes are very low and production and investment levels are also low. Some investment takes place to replace assets that have been completely depreciated in the economy. This has a multiplier effect on income. The increased level of income leads to an increased level of demand, which in turn leads to an increased level of investment to profit from the extra demand.

2 The boom period

As investment and demand increase, all of the unemployed labour and capital resources will become fully employed, and the economy reaches the peak of the trade cycle. Therefore, any further increase in demand cannot be met by increased production. Thus any further increase in demand will lead to inflation as demand outstrips the productive capacity of the economy. As prices begin to increase (inflation) demand will begin to drop.

3 The recession period

As demand continues to fall there is no incentive for entrepreneurs to invest in the economy. Therefore, the multiplier effect of investment is lost thus reducing incomes. As incomes decrease, demand decreases even further, leading to a decrease in production and an increase in unemployment. As unemployment increases incomes further decrease, demand decreases and so on.

4 The depression phase

Eventually income, demand and production will cease falling and will level out at a very low level. (Remember that demand would never fall to zero as we have to purchase the essentials for living even if this means using up any savings which we might have, or having to borrow to do so.) This depressed level of demand discourages any further investment and the economy drops to the trough of the trade cycle.

Eventually, the existing capital goods (machines, etc.) will become useless and will have to be replaced even if only to meet the present low level of demand. This new investment will now have a multiplier effect on incomes, causing demand to begin to increase slowly and this brings us back to the recovery period.

Trade cycles are often depicted on a diagram such as Fig 18.2.

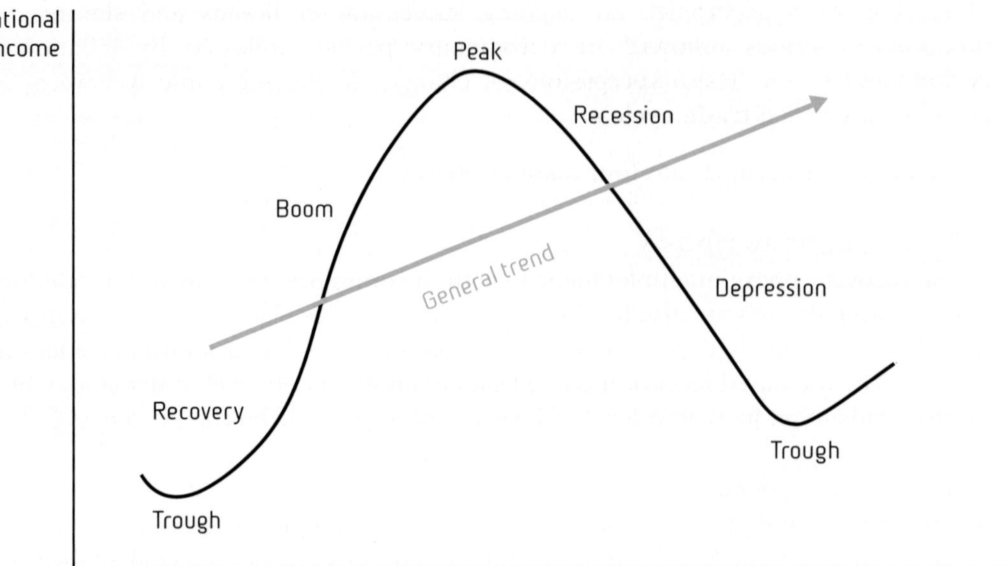

Fig 18.2 Example of a trade cycle

Note: Trade cycles may be examined in the Leaving Certificate exam as part of a question on national income or as part of a question on economic development or growth, which we will discuss in a later chapter.

LEARN THE KEY POINTS

1. Definition of the national income
2. The three methods of measuring the national income
3. Definition of depreciation
4. Definition of net factor income with the rest of the world
5. Know the effect of a change in indirect taxes on the GDP
6. Know the effect of a change in subsidies on GDP
7. Know why GNP rather than GDP is a better indicator of the standard of living in Ireland
8. Explain double counting
9. Explain transfer payments
10. Learn the uses of national income statistics

11 Understand the limitations of the use of the national income statistics when comparing the standard of living in different years within the same country

12 Know the limitations of the use of the national income statistics when comparing the standard of living in different countries

13 Understand the difference between national income at current prices and national income at constant prices

14 Know how the Human Development Index differs from the national income

Exam Q&A: See p. 395

Copy questions 1–5 into your answer book and complete each of the sentences by filling in the blank spaces.

1 National income is the total of all ____________ earned by the ____________ of a country who supply the ____________ in any given period.

2 The three methods of measuring the national income are the ____________ method, the ____________ method and the ____________ method.

3 The difference between gross domestic product and gross national product is ____________.

4 A decrease in indirect taxes would cause GDP at market prices to ____________ because people would be ____________.

5 Depreciation is the ____________ of ____________.

6 Distinguish between 'benefit-in-kind' and 'transfer payment'.

7 Explain fully why double counting must be avoided when calculating the national income using the production method.

8 If our national income, in money terms, increased from €1,000m in year 1 to €1,100m in year 2, does this have to mean that we achieved 10 per cent economic growth in year 2? Give a brief explanation of your answer.

9 Distinguish clearly the difference between national income at current prices and national income at constant prices.

10 What factors would you have to take into consideration when comparing the national income statistics of two countries in a given year to obtain a valid comparison of the average standard of living in both countries? Explain your answer.

11 How does the Human Development Index differ from our national income statistics as a means of measuring our welfare?

12 From the figures in Table 18.9 calculate, in the stated order:
(a) GDP at current market prices
(b) GNP at current market prices
(c) GNI at current market prices
(d) NNI at current market prices
(e) NNP at factor cost

Table 18.9

	€m
Depreciation	15,000
Net factor income with the rest of the world	– 20,000
Exports	110,000
EU subsidies	1,500
Imports	90,000
Non-EU taxes	25,000
Total expenditure	**160,000**
Non-EU subsidies	1,500
EU taxes	500

13 In Ireland, at the present time, is our GDP or our GNP the better guide to the standard of living in the country? Explain your answer.

14 In Ireland, at the present time, is our GDP or our GNP the better guide to the level of economic activity in the country? Explain your answer.

15 What are trade cycles? Name and explain the various stages in a typical trade cycle.

Chapter 19
Factors Determining the Size of the National Income

This chapter sets out to examine the factors which determine the size of a country's national income at any given time.

Examine Tables 19.1 and 19.2. Table 19.1 shows **the total national income** of a randomly selected group of countries. Table 19.2 shows the **average income per person** for the same group of countries. China and Ireland are highlighted for comparative purposes.

Table 19.1 *The total national income of a randomly selected group of countries*

	Subject Descriptor	Units	Scale	2005
Albania	Gross domestic product, current prices	US dollars	Billions	8
Argentina	Gross domestic product, current prices	US dollars	Billions	181
Australia	Gross domestic product, current prices	US dollars	Billions	708
Austria	Gross domestic product, current prices	US dollars	Billions	305
Canada	Gross domestic product, current prices	US dollars	Billions	1,132
China	**Gross domestic product, current prices**	**US dollars**	**Billions**	**2,234**
Cyprus	Gross domestic product, current prices	US dollars	Billions	16
Denmark	Gross domestic product, current prices	US dollars	Billions	259
Ethiopia	Gross domestic product, current prices	US dollars	Billions	11
France	Gross domestic product, current prices	US dollars	Billions	2,126
Ireland	**Gross domestic product, current prices**	**US dollars**	**Billions**	**200**
Lebanon	Gross domestic product, current prices	US dollars	Billions	22
Luxembourg	Gross domestic product, current prices	US dollars	Billions	36
Malta	Gross domestic product, current prices	US dollars	Billions	5
Pakistan	Gross domestic product, current prices	US dollars	Billions	110
Saudi Arabia	Gross domestic product, current prices	US dollars	Billions	309
United Kingdom	Gross domestic product, current prices	US dollars	Billions	2,229
United States	Gross domestic product, current prices	US dollars	Billions	12,455

Source: *IMF*

Note: The shaded areas in the figures are estimates by the IMF.

Table 19.2 The average income per person

	Subject Descriptor	Units	Scale	2005
Albania	Gross domestic product per capita, current prices	US dollars	Units	2,672
Argentina	Gross domestic product per capita, current prices	US dollars	Units	4,799
Australia	Gross domestic product per capita, current prices	US dollars	Units	34,740
Austria	Gross domestic product per capita, current prices	US dollars	Units	37,117
Canada	Gross domestic product per capita, current prices	US dollars	Units	35,133
China	**Gross domestic product per capita, current prices**	**US dollars**	**Units**	**1,708**
Cyprus	Gross domestic product per capita, current prices	US dollars	Units	20,214
Denmark	Gross domestic product per capita, current prices	US dollars	Units	47,984
Ethiopia	Gross domestic product per capita, current prices	US dollars	Units	153
France	Gross domestic product per capita, current prices	US dollars	Units	33,917
Ireland	**Gross domestic product per capita, current prices**	**US dollars**	**Units**	**48,604**
Lebanon	Gross domestic product per capita, current prices	US dollars	Units	6,033
Luxembourg	Gross domestic product per capita, current prices	US dollars	Units	80,288
Malta	Gross domestic product per capita, current prices	US dollars	Units	13,802
Pakistan	Gross domestic product per capita, current prices	US dollars	Units	727
Saudi Arabia	Gross domestic product per capita, current prices	US dollars	Units	13,409
United Kingdom	Gross domestic product per capita, current prices	US dollars	Units	37,023
United States	Gross domestic product per capita, current prices	US dollars	Units	42,000

Source: *IMF*

Note: The shaded areas in the figures are estimates by the IMF.

Ireland's average income per person is roughly 28.5 times greater than China's, but our total income is roughly 11 times less than that of China.

So why is China's total national income greater than Ireland's total national income?

The Factors Determining National Income

1 The stock of factors of production and the quality of that stock

Countries that have a vast land area have a bigger potential national income than those with only small tracts of land. However, the productive ability of the land depends on the quality of that land. Some countries have vast tracts of land which are frozen over and have no real capacity to produce products. Other countries have only small tracts of land which may be very arable or contain large quantities of mineral wealth. Similarly, the amount of labour and the quality of that labour will have a big influence on the size of the national income.

2 The state of technology in the economy

The quality of capital being used in a country will have a big influence on the size of the national income. Capital increases the productive capacity of labour. Thus as the state of technology improves, the potential level of production also improves. Imagine a building site in two different countries with different qualities of capital. One person using a mechanical digger can lay out a far greater area of foundations than a person using a shovel. Remember that both the shovel and the mechanical digger are examples of capital.

3 The productive capacity of the country

Every country has a limit, however great or small, to its productive capacity. Regardless of the quality of labour and capital available to it, it is impossible for a country to exceed this potential.

4 The national economic climate

If the effective level of demand for goods and services is increasing within a country, then the entrepreneurial spirit of the citizens will ensure that more goods and services are produced to satisfy the demand.

5 The international economic climate

When the level of income increases in other countries the level of demand will also increase. Therefore, we should be able to export more of those goods for which we have an absolute or a comparative advantage (see Chapter 25, International Trade). This extra production will increase our national income.

6 The level of aggregate demand

The level of aggregate demand in the country determines the actual value of the national income (Y) in any year.

✳ Aggregate demand (Y)

Aggregate demand refers to the total demand for all goods and services.

You should recall, from Chapter 18, that Ireland's national income is calculated by adding exports to, and subtracting imports from, total expenditure to get the GDP.

Total expenditure was explained in Chapter 18 so as to include spending on all goods, both consumer goods and capital goods by both the private and the public sector. Thus we could say that total expenditure is spending on consumer goods by the general public (C) plus spending on capital goods by the private and public sectors (I) and any other spending by the government (G).

Thus we can conclude that:

Y = C + I + G + X – M

Where:

C = the level of private consumption
I = the level of investment
G = government spending
X = the value of exports
M = the value of imports

Let us examine the factors which affect each of these variables.

✳Consumption (C)

The level of consumption is governed by the needs and wants of consumers. While some level of consumption is autonomous, i.e. independent of income, most people can only spend the amount that they earn. Thus the level of consumption is dependent on the level of income. Therefore, as income increases, consumption increases and vice versa.

However, this does not imply that all income is spent. Some people will want to set aside some income for future emergencies, or they may be influenced to save some of their income by the current rates of interest, or they may decide that they want to invest some of their income. The amount of income spent, therefore depends on the average propensity to consume (APC).

Definition of average propensity to consume (APC)

Average propensity to consume (APC) is the tendency to spend a given percentage of total income on consumer goods.

As an individual's income increases the extra amount spent on consumer goods is determined by the marginal propensity to consume (MPC).

Definition of marginal propensity to consume (MPC)

Marginal propensity to consume (MPC) is the tendency to spend a given percentage of the last increase in income on consumer goods. An individual's MPC depends on many factors.

Someone on a very low level of income will probably have a MPC of 100 per cent in order to satisfy all of his/her needs. Whereas someone on a very high income may not spend much of the increased income as all of his/her needs and wants are already satisfied.

People's MPC can also be affected by their attitude towards the future. Many people are pessimistic about the future and want to set aside as much money as possible. These people will have a small MPC. Other people may have a more optimistic attitude and decide to live for today and hope that tomorrow looks after itself. These people tend to have a high MPC.

The rate of interest which financial institutions offer on deposits will affect some people's MPC. These people would regard interest as an opportunity cost of spending. Thus they would weigh up the rate of interest against the rate of inflation before deciding on their level of spending of any increased income.

Therefore, we can conclude that the level of consumption depends on the level of income, the average propensity to consume and the marginal propensity to consume.

Circular Flow of Income

Let us now return to the circular flow of income mentioned in Chapter 18.

Definition of the circular flow of income

We can formally define the **circular flow of income** as the amount of income in circulation at any given time.

This income passes from one person to another. If our incomes remained unchanged then the sum of income in the circular flow of income would also remain unchanged as shown in Fig 19.1.

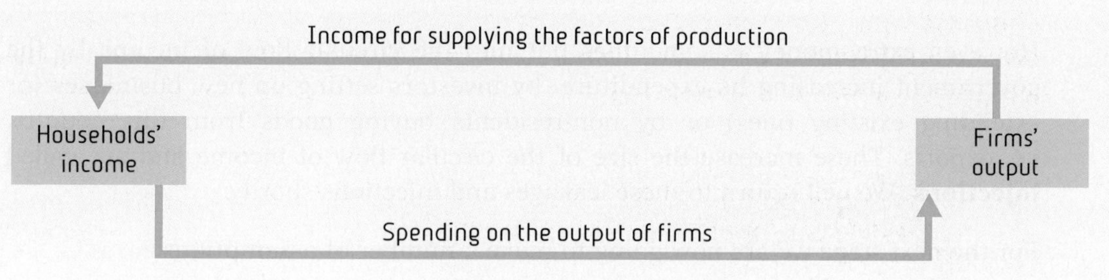

Fig 19.1 Circular flow of income without injections or leakages

In reality there is an ongoing injection of extra funds into the circular flow of income and a constant withdrawal or leakage of funds from it. The major injections are investments in new or existing firms, income earned from exports and extra money put into the economy by the government. The major withdrawals are money spent on imported goods, money saved and income taken from us in the form of taxation. These are illustrated in Fig 19.2.

People receive income for producing goods. They then spend this money on goods and services produced by other people, who in turn spend this same money on goods and services provided by another group of people.

People do not always pass on the full amount of money which they earn. Some of this is taken from them in taxation, some of it is saved and some of it leaves the country in the form of payment for imported goods. All of these reduce the size of the circular flow of income and are called **leakages** or **withdrawals**.

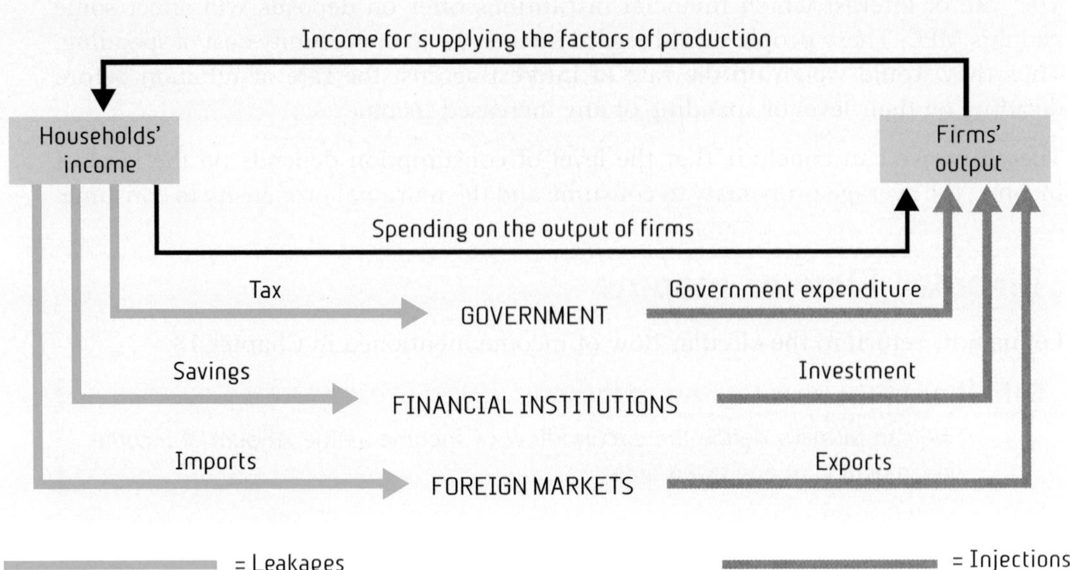

Fig 19.2 Circular flow of income with injections and leakages

However, extra money is sometimes put into the circular flow of income by the government increasing its expenditure, by investors setting up new businesses (or extending existing ones) or by non-residents buying goods from this country, i.e. exports. These increase the size of the circular flow of income and are called **injections**. We will return to these leakages and injections shortly.

For the next stage we are now going to make a number of assumptions.

Let us assume that extra income comes into the circular flow of income. For convenience sake, we will assume that it comes about by extra investment in the building of a new factory. This, logically, is an increase in income. To keep things simple, we will also assume that only one person, the builder, gets this extra income. We will call him Mr A and we will assume that the MPC is 80 per cent.

Table 19.3 *Incomes created by the increase in income*

Receiver of income	Spends on domestic consumer goods	Income created
A received €1,000	Which is income for him	€1,000
	A spends 80% of this which is income for B	€800
B received €800	B spends 80% of this which is income for C	€640
C received €640	C spends 80% of this which is income for D	€512

If this continued on it would eventually arrive at a total extra income created of €5,000. Thus this extra income put into the circular flow of income has created incomes greater than its own value.

✳ Injection

Any extra income put into the circular flow of income is called an **injection**. Therefore, we can say that an injection creates incomes greater than the value of the injection itself. This is known as the **multiplier effect**.

In a closed economy, i.e. one that does not trade with other economies, we use a formula to calculate the amount of income created by an injection. This formula is:

$$\frac{1}{1 - \text{MPC}}$$

where 1 represents 100 per cent of the injection.

Realistically some of this extra income will be spent on imported goods due to our marginal propensity to import (MPM).

✳ Marginal propensity to import

Definition of marginal propensity to import (MPM)

Marginal propensity to import (MPM) is the tendency to spend a given percentage of the last increase in income on imported goods.

Let us assume an MPM of 30 per cent and return to our table.

Table 19.4 *MPM decreases the multiplier effect*

Receiver	Spends on domestic consumer goods	Income created
A received €1,000	Which is income for him	€1,000
	A spends (80% – 30%) i.e. 50% of this which is income for B	€500
B received €500	B spends (80% – 30%) i.e. 50% of this which is income for C	€250
C received €250	C spends (80% – 30%) i.e. 50% of this which is income for D	€125

If this continued on it would eventually arrive at a total extra income created of €2,000.

Thus the money spent on imports, which caused money to leave the circular flow of income, reduced the multiplier effect.

Any expenditure which causes money to leave the circular flow of income is called a **leakage** or a **withdrawal**. Thus leakages reduce the multiplier effect. Injections and leakages take place at the same time in any economy.

Remember:

- An injection is anything which increases the size of the circular flow of income. The principal injections are exports and investments.
- A leakage is anything which decreases the size of the circular flow of income, e.g. imports. Taxes and savings are also leakages although these usually find their way back into the circular flow of income.

✳The multiplier formula

The economist, John Maynard Keynes (see p. 358) devised a formula for calculating the combined effects of the injections and leakages on incomes in an open economy, i.e. one which trades with other countries. This is known as the multiplier formula and it is:

$$\frac{1}{(1 - \text{MPC}) + \text{MPM} + \text{MPT}}$$

Where:

1 = 100% of any injection
MPC = the marginal propensity to consume
This is the percentage of the last increase in income spent on consumer goods.
MPM = the marginal propensity to import
This is the percentage of the last increase in income spent on imported goods.
MPT = the marginal propensity to tax

This is the percentage of the last increase in income taken in taxation.

✳Marginal propensity to save

Definition of marginal propensity to save (MPS)

The marginal propensity to save (MPS) is the tendency to save a given percentage of the last increase in income.

Remember that saving simply means not spending. Therefore, if you spend 80 per cent of your income then you must be saving 20 per cent of it. Likewise, if your MPC is 80 per cent then your MPS must be 20 per cent. So we can conclude that 1 – MPC = MPS.

Thus an alternative way of expressing the formula for the multiplier is:

$$\frac{1}{\text{MPS} + \text{MPM} + \text{MPT}}$$

From all of the above it is evident that it is very difficult to manipulate the level of consumption in any given period.

✳Investment (I)

The level of investment is mostly determined by entrepreneurs' expectations about future profits. While the government also invests money in the economy and can have some influence on the amount invested by others, the entrepreneurs in the private sector take the ultimate decision on the amount of investment in the economy. The factors which they take into account include: the rate of interest, the cost of capital goods, the state of technology, government policy and the domestic and international economic climate. (We will discuss, in detail, the factors which influence the entrepreneur's expectations in Chapter 29, Capital and Interest Rates.)

Thus it is evident that it is very difficult to manipulate the level of investment in any given period.

✳ Increased government current expenditure (G)

Government spending is independent of income.

The government can increase its expenditure at any time, even without increasing our taxes, by borrowing for the extra expenditure. It is simply a political decision. Hopefully, the government's decisions to borrow are taken for sound economic reasons.

Therefore, the level of government current expenditure can be changed very easily at any given time.

✳ Exports

The level of exports depends on:

- The level of incomes abroad.
- The ability of the country to manufacture, at internationally competitive prices, products for which there is an international demand.
- The marketing skills in the country.

Here, again, it is obvious that it is very difficult to manipulate the level of exports in any given period.

✳ Imports

The level of imports depends on the level of income in the country and on the marginal propensity to import. We can conclude that it is very difficult to manipulate the level of imports in any given period.

Summary

The only one of these variables which can be easily controlled at any given time is G.

$$Y = C + I + G + X - M$$

From this Keynes stated that our national income could be controlled by the government's fiscal policy, i.e. its policy on how it raises its income and its policy on expenditure.

An example of an exam question based on the components of the national income

The following table shows the level of national income, consumption, investment, exports and imports at the end of period 1 and period 2. For the purpose of this question you may ignore the government sector.

Table 19.5

	Y	C	I	X	M
Year 1	€80,000	€60,000	€10,000	€12,000	€2,000
Year 2	€90,000	€68,000	€12,000	€13,000	?

Calculate: (Explain and show all workings)

1. Imports in year 2
2. The MPC
3. The MPM
4. The MPS
5. The multiplier
6. The amount spent on domestically produced goods in each year.
7. The MPC(d)

The approach to the answer to this type of question is as follows:

Start with the statement that Y = C + I + X – M.

1. In year 2, €90,000 = €68,000 + €12,000 + €13,000 – M
   Therefore €90,000 = €93,000 – M
   Therefore imports = €3,000

2. MPC is the percentage of the last increase in income spent on consumer goods. In year 2 income increased from €80,000 to €90,000, i.e. an increase of €10,000. In this year consumption increased from €60,000 to €68,000, i.e. an increase of €8,000. Thus 80 per cent or 0.8 of the last increase in income was spent on consumer goods, i.e. MPC = 0.8.

3. MPM is the percentage of the last increase in income spent on imported goods. Imports in year 2 increased by €1,000 which is 10 per cent or 0.1 of the increase in income, i.e. MPM = 0.1.

4. The MPS is the percentage of the last increase in income saved. Consumption increased by 80 per cent of the increase in income, therefore the other 20 per cent must have been saved. Therefore the MPS is 20 per cent or 0.2.

Alternative answer

MPS = 1 – MPC, i.e. 1 – 0.8 = 0.2

5 In this context, because we are ignoring the government sector, the formula for the multiplier will exclude MPT. Thus the multiplier is:

$$\frac{1}{(1 - \text{MPC}) + \text{MPM}} = \frac{1}{(1 - 0.8) + 0.1} = \frac{1}{0.3} = \mathbf{3.33}$$

6 The total income spent on domestically produced goods is the income spent on total consumption less the income spent on imported goods.

Therefore in year 1 this equals total consumption of €60,000 less imports of €2,000 = €58,000.

Likewise in year 2 it is €68,000 less €3,000 = €65,000.

7 MPC(d) is the percentage of the last increase in income spent on domestically produced goods. As can be seen from answer 6 above, spending on domestically produced goods increased by €7,000 in year 2. This is 0.7 of the increase in income. Therefore the MPC(d) = 0.7.

Keynesian Graphical Presentation of National Income

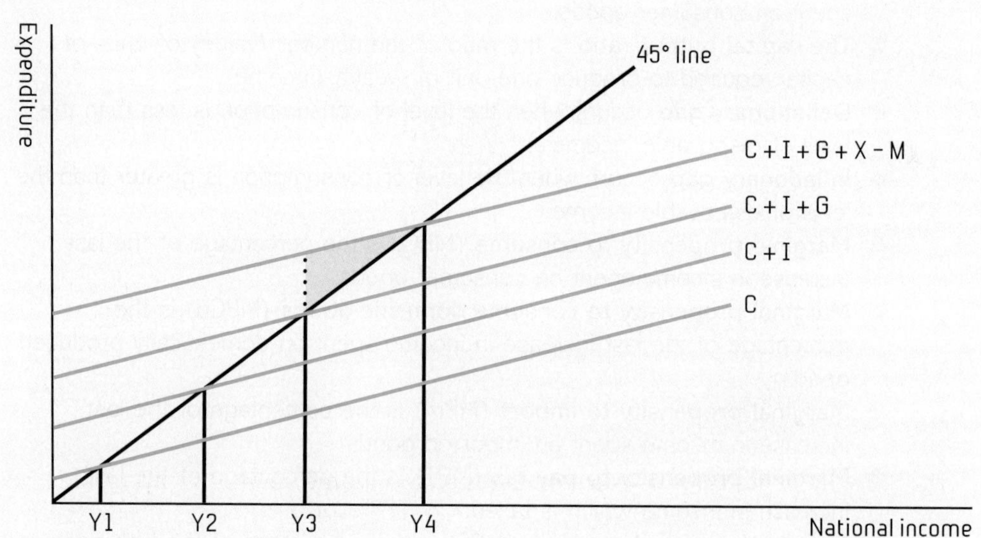

Fig 19.3 Keynesian graph showing national income

The 45° line is used to show all income being equal to all expenditure. This is sometimes called the **equilibrium** or **break-even level** of national income. This would imply that consumption is dependent on income.

However, this is not always true. **Autonomous consumption** is the level of consumption which is not dependent on income. This sometimes has to be financed out of past savings or from borrowings. When this happens **dissavings** are said to take place. Countries can of course also receive foreign aid to boost consumption

Line C (called the consumption function line) shows the different amounts spent at the different levels of income. Where line C intersects the 45° line this gives the equilibrium level of national income.

As **injections** are added into the circular flow of income, the national income increases and so too does the amount of expenditure. For example, the line C + I shows the consumption function after an additional injection of investment.

At any point where the relevant consumption function line is above the 45° line then consumption is greater than income and this is called an **inflationary gap**. This is represented by the shaded area in Fig 19.3.

At any point where the relevant consumption function line is below the 45° line then consumption is less than income and this is called a **deflationary gap**.

Definitions associated with national income

- **Autonomous consumption** is the level of consumption which is not dependent on the level of income.
- **Average propensity to consume** (APC) is the percentage of total income spent on consumer goods.
- **The capital output ratio** is the ratio of the number (value) of units of capital required to produce one unit of wealth (income).
- **Deflationary gap** occurs when the level of consumption is less than the level of disposable income.
- **Inflationary gap** occurs when the level of consumption is greater than the level of disposable income.
- **Marginal propensity to consume** (MPC) is the percentage of the last increase in income spent on consumer goods.
- **Marginal propensity to consume domestic goods** (MPCd) is the percentage of the last increase in income spent on domestically produced goods.
- **Marginal propensity to import** (MPM) is the percentage of the last increase in income spent on imported goods.
- **Marginal propensity to pay tax** (MPT) is the percentage of the last increase in income which is taxed.
- **Marginal propensity to save** (MPS) is the percentage of the last increase in income which is saved.
- **The multiplier** is that number by which an injection into the circular flow of income is multiplied to calculate the income created by the injection.
- **The productive capacity** is the capital stock divided by the capital output ratio.

The Accelerator Principle

The accelerator principle states that small changes in consumer spending can cause bigger percentage changes in investment.

The accelerator principle assumes that the number or value of units of equipment or capital needed to produce any given level or value of production remains unchanged, i.e. ratio of capital to output tends to remain constant.

Example

Let us make the assumption that it takes €100,000 worth of capital equipment to produce 50,000 units of a good in a year, i.e. a ratio of capital to output of 2:1. Let us also assume that there is 20 per cent wear and tear (depreciation) of capital equipment in each year. If there is no change in the level of production then there will be a need to invest €20,000 per annum to replace the depreciated equipment.

Finally, let us assume that in a given year, due to an increase in demand, production is to be increased by 20 per cent, i.e. to 60,000 units.

To keep the ratio of capital equipment at a ratio of 2:1 €20,000 worth of extra capital equipment will be required in that year plus the €20,000 required for the annual depreciation giving a total investment that year of €40,000. This is a 100 per cent increase on the previous year's investment.

Thus a 20 per cent increase in demand resulted in a 100 per cent increase in investment.

LEARN THE KEY POINTS

1. Know and explain, the five basic factors, other than aggregate demand, which influence the size of the national income
2. Know the components of aggregate demand
3. Explain the circular flow of income
4. Define injections and leakages and give examples of them
5. Know the main factors which influence the level of consumption
6. Clearly define each of the following: MPC, MPM, MPT, MPS
7. Define and give the formula for the multiplier
8. Outline the factors which effect the level of investment
9. Define and give an example of the accelerator principle
10. Outline the main factor which affects government spending

11 Outline the main factors which influence the level of exports and imports
12 On the Keynesian graphical model explain the importance of the 45° line
13 Know and explain autonomous consumption
14 Use the flow chart to explain the circular flow of income and the effect of leakages and injections

Exam Q&A: See p. 396

Copy questions 1–7 into your answer book and complete each of the sentences by filling in the blank spaces.

1 The circular flow of income is the total amount of ____________ in ____________ at any given time.

2 Average propensity to consume is the fraction of ____________ which is ____________ spent on ________________.

3 Marginal propensity to consume is the fraction of ____________ in income which is spent on ________________.

4 The fraction of the last increase in income spent on imported goods is called

____.

5 The marginal propensity to save is equal to 1 – ____________.

6 Aggregate demand is equal to ____________ + ____________ + ____________ + ____________ – ____________.

7 Autonomous consumption refers to the level of consumption which is ____________ of ____________.

8 Explain briefly why the amount of income in the circular flow of income is not the same as the amount of money in circulation.

9 Explain briefly the main factors which determine the potential size or value of a country's national income.

10 Explain briefly the factors which determine the level of exports.

11 What is the multiplier? Give the full formula for measuring it in an open economy.

12 'As the size (magnitude) of the MPC increases, the size of the multiplier also increases.'
Explain this statement using an example to illustrate your answer.

13 Why may government expenditure be independent of its income? Explain your answer.

14 Explain why the size of the multiplier is smaller in an open economy than in a closed economy.

15 The following figures apply to a country's national income.

Table 19.6

	GNP	C	I	X	M
Period 1	€7,800	€6,500	€1,550	€1,200	€1,450
Period 2	€8,400	€6,950	€1,650	?	€1,600

Ignoring the government sector, you are asked to calculate:

(a) Exports in period 2
(b) The MPC
(c) The MPM
(d) The value of domestically produced goods consumed in period 2
(e) The MPC(d)
(f) The value of savings in period 1
(g) The magnitude of the multiplier

16 State the accelerator principle and give an example to illustrate it.

Chapter 20
The Consumer Price Index and Inflation

Other than the weather, the rising cost of living (inflation) is probably one of the most frequent topics of conversation among adults. It is one of the most reported topics on national media. The increase in the cost of living is always somebody else's fault and everybody blames the government!

The rate of inflation is officially measured using the **consumer price index** (CPI).

The Consumer Price Index

Definition of the consumer price index (CPI)

The consumer price index (CPI) is an index drawn up by the Central Statistics Office (CSO) to measure the changes in the general level of prices over a period of time.

A price index, usually shown in table form, measures changes in prices over a period of time.

A simple price index measures the change in the price of one product only.

A composite price index measures the change in the price of a number of goods together.

✳How the CPI is compiled

As already noted the CPI measures the overall change in the prices of the goods and services that people typically buy over time. It does this by collecting the prices of a large number of goods and services every month and comparing these to the prices from the previous month.

As everyone has differing tastes and spending habits, the CPI measures prices for a huge assortment of items. Not only does the CPI measure price changes for goods but also for services, e.g. hairdressing, taxi fares and insurance. This collection is normally referred to as **the basket of goods and services**.

The basket does not apply to any particular person or family but represents the majority of households in Ireland. The goods and services that are included in the basket are determined from the five-yearly **Household Budget Survey**. The relative importance or weights of these goods and services are also decided from information collected in the Household Budget Survey. **Weighting** is determined by the fraction of income spent on the goods.

The HICP and how it differs from the CPI

The **Harmonised Index of Consumer Prices** (HICP) is the measure of price changes calculated by each member state of the European Union (EU). The index is based on a harmonisation and standardisation of practices within the EU. Its purpose is to allow for the comparison of different consumer price trends in the different member states.

Eurostat calculates the weighted indices for the EU13 (Eurozone) and the EU14 (other member states).

Certain items are excluded from the coverage of the HICP, which in essence makes the HICP a subset of the main CPI. The HICP expenditure covers 91 per cent of the total CPI expenditure and excludes mortgage interest, building materials, union subscriptions, motor taxation and the non-service elements of motor and house insurance. In addition, the weight of health insurance is lower in the HICP, where net rather than gross household expenditure on health insurance is used.

Source: *CSO*

Procedure for Drawing Up an Annual CPI

1. Every five years a household budget survey is conducted to establish:
   - The national average household shopping basket.
   - The fraction of income which the average household spends on each item in the basket.
   - The price of each item in the basket.

   These prices are, subsequently, checked every quarter.

2. A base year is chosen.

3. A simple index is made for each product using the price in the base year as 100.

4. Multiply the index for each product by its weighting and add the results to establish the CPI for that year.

Example

The following prices are established for three products.

Table 20.1 *Prices of products A, B and C*

Year	Product A	Product B	Product C
1	€1.00	€2.00	€0.20
2	€1.20	€2.50	€0.30
3	€1.25	€2.70	€0.35
4	€1.40	€2.80	€0.40

It is also established that 50 per cent of income is spent on A and 25 per cent each on B and C.

A simple index is next made for each product each year. The simple index is multiplied by the weighting of the product.

The weighted figures for each product each year are then added across to give the CPI for that year.

Table 20.2 *Calculation of CPI*

Year	Product A	Product B	Product C	CPI
1	100	100	100	
	× 0.5	× 0.25	× 0.25	
	50	25	25	100
2	120	125	150	
	× 0.5	× 0.25	× 0.25	
	60	31.25	37.5	128.75
3	125	135	175	
	× 0.5	× 0.25	× 0.25	
	62.5	33.75	43.75	140
4	140	140	200	
	× 0.5	× 0.25	× 0.25	
	70	35	50	155

This CPI measures the change in prices each year as a percentage of the prices which prevailed in the base year, i.e. prices in year 4 have increased by 55 per cent since year 1. It does not mean that the prices increased in year 4 by 15 per cent since year 3.

To calculate the annual rate of inflation between any of the above years use the formula:

$$\frac{\text{Current year's index minus previous year's index}}{\text{Previous year's index}} \times \frac{100}{1}$$

Using the figures for years 3 and 4 the rate of inflation in year 4 is:

$$\frac{155 - 140}{140} \times \frac{100}{1} = 10.71\%$$

✳The uses of the CPI

1 The CPI is used to measure the official rate of inflation. The official rate of inflation quoted by government sources is the rate of inflation as measured by the CSO when compiling the CPI.

2 The CPI is used as the basis for claims for wages and social welfare benefits increases. When trade unions look for wage increases they often base their claim

on the fact that the CPI has risen by a given percentage, so workers would need an increase in their wages of that percentage in order to maintain their real wages.

3 It is used as one of the economic indicators. An economic indicator is any statistic which reflects the performance of the economy. In this case, the CPI indicates Ireland's ability to control prices in the economy.

4 The CPI is used to assess Ireland's price competitiveness on the international market (see also note on HICP above). The international competitiveness of Ireland's economy can be gauged by comparing its rate of inflation, as shown by the CPI, with the rate of inflation of other countries. If Ireland's rate of inflation is higher than that of our trading partners, then we will find it increasingly difficult to sell our exports, and our domestic industries may find it difficult to compete with imported goods.

5 The CPI is used as a basis for indexation of interest rates. (This is now done in conjunction with the ECB.) The rate of interest offered by financial institutions cannot be allowed to drag too far behind the rate of inflation, as this could result in a negative interest rate and thus discourage savings.

Limitations on the use of the CPI as an economic indicator

1 A limited range of products is included in the CPI. Most families spend their income on a very large range of goods. Only twelve categories of goods are included in the CPI comprising roughly 8,000 different goods. There are tens of thousands of different goods on the market at any given time.

2 The CPI does not include any new products which have come on the market since the household survey. The household survey is carried out once every five years. In the interim between these surveys many new products come onto the market and are widely consumed. These new products are not included in the CPI until the next household survey is carried out.

3 It overstates the cost of living. As products included in the CPI increase in price consumers switch to cheaper substitute goods, thus distorting the weighting given to these products.

4 The survey establishes the basket of goods of the average household only. There is no such thing as the average household as 'the average' is merely a mathematical concept. If families do not consume many of the items included in the household basket then the CPI is irrelevant to that family. For example, if a family does not buy cigarettes, alcohol, petrol and meat then the CPI does not accurately reflect its cost of living.

5 The CPI does not take account of changes in the quality of goods. Real price increases are often hidden by changes in the quality of the goods being sold. If the average size of a bar of chocolate is reduced by 10 per cent while its price remains unchanged then this really constitutes a hidden price increase.

6 It does not make any allowance for differences in rural and urban lifestyles. Many rural dwellers are not affected by the change in price of such things as potatoes and eggs as they produce these goods themselves for their own consumption. Urban dwellers may spend a relatively large percentage of their income on these

goods, thus increasing their cost of living. On the other hand, transport costs tend to be greater in rural areas than in urban areas.

7 The CPI makes no allowance for price increases due to increased indirect taxes. Price increases are often caused by increases in indirect taxes. If the extra taxes are used to provide extra services free of charge to the consumers then their real cost of living has not increased.

Table 20.3 *Consumer Price Index, May 2007*

	Weights	Base year Dec 2006	Percentage change One month	Percentage change Three months	Percentage change Twelve months
Food and non-alcoholic beverages	11.742	102.1	+ 0.6	+ 2	+ 1.4
Alcoholic beverages and tobacco	6.048	101.4	—	+ 0.4	+ 5.4
Clothing and footwear	5.416	96.9	+ 0.6	+ 1.8	– 3.1
Housing, water, electricity, gas and other fuels	16.509	108.5	+ 0.7	+ 4.4	+ 22.6
Furnishings, household equipment and routine house maintenance	4.442	98.6	+ 0.1	– 0.5	– 2.0
Health	3.154	101.8	+ 0.4	+ 0.5	+ 2.8
Transport	13.293	103.8	+ 0.1	+ 2.9	+ 1.6
Communications	3.419	99.9	—	+ 0.1	– 0.1
Recreation and culture	10.104	100.6	—	– 0.1	+ 1.5
Education	2.043	100.6	—	+ 0.1	+ 4.8
Restaurants and hotels	15.425	103.2	+ 0.6	+ 2.7	+ 4.9
Miscellaneous goods and services	8.426	99.4	+ 0.1	– 0.5	+ 0.4
All items	**100**	**102.6**	**+ 0.4**	**+ 1.9**	**+ 5**

Source: *CSO*

Note: Some weights are rounded up to the nearest third decimal place.

Note: The figures in the column 'Base Year 2006' show the index for May 2007 taking mid-December 2006 as the base year. December 2006 was the start of a new five-year cycle.

It is of interest to note that the EU Harmonised Index of Consumer Prices (HICP) increased by 0.3 per cent in the month of May 2007 and that the annual increase was only + 2.7 per cent.

A Constant Tax Price Index

A Constant Tax Price Index (CTPI) is one that omits price increases due to increases in indirect taxes when compiling the CPI.

Argument for CTPI

Governments claim that extra services are given for these taxes. Therefore, people are enjoying a higher standard of living by paying the extra taxes.

Argument against CTPI

Not all people benefit from these services. If extra primary school facilities are provided from the extra taxes then there is no gain to old age pensioners from the extra taxes.

Inflation

Definition of inflation

Inflation refers to the increase in the general level of prices.

✳Forms of inflation

Demand-pull inflation

Demand-pull inflation occurs when total (or aggregate) demand in the economy exceeds total supply resulting in an increase in the general level of prices.

Cost-push inflation

Cost-push inflation occurs when increases in the costs of production are passed on to the consumer in the form of increased prices. The most common causes are:

- Increased wages.
- Increased indirect taxes.
- Increased cost of imports.

✳Control of demand-pull inflation

Reduce demand in the economy by:

1. **Increasing direct taxes:** This leaves people with a smaller take-home pay, therefore they have less purchasing power.
2. **Introducing credit controls:** If consumers cannot obtain loans from the credit institutions this will result in a decrease in the demand for expensive consumer durable goods.

3 **Increasing interest rates:** Interest is the price of credit. When the price of any commodity increases the demand for it goes down. Thus increased interest rates will result in less money being borrowed for consumption purposes.

4 **Reducing government expenditure:** The biggest spender in the economy is the government. Thus any decrease in its expenditure will have a significant effect on the overall demand within the economy.

An alternative approach to the control of this form of inflation would be to increase supply, thus bringing supply equal to demand. In the immediate short term it may be difficult to do this by using domestic resources. However, if there is a demand for goods and it is profitable to supply these goods this demand will be met by importers. Thus, in the short term, increasing imports may increase supply. However, this could have a detrimental effect on the balance of payments, as the increased supply will result in an outflow of funds from the country.

Control of cost-push inflation

Cost-push inflation is a much more difficult form of inflation to control. However, if we look at the causes of cost-push inflation we can see some of the more theoretical means of controlling it.

Increased indirect taxes

We stated that one of the causes of inflation was the imposition of indirect taxes on goods and services by the government. Thus if the government were to decrease these taxes prices would automatically decrease. However, from a realistic and practical point of view this is most unlikely to happen, as the government normally needs the revenue from these taxes and would be unwilling to replace indirect taxes with direct taxes.

Increased wages

The increasing of wages is by far the most common form of cost-push inflation. When wages increase suppliers tend to pass on this increase in cost to the consumer in order to maintain their profit margins. This in turn leads to increased prices, thus negating the benefit of the wage increase. This can lead to an ongoing wages/prices spiral. Thus if the increase in wages can be controlled this vicious circle will be broken. One way of doing this is to link wage increases to increases in productivity. In the following example we are making the simplistic assumptions that wages are the only cost of production and that the cost of production is the selling price.

Example

- Initial wage bill = €10,000 and initial production is 10,000 units. Therefore the selling price is €1.
- Wage bill increases to €20,000 and production remains at 10,000. Therefore the selling price is €2. This is inflationary.

However, if production increased to 20,000 units when the wages increased to €20,000 then the selling price would remain at €1. This is not inflationary. In fact in this situation everybody gains. More goods are produced, thus the wealth of the nation has been increased. The employees also have an increase in their real wages as their purchasing power has now increased. Prices have not gone up and they have more money!

An alternative measure may be to implement a prices and incomes policy. This type of policy sets a maximum price for goods and the providers of goods and services are not allowed to exceed these prices. If prices do not increase the government and the employers can claim that there is no need for any wage increases. The biggest problem with this solution is that the maximum prices tend to become the minimum prices. This policy has never been successful in Ireland.

National wage agreements

National wage agreements are agreements between the Social Partners. The main parties to these agreements – as far as wages are concerned – are the Irish Congress of Trade Unions, the Irish Business and Employers Confederation, various farming organisations and the government. These agreements have been operating in Ireland since the 1970s and have carefully controlled the cost of labour, producing a highly skilled yet competitively priced labour force. The agreements are for a certain number of years and the increase in the wage rate is spread over the agreed period of time. They have led to predictable wage costing which can be incorporated into any business plan.

In extreme situations the government could order a wage freeze, i.e. if it did not want to be returned to power at the next election!

Increase in the cost of imports

The prices that we pay for our imported goods are determined by the international demand for and supply of these goods. Therefore, we have no control over these prices. We either pay the international price for these goods or do without them.

✻Problems caused by inflation

1. Because of the higher cost of living caused by inflation, people have reduced purchasing power, which causes a reduction in their standard of living.
2. Inflation may cause unemployment if employers, who are faced with demands for increased wages and possible loss of markets, are forced to reduce costs by reducing their labour force.
3. Inflation causes demands for wage increases to compensate for the inflation that, ironically, can further fuel cost-push inflation.
4. If there is a negative interest rate, i.e. if the rate of inflation is greater than the rate of interest, savings will decrease leading to less investment funds being available.
5. If interest rates are less than the rate of inflation borrowing may increase, leading to further demand-pull inflation.

6 Adverse effects on the balance of trade:
- Exports become more expensive making them less competitive on the international market.
- Imports become relatively cheaper, thus creating a greater demand for them.

7 People on fixed incomes suffer most. These people's real income decreases as inflation increases, e.g. people on fixed pensions. People in employment may be able to obtain wage increases to compensate for the inflation. This causes disparity between different sectors of the population.

8 Speculation in fixed assets, increases, e.g. property, as these tend to increase in value during a period of inflation.

9 As a result of point 8, money moves away from investment in wealth-creating projects, thus reducing the potential productive capacity of the country.

10 Rising inflation creates uncertainty in the economy that is unfavourable to investment decisions.

11 There may be pressure on the European Central Bank to raise interest rates. Rising inflation may force the Central Bank to take corrective action and increase interest rates. This would have adverse effects on investors and on people buying houses on mortgages.

LEARN THE KEY POINTS

1 Explain the difference between each of the following:
- A price index
- A simple price index
- A composite index
- A consumer price index (CPI)

2 Know the procedure followed for drawing up a consumer price index

3 Draw up a CPI using your own figures

4 Interpret a CPI

5 Know the uses and users of the CPI

6 Know the limitations of the CPI as an economic indicator

7 Know the limitations of the CPI as a means of comparing the standard of living in a country between different years

8 Define inflation

9 Know the difference between cost-push and demand-pull inflation

10 Know the means by which demand-pull inflation can be controlled

11 Know the means by which we can attempt to control cost-push inflation

12 Explain the problems caused by inflation

13 Explain the HICP and how it differs from the CPI

Questions

Exam Q&A: See p. 399

Copy questions 1–6 into your answer book and complete each of the sentences by filling in the blank spaces.

1 The Consumer Price Index (CPI) is used to measure ____________ in the ____________ of prices over a period of time.

2 The goods and services included in the CPI are determined from the five-yearly ____________ Survey.

3 The weighting given to each category of goods in the CPI is determined by the ____________ of ____________ spent on the goods.

4 Cost-push inflation occurs when ____________ in the costs of ____________ are passed on to the consumer in the form of ____________ prices.

5 Demand-pull inflation occurs when total ____________ in the economy exceeds total ____________ resulting in an increase in ____________ of prices.

6 The CPI at constant taxes omits ____________ in prices caused by ____________.

7 Outline the steps involved in compiling the CPI.

8 What purposes do the CPI statistics serve? Explain your answer.

9 Outline fully the limitations on the reliance of the CPI statistics when attempting to compare the standard of living in Ireland today with the standard of living in Ireland ten years ago.

10 What is the Harmonised Index of Consumer Prices and how does it differ from the CPI?

11 From the following information compile the CPI for years 1 to 4, taking year 1 as the base year. The following prices were established for three products, namely A, B and C.

Table 20.4

Year	Product A	Product B	Product C
1	€0.50	€3.00	€4.00
2	€0.65	€3.60	€4.80
3	€0.80	€3.90	€4.80
4	€1.00	€4.20	€4.60

60 per cent of income was spent on Product C, 30 per cent was spent on Product B and 10 per cent on Product A.

12 Outline the problems encountered in any attempt to control cost-push inflation.

13 Discuss the problems caused by a high rate of inflation for each of the following sectors of the economy:

(a) Employees
(b) Exporters
(c) Consumers
(d) Savers

Chapter 21
Taxation and Government Finances

There is an old proverb which states that the only two certainties in this life are death and taxes. We have no control over death but we vote for taxes! Therefore, we must be able to justify taxation.

Functions of Taxation

1. **To raise money for government expenditure:** Without taxation the government could not function on a day-to-day basis. Government current expenditure is approximately €50 billion a year.
2. **To redistribute wealth:** This means taxing people who are earning good incomes to provide an income for those who cannot earn it themselves.
3. **To achieve desirable social objectives:** For example, increasing taxes on tobacco to discourage smoking and promote healthier living.
4. **To provide merit goods:** These are goods which society deems should be available to everybody at some minimum quantity, regardless of their income. These include food, clothing, shelter, education and medical services.
5. **To provide public goods:** These are goods provided by the government which benefit everybody, e.g. our security system and defence.
6. **Taxation can act as an automatic stabiliser:** This occurs when changes in government expenditure and tax revenue happen without any change in government policy as national income changes. As national income increases tax revenue automatically increases. This has the effect of dampening inflation in the economy and also providing the government with the extra funds needed to finance its current expenditure.

Example

During a period of inflation, prices will increase so pushing up the absolute cost of government expenditure. However, as prices rise government income from indirect taxes will automatically increase, thus giving it the extra income it needs to finance its expenditure and at the same time the increase in prices will slow down demand-pull inflation.

7 **To achieve economic objectives:**

- Reduce inflation, e.g. by cutting indirect taxes the government can reduce cost-push inflation, or by increasing direct taxes it can reduce demand-pull inflation.
- Encourage investment in certain industries, e.g. oil exploration companies in Ireland are given generous tax incentives.
- Stabilise the balance of trade, e.g. by increasing customs duties the government can discourage the importation of goods.
- Protect particular domestic industries, e.g. decreasing taxes on profits for some firms can protect these industries from foreign competition.

Adam Smith's Canons of Taxation

The renowned eighteenth-century writer and economist Adam Smith laid down guidelines for the implementation of any tax system. These are referred to as the *Canons of Taxation*.

- There should be **equity** of taxation, i.e. the tax should take into account the ability of people to pay the tax. Thus people on large incomes should pay more in taxation than those on small incomes. He wrote, 'It is not very unreasonable that the rich should contribute to the public expense, not only in proportion to their revenue, but something more than in that proportion.'
- There should be **certainty** of taxation, i.e. people should know their tax liability at the start of the year so that they can set aside money to pay their taxes as they become due.
- There should be **convenience** of taxation, i.e. the method of payment of the tax should suit the taxpayer not the government.
- There should be **economy** of taxation, i.e. the revenue from the tax should far exceed the cost of collecting it.

In modern economies we also agree that:

1. Taxes should not act as a disincentive to work. If the marginal rate of tax is very high people may be reluctant to take on extra work. For example, if people have to pay 55 per cent of their income on taxation they may be reluctant to work overtime as they will only pocket 45 per cent of the income earned from the overtime. This would have a detrimental effect on the supply of labour.

2. Taxes should not act as a disincentive to investment. If potential investors feel that too much of the profit which they could earn is to be deducted as tax, they may consider that the risk which they undertake in investing their money is not properly rewarded. This would result in a loss of extra productive capacity and a loss of potential employment.

3 Taxes should not act as a disincentive to save. If the rate of taxation on the interest earned on savings results in a negative rate of interest then dissaving would take place. This may result in a lack of funds available for investment and insecurity for people in later life.

Progressive, Regressive and Proportional Taxes

✳Progressive tax

A progressive tax takes a higher percentage of income from a person as that person's taxable income increases. This form of taxation takes into account a person's ability to pay taxes, e.g. PAYE.

✳Regressive tax

A regressive tax takes a higher percentage of income from a low-income earner than from a high-income earner, e.g. VAT.

Fig 21.1 VAT is a regressive tax

Example of a regressive tax

Mary earns €500 per week and John earns €200 per week.

Both purchase a television on which there is €80 VAT.

This €80 represents 40 per cent of John's income while it represents only 16 per cent of Mary's income.

✳Proportional tax

A proportional tax is one which takes a constant rate of tax from income as income rises.

The Imposition of Taxation

The imposition or impact of taxation refers to the people or companies on whom the tax is actually levied, i.e. imposed. They have to pay the tax directly to the government, e.g. the excise duty on petrol is levied on the petrol companies.

The Effective Incidence of a Tax

The effective incidence of a tax refers to the people who bear the burden of the tax, e.g. the tax on petrol is levied on the petrol companies. They pass this on to the motorists in the form of increased prices. The effective incidence of the tax is on the motorists.

Tax Avoidance and Tax Evasion

Tax avoidance is the practice of using the Tax Code (the tax laws) to the best possible advantage in order to reduce your tax liability to the minimum. This is legal.

Tax evasion is the non-payment of taxes due by either making no tax returns or making false tax returns. This is illegal.

Direct and Indirect Taxes

Direct taxes are taxes on all forms of income, e.g. PAYE, capital gains tax, capital acquisition tax and DIRT.

Indirect taxes are taxes on transactions, e.g. VAT, customs duties, excise duties and stamp duties.

Advantages of direct taxes

- They are a form of progressive tax, therefore there is equity of taxation.
- They are a convenient form of taxation for most PAYE workers.
- They are an economical form of taxation, as employers collect the tax and pass it on to the revenue commissioners. No fee is paid to the employer.
- There is certainty of liability. Tax rates and tax bands are announced in the budget before the commencement of the tax year.
- They make government budgeting of income easy, as national levels of income are easy to forecast, thus simplifying the forecasting of revenue from income taxes.

Disadvantages of direct taxes

- High rates of tax may discourage work and investment.
- Those working in the black economy can avoid direct taxes.
- If there is a small tax base then the burden of tax may be great on those paying the taxes. (The tax base refers to the number of people paying income tax.)

Advantages of indirect taxes

- People can reduce the amount of tax they pay by altering their consumption to those goods which carry a low rate of VAT and other indirect taxes.
- Evasion of tax is almost impossible as everybody spends money in shops, so even people working in the black economy will have to pay some taxes.
- They are a cheap form of tax to administer as producers and retailers collect them free of charge and pass them on to the revenue commissioners. Thus there is economy of taxation.
- The taxpayer often does not realise that tax is being paid as it is incorporated into the price of the good. Thus there is convenience of taxation.
- They are unlikely to act as a disincentive to work. They may even act as an incentive to work, because as indirect taxes increase people need more money to purchase the same amount of goods, and therefore they may undertake more work.

Disadvantages of indirect taxes

- They are a regressive form of taxation. These taxes do not take into account a person's ability to pay the tax.
- They lack certainty, i.e. from the government's point of view it is difficult to accurately forecast its revenue from these taxes.
- Indirect taxes add to inflation. This may make Irish goods less competitive on both the foreign and the domestic markets.
- These taxes increase the cost of living. They often lead to demands for wage increases, which add further to cost-push inflation. Thus these taxes are said to be inflationary.
- Indirect taxes add to the administration costs of the business community and take up much labour time for which there is no return.

Definitions of some taxes

- An ***ad valorem* tax** is an indirect tax which takes a given percentage of the price of the good, e.g. VAT.
- **Capital acquisition tax** is a tax on gifts received or on inheritances above a certain value.
- **Capital gains tax** is a tax on the profits from the sale of assets.
- A **lump-sum tax** is a fixed sum of tax levied on a firm irrespective of its level of income or profit.
- A **specific tax** is levied at a given absolute amount on each unit of a good sold, e.g. 10c on a litre of petrol.
- **Stealth taxes** are charges made for the use of services provided by the government or by a local authority, e.g. bin charges and outpatients' hospital charges.

Difference between Exchequer Balance and General Government Balance

The **Exchequer balance** is the difference between total current and capital expenditure and total income of the central government.

The **general government balance** (GGB) is total income minus expenditure of all arms of government, i.e. central government, local authorities, vocational education committees and non-commercial state sponsored bodies. Government agencies also manage funds such as the Social Insurance Fund and the National Pensions Reserve Fund. This is the equivalent of the public sector borrowing requirement, if the GGB is in deficit.

The GGB does not include financing for commercial state sponsored bodies as these agencies are classified as being outside the general government sector.

Under the Maastricht Treaty, the GGB is calculated in a standard manner, developed by the EU, to facilitate budgetary comparisons between EU member states.

The National Debt

Definition of the national debt

The **national debt** is the total outstanding amount of money borrowed by central government and not repaid to date, less liquid assets available for redemption of those liabilities at the same date.

The general government debt (GG debt) includes the national debt, as described above, as well as local government debt and some other minor liabilities of government. It is another standard measure used within the EU for comparative purposes.

The national debt at the end of September 2007 was €39.007 billion. (Source: *National Treasury Management Agency*)

There are two elements to the national debt.

1. The internal or domestic debt, i.e. money borrowed from citizens and institutions in the country.
2. The external or foreign debt, i.e. money borrowed from abroad. In 2007 this was a zero figure.

Reasons for the national debt

The national debt arises because money is borrowed to finance various types of projects.

Productive investment

Productive investment is spending on projects which become self-financing. These investments eventually create incomes which are then taxed to repay the borrowings. This form of borrowing causes no problems for the country in the long term.

Social investment

Social or non-productive investment involves financing projects which can never be self-financing, but which are desired and required by society, e.g. expenditure on schools and hospitals. This type of investment could benefit the economy in the long run if it results in a better-educated and healthier workforce.

Current budget deficit

Current budget deficit is borrowing to finance current government expenditure, e.g. payment of civil servants' wages, heating government buildings. This is an undesirable form of borrowing as it simply delays taxation to a future date. Some of our national debt arose from our governments' decisions to operate these deficit budgets during the 1970s and 1980s.

Problems associated with the national debt

- It is deferred taxation, i.e. it must be repaid out of future taxes.
- Domestic borrowing may increase interest rates as the availability of loanable funds decreases.
- There may be a large opportunity cost to the borrowings if the scarce funds could be better used by the private sector.
- Repayment of the actual debt may cause problems in the future and may result in rolled over debts, i.e. replacing one debt with another.
- Changes in the rate of exchange could increase the external (foreign) debt itself and the cost of servicing it.
- Lenders may be able to influence government policy to protect their loans, i.e. too great a stress may be put on the repayment of the debt at the expense of other pressing needs of the economy.
- Payment of interest on the internal (domestic) debt may result in an unequal distribution of wealth in the economy. It is normally the wealthy section of the population which lends money to the government. The interest paid to these people comes from general taxation.
- The government is unable to recoup any of the interest paid on the external (foreign) debt through taxation.
- Servicing and repayment of the external (foreign) debt may result in a depletion of the country's foreign reserves. (In 2007, there was no foreign debt.)

The National Treasury Management Agency

The National Treasury Management Agency Act, 1990, established the National Treasury Management Agency (NTMA). This Act allows the government to delegate the borrowing and debt management functions of the Minister for Finance to the NTMA. The actions taken by the NTMA have the same status in law as those undertaken by the Minister for Finance.

✳Functions of the NTMA

1. The essential role of the NTMA is managing the national debt on behalf of the government.
2. It manages the National Pensions Reserve Fund and other government funds such as the Social Insurance Fund, and the Dormant Accounts Fund, as well as borrowing on behalf of the Housing Finance Agency.
3. The provision of financial advice, funding and providing guarantees for all major public investment projects is carried out by the National Development Finance Agency operating through the NTMA.
4. The NTMA also provides a central treasury service by taking deposits and lending to local government bodies and liquidity management for the Central Bank and Financial Services Authority of Ireland.
5. It manages all personal injuries claims brought against government departments and other state authorities.

Source: *NTMA*

General Government Debt/GDP Ratio

This is the ratio of general government debt to gross domestic product (GDP). In other words, it reflects our debt as a percentage of what we produce or earn in a year. At the time of writing this was approximately 1:4, or the debt represents approximately 25 per cent of our GDP.

The debt has remained stable and there has been a rapid growth in the Irish economy in recent years. Because of these factors the debt GDP ratio has fallen from over 90 per cent during the first half of the 1990s to an estimated 27.4 per cent at the end of 2005.

Current and Capital Government Expenditure

✳Government current expenditure

Government current expenditure in a year is spending by the government on the provision of goods and services which will be totally consumed in that year. The government spends money every week paying the salaries of nurses and doctors working in hospitals. This is an example of current expenditure. Other examples of current expenditure are social welfare payments, the heating and lighting in government buildings, interest payments on the national debt and the payment of wages to members of the Defence Forces.

Fig 21.2 The wages of hospital workers are part of current expenditure

It is highly desirable that the current expenditure in any one year comes from the government's income in that year. Otherwise, the government would have to borrow to pay for these services. This would be the equivalent of a family having to borrow to pay for its food. In this situation, part of future earnings will have to go on paying for goods and services which have already been used.

Government capital expenditure

Government capital expenditure is spending by the government on assets which will benefit the country for some time into the future. When the government builds a new hospital it will benefit the citizens for many years to come. This is a form of capital expenditure. Other examples include spending on social housing, the building of new government offices, and the provision of new schools.

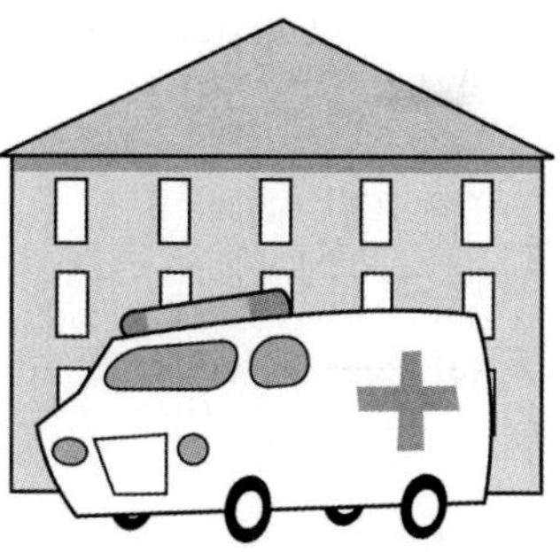

Fig 21.3 The cost of building hospitals is part of capital expenditure

Borrowing for capital expenditure can be justified as the citizens of the future will benefit from this expenditure and so their future taxes can be used towards the repayment of the loans incurred. This is the equivalent of taking out a mortgage to purchase a house. You continue to obtain a benefit (utility) from the loan repayment during the lifetime of the mortgage. Of course, if you have the money to pay for your house without borrowing then this will save you any interest payments in the future and all your future income will be your own, i.e. not partly due to a building society or financial institution. Likewise, the government sometimes pays for capital projects out of its own income without having to borrow to finance the expenditure.

Keep in mind that under the Maastricht Agreement borrowings in any one year by the government for any form of expenditure is restricted to 3 per cent of its GDP.

In recent years, the Irish government has been operating a current budget surplus, i.e. it takes in more in current revenue than it spends on current expenditure. This can be seen in Table 21.1 (see p. 220).

Table 21.1 *Summary of budgets 2007 to 2010*

	Estimated outturn	Post budget Estimate	Projection	Projection
	€m	€m	€m	€m
Current expenditure				
Departmental expenditure	41,265	45,198	47,255	49,149
Expenditure from Social Insurance Fund	7,051	7,678	8,188	8,812
Expenditure from National Training Fund	396	410	417	425
Central Fund Expenditure (non-voted)	3,990	4,437	4,857	5,129
Gross current expenditure	**52,701**	**57,722**	**60,717**	**63,514**
Less Appropriations-in-aid	11,612	12,865	13,384	14,042
Less Departmental balances	151	30		
Net current expenditure	**40,938**	**44,827**	**47,333**	**49,472**
Current receipts				
Tax revenue	47,325	48,910	51,790	55,150
Non-tax revenue	674	684	708	689
Total current receipts	**47,999**	**49,594**	**52,498**	**55,839**
Current budget balance	**7,061**	**4,767**	**5,165**	**6,367**

Source: *The Department of Finance*

Note: Due to rounding up of figures totals may not tally exactly in all cases.

Advantages of operating a current budget surplus

Reduced inflationary pressures

The government is withdrawing more money from the economy than it is putting in. This tends to have a deflationary effect in the economy thus reducing demand-pull inflation.

Managing our finances

The existence of a budget surplus means that government does not have difficulty in controlling its finances. This can lead to confidence in the economy and attract investment.

Adhering to EU guidelines

The fact that a budget surplus exists indicates that the country is meeting the EU agreed guidelines without any difficulty. This alleviates the need for the EU to comment adversely on government economic policy.

Scope for taxation reforms

The fact that a surplus exists indicates that there is scope for reform in the taxation system in the country. This should allow for improvements in the tax system allowing people to retain more of their income through decreased rates of direct taxes and even a reduction in indirect taxes. Recently we have seen the abolition of stamp duty on the purchase of houses by first-time buyers.

Uses of this increased government revenue

The surplus gives the government the option of using this money to pay for more current activities or to spend it on long-term projects, e.g. infrastructure.

Disadvantages of a current budget surplus

Rise in conflicting expectations

When citizens observe the budget surplus they may demand improvements in state services, e.g. health services and education provision. However, the demands made on the government may conflict with each other, causing further problems for the government. It is not always possible to satisfy everybody's demands.

Public sector workers

When public sector workers see this budget surplus they may see it as an opportunity for wage negotiations. These workers may thus demand pay increases and demand an increase in the level of the workforce.

Tax reductions

Taxpayers who feel that they are paying too much tax may feel aggrieved. They may demand reductions in their taxes or look for improved equity in the tax system.

Discontinuity in social partnership

Trade unions, observing the surplus, may feel that some other sectors of the economy are benefiting more from government policies. Employers and industrialists in the private sector may however regard the surplus as prudent management of the public finances. This may make it difficult to negotiate new national wage agreements.

Government financial planning

The actual surplus at the end of a year, if it is greater than the planned surplus, may indicate inefficiency in the preparation of the budget.

Opportunity costs of a surplus

The budget surplus may have been achieved by the reduction of expenditure on services within the country. Thus essential services such as health or education may have deteriorated.

The Formal Organisation of the Government's Finances

Every year each government department makes an estimate of all of its expenditure for the coming financial year. These estimates are then submitted to the Department of Finance for approval.

The Department of Finance then calculates its estimated income for the coming financial year based on the current revenue structure, i.e. if there was to be no change in current taxes.

In October, the government publishes detailed pre-budget estimates of the resources required to maintain the existing level of public services in the following year. These pre-budget estimates form part of the new **Pre-Budget Outlook (PBO)** which sets out the economic and fiscal outlook for the next three years.

In December, all policy initiatives involving an increase in public expenditure, above and beyond the 'existing level of service' figures, are published in **The Budget**, along with the social welfare increases and any new tax measures which are to be introduced.

This budget must get the formal approval of the Dáil by the passing of two pieces of legislation. **The Finance Act** gives the government permission to raise revenue as outlined in the budget. **The Appropriation Act** gives the government permission to spend money as outlined in the budget. If either of these Acts failed to pass a vote in the Dáil then the government would have to resign as it could not function if it could not raise income or spend that income.

Finally, the government's accounts are examined at the end of the year by the **comptroller and auditor general** to ensure that all income raised and all money spent was done so in accordance with the measures outlined in the Finance and the Appropriation Acts.

Local Taxation

All of the discussions so far have been on central government finances. However, we must also remember that local government – your local county council – also plays an important part in our lives. The activities entrusted to these authorities also have to be financed.

While the extent of activities and finances involved vary from one local authority to another, depending on their size, they share many common activities and sources of finance.

A typical large local authority will carry out many programmes in a year. For example, Fingal County Council operates eight programmes:

Programme Group 1 Housing and Building
Programme Group 2 Road Transportation and Safety
Programme Group 3 Water Supply and Sewerage
Programme Group 4 Development Incentives and Controls
Programme Group 5 Environmental Protection
Programme Group 6 Recreation and Amenity
Programme Group 7 Agriculture, Education, Health and Welfare
Programme Group 8 Miscellaneous Services

For the year 2007, the council drafted a budget for these programmes of €230.16m. The council expected to finance this expenditure as follows in Table 21.2.

Table 21.2 *Fingal County Council*

Commercial rates	€102.78m
Local Government Fund	€32.66m
Road grants	€7.32m
Other grants	€16.97m
Rents/repayments	€16.98m
Agency services/recoup other local authorities	€7.81m
Water charges[1]	€6.98m
Environmental charges	€12.75m
Income from other services	€25.91m
Total	**€230.16m**

Source: *Fingal County Council website*

[1]At the time of writing, water charges do not apply to private households in this council.

Without over analysing these figures there are some interesting features contained within them.

Commercial rates are a tax levied on properties which are used for business purposes. So, in this case, these business operators are paying almost 47 per cent of the operating costs of the council.

The figure for the **Local Government Fund** comes from the central government's Department of the Environment, Heritage and Local Government. This department operates a fund known as the Local Government Fund. Thus it is coming out of the taxes we pay to the central government.

Other interesting figures mentioned are **water charges**[1] and **environmental charges**, which are more commonly referred to as bin charges. These have to be paid by residents of each council. Remember that these have to be paid out of the family's net income, i.e. the income received after paying taxes to the central government. Thus they are a form of **double taxation**. Assume these charges total €500 per household per year and that the taxpayer is paying 42 cents in the euro in income tax plus another 7.5 per cent in PRSI. Thus this taxpayer will have to earn almost €1,000 gross to pay the €500 charges. These types of taxes are sometimes known as **stealth taxes**.

Definitions associated with government finances

- **Balanced current budget** is one where planned current income = planned current expenditure.
- **Surplus current budget** is one where planned current income > planned current expenditure.
- **Deficit current budget** is one where planned current income < planned current expenditure.
- **Balanced budget*** is one where planned total income = planned total expenditure.
- **Surplus budget*** is one where planned total income > planned total expenditure.
- **Deficit budget*** is one where planned total income < planned total expenditure.
- A **neutral budget** is one which is neither inflationary nor deflationary.
- The **Exchequer borrowing requirement** (EBR) is the amount of money which the government borrows to finance both its current and capital expenditure in a year.
- The **public sector borrowing requirement** (PSBR) or **general government balance** (GGB) is the EBR plus borrowings for the non-commercial state sponsored bodies and local authorities in any one year.
- The **national debt** is the total amount of money owed by the national government at any given time less liquid assets available for redemption of these debts (see p. 216).
- **Deadweight debt** or borrowing is borrowed money which when it is spent adds nothing to the revenue of the government, i.e. it is not self-financing.
- **Rolled over debt** is substituting an old debt with a new one, e.g. if the government owes €1m to A it can borrow €1m from B to pay A.
- **Appropriations-in-aid (A-in-As)** are any incomes which a department receives directly from the general public and which are kept by that department rather than being paid into the central Exchequer Funds, e.g. PRSI receipts accrue to the Social Insurance Fund.
- **Departmental balances** are any funds which were allocated to a department in one year and were not fully spent. The department keeps the balances for spending in the following year.

* Includes current and capital income and expenditure.

LEARN THE KEY POINTS

1. The functions of taxation
2. Understand Adam Smith's *Canons of Taxation*
3. Know the additional modern features of taxes
4. Understand the difference between a progressive, a regressive and a proportional tax
5. Distinguish between the imposition and the effective incidence of a tax
6. Distinguish between tax avoidance and tax evasion
7. Know the difference between a direct and an indirect tax
8. Explain the advantages and disadvantages of both direct and indirect taxes
9. Learn the terminology associated with government finances
10. Understand the Exchequer balance versus general government balance versus general government debt
11. Know the functions of the National Treasury Management Agency
12. Explain the advantages and disadvantages of the government's policy of operating a surplus current budget
13. Understand the problems caused by the national debt
14. Know the formal organisation of the government's finances
15. Explain local government finances
16. Understand double taxation or stealth taxes

Exam Q&A: See p. 403

1. State and explain the functions of taxation.
2. State and explain Adam Smith's four *Canons of Taxation*.
3. Explain the difference between direct and indirect taxes.
4. Explain the difference between a progressive and a regressive tax.
5. 'Taxation should not act as a disincentive to investment nor act as a disincentive to work.' Explain the importance of this statement.
6. Explain fully why regressive taxes are regarded as being inequitable.

7 Outline a situation where a company on which a tax has been imposed would be reluctant to pass on the effective incidence of this tax to its customers.

8 Distinguish between the Exchequer balance and the general government balance.

9 Distinguish between deadweight debt and rolled over debt.

10 Why is it important that current government expenditure should be fully financed from its current income?

11 Outline four problems which could arise for the government from its policy of operating surplus current budgets.

12 Outline a situation where the government would be justified in borrowing for capital expenditure in a given year. Is there any restriction on the amount that the government can borrow? Explain your answer.

13 How has our national debt arisen? Outline some of the problems which our national debt could cause.

14 Outline the role of the National Treasury Management Agency.

15 Explain why the charges imposed by local authorities for the services which they provide are often referred to as 'double taxation'.

Chapter 22
The Role of Government in the Economy

The Role of Government

There is much debate about the role of the government in our modern economic system. One school of thought, advocated by the followers of John Maynard Keynes (see p. 358), argues that the government should directly intervene in the working of the economy to achieve a stable level of growth in the economy. They state that this would help to avert recessions, avoid high levels of unemployment and stabilise prices. Another school of thought, advocated by the followers of Milton Friedman (see p. 360), argues that government involvement and intervention in economic affairs should be minimal and that economic issues should be determined by market forces, i.e. by the interaction of total demand and supply in an economy.

When a government does intervene in the running of an economy there are certain policies or instruments it can use to do so.

The Instruments of Government Economic Policy

1. **Fiscal policy** is policy on expenditure and taxation.
2. **Monetary policy**, which is carried out by the Central Bank on behalf of the European Central Bank (ECB), is the policy on the money supply, interest rates and credit creation.
3. **Exchange rate policy** refers to devaluing or revaluing our currency in terms of other currencies. This policy is now directly controlled by the ECB. Therefore, while we mention this policy as a government policy it can only be implemented by full agreement with all other Eurozone countries.
4. **Direct intervention** refers to the setting up of semi-state bodies to provide goods or services on the open market and the passing of legislation, e.g. minimum wages.
5. **Deregulation** is the changing of laws and practices which are detrimental to competition. It is also regarded as a form of direct intervention. An example of this was the abolition on the restriction of the number of taxi licences which could be issued.

6 **Prices and incomes policy** is the way the government implements price control regulations and freezes or limits wage increases.

7 **Economic planning** includes consultations with the social partners to achieve realistic economic targets over an agreed period of time, e.g. the **National Development Plan** (NDP) and **Towards 2016**.

Let us now study (a) the economic aims of the government, (b) the reasons why the government regards each of them as an economic aim and (c) the instruments which the government uses to achieve the aims. Remember that each one is being taken as a 'stand alone' aim and that we are examining the theoretical possibilities. Any decision taken by the government to achieve one economic aim may have a detrimental effect on one or more of its other economic aims.

The Economic Aims of the Government

Aim 1: To create full employment

Reasons

The reduction of unemployment decreases government current expenditure on the dole (unemployment benefit) and other social welfare benefits. The creation of full employment increases government revenue from PAYE taxes, it reduces the social costs of unemployment and the government also benefits from the extra spending, e.g. from VAT, by the newly employed people.

Instruments used

- Fiscal policy, i.e. reduce direct and indirect taxes to encourage domestic demand which should result in more production and more employment.
- Monetary policy, i.e. reduce interest rates to encourage investment. The extra investment should create more employment.
- Exchange rate policy, i.e. devalue the currency to make exports cheaper which should increase the level of exports and could even result in import substitution, thus creating more jobs.
- Direct intervention, i.e. increase employment in the public sector and provide retraining and resettlement allowances to encourage mobility of labour.
- Prices and incomes policy, i.e. link wage increases to increased productivity so that average cost and prices are not affected. (This is to maintain employment.)

Aim 2: The control of inflation

Reasons

The control of inflation stabilises the cost of living, it prevents demands for wage increases and it keeps Irish industry internationally competitive.

Instruments used

- Fiscal policy, i.e. increase direct taxes to decrease demand and also reduce government expenditure.
- Monetary policy, i.e. increase interest rates to decrease the demand for loans for consumption purposes.
- Prices and incomes policy, i.e. impose a wage freeze and at the same time impose price control orders.
- Economic planning, i.e. negotiate national wage agreements to control the wages and prices spiral, e.g. Towards 2016.

*Aim 3: To achieve equilibrium of the balance of payments

Reasons

A balanced balance of payments is important in keeping the value of imports and exports equal to each other. This maintains employment, production and the standard of living at a high level, without a net outflow of funds from the country.

Instruments used

- Fiscal policy, i.e. the government could increase direct taxes to lower income, thus decreasing the demand for imports. The government could also decrease the tax on profits from exports to encourage more firms to enter the export market.
- Monetary policy, i.e. increase interest rates on loans for consumption purposes, thus less money can be spent on imports.
- Exchange rate policy, i.e. in conjunction with ECB, devalue currency. This should lead to cheaper exports and dearer imports, thus hopefully increasing our exports and decreasing our imports. This will only work if the **Marshall-Lerner condition** holds good. This states that devaluation will improve the balance of payments only if the sum of the price elasticities of demand for exports and for imports is greater than one.

*Aim 4: Control of government finances

Reasons

Better control of government finances is aimed at reducing the national debt in order to reduce the cost of servicing the debt. This would allow the government to make better use of our own resources. If less interest has to be paid on the debt then the government can either reduce taxes or use the money saved to provide more or better services.

Instruments used

- Fiscal policy, i.e. decrease government expenditure and decrease government borrowings to control the national debt, as is being done by the National Treasury Management Agency.

✳Aim 5: To achieve a just social policy

Reason

Social policy is often referred to as 'the redistribution of wealth'. It is aimed at providing an income for those people who cannot provide an adequate income for themselves. This has definite economic consequences as the marginal propensity to consume of very low-income earners is 100 per cent, whereas the marginal propensity to consume of high-income earners is roughly 80 per cent. (Refer to Chapter 18, 'Methods of Measuring National Income', p. 169).

Instruments used

- Fiscal policy, i.e. implement a progressive income tax policy and increase social welfare expenditure.

✳Aim 6: The provision of an adequate national infrastructure

Reason

The infrastructure of a country is capital, which in itself is not directly productive, but without it the provision of goods and services could not take place efficiently, e.g. roads, waste disposal, hospitals and telecommunications.

Instruments used

- Fiscal policy, i.e. increase government capital expenditure on all of the above goods and services (see 'Government Long-Term Economic Planning' on p. 232).
- Direct intervention, i.e. cooperate with private enterprise in the provision of facilities such as telephone services, waste disposal services, hospitals and roads. When government and private enterprise work together in the provision of any goods or services the partnerships between them is known as **Public Private Partnerships (PPPs)**.

  Public Private Partnerships are defined in the National Development Plan as:

  > Partnerships between public sector organisations and private sector investors and businesses for the purposes of designing, planning, financing, constructing and operating infrastructure projects, particularly projects which are normally provided through traditional procurement mechanisms by the state or other government bodies.

✳Aim 7: The achievement of economic growth

Reason

Economic growth is aimed at increasing the average income per head of the population without any radical change in the structure of society.

Instruments used

- Economic planning, i.e. negotiate with the social partners to set realistic targets for growth, e.g. the National Development Plan and national wage agreements.

- Fiscal policy, i.e. increase expenditure on the identified targets.
- Monetary policy, i.e. ensure that the money supply is adequate when needed.

✳Aim 8: Regional development

Reasons

Regional development is aimed at ensuring that all regions of the country share in the economic development of the country and that all the population has an adequate infrastructure suited to its needs.

Instruments used

- Fiscal policy, i.e. ensure the payment of higher grants to companies setting up in the less developed areas of the country and the provision of temporary employment subsidies to these companies.
- Economic planning, i.e. implement The National Spatial Strategy for Ireland 2002–2020.

Conflicts between Government Aims

✳Full employment vs control of inflation

To achieve full employment the government would increase expenditure and lower interest rates. These two actions would actually fuel inflation. Similarly, to control inflation the government would increase interest rates, decrease expenditure and increase direct taxes. These actions would be counter-productive to the creation of employment.

✳Economic growth vs just social policy

To achieve a just social policy the government may impose high taxes on the high-income earners and transfer this income to those on social welfare. These high-income earners are usually the wealth creators in the economy. High taxes could force these people out of the economy and so seriously stunt the effort to achieve economic growth. Some people would also argue that the welfare payments might act as a disincentive to get people back onto the workforce.

✳Provision of infrastructure vs control of government finances

Expenditure on the infrastructure is frequently financed by government borrowings. This expenditure does not always bring a direct or immediate return to the government. Thus the burden of the national debt is increased, which requires extra servicing of the debt, thereby increasing current expenditure.

✳Full employment vs balance of payments equilibrium

The creation of employment results in the increasing of the general level of income in the economy. As Ireland has a high marginal propensity to consume this could have a detrimental effect on the balance of payments as the increased imports will result in an outflow of funds from the country.

✳Control of government finances vs full employment

If the government prioritises control of its finances over all other aims, then it will be reluctant to give grants, subsidies or any other financial incentives to firms to create employment. This happened in the late 1980s and early 1990s, when the government saw control of its finances and inflation as its top priorities, even though Ireland had a very high level of unemployment at that time.

Government Long-Term Economic Planning

✳The National Development Plan 2007–2013

The €184 billion National Development Plan (NDP) 2007–2013 was launched in January 2007, and is entitled *Transforming Ireland – A Better Quality of Life for All*. The Plan is the largest and most ambitious investment programme ever proposed for Ireland and provides for five 'Priorities Programmes'.

The following is a summary of these priorities as outlined in the National Development Plan.

✳Priority 1: Economic infrastructure

The National Development Plan states that dealing with the shortfalls or deficiencies in our infrastructure is crucial to our future economic growth, and regional development. Total investment at current prices (2007) is outlined below.

Transport (€32,914m to be invested)

The investment in transport includes spending on national and non-national roads, investment in the three major airports and the six regional airports which includes Derry airport. There is also to be investment in public transport, in particular in the Greater Dublin Region as well as expenditure on the rural Transport Initiative. Finally, there is to be increased investment in upgrading strategic ports facilities and regional harbours. Many elements of this are included in Transport 21, details of which are given on p. 236.

Energy (€8,526m)

The Plan aims to have a guaranteed supply of competitively priced and environmentally friendly energy by the end of the Plan period. Major capital investments will be undertaken by the ESB, Bord Gáis Éireann, Bord na Móna and EirGrid plc. There will also be investment in the east/west and north/south electricity interconnectors. There is ongoing investment in sustainable energy in order to meet the target of 15 per cent of electricity production from renewable sources by 2010.

Environmental services (€5,772m)

Under environmental services the Plan entails investment in water services, waste management and also investment in projects arising from the problems associated with climate changes.

Communications and broadband programme (€435m)

€435 million is to be spent in supporting regional economic development and to address market failures in the provision of broadband in certain parts of the country.

Government buildings infrastructure (€1,413m)

This includes investment in the acquisition of new sites for, and the construction of new government offices. It also includes €830 million for the decentralisation programme up to 2011.

Local authority development contributions (€2,100m)

Local authorities are to receive €1.2 billion as compensation for providing infrastructure for private developers. Most of this money will be raised by levying charges on planning permission applications.

There is an interesting figure of €3,500m in this section entitled 'Unallocated Capital Reserve'.

*Priority II: Enterprise, science and innovation (€20 billion)

The Plan intends an investment of circa €20 billion in enterprise, science and innovation and states that this is essential if Ireland is to attract high-quality foreign direct investment and to develop our own indigenous (native) companies. It stresses the need to encourage the establishment of Irish companies capable of becoming world leaders in given industries; and the establishment of companies specialising in products based on our natural resources. The investment will also include the modernisation of the agriculture sector, the development of the tourism industry and support for the rural economy.

*Priority III: Human capital (€25,796m)

Ireland's track record in education investment has been fundamental to generating our economic success.

The main objective of the proposed investment of €25.8 billion is to ensure access for everybody in our society to the highest standards of education to enable us to meet the labour skills requirement of the future. The investment is to focus on developing the third level sector. Particular attention is to be given to postgraduate studies.

*Priority IV: Social infrastructure (€33,612m)

Investment in social infrastructure aims to achieve a fair and equitable redistribution of the wealth created by the recent economic success among all sections of our community.

Over €21 billion will be invested in housing to include the provision of 100,000 new social and affordable units and a rent supplement scheme to other households.

Just under €5 billion is to be invested in health infrastructure, including acute hospitals and primary and community care facilities.

Roughly €2.3 billion is to be spent to deliver a modernised prison infrastructure, a new criminal courts complex and improvements to Garda Stations and Garda infrastructure generally.

There is to be an investment of over €3.6 billion for sports, culture and heritage infrastructure, including the first phase of the Abbotstown sports complex and the redevelopment of the Lansdowne Road stadium.

✳Priority V: Social inclusion (€49,636m)

Investment in social priorities is seen as being central to the National Development Plan. This Plan does not deal with normal social welfare payments. These payments are dealt with in the annual current budget.

The main areas of investment in this priority are:

1. €12 billion is allocated to Children's Programmes dealing with childcare services, child protection and recreational facilities. It also aims to provide funds for the education of children from disadvantaged communities and those with special needs.
2. Over €4 billion is to be spent on Working Age Education Support programmes to support further education, student support and third level access.
3. €9.7 billion is to be provided to help older people live independently at home and to provide quality residential care facilities for older people who are no longer able to live at home.
4. €19 billion is to be provided to support the provision of programmes and services for people with disabilities.
5. Extra funds are to be provided for the RAPID (Revitalising Areas by Planning, Investment and Development) programme, which prioritises investment in forty-six of the most disadvantaged urban areas and provincial towns.

Funding

This new Plan is almost completely funded from domestic sources, the vast bulk of it by the Central Exchequer.

It is estimated that €3 billion in EU rural development and structural funding will be made available over the period 2007–2013. This funding will be the subject of separate programmes to be agreed between Ireland and the European Commission.

The National Spatial Strategy (NSS)

The National Spatial Strategy is a twenty-year planning framework aimed at creating a more balanced social, economic and physical development of the country.

The basic concept underlying this programme is to support and create a better balance between those areas (hence the word 'spatial') in the country, which are experiencing rapid development, and thus congestion, and those areas that are economically under-utilised.

The Strategy, in conjunction with the Regional Development Strategy for Northern Ireland, sets out how all areas of the country will have the opportunity to develop to their full potential.

The rate at which the NSS can be implemented will be 'subject to overall macro-economic and budgetary considerations'.

Summary

The NSS has identified nine main 'gateways' which are areas of, or will be areas of very high levels of economic and social activity.

Many larger towns (hubs) within a reasonable distance of the gateways are to be developed to feed into the gateways and benefit from them.

Beyond these hubs, 'complementary towns' will be developed to provide services, e.g. housing, shopping and educational services, for those working in the gateways and hubs, as well as providing these services for the outlying rural communities.

However, development funds will only be invested in those areas which have the natural potential and the critical mass (population level), as well as having a reasonably good transport, communications and energy network, i.e. linkages.

Key concepts

Under this strategy the key concepts which will be taken into account when assessing the future development of an area or region are:

1. Potential
2. Critical mass
3. Gateways
4. Hubs
5. Complementary roles
6. Linkages

1 Potential

Potential here refers to the natural capacity that a region has for development. This potential could be determined by its natural resources, its population, its labour, its economic and social capital, its infrastructure and its location relative to markets. In other words, the areas which can prove their potential economic and social value will be prioritised for the receipt of development funds.

2 Critical mass

Critical mass means that the size and concentration of population is sufficient to ensure that a full range of services and facilities can be supported. This population must be large enough to attract and support higher levels of economic activity and improved quality of life.

3 Gateways

Gateways are strategic locations such as cities or major towns, which can provide large scale social and economic infrastructure and support services. These have been identified as the five existing gateways of Dublin, Cork, Limerick/Shannon, Galway and Waterford. There are four new national level gateways, the towns of Dundalk and Sligo, the linked gateways of Letterkenny/Derry and the Midland towns of Athlone, Tullamore and Mullingar. These are key components of the NSS.

4 Hubs

Hubs are large towns, close to the gateways, which can, in turn, energise smaller towns and rural areas within close proximity to them.

5 Complementary roles

There are complementary roles for other towns in relation to villages and rural areas. This means the development of various medium-sized towns in each region. These towns will act as 'local capitals' in providing a range of services and opportunities for employment.

Within the spatial framework proposed by the NSS, 'rural potential will draw upon local economic strengths, supported by a stronger structure of smaller towns and villages as a focus for economic and social activity and residential development' (*National Spatial Strategy* document).

6 Linkages

Linkages refer to the need for good transport, communications and energy networks in the areas to be developed.

Transport 21

Transport 21 is a government capital investment programme of €34 billion over the period 2006–2015. This capital investment will be used to transform Ireland's transport system. In particular it will provide finance to:

- Complete the development of the inter-urban motorway network by 2010.
- Bring about improvements in the rest of the national road network, particularly in the regions identified in the National Spatial Strategy.
- Complete the safety programme on the national rail network.
- Bring about a radical improvement in the level and quality of rail services.
- Transform the public transport system in the Greater Dublin Area.
- Develop the public transport system in the provincial cities.
- Improve regional and rural public transport services.
- Fund essential capital works at the six existing regional airports.
- Improve accessibility to public transport for people with mobility, sensory and cognitive impairments.

Source: *Transport 21* website

Privatisation

Privatisation is the sale of government owned companies and assets to the private sector. In recent times the two most notable privatised companies are Eircom and Aer Lingus.

Advantages of privatisation

- The sale of these companies can raise money for the government which can be used to reduce the national debt.
- Many of these semi-state companies are loss-making enterprises which are supported by taxation. Their sale would reduce the need for taxation or the money could be spent providing other services.
- Some semi-state companies' activities are restricted by the Act which set them up. This restricts their expansion and thus their profitability. By selling the semi-state company a new Memorandum of Association and Articles of Association can be drawn up allowing the business to expand.
- Privatisation gives Irish people the opportunity to invest in major Irish companies. The government can discriminate in favour of investors seeking small numbers of shares and against large institutional investors.
- Employees are often given shares in the company being privatised. This affords them a chance to earn capital gains on the Stock Exchange, if the company is successful.

Disadvantages of privatisation

- The government will only succeed in selling profitable or potentially profitable semi-state bodies which will leave it supporting the loss-making bodies.
- The new companies could fall into foreign control and could make decisions which are not in the national interest.
- The new company could discontinue the provision of services, which the semi-state body deemed socially desirable, but which are unprofitable.
- The privatised company may reduce staffing levels, thus creating more unemployment, thus causing an extra burden on government resources, i.e. more dole payments.
- If the new privatised firm is still a monopoly, it could restrict production to increase prices to the consumers.

Nationalisation

Nationalisation is the complete opposite to privatisation. In this situation, the government acquires ownership of privately owned businesses. This may be done to ensure the continuity of supply of an essential product or service (e.g. water) to all citizens at a reasonable price. Nationalisation is a means of counteracting the potential exploitation of consumers by private monopolies and oligopolies.

LEARN THE KEY POINTS

1. Understand the instruments of government economic policy
2. Learn the economic aims of the government and the instruments used to achieve them
3. Understand the conflicts between government aims
4. Know about Public Private Partnerships
5. Understand the National Development Plan 2007–2013 and its five priorities
6. Explain The National Spatial Strategy
7. Know about Transport 21
8. Explain privatisation plus its advantages and disadvantages

Exam Q&A: See p. 405

1. Distinguish between monetary policy and fiscal policy.
2. Give a brief description of the other main instruments of government economic policy.
3. Give a brief description of the main economic aims of the government.
4. Why have the traditional instruments of government policy, i.e. those of 'devaluation' and 'monetary policy', become less effective policies for the Irish government?
5. Why is the control of inflation always one of the most important elements of government policy? Give a full explanation of your answer.
6. Describe fully how the government's aim of controlling inflation could conflict with its aim of creating full employment.
7. What are Public Private Partnerships?
8. What is meant by 'privatisation'? Outline any four arguments for and against the privatisation of semi-state bodies.
9. What are the five 'priorities' stated in the National Development Plan 2007–2013?
10. Which specific government policy is addressed by the National Spatial Strategy? Give reasons for your answer.
11. List three semi-state bodies and write a brief note on each.

Chapter 23
The European Union

The Common Market

'We are joining into the Common Market' was the colloquial phrase used in Ireland in 1973 when we first joined what is now the European Union (EU). In fact it was not a common market at that time. So firstly let us clarify the distinctions between three different types of trading agreements.

1. **A free trade area:** This is an agreement between a number of countries to permit the free trading of goods between them without any quotas, customs duties or any other tariffs.
2. **A customs union:** This is a free trade area which also imposes common restrictions on goods coming into the area from non-member countries.
3. **A common market:** This is a customs union which also allows the free movement of the factors of production between the member countries.

The Structure of the EU

The EU is a group of democratic European countries working together for peace and prosperity. Its member countries have established bodies that enable them to carry out common policies on issues which are of mutual interest and benefit.

✳The European Parliament

The European Parliament, which is elected every five years by the people of Europe, has 785 members from the twenty-seven EU countries. The main job of Parliament is to pass European laws. It shares this responsibility with the Council of the European Union. The proposals for new laws come from the European Commission. The Parliament, along with the Council, also has the responsibility of approving the EU's annual budget (see p. 242).

The European Parliament buildings in Brussels (left) and Strasbourg (right)

The Council of the European Union

Ministers from the national governments of all the EU countries sit on this Council. The topic being debated at a Council meeting will determine which minister from the national governments will attend. For example, if the topic is dealing with finance then the Ministers of Finance will attend.

The Council and the Parliament share the responsibility for passing laws and taking policy decisions. The Council also bears the main responsibility for the EU common foreign and security policies.

When the presidents and prime ministers of the member states meet at a Council meeting the meeting is referred to as the **European Council**. These summit meetings set overall EU policy.

Each country has a number of votes in the Council. The number of votes usually reflects the size of the population of the respective countries with a slight weighting in favour of the smaller countries. However, it must be remembered that decisions are seldom put to a vote and are usually taken on a consensus basis. The speaking time of any member is not in proportion to that country's voting rights, therefore a small country with a very persuasive argument could 'swing' an issue.

If an issue has to be voted on a simple majority is needed. If a vote has to be taken on any sensitive issues in areas such as taxation, immigration, or foreign and security policy, a unanimous decision is needed.

Fig 23.1 *Map showing the EU member states in January 2008*

⁕The European Commission

The European Commission is almost the equivalent of a Cabinet in a national government. Each member of the Commission is appointed by its own national government, but acts independently from its government. Each of the commissioners has responsibility for a particular EU policy area, e.g. there is a commissioner for agriculture and a commissioner for fisheries. They are responsible for the day-to-day affairs of that area, as well as implementing EU policies and managing the budget allocated to that area.

⁕The Court of Justice

Like any national government the EU also operates a judicial system known as the **Court of Justice**. It is the role of this Court to ensure that all national governments enforce all EU legislation and that the legislation is correctly interpreted.

⁕The Court of Auditors

The Court of Auditors has the same responsibility as the comptroller and auditor general in Ireland, that is responsibility for ensuring that all expenditure is undertaken legally and in accordance with budgetary policy.

There are also very many consultative bodies within the EU such as The European Economic and Social Committee and The Committee of the Regions. We must not forget the European Central Bank (ECB) which we have already discussed in detail (see pp 151–153).

⁕The EU budget

Like all major organisations the EU must operate within a budget. The estimated total expenditure for 2008 was €129.2 billion. This is financed as follows.

- **Traditional own resources (TOR)** are duties that are charged on imports of products coming from a non-EU state. They bring in approximately 15 per cent of the total revenue.
- **The resource based on value added tax (VAT)** is a uniform percentage rate that is applied to each member state's harmonised VAT revenue. The VAT-based resource accounts for 15 per cent of total revenue.
- **The resource based on gross national income (GNI)** is a uniform percentage rate (0.73 per cent) applied to the GNI of each member state. This is the largest source of revenue and accounts for 69 per cent of total revenue.
- **Miscellaneous resources:** The budget also receives other revenue, such as taxes paid by EU staff on their salaries, contributions from non-EU countries to certain EU programmes and fines on companies that breach competition or other laws. These miscellaneous resources add up to about 1 per cent of the budget.

Common Policies of the EU

*The Common Agricultural Policy (CAP)

According to Europa.eu, the official website of the EU, the aim of the common agricultural policy is to provide farmers with a reasonable standard of living, to provide consumers with quality food at fair prices and to preserve our rural heritage. The policy has evolved to meet society's changing needs, so that food safety, preservation of the environment, value for money, and agriculture as a source of crops to convert to fuel, have acquired steadily growing importance.

To understand the common agricultural policy in its present form it is necessary to take a brief look at its evolution.

1957 The Treaty of Rome

In 1957, when the Treaty of Rome was signed, most Europeans still had a very vivid memory of the post-war food shortages and were determined that these shortages would never reoccur.

Therefore, the community encouraged an increase in the production of most agricultural goods through a system of guaranteed minimum prices and market intervention. This meant that farmers were guaranteed a minimum price for their output. If market forces resulted in a price below this minimum price the oversupply was taken off the market and 'put onto intervention'. Thus it encouraged production, stabilised the markets and protected farmers from fluctuations in world markets.

However, it also led to an oversupply of most products which had guaranteed minimum prices. Who would not keep on producing any good if there was a guaranteed market for it at a guaranteed price? This led to the creation of the infamous beef and butter mountains and wine lakes.

EU spending in agriculture increased at an alarming rate and accounted for roughly 50 per cent of the total EU budget. As a result, in its four-decade existence, the CAP has undergone several reforms.

1968 The Mansholt Plan

In 1968 The Mansholt Plan was introduced. The Plan sought to reduce the number of people employed in agriculture and to promote the formation of larger and more efficient farm sizes. However, this had very little impact on the problem of oversupply and despite further efforts in 1972, 1983, 1991 and 1992, it was not until 2000 that any significant progress was made.

Agenda 2000

Agenda 2000 has been the most radical and comprehensive reform of the Common Agricultural Policy since its inception. In particular, the reform comprises measures for:

- The reinforcement of the competitiveness of agricultural commodities in domestic and world markets.
- The promotion of a fair and decent standard of living for the farming community.
- The creation of substitute jobs and other sources of income for farmers.
- The formation of a new policy for rural development, which has become a major element of the CAP.
- The integration of more environmental and structural considerations into the CAP.
- The improvement of food quality and safety.
- The simplification of agricultural legislation and the decentralisation of its application, in order to make rules and regulations clearer, more transparent and easier to access.

June 2003 Reform

The major element of the June 2003 reform was the introduction of **decoupling** and **single farm payments**. This major CAP reform alters the basis of direct aid to producers by decoupling it from production. This decoupling, which began on 1 January 2005 separates grants received from production.

The new system is intended to balance producers' income more effectively, through the single farm payment scheme.

The decoupling is intended to eliminate surplus overproduction and thereby balance supply and demand, leaving farmers' incomes unaffected.

The reforms allow a transitional period beginning no later than 2007.

Continuation of CAP reforms in 2004

The Commission has proposed a radical reform package for many of the Mediterranean products and for sugar.

The reform of the sugar sector aims to reduce sugar exports and export refunds (see note on p. 245) by removing intervention and capping Community production of sugar and its domestic price. This reform has already taken its toll on the Irish economy and the accompanying compensation measures have caused much disquiet between the producers and the processors of beet in Ireland. Similar reforms have been introduced for many Mediterranean products.

Note: An **export refund** is a payment to the exporter of a product produced within the EU which has a guaranteed minimum price. If the price received on the export market is less than the guaranteed minimum price, then the difference in the two prices is paid directly to the exporter.

✳The Common Fisheries Policy (CFP)

The first common measures in the fishing sector date from 1970. The common fisheries policy in place today is based on the stated fisheries policy outlined by the EU:

> The Common Fisheries Policy shall ensure exploitation of living aquatic resources that provide sustainable economic, environmental and social conditions. For this purpose, the Community shall apply the precautionary approach in taking measures designed to protect and conserve living aquatic resources, to provide for their sustainable exploitation and to minimise the impact of fishing activities on marine ecosystems.

Common measures are agreed in the following main areas.

Conservation of the environmental impact of fishing

The conservation and limitation of the environmental impact of fishing is aimed at protecting fish resources by regulating the amount and physical size of fish taken from the sea. These maximum quantities, called **total allowable catches (TACs)**, are divided among member states. Each country's share is called a **national quota**. This policy attempts to ensure that the EU has sufficient numbers of mature fish to renew stocks. It also ensures that sufficient amounts of small fish must be left to grow and reproduce. Policies are also put in place to ensure that these measures are respected.

Structures and fleet management

The European Fisheries Fund will provide financial assistance for projects in all branches of fishing and aquaculture and for measures to identify and promote new market outlets. Funding is available for modernisation of the fishing fleets as well as for getting rid of excess fishing capacity.

Common organisation of markets

The common organisation of markets was part of the first set of common measures. The objective is to create a common market inside the European Union and to match production to demand for the benefit of both producers and consumers. These original objectives have been complemented by the creation of the European single market and the gradual opening up of world trade.

Economic and Monetary Union (EMU)

EMU is the process of harmonising the economic and monetary policies of the member states and for the introduction of a single currency.

✳ The monetary union element

There were three stages in the process of monetary union.

Stage 1: 1 July 1990–31 December 1993

Stage 1 culminated in the implementation of The Single European Act adopted in 1998. It saw the removal of all barriers to the free movement of capital within the EU as well as a better coordination of economic policies and closer cooperation between the Central Banks.

Stage 2: 1 January 1994–31 December 1998

Stage 2 began with the establishment of the European Monetary Institute (EMI). It was dedicated to technical preparations for the introduction of the single currency and the avoidance of excessive deficits, and an enhanced convergence of economic and monetary policies to ensure stable prices and sound public finances. This culminated in the establishment of the European Central Bank (ECB) in 1998.

Stage 3: 1 January 1999–

Stage 3 began with the irrevocable fixing of exchange rates, the transfer of responsibility for monetary policy to the ECB. January 2000 saw the introduction of the euro as the single currency which was initially introduced in eleven member countries: Austria, Belgium, Finland, France, Germany, Ireland, Italy, Luxembourg, the Netherlands, Portugal and Spain. Since then both Greece and Slovenia have joined the Eurozone. (See Chapter 17, Money and Banking, for the benefits of the euro system, p. 142.)

✳ The economic union element

The Single European Market

The Single European Market has as its main aim the 'free movement' of people, goods, services and capital.

The EU flag

People

The principle of free movement of people dates back to the creation of the European Community. This principle was initially introduced to open Europe's labour markets to migrant workers and their families. Over the years, this right was extended to cover all categories of citizens.

Fig 23.2 Citizens of EU countries are entitled to freedom of movement between member countries

Today, with the lifting of most internal border controls, we can move as freely around Europe as we can within a member state. Thus all EU citizens can decide to study, work, or retire in another EU country.

Goods

One of the 'four freedoms' of the single market is the free movement of goods. Member states may restrict the free movement of goods only in exceptional cases, for example, when there is a risk resulting from issues such as public health, environment or consumer protection.

Approximately half of the trade in goods within the EU is covered by harmonised regulations, while the other half is either regulated by national technical regulations or not specifically regulated at all.

Services

Services account for over 60 per cent of economic activity in the EU and a similar (and rising) proportion of overall employment.

Under the free movement of services, all EU companies providing services are guaranteed the freedom to establish themselves in, or the freedom to provide services in, the territory of another EU country.

Capital

Not so long ago, Europeans were in principle obliged to manage and invest their money predominantly in their home country. Now with the free movement of capital and payments all EU citizens can, in theory, conduct most financial operations anywhere within the EU. These can vary from simply opening bank accounts to buying shares in non-domestic companies, or from purchasing property in any EU country to purchasing life assurance policies.

However, the rules concerning some of these rights can presently be restricted by domestic governmental regulations in member countries. These vary from one member state to another. In 2005, the Commission, recognising this problem, created an action plan aimed at developing a true European-wide market in financial services and is now drawing up a strategy to achieve this end.

Free movement of capital is an essential condition for the proper functioning of the single market. It enables a better allocation of resources within the EU, making it easier for businesses to raise the money they need to start and grow.

Free movement of capital is also an essential condition for the cross-border activities of financial services companies. The success of the International Financial Services Centre in Dublin is heavily reliant on the free movement of capital.

Benefits of the single market

Overall economic benefits

1. Since its establishment the single market has created over 2.5 million jobs and over €877 billion of extra income. This equates to an average of €5,700 per household.
2. The single market has enhanced the ability of EU firms to compete on the worldwide markets.
3. EU exports to non-EU countries have increased from 6.9 per cent of EU GDP in 1992 to 11.2 per cent in 2001.
4. The single market has made Europe a much more attractive location for foreign investors. New inflows of foreign direct investment into the EU have more than doubled as a percentage of GDP.

Benefits for citizens

1. EU citizens can travel across most of the EU without carrying a passport and without being stopped for checks at the borders. (Because the UK opted out of this element Ireland also had to opt out.) Shoppers have full consumer rights when shopping anywhere within the EU and there are no limits on the quantities they can buy and take home with them, as long as the products purchased are for personal use.
2. There is now less bureaucracy for people wishing to study, work or retire in another EU country. Nearly 2 million young people have already taken advantage of EU programmes, such as the Erasmus Programme, to pursue their studies in another European country. The gradual movement towards mutual recognition of educational and professional qualifications is now making labour more occupationally and geographically mobile.
3. There is wider choice for consumers. The range of products and services on sale across the EU is greater than ever and in most cases prices are easily compared thanks to the euro.
4. The prices are more competitive. Manufacturers and service providers are now selling in a single competitive market of 480 million people. In order to gain more market share many producers have had to lower their prices in the hope of

increasing total revenue. Recall the theory of price elasticity of demand (see Chapter 6, Elasticity of Demand, p. 40). In particular phone calls, internet access and air travel have all become cheaper. The competition has resulted in the improved use of technology in the attempt to lower price. This has been so successful that the prices charged by the old national monopolies for national calls have been brought down to a fraction of what they were ten years ago.

5. With more financial integration and liberalisation of capital movements within the EU, citizens can benefit from a wider range of financial products and service and at a lower cost. However, this is probably the slowest changing sector for the consumer.

6. More competition in public procurement means better value and higher quality services for the taxpayer. The change in relation to public procurement contracts means that all major contracts for state and local authority work must now be open to quotations from all companies within the EU.

Benefits for business

1. Trade within the EU has become much easier. The absence of border bureaucracy has cut delivery times and reduced costs. Before the frontiers came down, the tax system alone required 60 million customs clearance documents annually, these are no longer needed.

2. The 'mutual recognition principle' means that in most cases companies can do business across the EU by complying with the rules in their home member state.

3. New export markets have been opened up to small and medium-sized enterprises (SMEs) who previously would have been prevented from exporting by the costs and difficulties involved.

4. Companies are now able to bid for contracts to supply goods and services to public authorities in other member states, thanks to the opening up of public procurement (see above).

5. Capital or money now flows more easily within the single market providing more start-up capital for new businesses and more capital for expansion purposes. It also ensures that investment funds are not lying idle in one region of the EU when they are needed in another region.

6. SMEs have benefited from lower electricity costs in those member states where this segment of the market has been opened up to competition. This has happened on the Irish market with the entry of Airtricity.

7. Any competitive business in the EU should be able to benefit from the huge open market in twenty-seven countries with over 480 million potential customers!

Improvements needed in some sectors

1. Improvements are still needed in certain sectors. For example, the services sector has opened up more slowly than the markets for goods. This was particularly the case for a wide range of financial services, and for transportation, where separate national markets still exist – especially for rail and air transport.
2. There are still some administrative and technical barriers to the free flow of goods and services. These include the reluctance of some EU countries to accept each other's standards of production or specifications. There is still some reluctance to mutually recognise professional qualifications. In particular, these apply in countries where domestic unemployment is still a source of concern.
3. The slow movement towards tax harmonisation of national tax systems has also slowed down market integration and efficiency.

Other European Institutions

The European Investment Bank, see Chapter 17, Money and Banking, pp 165–166.

✳The European Regional Development Fund (ERDF)

As part of its task to promote regional development, the ERDF contributes towards financing the following measures:

1. Productive investment to create and safeguard sustainable jobs.
2. Investment in infrastructure which contributes to the development of sustainable jobs in all eligible regions, and the revitalisation, improved access and regeneration of economic sites and industrial areas suffering from decline.
3. Development of local employment initiatives and the activities of small and medium-sized enterprises.
4. Investment in education and health in regions whose development is lagging behind the rest of the EU.

Projects in Ireland

Some of the projects in Ireland which benefited from the European Regional Development Fund include:

- The Technical Assistance Operational Programme (2000–2006) received €4.9 million out of the programme's total cost of €9.8 million.
- The Economic and Social Infrastructure Operational Programme (2000–2006) (ESIOP) received €905.621 million out of the programme's total cost of €1,566.944 million.
- The Productive Sector Operational Programme received €282.4 million out of the programme's total cost of €844.3 million.

The European Social Fund (ESF)

The European Social Fund (ESF) helps people improve their skills and, consequently, their job prospects. Created in 1957, the ESF is the EU's main source of financial support for efforts to develop employability and human resources. It helps member states combat unemployment, prevents people from dropping out of the labour market, and promotes training to make Europe's workforce and companies better equipped to face new, global challenges.

According to the new European Social fund regulation for 2007–2013, the ESF will provide support for anticipating and managing economic and social change. Its intervention will focus on four key areas for action:

1. Increasing adaptability of workers and enterprises.
2. Enhancing access to employment and participation in the labour market.
3. Reinforcing social inclusion by combating discrimination and facilitating access to the labour market for disadvantaged people.
4. Promoting partnership for reform in the fields of employment and inclusion.

Example of Ireland's Gain from the ESF

Ireland

Project name: Third Level Access Funding
Project duration: 2000–2006
ESF funding: €45,375,000

The Third Level Access Fund was set up to help to maximise the opportunities of certain target groups to access further and higher education and as a consequence to participate fully in the economy, in employment and society through the acquisition of the necessary skills and qualifications required by the economy.

The development of third level access has promoted and continues to promote the participation of students with disabilities, students from disadvantaged backgrounds, including those from the Traveller community, ethnic minorities and mature 'second chance' students, in third level and further education courses.

Source: *European Commission – DG Employment, Social Affairs and Equal Opportunities*

Other projects in Ireland which benefited from ESF finding include:

- The National Framework of Qualifications €7.759 million
- National Traineeship Programme €85.55 million

Table 23.1 shows the total gains which have accrued to Ireland since our accession to the EU in 1973.

***Table 23.1** Statistics on Ireland's Net EU Receipts*

Year	Receipts from EU budgets (€m)	Payments to EU budgets (€m)	Net EU receipts (€m)	% of GDP
2003	2,810.4	1,365.0	1,445.4	1.1%
2002	2,513.1	1,101.7	1,411.4	1.2%
2001	2,488.8	1,220.0	1,268.8	1.1%
2000	2,602.1	1,075.0	1,527.1	1.5%
1999	2,678.9	1,051.0	1,627.9	1.9%
1998	3,015.9	989.4	2,026.5	2.9%
1997	3,179.9	652.0	2,527.9	4.1%
1996	2,818.2	687.1	2,131.1	4.0%
1995	2,568.7	689.2	1,879.5	3.8%
1994	2,338.1	641.9	1,696.2	3.8%
1993	2,850.9	575.8	2,275.1	5.5%
1992	2,531.9	448.7	2,083.2	5.5%
1991	2,795.0	442.2	2,352.8	6.5%
1990	2,210.6	359.2	1,851.4	5.4%
1989	1,644.7	362.6	1,282.1	4.0%
1988	1,474.9	314.6	1,160.3	4.0%
1987	1,397.1	324.0	1,073.1	4.0%
1986	1,455.9	305.1	1,150.8	4.6%
1985	1,433.2	270.9	1,162.3	4.9%
1984	1,100.5	257.1	843.4	4.0%
1983	924.0	234.5	689.5	3.6%
1982	764.5	173.6	590.9	3.5%
1981	643.6	133.8	509.7	3.5%
1980	711.8	112.9	598.9	5.0%
1979	671.8	76.9	594.9	5.9%
1978	520.8	58.5	462.3	5.4%
1977	346.5	28.0	318.5	4.4%
1976	151.7	17.0	134.7	2.3%
1975	138.5	12.4	126.1	2.6%
1974	85.6	7.0	78.6	2.0%
1973	47.1	5.7	41.4	1.2%
1973–2003	**50,914.7**	**13,992.8**	**36,921.9**	

Source: *The Department of Finance*

In this chapter, the information on EU institutions, EU policies and statistics relating to the EU is based on articles on the Europa website, the official website of the EU.

LEARN THE KEY POINTS

1. Explain a free trade area
2. Explain a customs union
3. Understand the Common Market
4. Know the structures of the EU
5. Understand the sources of revenue for the EU budget
6. Learn the Common Agricultural Policy
7. Learn the Common Fisheries Policy
8. Explain the four 'Freedoms of Movement' of the Single European Market
9. Know the benefits of the Single European Market
10. Understand the issues still to be addressed by the Single European Market
11. Understand how the European Investment Bank works (Refer to Chapter 17)
12. Understand how the European Regional Development Fund (ERDF) works
13. Explain what the European Social Fund does

Exam Q&A: See p. 407

1. Distinguish between free trade areas, customs unions and common markets.
2. What are the main functions of the European Parliament?
3. Outline the role of the Council of the European Union.
4. Give a brief outline of the financing of the EU activities.
5. What has been the major shift in the CAP regarding payment to farmers and production levels?
6. Outline the three main elements of the Common Fisheries Policy.
7. Explain the major benefits for consumers of the Single European Market.
8. Explain the major benefits of the Single European Market for the business sector of the economy.
9. Give a brief description of the activities of the European Regional Fund.
10. Outline the role of the European Social Fund.
11. In your opinion. has the enlargement of the EU since 2004 been beneficial, or detrimental, to the Irish economy? Give reasons for your answer.

Chapter 24
Economic Development and Growth

Economic Development

The figures in Table 24.1 are used to give you some idea of the vast difference in the average wealth per person between the rich and the poor nations.

The GDP (gross domestic product) figures are at purchasing power parity (PPP) values. For example, if every product had a price of $1 then the average person in Ireland, based on Table 24.1, could purchase 40,610 products in a year, while the average person in Malawi could only buy 600 products in that year.

The GDP figures at PPP are calculated by various organisations, including the International Monetary Fund and the World Bank. As estimates and assumptions have to be made, the results produced by different organisations for the same country tend to differ. PPP per capita figures are estimates rather than hard facts, and should be used as a guideline to the differing purchasing powers of the citizens of the various nations.

Table 24.1 *Contrasting national incomes*

Rank	Country	GDP (PPP) $ Per Head	Rank	Country	GDP (PPP) $ Per Head
224	Sierra Leone	800 (est.)	1	Luxembourg	69,800
225	Guinea-Bissau	800 (est.)	2	Norway	42,364
226	Burundi	700 (est.)	3	United States	41,399
227	Tanzania	700 (est.)	4	**Ireland**	**40,610**
228	Democratic Republic of The Congo	700 (est.)	5	Iceland	35,115
229	Solomon Islands	600 (est.)	6	Denmark	34,740
230	Comoros	600 (est.)	7	Canada	34,273
231	Somalia	600 (est.)	8	Hong Kong	33,479
232	**Malawi**	**600 (est.)**	9	Austria	33,432
233	Gaza Strip	600 (est.)	10	Switzerland	32,571

Source: *IMF 2005 figures*

In Ireland in 2007, the state contributory old age pension was roughly €10,920, i.e. more than eighteen times the average GDP per person in Malawi.

We no longer make the simple distinction between developed and underdeveloped countries. We now look at two different groupings depending on their state of development. These are **least developed countries** and **developing countries**.

Least developed countries

Least developed countries (LDCs or Fourth World countries) are countries which according to the United Nations exhibit the lowest indicators of socioeconomic development with the lowest Human Development Index ratings of all countries in the world.

The Human Development Index (HDI) is a comparative measure of life expectancy, literacy, education and standard of living for countries worldwide.

A country is classified as a least developed country if it meets three criteria based on:

1. Low-income GNP (gross national product) per capita of less than US$750.
2. Human resource weaknesses based on indicators of nutrition, health, education and adult literacy.
3. Economic vulnerability based on (a) instability of agricultural production, (b) instability in the exports of goods and services, (c) economic importance of non-traditional activities, (d) exports based on one product, (e) the very small size of the economy, and (f) the percentage of population displaced by natural disasters.

Developing countries

A developing country displays the following characteristics:

- They have a relatively low standard of living.
- They have an undeveloped industrial base.
- They have a moderate to low score on the Human Development Index.
- They have low income per head of the population resulting in widespread poverty.
- They have low capital formation.

There is a distinction between economic development and economic growth.

Definition of economic development

Economic development is the process of increasing average income per head while changing the structure of the economy.

Definition of economic growth

Economic growth is the process of increasing average income per head without changing the structure of the economy.

Characteristics of Least Developed and Developing Countries

1. **Poverty trap:** Most people earn subsistence level of income only, i.e. just enough income to keep alive. Therefore, they do not have any savings which are essential to improving their standard of living and they cannot afford to borrow as they could not meet the repayments.

2. **Economic dualism:** The majority of people live in the poverty trap, while there is one region which is very rich, based on some natural wealth, e.g. a mineral ore, which is normally exported. The income from this sector is owned by a very small percentage (usually less than 5 per cent) of the population.

Four imbalances

3. **Imbalanced economy:** The economy is mostly based on agricultural production with little or no manufacturing, construction or service industries.

4. **Imbalanced population structure:** There is a very high proportion of young people and the average life expectancy is 40 years.

5. **Imbalanced distribution of wealth:** This usually translates into roughly 80 per cent of the wealth being owned by 5 per cent of the population.

6. **Imbalanced employment structure:** The vast majority of people work in agriculture. This arises from point 3 above.

Four lacks

7. **Lack of education:** Most people are illiterate and innumerate. These countries cannot afford to establish a national educational system as this requires government income. The governments' income is very low because of the subsistence level of income of the citizens. An uneducated and untrained workforce is not very productive; therefore output per person employed tends to be very small. This also makes it more difficult to attract inward investment from foreign multinational firms.

8. **Lack of infrastructure:** This means very poor roads, and little or no telecommunications. The reason is the same as above. This makes it very difficult for firms to get their products to the consumers.

9. **Lack of capital:** Most production methods are very primitive with little or no machinery used. Capital formation requires savings. As income levels tend to be at subsistence level saving is almost impossible.

10. **Lack of demand:** Because income is very low there is very little demand within the economy, hence no industries are set up, as there is no one to sell to. This makes job creation very difficult.

✳ Sundries

11 **Political corruption.**

12 **Political instability.**

13 **Poor health facilities.**

14 **No financial services sector**, i.e. no banks, insurance companies etc.

15 **High national debt** as a percentage of GNP.

16 **Unfavourable terms of trade:** The export of crops which tend to have low prices internationally and the import of capital goods which, internationally, tend to have high prices.

Requirements for Economic Development

✳ Desire for economic development

Very few people, even in developed countries, become wealthy by accident. They are motivated by a desire to prove that they can accomplish something or simply by a need to improve themselves. Many see opportunities and have the drive and enthusiasm to take advantage of them. In other words, they possess an entrepreneurial spirit.

Likewise, many good political leaders are driven by the desire to improve the living standards of the citizens of their country and appreciate the importance of the creation of wealth. Without this desire by individuals and governments, economic development cannot take place.

Therefore, the first and most essential requirement for any country to achieve economic development is to create this desire among its citizens. This may arise from a demonstration effect from other countries or from political leadership. In particular, it may require a change in cultural, religious and social practices.

✳ Education

Education should be of a utilitarian nature and expenditure should increase in line with the requirements of the economy.

All money spent on education should initially be spent on primary education to create a literate and numerate population. This is essential if people are to learn to improve their agricultural production methods. When this is done, some people can be released from agriculture and become available to work in the manufacturing sector.

As the manufacturing sector begins to develop governments should increase their spending on education and the increased expenditure should go to the secondary sector in order to train people in the skills needed in that sector, e.g. trades and basic office skills.

Likewise, as the services sector begins to develop governments should further increase their expenditure on education and the increased amount should be spent on third level education to provide the professions needed, e.g. the technicians, engineers and scientists.

✳Capital

The development of enterprise is essential to the development of all countries. However, effective enterprises need capital. Initially, this capital may be put in place by attracting direct foreign investment into the countries. This will create employment in these economies and eventually increase incomes to such a level that some savings can take place. These savings can then be invested in indigenous industries ensuring that the profit from these industries remain in the country.

As native industries begin to grow governments' revenue from taxation should increase. This will allow the governments to borrow money from abroad and this can then be used to assist enterprises (businesses), which could create sustainable jobs. Governments should also undertake simple but effective medium-term economic development plans to ensure that the money needed for capital formation is available as required.

✳Increase agricultural production and introduce agricultural reform

The governments should encourage farmers to diversify production so that they are not totally dependent on one cash crop.

Grants and aid should be given to farmers to improve their productivity by using more modern production methods. This would release more workers to be available for employment in manufacturing industries.

Ownership of land tends to be in the hands of a small percentage of the population in these countries. Schemes should be devised to have a more diverse ownership of the land.

✳Infrastructure

Infrastructure would entail the provision of clean water and basic sanitation facilities, the provision of public housing and the development of roads, power supplies and basic communications systems. This is important because no production can take place without a reasonable infrastructure.

✳Trading opportunities

These countries should endeavour to enter trade agreements with other countries to earn foreign currency from exports to pay for imports.

✳Foreign aid

There are many international governmental and non-governmental organisations (NGOs), which can offer and provide technical and financial aid, with no strings attached.

✳ Political stability

Political stability is essential. Thus there must be an end to civil and tribal warfare and a proper political system must be established.

✳ Decrease in birth rate

A smaller number of people sharing the wealth will result in a higher average income. This can be a controversial point, as there are moral, ethical and human rights issues involved.

Note: A question which features occasionally on the Leaving Certificate examination is: 'How can governments of less developed countries help to promote economic development in their own countries?'

To answer this question simply extrapolate the following points from the list and expound on them.

1. Improve basic infrastructure
2. Spend more on education and training
3. Reform agriculture
4. Invest in industrial capital
5. Create incentives for entrepreneurs
6. Promote population control

Developed Countries Helping LDCs

There are various means by which the governments of developed countries can help to promote the economic development of LDCs.

1. **Foreign aid programmes:** Governments can continue with aid to help in emergency situations. They can also provide more long-term aid to help with the development of infrastructure and provision for education and health programmes.
2. **Restructure national debts:** If the respective national debts of these countries were cancelled or restructured the money presently being spent on servicing the debt would become available to each country to use for its own development. (See 'HICP Initiative', p. 261.).
3. **Improve trading opportunities:** The developed countries should improve access to markets in the developed world in order to provide outlets for the exports of the developing countries. Most underdeveloped countries suffer from unfavourable terms of trade. Developed countries could improve the terms of trade available by paying higher prices for the exports of the underdeveloped countries, e.g. 'Fair-Trade'.
4. **Encourage multinationals to set up firms in LDCs:** These could provide the workers with skills. The (fair) wages received could help boost domestic demand and provide tax revenue for the state.
5. **Assist LDCs with available technologies:** The provision of simple technologies to the LDCs could help improve standards of living and increase productive capacity.

Role of the EU

The EU set up **EuropeAid** in 2001. EuropeAid is responsible for implementing all external assistance outside the EU. It is committed to delivering high-quality aid programmes that will have a practical impact on the quality of people's lives, and that will achieve a level of efficiency to meet the highest international standards.

In 2005, the EuropeAid programme managed funds valued at €7.5 billion.

✳The EU and trade with less developed countries

An important issue in enhancing development through trade is that of trade preferences. Preferences mean that developing countries can export a wide range of products to the EU with a preferential customs toll, i.e. paying lower customs duties than other countries. The EU commits around €700 million per year to trade-related assistance.

Fig 24.1 The EU imports from developing countries and from least developed countries

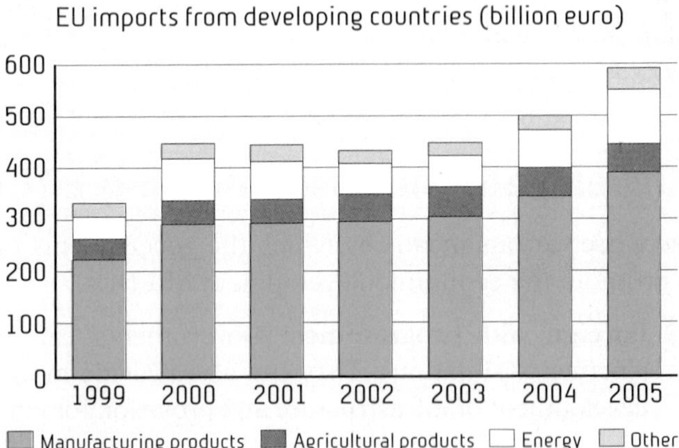

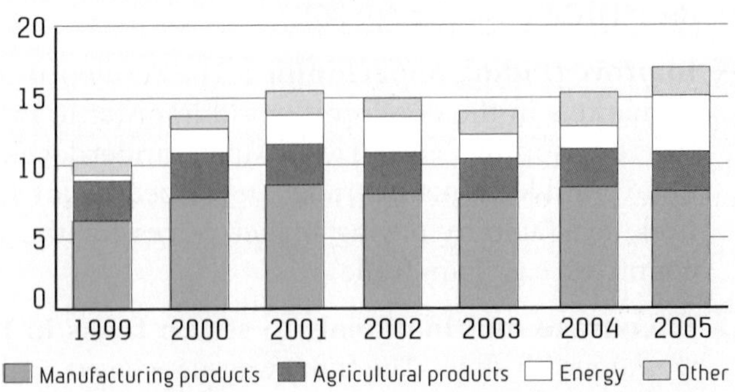

Source: *Europa: EU and World Trade*

Role of the IMF and World Bank

✳The Heavily Indebted Poor Countries (HIPC) Initiative

The HIPC Initiative was first launched in 1996 by the IMF and World Bank, with the aim of ensuring that no poor country faces a debt burden it cannot manage.

To be considered for HIPC Initiative assistance, a country must:

1. Be eligible for IDA assistance (see p. 164).
2. Face an unsustainable debt burden.
3. Establish a track record of reform and sound policies through IMF- and IDA-supported programmes.
4. Have developed a Poverty Reduction Strategy Paper (PRSP). A Poverty Reduction Strategy Paper is a plan for economic development.

Once a country has met or made sufficient progress in meeting these criteria the IMF and IDA formally decide on its eligibility for debt relief, and the international community commits itself to reducing the debt to an agreed sustainable level. This is called the **decision point**. Once a country reaches its decision point, it may immediately begin receiving interim relief on its debt service, i.e. the interest due on the debt.

In order to receive the full and irrevocable reduction in debt available under the HIPC Initiative, however, the country must:

1. Establish a further track record of good performance under IMF- and IDA-supported programmes.
2. Implement satisfactorily key reforms agreed at the decision point.
3. Adopt and implement the PRSP for at least one year.

Once a country has met these criteria, it can reach its completion point, at which time lenders are expected to provide the full debt relief committed at decision point.

Forty countries have been found to be eligible or potentially eligible for HIPC Initiative assistance. These are listed in Table 24.2, on p. 262.

The total cost of providing assistance to the forty countries was estimated to have been about US$64 billion by the end of 2005.

Source: *IMF*

Table 24.2 *List of countries that have qualified or are eligible for HIPC Initiative assistance (as of end of December 2006)*

Post-completion-point countries (21)		
Benin	Honduras	Niger
Bolivia	Madagascar	Rwanda
Burkina Faso	Malawi	Senegal
Cameroon	Mali	Sierra Leone
Ethiopia	Mauritania	Tanzania
Ghana	Mozambique	Uganda
Guyana	Nicaragua	Zambia
Interim countries (between decision and completion point) (9)		
Burundi	Democratic Republic of the Congo	Guinea-Bissau
Chad	The Gambia	Haiti
Republic of Congo	Guinea	São Tomé & Príncipe
Pre-decision-point countries (10)		
Central African Republic	Kyrgyz Republic	Sudan
Comoros	Liberia	Togo
Côte d'Ivoire	Nepal	–
Eritrea	Somalia	–

Source: *IMF*

However, some difficult problems still remain. For example, in countries ravaged by war or natural disasters, the urgent reconstruction, which needs to be undertaken, may mean large new loans at the same time that old debt is being reduced.

Other countries face challenges to meet the criteria for reaching the decision point, due to poor policy records or poor governments resulting from civil conflict.

Finally, some countries (such as Liberia and Sudan) have very large debts and are running arrears to various creditors that will require additional funding for the Initiative to deal with those arrears.

Rostow's Stages of Economic Development

There have been many research studies undertaken to explain the achievement of economic development. The most famous of all of these is that of Walt Rostow (1916–2003), which he originally published in 1995 and was later included in his famous book *The Stages of Economic Growth: A Non-Communist Manifesto*. This is a linear theory of development, i.e. an economy progresses from being a producer of primary goods through to being a producer of secondary goods and finally to being a provider of tertiary services. His research is based on a study of the history of developed countries and he suggests that there was a common pattern of structural change in these economies as outlined below.

✳ 1 The traditional society

In a traditional society all economic activity is carried on at a subsistence level, i.e. the society is a self-sufficient one where people consume the products which they produce. What little trade takes place is done on a barter basis. Labour intensive agriculture is the dominant industry.

✳ 2 The preconditions for take off

At this stage of development specialisation begins to take place and producers produce more than their own requirements. This leads to a growth in trading within the economy and a transport infrastructure is put in place to accommodate this trade. Incomes begin to grow to a level where some savings can take place. These savings are utilised by an emerging entrepreneurial sector and international trade begins to take place based on the exportation of primary products.

✳ 3 The take off

The level of productivity in agriculture increases, thus releasing labour to be employed in the growing industrial sector. The rise of the industrial sector sees a change in the structure of the society with a decline in the rural population and an increase in the urban population. This industrial sector tends to be based in a small number of regions in the country and production is limited to a small number of manufacturing industries. However, investment in the economy is now in the region of 10 per cent of the national income. The increased level of investment leads to increased incomes, which in turn leads to increased level of demand. This becomes self-sustaining in the sense that the increase in demand leads to an increase in investment, which in turn leads to an increased level of income, which in turn leads to more savings and so on.

At the same time, political and social structures are put in place, which assist this sustained level of economic activity.

✳ 4 The drive to maturity

Incomes continue to rise and the economy now diversifies into new industries, many of them being import substitutes. The use of technological innovation creates a new range of investment opportunities and the economy now produces a wider range of goods and services. The level of international trade increases both in value and in volume. This is accompanied by a growth in the infrastructure required for such a level of economic activity, e.g. harbours, airports and communications. The movement of population from the rural areas to the towns and cities continues. At this stage up to 20 per cent of national income is reinvested in the economy.

✳ 5 The age of mass consumption

In the age of mass consumption, a large part of the population has moved beyond meeting their basic needs. Leading sectors of the economy are producing consumer durable goods, e.g. cars. The service sector becomes increasingly dominant and accounts for the highest proportion of employment. The society is now predominantly an urban or even suburban society. The infrastructure is now highly developed providing very good transport, communications and social services.

✳The post-industrial society

Many modern economists add in a sixth stage, i.e. the post-industrial society. This is characterised by a very high level of productivity due to the use of very sophisticated technology. Thus more goods can be produced in less time. This leads to a greater emphasis on a shorter working week and a greater desire for more leisure time. At this stage of development, people's desire for an improvement in their quality of living is greater than their desire for the acquisition of more goods.

Governments are also aware of the need to provide better social welfare benefits for the less privileged sector of society and also to prioritise spending on health and advanced education.

✳Criticisms of Rostow's theory

1. His analysis of the take off and drive to maturity stages are very vague.
2. His analysis is based on a historical study of developed countries. Economic problems are, by their very nature, dynamic. What worked for other countries years ago may not work in today's environment.
3. Many development economists argue that Rostow's model was developed with Western cultures in mind and may not be applicable to many of the LDCs.
4. His analysis ignores the needs of individuals and concentrates on theoretical models. Increased output does not always 'trickle down' to increase the average income per head.
5. His analysis based a great amount of emphasis on the ability of the developing nations to save up to 20 per cent of their national income for investment and capital acquisition purposes. The global movement of capital investment decreases this necessity as multinational companies often provide this capital. Likewise, there are now very many international aid organisations which can speed up this process for the LDCs.

Economic Growth

So far in this chapter we have only dealt with economic development. You may recall that we distinguished between economic development and economic growth at the start of the chapter and stated that economic growth was the process of increasing the average income per head of the population without changing the structure of the economy or society. The concept of economic growth assumes that we are dealing with a developed economy. Thus it is dealing with measures which increase our national income. We have already dealt with this in Chapter 19, Factors Determining the Size of the National Income. Thus it is through the management of C + I + G + X – M that we achieve this growth.

However, it is important to understand that a country's economy cannot just develop and then remain at a standstill. It either progresses or regresses. This is due to the nature of capital investment. If a country's economy does not maintain a certain level of reinvestment its productive capacity will decrease as its older capital goods lose their efficiency. Also technology is improving on an ongoing basis. If a country does not invest in the new technology it will lose its international competitive edge.

To achieve economic growth a country needs to invest and reinvest more and more of its resources in capital goods. However, the production of capital goods has an opportunity cost on the amount of consumer goods we purchase. Remember that the resources of any economy are scarce and have alternative uses. This is highlighted by the productive possibility curve (PPC), see Fig 24.2.

Definition of a production possibility curve (PPC)

A **production possibility curve (PPC)** is a graph that shows the different quantities of two goods that an economy could produce with limited productive resources. Points along the curve describe the trade-off between the two goods. The curve shows that increasing the production of one good reduces production of the other good.

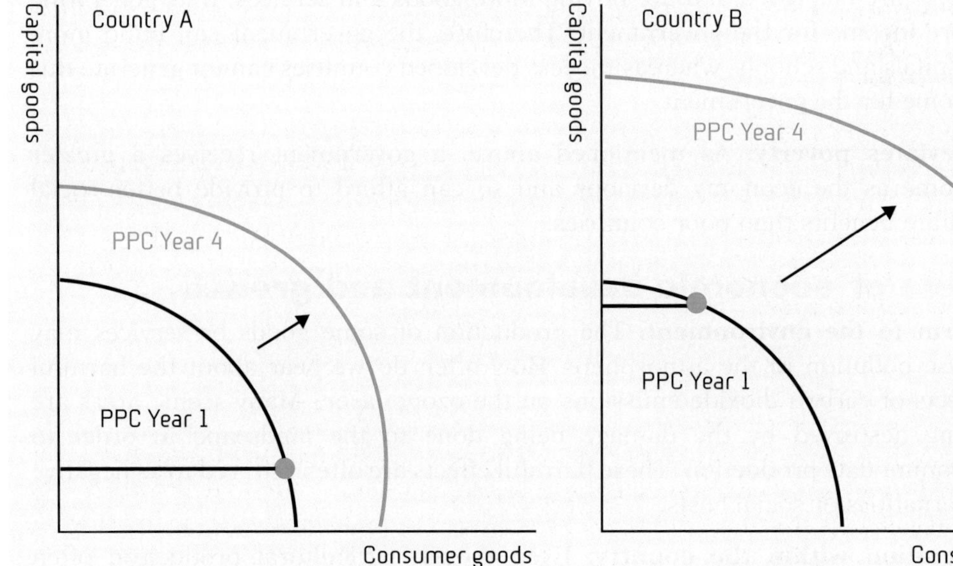

***Fig 24.2** The productive possibility curve (PPC)*

These diagrams show that if we sacrifice consumer goods for capital goods in the short term our options become greater in the succeeding years. The diagram on the right shows that the extra investment made in Country B in Year 1 gave it a greater productive capacity in Year 4 than Country A.

✳ Balanced vs unbalanced development

Balanced development refers to the development of all sectors of an economy at the same time, so that the producers in one sector become the consumers in another sector.

Unbalanced development refers to the development of certain sectors of the economy only. The sectors developed would be those sectors in which the country had some natural or native advantage, e.g. mining or crop growing. This would leave gaps in the economy which would eventually be filled by entrepreneurship.

✳ Benefits of economic development and growth

1. **Improves the standard of living:** As average income per person increases this gives greater purchasing power to consumers. Thus they will be able to purchase more and better food, improve their own housing and purchase more consumer goods such as televisions, fridges and cars.
2. **Provides more employment:** As demand increases in an economy this creates not only more jobs but also a greater range of jobs. Thus people with different skills can be used to greater advantage as the economy develops and grows.
3. **Generates more tax revenue for the government:** As a country develops more people are employed and are buying more goods and services, thus generating more income for the government. Therefore, the government can build more hospitals and schools, whereas the less developed countries cannot generate this income for the government.
4. **Alleviates poverty:** As mentioned above, a government receives a greater income as the economy develops and so can afford to provide better social welfare benefits than poor countries.

✳ Costs of economic development and growth

1. **Harm to the environment:** The production of some goods or services may cause pollution in the atmosphere. How often do we hear about the harmful effects of carbon dioxide emissions on the ozone layer? Many scenic areas are being destroyed by the damage being done to the landscape in order to accommodate production. These harmful effects are often referred to as negative externalities or social costs.
2. **Migration within the country:** Even though agricultural production often increases as the economy develops, the increased production is due to the extended use of technology. Thus the employment opportunities in rural areas decrease. This causes migration into the larger towns and cities which are

probably already overcrowded. Increase in wealth does not guarantee an improvement in the quality of life. Thus the urban population increases at the expense of the rural population. This can have detrimental effects on the structure of our society.

3 **The benefits of economic development are not always evenly distributed:** The concept of 'trickle down economics' does not always apply. This often causes a greater divide in society where the gap between the wealthy and the not so wealthy people increases.

4 **Standard of living versus quality of living:** While the standard of living may improve, the quality of living may not improve accordingly. As individuals become more successful in the commercial world they may have to work under very stressful conditions and this may take its toll on their health. Many others have to commute long distances to and from work leaving them little or no time to enjoy home-life or to engage in their hobbies. One of the growing problems facing Irish society is the dwindling number of people who can offer their time in the voluntary sector of our communities.

LEARN THE KEY POINTS

1. The definition of economic development
2. The definition of economic growth
3. Learn the characteristics of less developed countries
4. Understand the requirements for economic development
5. Explain how the governments of the LDCs can assist in the economic development of their own countries
6. Explain how the governments of foreign countries can assist the LDCs in the economic development of their countries
7. Understand the role of the IMF and the World Bank in assisting LDCs
8. Explain the role of capital investment in economic growth
9. Define a production possibility curve and give an example
10. Understand the benefits of economic development
11. Understand the costs of economic development

Questions

Exam Q&A: See p. 408

1 Distinguish between least developed countries and developing countries.

2 Distinguish between economic development and economic growth.

3 Distinguish between balanced and unbalanced development.

4 What is the Human Development Index?

5 Give a detailed account of the characteristics of least developed and developing countries.

6 The desire to acquire wealth, a good utilitarian system of education and a growth in capital are essential for economic development. Explain the role of these three factors in the achieving of economic development.

7 Discuss any other four factors which are required to achieve economic development.

8 Name and explain the five stages of economic development as identified by Rostow.

9 What are the weaknesses in Rostow's theory of development? Explain your answer.

10 Describe the role of the Heavily Indebted Poor Countries (HIPC) Initiative.

11 Give a brief description of the means by which the EU assists LDCs.

12 'Multinational companies who locate to underdeveloped countries simply exploit the cheap labour available in these countries and do not assist in the economic development of these countries.' Comment on this statement.

13 Why is continuous investment necessary to maintain economic growth? Explain your answer.

14 Economic development can carry certain costs. Give an explanation of these costs.

Chapter 25
International Trade

We are all familiar with the concept of international trade and we use words associated with international trade in our everyday language. However, these words are frequently misused so we will start this topic by defining some of these terms.

Definitions

- **Exports** are any goods or services provided by the residents of a country which cause money to come into the country.
- **Imports** are any goods or services purchased by the residents of a country which cause money to leave the country.
- **Visible exports** are any physical (merchant) goods provided by the residents of a country which cause money to come into the country, e.g. food, computer chips and pharmaceutical goods.
- **Invisible exports** are any services provided by the residents of a country which cause money to come into the country, e.g. tourists coming into Ireland, winnings by Irish golfers playing abroad which are returned to Ireland and non-residents using an Irish airline.
- **Visible imports** are any physical goods purchased by the residents of a country which cause money to leave the country, e.g. cars, timber and electrical products brought into the country.
- **Invisible imports** are any services purchased by the residents of a country which cause money to leave the country, e.g. residents of a country going on holidays abroad, foreign pop groups playing in Ireland and repatriating the income earned here.

Reasons for International Trade

Countries participate in international trade for the following reasons:

1. Countries import in order to obtain raw materials and capital goods which are not available in their own country.
2. Countries import in order to obtain consumer goods which cannot be made, or cannot be made at a reasonable price, in their own country.

3. Countries export in order to earn foreign currency to pay for their imports.
4. Countries export in order to increase their production levels to obtain the benefits of the economies of scale.
5. Countries export in order to sell off their surplus production.
6. Countries export in order to create employment in their own country, which would not otherwise be created.
7. Countries export in order to increase their national income and thus their standard of living.
8. Countries export in order to create economic growth or to stimulate economic recovery.

The Balance of Payments

The balance of payments is a record of the economic transactions of a country with the rest of the world. It is made up of three sections or accounts, the **current account**, the **capital account** and the **financial account**. The balance of payments should balance in the accounting sense, because if all of the transactions result in a movement of money out of the country, this can only be done by showing the change in our international debt or by decreasing our holding of foreign currency, i.e. our external reserves and vice versa.

The current account

The current account shows:

1. The difference between the value of visible exports and visible imports, known as the **balance of trade** or the balance on visible trade.
2. The difference between the value of invisible exports and invisible imports, known as the **balance on invisible trade**.
3. Net factor income from abroad which covers items such as interest and dividends and repatriation of profits as explained in Chapter 18, Measuring the National Income.
4. Net current transfers from abroad such as subsidies and other current transfers receivable from and taxes payable to the EU; also payments under Third World aid programmes operated by non-governmental organisations (NGOs) and transfers related to non-life insurance business.

The capital account

The capital account covers amounts receivable under the EU Regional Development Fund and the Cohesion Fund and all other transfers intended for capital purposes.

✳The financial account

The financial account is concerned with transactions in foreign financial assets and liabilities under four headings, i.e. direct investment, portfolio investment, other investments and reserve assets.

A summary of all of these transactions is shown in Table 25.1.

Table 25.1 *Ireland's balance of payments for 1 January 2007 to 31 March 2007*

Current account	€m
Balance on visible trade	5,336
Balance on invisible trade	– 880
Net factor income	– 6,999
Current transfers	– 728
Capital account balance	30
Balance on current account	– 3,241
Financial account	
Direct investment	3,654
Portfolio investment	– 6,331
Other investments	2,220
Reserve assets	– 47
Balance	– 504
+ Net errors and omissions	3,745
Balance on financial account	3,241

Source: *CSO*

Definitions

- **Direct investment** refers to the net difference between the amounts of money invested in Irish-based enterprises by non-residents of Ireland and the amounts invested by residents of Ireland in foreign-based enterprises.
- **Portfolio investments** cover the buying and selling of shares and other forms of ownership of businesses other than directly setting up enterprises.
- **Other investments:** The bulk of the transactions under this heading deal with the interest flows of credit institutions, i.e. the difference between interest paid into these institutions from abroad and the amount of interest sent out of the country by them.

- **Reserve assets** have been defined by the ECB as: '(a) qualifying assets which are under the effective control of the national monetary authority (i.e. the Central Bank and Financial Services Authority of Ireland), and (b) consisting of highly liquid, marketable and credit-worthy foreign (non-euro) currency denominated claims on non euro-area residents together with gold, special drawing rights (SDRs) and the reserve position in the IMF.'
- **Net errors and omissions:** Arise from the incomplete reporting of balance of payments transactions and to the difficulty of tracking increasingly complex international financial transactions. They can only be calculated by subtracting the actual change in the value of our Reserve Asset from the change which should have occurred from the known transactions. This is frequently referred to as either 'the net residual' or 'the black hole in the economy'.

Source: *CSO*

The Terms of Trade

The terms of trade is the relationship between the average price received for a unit of exports and the average price paid for a unit of imports. It reflects the number of units of imports which can be purchased with a unit of exports.

The formula used to measure it is:

$$\frac{\text{The Index of Export Prices}}{\text{The Index of Import Prices}} \times 100$$

If the answer to this is **> 100** we are then said to have **favourable terms of trade**, i.e. the average price of a unit of exports is greater than the average price of a unit of imports.

If the answer to this is **< 100** we are then said to have **unfavourable terms of trade**, i.e. the average price of a unit of imports is greater than the average price of a unit of exports.

In Table 25.2 on p. 273 we can see how the terms of trade was calculated. In 2002, The Index of Export Prices of 118.5, divided by the Index of Import Prices of 126.7 and multiplied by 100 = 93.5 to the nearest decimal place.

A **favourable movement** in the terms of trade occurs when the index increases in value regardless of whether the numbers are > or <100. For example, if the index changes from 89 to 94 this is a favourable movement in the terms of trade.

An **unfavourable movement** in the terms of trade occurs when the index decreases in value. For example, if the index changes from 110 to 108 this is an unfavourable movement in the terms of trade.

It is possible for a country to have unfavourable terms of trade and at the same time to have a favourable balance of trade.

Table 25.2 Volume, price and terms of trade indices

Year	Volume index		Price index		Terms of trade
	Imports	Exports	Imports	Exports	Index
1990	100.0	100.0	100.0	100.0	100.0
1991	100.8	105.6	102.3	99.3	97.0
1992	105.6	121.1	100.2	96.6	96.4
1993	113.0	133.4	105.4	103.9	98.6
1994	127.9	153.2	108.1	103.8	96.0
1995	146.3	184.0	112.7	105.7	93.7
1996	160.9	202.2	111.4	105.1	94.3
1997	184.8	232.4	112.0	106.3	94.9
1998	218.3	289.2	114.6	109.1	95.2
1999	236.5	336.5	118.0	109.5	92.8
2000	275.2	401.4	128.0	115.0	89.9
2001	274.2	422.0	131.8	120.9	91.7
2002	276.6	435.1	126.7	118.5	93.5
2003	259.7	418.4	116.1	108.0	93.0
2004	283.6	446.5	113.5	104.0	91.7
2005	316.3	456.7	114.4	104.5	91.3
2006	317.7	457.4	120.0	104.4	87.0

Source: *CSO*

Note: The indices for import and export prices are given to the nearest single decimal place and may not exactly tally, in all cases, with the Terms of Trade Index.

Example

The average price received for a unit of exports = €10
The average price paid for a unit of imports = €15
This = unfavourable terms of trade

Total quantity of exports = 2,000 units, therefore value of exports = €20,000
Total quantity of imports = 1,000 units, therefore value of imports = €15,000
This = favourable balance of trade

It is possible for a country to have favourable terms of trade and at the same time to have an unfavourable balance of trade.

Example

The average price received for a unit of exports = €15
The average price paid for a unit of imports = €10
This = favourable terms of trade

Total quantity of exports = 1,000 units therefore value of exports = €15,000
Total quantity of imports = 2,000 units therefore value of imports = €20,000
This = unfavourable balance of trade

Laws Governing International Trade

✳The Law of Absolute Advantage

Definition of the Law of Absolute Advantage

The **Law of Absolute Advantage** states that countries will benefit from trade so long as each of the countries trading has an absolute advantage in the production of one of the goods.

A country has an absolute advantage when it uses less of its resources to produce one unit of a product than the other country uses.

Example

Assume there are two countries A and B and that they produce two products X and Y and that each can produce the following quantities with a given amount of resources:

Table 25.3 *Position before specialisation*

	Product X	Product Y
Country A	300	100
Country B	600	50
Total production	**900**	**150**

Here country A has an absolute advantage in the production of Y and country B has an absolute advantage in the production of X (i.e. a ratio of 2:1 in each case).

They now specialise in the production of these products and, allowing for constant returns to scale (i.e. if you double the inputs output will double), the figures will now read as follows.

Table 25.4 *Position after specialisation*

	Product X	Product Y
Country A	0	200
Country B	1,200	0
Total production	**1,200**	**200**

It can be seen that the total production of both products has increased.

The countries now trade with each other and the final figures are as shown in the table below.

Table 25.5 *Position after trade*

	Product X	Product Y
Country A	400	120
Country B	800	80
Total production	**1,200**	**200**

Both countries have gained from the trade.

✳The Law of Comparative/Relative Advantage

David Ricardo (see p. 353) first stated the Law of Comparative/Relative Advantage in 1817 in Chapter 7 of his publication *On The Principles of Political Economy and Taxation*.

Definition of the Law of Comparative/Relative Advantage

The **Law of Comparative/Relative Advantage** states that countries should trade with each other and will gain mutual benefit from the trade if they specialise in the production of those goods and services in which they are relatively most efficient and obtain their other requirements through trade.

The actual words used by Ricardo were that trade 'diffuses general benefit' to the participating countries.

Example

Make the same assumptions as in the Law of Absolute Advantage. The figures before specialisation are as shown below.

Table 25.6 *Position before specialisation*

	Product X	Product Y
Country A	1,000	2,100
Country B	250	700
Total production	**1,250**	**2,800**

It can be seen that country A has an absolute advantage in the production of both products, however it is relatively more efficient in the production of X, i.e. 4:1 compared to 3:1. Therefore, A should produce X and leave the production of Y to B (B is least inefficient in the production of Y).

The figures after specialisation are shown in Table 25.7. These assume that there are constant returns to scale, i.e. if you double the resources used to produce a product you will double the output

Table 25.7 *Position after specialisation*

	Product X	Product Y
Country A	2,000	0
Country B	0	1,400
Total production	**2,000**	**1,400**

They now trade with each other and the figures after trade are as shown in Table 25.8.

Table 25.8 *Position after trade*

	Product X	Product Y
Country A	1,600	1,050
Country B	400	350
Total production	**2,000**	**1,400**

⁎Proof of gain

Country A

Before specialisation A had 1,000 units of X, it now has 1,600, a gain of 600/1,000, i.e. **+ 60%**

Before specialisation A had 2,100 units of Y, it now has 1,050, a loss of 1,050/2,100, i.e. **– 50%**

This gives A an overall gain of 10%.

Country B

Before specialisation B had 250 units of X, it now has 400, a gain of 150/250, i.e. **+ 60%**

Before specialisation B had 700 units of Y, it now has 350, a loss of 350/700, i.e. **– 50%**

This gives B an overall gain of 10%.

Note: Adopt the following procedure when trading the goods to ensure mutual benefit from the trade. Distribute the goods so that the countries maintain the same ratio of the goods as they had before any specialisation took place. For example, before specialisation the ratio between countries A and B for product X was 4:1. Distribute the 2,000 units of X produced by A after specialisation in the ratio of 4:1 between A and B, i.e. 1,600 to A and 400 to Y. Distribute Y in the ration of 3:1.

Assumptions Governing the Laws of Absolute and Comparative Advantage

1. There is free trade between the countries. This means that there are no restrictions on the importation of goods and governments do not place any taxes on the imports. See below.
2. Transport costs are negligible. This assumes that the cost of transporting the goods from one country to the other does not negate the absolute or comparative advantage which the exporter enjoyed.
3. There is mobility of the factors of production. When specialisation takes place in a country it is assumed that the factors of production, which were made redundant by the closure of one industry, can be employed in the 'specialised' industry.
4. The benefits of the trade are distributed throughout the economies. This assumes that both countries will benefit equally from the trade and that all citizens in both countries will share the benefits of the trade.
5. There are constant returns to scale. This states that production of a good will increase in proportion to the increase in the factors of production being used to produce it, e.g. if you double the resources being used to produce a product you will double the production of that good.

Free Trade

✳Arguments for free trade

The arguments for free trade are based on the gains arising from the Laws of Absolute and Comparative Advantage so that countries can engage in international trade for the reasons mentioned earlier (see p. 269).

✳Arguments against free trade

The arguments against free trade are sometimes referred to as **protectivism**.

To protect employment

Trade unions often argue that the importation of goods results in the closure of domestic firms, thus creating unemployment. Unemployment also has adverse effects on the government's budget as it gets in less revenue in income taxes and has to pay out more money in dole payments. For these reasons, people call for the banning of imported goods which could be substituted for domestically produced goods.

Infant industry argument

If a country establishes a new industry, which has the potential to be internationally competitive, it may protect this industry on the domestic market against competition from similar foreign goods until that industry grows and obtains the benefits of the economies of scale. Then the protection is removed and the industry should be able to compete against similar industries in other countries.

To protect the balance of payments

If a country has a continuous deficit on its balance of trade, one of the simplest ways of rectifying this, in the short run, is to curtail imports until the basic flaw in the economy can be corrected. This is used as an argument for protectionism in the short run.

To protect against competition from low wage countries

It is often argued that developed countries with reasonably high wage rates cannot compete with goods coming from countries with very low wage rates. It is argued that employees in these low-wage-rate countries are being exploited and therefore we should not trade with them until the employees are paid a decent wage rate.

To maintain government revenue

Some countries might argue that their governments have come to depend on the revenue generated by customs duties and that they may have to operate deficit budgets and increase their national debt if these duties were abolished.

For strategic purposes

Many countries do not want to be dependent on other countries for the supply of essential products such as food and oil. Therefore, they call for protection of these industries in their own countries to ensure a supply of them in emergency situations, e.g. during a war.

To prevent dumping

Dumping occurs when a country sells its surplus production on a foreign market at less than cost price, or at a price lower than that prevailing on the domestic market. This is done to increase revenue from a batch of goods which has already yielded a profit on its own domestic market.

Retaliatory measure

A country can use a lack of free trade as a retaliatory measure for not having access to another country's market. Sometimes countries may have free access to sell their goods on foreign markets, but they in turn do not grant free access to their own domestic markets to other countries. Therefore, the countries that are deprived access to these markets will refuse to continue importing until access is granted, 'If you do not take our goods we will not take your goods!'

Strict domestic laws governing production

Some countries have to abide by strict production, environmental and labour laws which do not apply to their competitors.

Irish beef producers would argue the EU regulations governing the production and distribution of beef impose additional costs which do not apply to Brazilian beef producers. While these regulations benefit the consumer in the form of a guaranteed, high-quality product, many consumers may opt to purchase cheaper imported beef. The additional costs involved in complying with these regulations mean that Irish beef producers cannot compete on a price basis, thus giving the importers an unfair advantage.

Means of restricting free trade

1. **Customs duties/tariffs:** These are taxes levied on imported goods to make them more expensive than domestically produced goods. When price goes up demand usually goes down. Therefore, these tariffs should reduce the demand for imported goods.

2. **Embargoes:** This is a complete ban on the importation of certain goods.

3. **Quotas:** This is setting a limit on the number of units of a product which can be imported.

4. **Exchange control regulations:** This is a system where the Central Bank does not make foreign currency available to importers to pay for their goods. Therefore, they are unable to place orders for imports.

5. **Administrative regulations:** Here the government imposes so many regulations on specifications, certificates, form filling and so on that it discourages importers from importing.

6. **Subsidies to domestic producers:** Here the government pays a subsidy, i.e. direct payment per unit produced, to domestic producers of goods so that

they can sell their products on the home market at a cheaper price than the imported goods.

It must be remembered that none of these measures can be used for trade between EU member countries.

The World Trade Organisation and the General Agreement on Tariffs and Trade

The original General Agreement on Tariffs and Trade, now referred to as GATT 1947, provided the basic rules of the multilateral trading system from 1 January 1948 until the World Trade Organisation (WTO) was established in 1995.

The World Trade Organisation aims to lower trade barriers and encourage multilateral trade. It monitors members' adherence to GATT agreements and negotiates and implements new agreements.

Multilateral trade means trade between many countries, as distinct from bilateral trade, which is trade between two countries only. In a multilateral trade situation a country does not necessarily import from the countries to which it exports.

In order to prevent two countries negotiating bilateral trading arrangements that could be detrimental to the interests of a third country, the concept of 'The Most Favoured Nation' was introduced. Under the WTO agreements, countries cannot normally discriminate between their trading partners. If one country grants another country a particular concession, e.g. the removal of customs duties, then that concession must be granted to all other members of the World Trade Organisation.

The work of the WTO is carried out by means of rounds of negotiations. The two most important of these were the Uruguay Round and the more recent Doha Round.

But the WTO is not just about liberalising trade. In some circumstances its rules support maintaining trade barriers, e.g. to protect consumers or to prevent the spread of disease.

Factors Affecting the Competitiveness of Irish-Based Firms in International Trade

1. **The rate of inflation in Ireland versus the rate of inflation in competitors' countries:** If the Irish rate of inflation is higher than that of our competitors on the export market then the Irish-based firms' goods are at a price disadvantage and vice versa.

2. **The value of the euro versus the value of other currencies:** If the value of the euro rises against other currencies then the price of Irish goods will increase on non-EU markets, thus putting them at a price disadvantage and vice versa.

3 **Transport costs:** As Ireland is an island away from the mainstream big markets, Irish firms have additional transport costs, which have to be added to the selling price of the goods.

4 **Labour costs:** The scarcity of labour in Ireland has put upward pressure on the wage rate, thus increasing the costs of production for Irish-based firms. Unless these costs are matched by similar increases in productivity the prices of goods produced here will rise thus putting Irish-based firms at a disadvantage on the international market. Immigration into Ireland has helped to reduce this pressure in recent times.

5 **Social partnership agreements and national wage agreements:** Up to recently (2007) these have ensured a relatively peaceful industrial climate in Ireland and have helped to control the rate of inflation here. However, there are signs that these agreements may be nearing an end. Unless they are replaced with some meaningful alternative there could be industrial chaos in the country resulting in an adverse effect on the international competitiveness of Irish-based firms.

6 **Poor infrastructure:** It is often stated that Ireland has a First World productive economy but a Third World infrastructure. This is an external diseconomy of scale for Irish-based firms, thus reducing their competitiveness on the international market. However, this problem is addressed in the National Development Plan (see p. 232).

7 **Government policies:** These can have a mixed effect on the competitiveness of Irish-based firms. For example, increases in VAT have caused prices to rise, but low profit taxes are a boost to these firms.

Statistics Relating to Irish Trade

Table 25.9 *Ireland's main trading partners, 2006*

Country	Imports €m	Exports €m
Great Britain and Northern Ireland	19,393.6	15,550.1
Other EU countries	17,139.2	39,291.0
USA	6,811.3	16,207.1
Rest of World	17,423.9	15,810.6
Total	**60,768.0**	**86,858.8**

Source: *CSO*

Table 25.10 *Ireland's main trading partners 2003*

Country	Imports €m	Exports €m
Great Britain and Northern Ireland	14,680.0	14,870.2
Other EU countries	11,822.6	35,470.4
USA	7,390.0	16,923.8
Rest of World	13,632.4	14,911.1
Total	**47,525.0**	**82,175.5**

Source: *CSO*

Note: The increase in imports is far greater than the increase in exports.

LEARN THE KEY POINTS

1. The definition of an export
2. The definition of an import
3. The definitions of visible imports and exports
4. The definitions of invisible imports and exports
5. Explain the reasons countries engage in international trade
6. Define the balance of payments
7. Define the balance of trade
8. Define the balance on the current account
9. Define the capital account
10. Explain the net residual or the 'black hole' in the balance of payments
11. Define the terms of trade
12. Know the difference between favourable and unfavourable terms of trade
13. Define and give an example of the Law of Absolute Advantage
14. Define and prove the Law of Comparative Advantage
15. Know the assumptions governing these two laws
16. Know the arguments for and against free trade
17. Know the means of restricting free trade
18. Understand the aims of the World Trade Organisation
19. Know what is meant by 'The Most Favoured Nation' concept

Exam Q&A: See p. 411

Copy questions 1–5 into your answer book and complete each of the sentences by filling in the blank spaces.

1 A visible export is any __________ product provided by the __________ of a country which causes money to __________ the country.

2 An invisible import is any __________ purchased by the __________ of a country which causes money to __________ the country.

3 The balance of trade is the difference between the __________ of a country's __________ exports and the __________ of its __________.

4 The balance of invisible trade is the difference between the __________ of a country's __________ exports and the __________ of its __________.

5 A country has favourable terms of trade when the __________ received for a unit of __________ is greater than the __________ paid for a unit of __________.

6 Distinguish between a country's balance of trade and its terms of trade.

7 Explain the term 'a favourable movement in the terms of trade'.

8 Distinguish between net factor income and current transfers as used in calculating the balance on the current account.

9 Distinguish between embargoes and quotas as means of restricting free trade.

10 How has Ireland's participation in international trade benefited its economy?

11 Two countries, A and B, can produce the following quantities of goods with any given amount of resources:

Table 25.11

	Product X	Product Y
Country A	5,000	500
Country B	600	6,000
Total production	**5,600**	**6,500**

(a) State the law which dictates that these countries should trade with each other.

(b) Show and explain how these countries will benefit from the trade.

12 Two countries, A and B, can produce the following quantities of goods with any given amount of resources:

Table 25.12

	Product X	Product Y
Country A	100	200
Country B	400	600
Total production	**500**	**800**

(a) State the law which dictates that these countries should trade with each other.

(b) Apply this law to this situation and show how each country gains from the trade.

13 Using the figures in question 11 calculate the limits within which the terms of trade would lie for both products X and Y.

14 The following prices apply to a country's export and import prices: the average price received for a unit of export is €20 and the average price paid for a unit of imports is €25. Is it possible for this country to have a favourable balance of trade? Explain your answer with the aid of absolute figures.

15 (a) State and explain the assumptions governing the Law of Comparative/Relative Advantage.

(b) Do all of these assumptions hold true for Ireland? Explain your answer.

16 Give a brief outline of the role which the World Trade Organisation plays in international trade.

17 Give a brief outline of the arguments which are used against free trade between countries.

18 Give a brief outline of what you believe are Ireland's competitive advantages in international trade.

Chapter 26
Demand for Factors of Production

Derived Demand

The demand for a factor of production is a derived demand. It is derived from the demand for the goods being produced by a firm. Therefore, as the demand for the firm's product increases there is the tendency to employ extra units of a factor of production.

Briefly let us remind ourselves of two concepts which we have already discussed.

Definition of marginal physical product (MPP)

Marginal physical product (MPP) of a factor of production is the addition to total production caused by employing an extra unit of a factor of production.

Definition of marginal revenue product (MRP)

Marginal revenue product (MRP) of a factor of production is the addition to total revenue (income) caused by employing an extra unit of a factor of production.

A Factor of Production

A firm will employ a factor of production when the cost of employing it is not greater than the extra revenue it creates, i.e. its MRP. In this way, the firm is either making a profit from employing the extra factor or at least breaking even on it. If the cost is greater than the extra revenue then it would not pay the firm to employ the extra factor.

Let us look at the production and revenue figures for a firm as it employs extra units of a given factor of production. Here we are assuming that the price (AR) remains constant no matter how many units are produced and sold. You may remember that this holds true in perfect competition.

Note that these output figures are the same as those used when demonstrating the Law of Diminishing Returns in (see p. 71).

Table 26.1 *Production and revenue figures of a firm*

Qty of a factor	Total output	MPP	AR (price per unit sold)	TR (total output x AR)	MRP, (MPP x AR)
1	500	500	€100	€50,000	€50,000
2	1,200	700	€100	€120,000	€70,000
3	1,950	750	€100	€195,000	€75,000
4	2,400	450	€100	€240,000	€45,000
5	2,800	400	€100	€280,000	€40,000
6	3,000	200	€100	€300,000	€20,000
7	3,100	100	€100	€310,000	€10,000

The graph in Fig 26.1 is roughly based on the figures above and is the normal graph showing the total production for a factor of production. Notice that total production increases at a decreasing rate as each extra unit of the factor is employed. This is due to the Law of Diminishing Returns, as we are adding a variable factor to another fixed factor or factors.

Fig 26.1 *Total product curve*

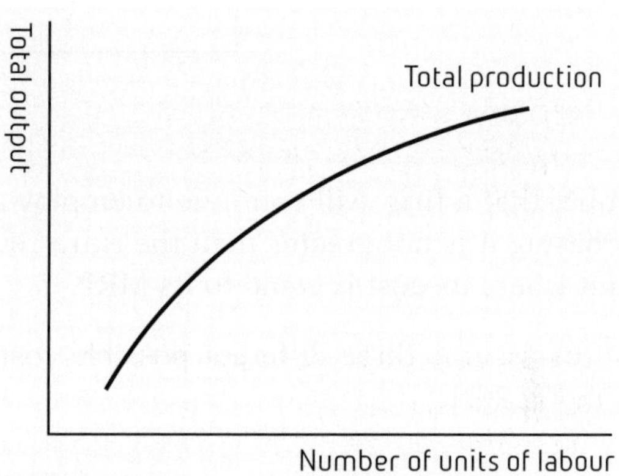

Now let us draw a graph of the MPP of this factor based on the figures above. This is shown in Fig 26.2.

Fig 26.2 *MPP curve*

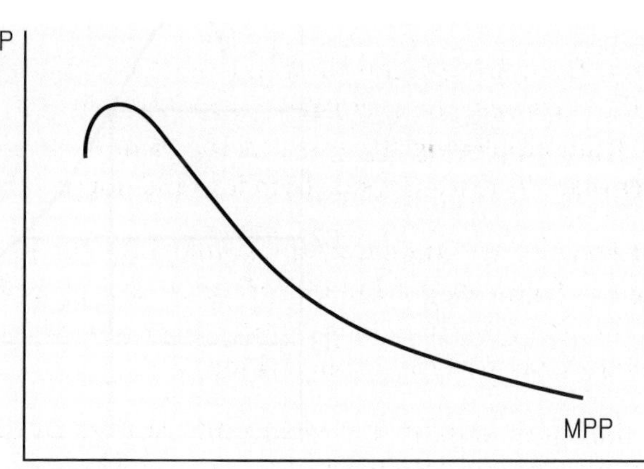

In order to meet the extra demand for its product the firm is obviously interested in the extra production created by each extra unit of the factor. However, it is even more interested in the extra revenue, MRP, which this brings in to the firm, as the extra revenue must be balanced against the cost of that extra unit of the factor.

If we multiply the MPP by the price we get the MRP. This is shown in the figures above. If we were to graph these MRP figures the graph would be shaped as that shown in Fig 26.3.

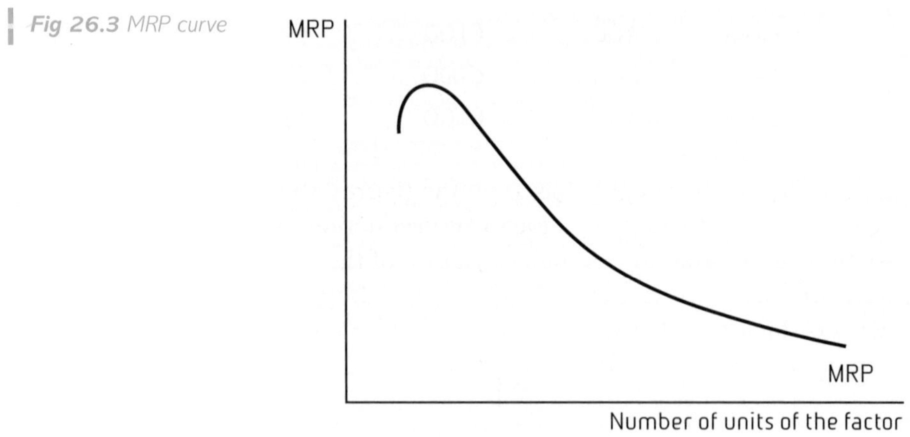

Fig 26.3 *MRP curve*

Remember that a firm will continue to employ a factor of production until the cost of purchasing it is not greater than the extra revenue it creates (its MRP), i.e. up to the point where its cost is equal to its MRP.

Now let us assume three different possible costs for this factor: C1, C2 and C3, as shown in Fig 26.4.

Fig 26.4 *MRP curve equals demand curve for a factor of production*

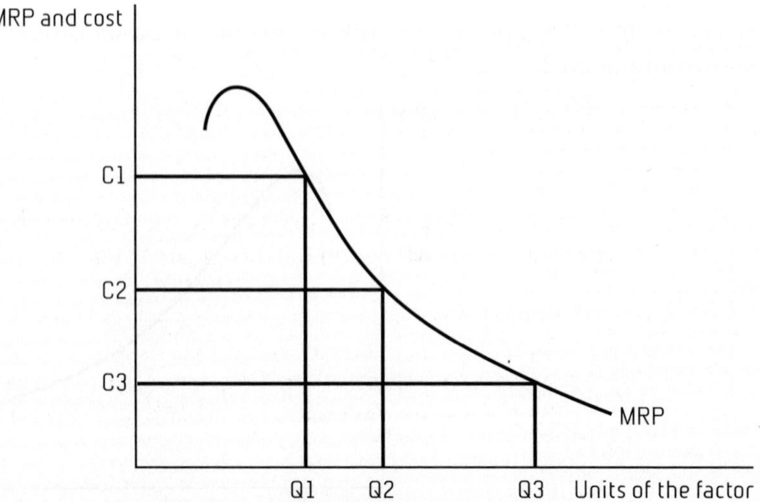

Thus we can see that at C1 the firm would employ Q1, and at C2 and C3 respectively it would employ Q2 and Q3. The MRP curve shows the relationship between the price (cost) of the factor and the number of units of the factor demanded. A curve showing this relationship is a demand curve. Therefore, the MRP curve of a factor of production is its demand curve and as you can see it slopes downwards.

Thus we can generalise and say that the demand curve for a factor of production slopes downwards from left to right. For convenience purposes we usually show it like an ordinary demand curve.

The Factors Affecting the MPP of a Factor of Production

1. **The quality or specialised nature of the factors:** If the quality of the factors of production used improves then they become more efficient and additional output will be produced.

2. **The training or education provided for labour:** If the labour force is highly trained it becomes more skilled resulting in increased efficiency and more output.

3. **Expertise of the entrepreneur:** If the entrepreneur is expert in organising the production unit then each factor will be more productive and work to their maximum efficiency.

4. **Law of Diminishing Marginal Returns:** As each additional unit of a factor of production is used a point will be reached where the additional output per unit produced will decline.

The Factors Affecting the MRP of a Factor of Production

1. **The productivity of the factor**: Let us take a very simple example of labour. Employees may undertake a training course which makes them more efficient. This will result in a greater quantity being produced by labour, thus increasing its MRP.

2. **The AR or selling price of the output:** If the selling price obtained on the market is rising then the MRP will automatically increase.

3. **The law of demand:** On the market, the law of demand dictates that in order for more units of a good to be sold the price of that good must be decreased. If this happens then the MRP will again automatically decrease. Note that the exception to this is in perfect competition which we discussed in Chapter 12.

LEARN THE KEY POINTS

1. Explain derived demand
2. Define the marginal physical product (productivity)
3. Define the marginal revenue product (productivity)
4. Know the derivation and shape of the total production curve
5. Know the derivation and shape of the MPP curve
6. Know the derivation and shape of the MRP curve
7. Explain the relationship between the cost of a factor of production and the number of units of that factor employed
8. Know the factors affecting the MPP of a factor of production
9. Know the factors affecting the MRP of a factor of production

Exam Q&A: See p. 415

Copy questions 1–4 into your answer book and complete each of the sentences by filling in the blank spaces.

1. The demand for a factor of production is a ____________ as its demand arises from the ____________ for ____________.
2. The MPP of a factor of production is the ____________ to total ____________ caused by the employment of an ____________ of that factor.
3. The MRP of a factor of production is the ____________ to total ____________ caused by the employment of an ____________ of that factor.
4. A total production curve shows the relationship between the level of ____________ and the number of ____________ of a factor of production which are ____________.
5. Explain briefly why employers are reluctant to pay employees a wage greater than their MRP.
6. Explain why the MPP curve of a factor of production tends to slope downwards from left to right.
7. Explain fully why the MRP curve of a factor of production represents its demand curve.
8. State and explain the factors which influence the MPP of a factor of production.
9. State and explain the factors which influence the MRP of a factor of production.
10. Is it always possible to calculate an employee's MRP? Explain your answer.

Chapter 27
Land

Land

All factors of production are important, however land is probably the most essential factor. We need land to provide food, we need land to supply mineral wealth and we need land on which we can build houses, factories, offices, schools and all other forms of accommodation.

Definition of land

> **Land** is anything provided by nature that helps to create wealth. The return to (or price of) land is called **rent**.

In Chapter 1 (see p. 3), we stated that land has two particular characteristics, namely that it is **fixed in supply** and has **no cost of production**.

Fixed in supply

Land has many uses and is fixed in supply. Because of these factors, land has been the cause of much strife throughout history. People have murdered for land, families have feuded over land, countries have gone to war with each other over land and countless numbers of court cases have been about the ownership of land. Land has been the basic theme of numerous novels, plays and films.

As the world's population grows the need for land also grows. As the wealth of an economy increases so too does the demand for land. Some people are so preoccupied about the ownership of land that they engage solicitors to ensure that any land they buy is legally registered in their names.

In Ireland, as in most other developed countries, the use of land is controlled nationally or at local level by planning laws. The theory governing the planning laws is that the use of the fixed supply of land must be decided by society rather than by individuals.

Commercial Rent

We have stated that the return to (the price of) land is called **rent**. Because it is a price, it is determined by the interaction of the total supply of and the total demand for land.

Land is fixed in supply, therefore its supply curve is a perpendicular curve as shown in Fig 27.1. This is identical to the supply curves of products in fixed supply as discussed in Chapter 7, Supply and Elasticity of Supply.

Fig 27.1 Supply curve of land

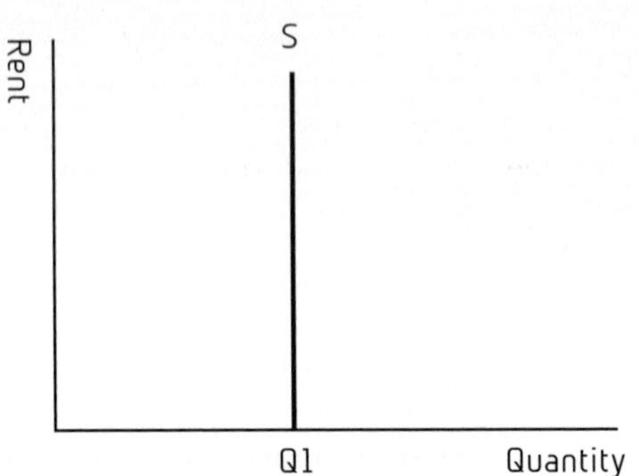

In Chapter 26, Demand for Factors of Production, we saw that the demand curve for a factor of production is based on its marginal revenue product (MRP) and so is a normal downward sloping one. So if we superimpose the demand curve onto the supply curve we will determine the rent (price) of land. We will call this price R1 as shown in Fig 27.2.

Fig 27.2 Interaction of D and S determines rent

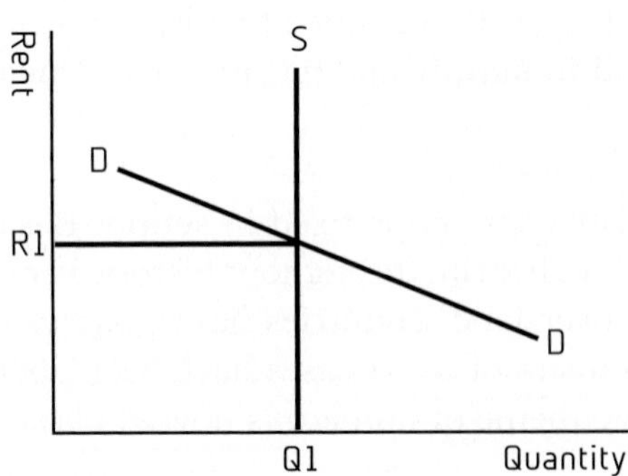

The supply of land is fixed. Thus the only variable in the relationship between the supply of and the demand for land is the demand. Therefore, it is really the demand for land that determines its price.

The demand for land is based on its MRP. Therefore, the higher the selling price of the commodity for which the land is used, the higher its MRP will be.

Example

Assume that there is an acre of land for sale on the outskirts of a highly populated town and that this land can be used either for agricultural purposes or for house-building purposes. The revenue that a farmer can get from the use of this land will be far less than the revenue that a property developer can generate from it. Thus the MRP of the land for the property developer is greater than the MRP of the land for the farmer. Therefore, the property developer will pay a higher price than the farmer for the land. This means that the property developer's demand curve for the land is to the right of the farmer's, resulting in the higher price that the developer will pay. Thus the price of the land will increase from R1 to R2 as shown in Fig 27.3. Therefore, it is the high prices which can be charged for products which drive up the rent and not vice versa. This is stated in the old saying, 'it is high prices which cause high rents and not high rents which cause high prices'.

Fig 27.3 Changes in D cause change in rent

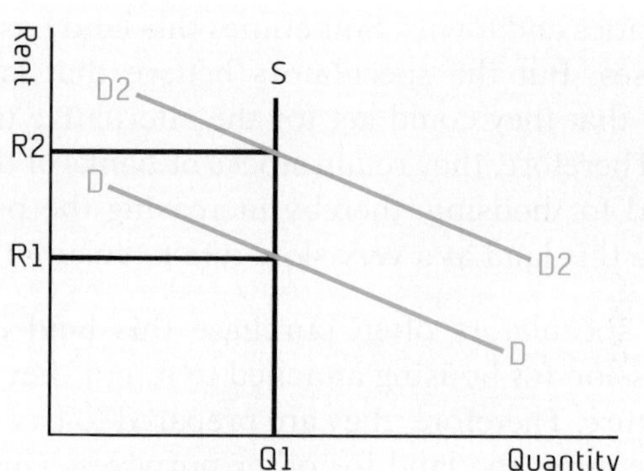

✳Reasons for the high price of land in Ireland

Planning laws

We have already seen that land has many alternative uses. Some of these uses are more profitable than others. The price paid for land is based on the MRP of that land. However, land can be zoned for particular uses only. When this happens, it restricts the alternative uses of that land. This reduces the potential of the land, thus reducing its value.

On the other hand, if some of our land is restricted to certain uses then it reduces the supply of land which is required for other purposes, thus increasing the value of these other tracts of land. Therefore, the price of land is greatly influenced by the planning restrictions placed on it and the supply of suitable land for any given purpose.

Increase and change in structure of population

As the size of Ireland's population increases and the average family size decreases, there is a growing demand for land for housing purposes. This growth in demand for housing has led to an increase in the demand for land with planning permission, thus driving up its price. At the same time, the percentage of the population in the age group that constitutes the market for first-time buyers has also increased.

Increasing levels of income and low interest rates

The increased level of economic activity in Ireland since the 1990s has resulted in a substantial increase in incomes in real terms. At the same time, interest rates fell to a historically low level. All of this meant that many people could afford to purchase a second home or a holiday home. This of course has resulted in a greater demand for the land on which to build these houses. This extra demand has resulted in higher prices for the land.

Land speculators

1. Many speculators have been buying up vast tracts of land on the periphery of large cities and towns. Sometimes this land has planning permission for housing purposes. But the speculators believe that land inflation is greater than the return that they could get for the alternative uses of the money invested in the land. Therefore, they retain stocks or banks of this land, thus reducing the supply of land for housing, thereby increasing the price of the remaining land. They release this land at a very slow rate to ensure that supply is kept at a low level.

2. These speculators often purchase this land even when there is no planning permission for housing attached to it, but they hope to have the land rezoned in the future. Therefore, they are prepared to pay more for the land than somebody who requires the land for other purposes. This has the effect of driving up the price of all land located on the periphery of these cities and towns.

Increase in economic growth

Ireland's economy has been growing, on average, at a rate of above 5 per cent per annum. This has created an increase in the demand for land which is zoned for commercial purposes. This increase in demand has led to an increase in the price of the limited supply of land suitable for this purpose.

More land required for infrastructural purposes

In Chapter 22, The Role of Government in the Economy, we saw that the National Development Plan, the National Spatial Strategy and Transport 21 all identified the need to develop Ireland's infrastructure. Thus more land is required for these purposes. Not only is there a limited supply of the land suitable for these programmes, but the government will also have to compete with all other sectors of the economy seeking land. This is putting further upward pressure on the demand for land.

Decentralisation

The government's policy to decentralise many of its departments to regions outside Dublin, not only creates a demand for land for its offices in these regions, but also increases the demand for land for the housing requirements of the people moving to these regions. Again this puts upward pressure on the price of land.

Economic Rent

Firstly, let us introduce two new terms: supply price and economic rent.

Definition of supply price

The **supply price** of a factor of production is the minimum payment which must be made to bring a factor of production into existence and to maintain it in a particular employment.

If there is a statutory minimum wage rate, then that is the price which an employer must pay to get the supply of labour required, otherwise no labour will be supplied. If the minimum wage rate is increased, then this new rate must be paid to keep the employees employed.

Definition of economic rent

Economic rent is any payment made to a factor of production above its supply price.

Let us assume that the owner of the acre of land mentioned earlier was willing to sell it at a price of R1, then the supply price of the land is R1. However, because of the competition between the farmer and the property developer the price increased to R2. Thus the seller received an economic rent of the difference between R1 and R2.

The economist David Ricardo (see p. 353) first introduced this concept of economic rent. He observed the price of fertile land increasing when there was a shortage of food during the Napoleonic Wars.

Let us examine the concept of economic rent under three different headings: (a) mankind-in-general and economic rent, (b) competing industries and economic rent and finally (c) the individual and economic rent. The simplest way of understanding the progress through these three headings is to regard it as an exercise in logic based on the definitions of supply price and economic rent.

⁕Mankind-in-general and economic rent

Land is a gift of nature, i.e. it has no cost of production. Therefore, to mankind-in-general it has no supply price. Thus any payment made by mankind for land must be economic rent as it is a payment above its supply price.

⁕Competing industries and economic rent

The **transfer cost** (sometimes referred to as the transfer earnings) of a factor of production is the minimum payment which must be made to transfer a factor from one industry or activity to another. Assume a landlord is renting a piece of land to one group of people, e.g. crop-growers at €100 per acre. If another group of people, e.g. cattle breeders, want to obtain that piece of land then the landlord will not transfer the land from the crop-growers to the cattle breeders unless he receives a minimum of €100 per acre from them.

When land is transferred from one industry to another the minimum payment for the land is its transfer cost. This is its **supply price**. Therefore, only that part of any payment above its transfer cost would constitute economic rent.

✳The individual and economic rent

It is assumed that people act rationally. An individual, when acquiring land, will only pay the minimum price which guarantees that the land will be supplied to him/her. He/she is only paying its supply price. Therefore, no part of the payment made by an individual for land would constitute economic rent.

The concept of economic rent can also be applied to labour and enterprise.

✳Economic rent as applied to labour and enterprise

Labour and economic rent

Definition of quasi-rent

Quasi-rent is economic rent earned by labour in the short run.

This happens when the demand for that form of labour is temporarily greater than its supply. Because the demand is greater than the supply this type of labour may command a higher wage than normal. Thus the labour is receiving a payment above its supply price.

However, the existence of these high wages will attract others to acquire the necessary skills and so the supply of that labour will increase and will eventually eliminate the quasi-rent.

Rent of ability

Definition of rent of ability

Rent of ability is economic rent earned by labour in the long run.

It happens when an individual has a unique talent for which there is a great demand. Because the skill is unique the supply of it cannot be increased in the long run. Therefore, this form of labour will continue to earn rent of ability in the long run. This would apply to individuals who have exceptionally brilliant organisational skills.

Enterprise and economic rent

Normal profit, by definition, is the supply price of enterprise in the long run. Thus in the long run supernormal profits (SNPs) must be regarded as economic rent as they are a payment above the supply price of enterprise.

LEARN THE KEY POINTS

1. The definition of land
2. Understand the difference between commercial rent and economic rent

3. Know the definition of transfer cost
4. Know the definition of economic rent
5. Explain the part of any payment which is regarded as economic rent when a payment is made for land by (a) mankind-in-general, (b) by industries competing for land and (c) an individual person
6. Know and explain the concept of quasi-rent
7. Know and explain the concept of rent of ability
8. Explain why SNPs are regarded as economic rent
9. Explain how the existence of high market prices causes the high rents for properties and not vice versa

Exam Q&A: See p. 416

Copy questions 1–4 into your answer book and complete each of the sentences by filling in the blank spaces.

1 Land is __________ in supply and has no __________.

2 The supply price of a factor of production is the __________ which must be made to bring a factor of production __________ and to __________.

3 Economic rent is any payment made to a __________ above its __________.

4 The transfer cost of a factor of production is the __________ which must be made to transfer a factor from one __________ or __________ to another.

5 Distinguish between quasi-rent and rent of ability.

6 Why are supernormal profits regarded as a form of economic rent?

7 Explain why the demand for land is the predominant factor which determines its price (rent).

8 'The retailers on a fashionable shopping street must charge high prices for the products which they sell because these retailers are being charged very high rents for their premises.' Comment on the validity of this statement.

9 Fifty per cent of the economic rent earned by the supplier of a factor of production is to be taken from that supplier in the form of taxation. Would this tax have any effect on the selling price of the factor of production? Explain your answer.

10 'The seller involved in a transaction for land may earn economic rent, yet the buyer in that transaction may not pay any economic rent.' Explain this statement.

Chapter 28
Labour and the Wage Rate

Labour

The word **labour** tends to conjure up different images in the minds of different people. Some people associate it with hard work, while others associate it with political parties. Let us explain what we mean by labour.

Definition of labour

Labour is any human effort that helps in the production of wealth.

Definition of the labour force

The **labour force** is comprised of all of those people who are working and all of those available for work at the present wage rate. This is normally measured in 'man-hours'. Therefore, we could say that the workforce at any given time is the number of people who are working multiplied by the number of hours they work.

- **Full employment** exists when everybody who is available for work, at the present wage rate, is employed.
- The **return to labour**, i.e. its share of the wealth created, is called **wages**.

Definition of the wage rate

The **wage rate** is the price of one man-hour's labour.

Like all prices the wage rate is determined by the interaction of supply and demand, in this case the relationship is between the supply of and the demand for labour. If the supply is greater than the demand then the wage rate will decrease, and if the demand is greater than the supply then the wage rate will increase.

The Demand for Labour

We saw in Chapter 26, Demand for Factors of Production, that the demand for a factor of production is determined by its marginal revenue product (MRP). Thus we can state that the demand for labour is determined by its MRP, i.e. the addition to total revenue brought about by the employment of an extra unit of labour. It would not pay an employer to employ labour if its MRP was less than the wage rate. Therefore, when the wage rate increases the demand for labour decreases. This means that the demand curve for labour is the normal downward sloping demand curve as shown in Fig 28.1.

Fig 28.1 *Demand curve for labour*

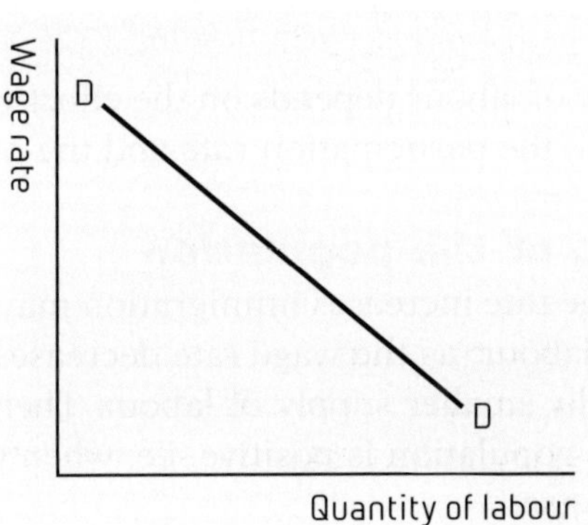

✻Factors affecting a firm's demand for labour

1 **A derived demand:** The demand for labour is derived from the demand for the product that the firm is producing. As the demand for the firm's product increases it is likely that the demand for labour will also increase.

2 **The cost of capital goods:** Capital and labour can be substitutes for each other. Thus as the cost of capital goods decreases the demand for them will increase at the expense of labour. Therefore, this firm may replace labour with capital.

3 **Improvements in technology:** While the cost of capital goods may not change at any given time, their marginal physical productivity (MPP) might increase. This lowers the cost of the capital per unit produced. This could cause a decrease in demand for labour by that particular firm.

4 **The availability of other factors of production:** Even if the demand for the firm's product was very high, the firm could not produce sufficient amounts of the good to meet the demand if there was a scarcity of raw materials. Thus this would decrease this firm's demand for labour.

The Supply of Labour

The supply of labour (the labour force) means all of those people who are working and who are available for work at the current wage rate. Let us discuss two new terms which are appropriate to this topic.

Definition of a positive wage effect

A **positive wage effect** means that as the wage rate increases the supply of labour also increases and vice versa.

Definition of a negative wage effect

A **negative wage effect** means that as the wage rate increases the supply of labour decreases and vice versa.

The supply of labour depends on the effect which the wage rate has on the size of the population, the participation rate and the number of hours worked by each person.

The size of the population

As the wage rate increases immigration may occur, thus causing a potentially greater supply of labour; as the wage rate decreases there could be emigration thus causing a potentially smaller supply of labour. Therefore, the effect of the wage rate on the size of the population is positive, i.e. when wage rate increases population increases and vice versa.

The participation rate

The participation rate refers to the number of people between the ages of 16 and 65 who are willing to work. This age group is taken as a general guideline, because those under 16 are obliged to attend full-time education and 65 is regarded as the average age of retirement from the workforce. As the wage rate increases more people are usually willing to work.

- More married women are attracted back into the workforce because the opportunity cost of staying at home increases.
- In a like manner, some people who are on the dole on a 'voluntary' basis will be attracted back into the workforce; this of course assumes that the gap between the new wage rate and the dole payment is attractive enough!
- Some people's pensions are based on a percentage of their earnings at retirement. Therefore, as the wage rate increases some people will be tempted to stay in the workforce for a longer period of time, thus increasing the labour force.

Therefore, the wage rate has a positive effect on the number of people willing to work.

The number of hours worked by each person

As the wage rate increases those who prefer an increase in wealth will work more hours, whereas those who prefer an increase in leisure time will work fewer hours. Thus the effect of the wage rate on the number of hours worked by each person can be either **positive** or **negative**.

The three possible overall positive effects of the wage rate outweigh the one possible negative effect, ensuring that an increase in the wage rate leads to an increase in the supply (S) of labour. Therefore, the supply curve of labour is the normal upward sloping supply curve as shown on Fig 28.2(a), see p. 299.

Fig 28.2(a) Supply of labour increases as the wage rate increases

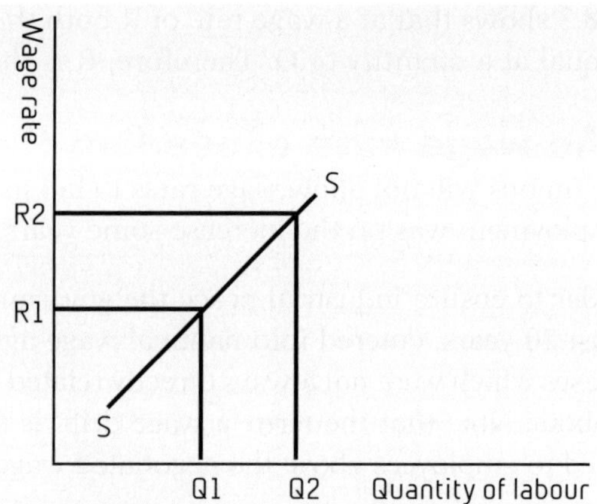

A statutory minimum wage rate can alter the shape of the supply curve. If there is a minimum wage rate then no labour will be supplied below that rate. This is shown in Fig 28.2(b), where R1 is the minimum wage rate.

Fig 28.2(b) Supply curve of labour subject to minimum wage rate

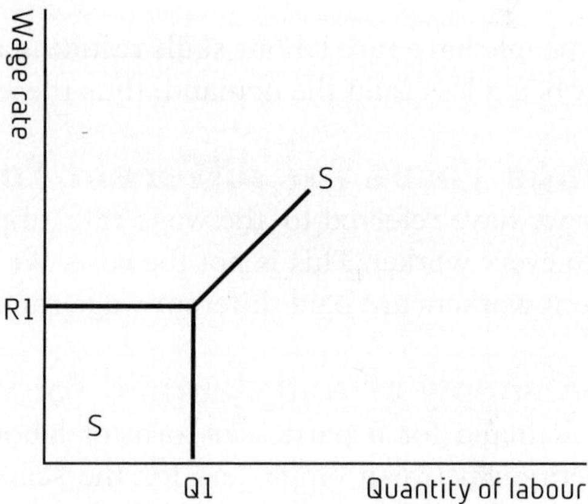

Now if we superimpose the D (demand) and the S curves on each other we can ascertain the equilibrium wage rate, i.e. that wage rate which brings about an equal supply of and demand for labour. This is shown in Fig 28.3.

Fig 28.3 The equilibrium wage rate

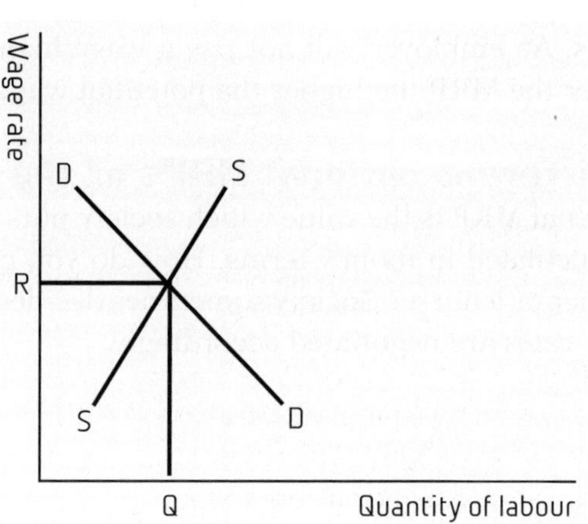

Fig 28.3 shows that at a wage rate of R both the demand for and the supply of labour are equal at a quantity of Q. Therefore, R is the **equilibrium wage rate**.

✳The wage rate exceeding the equilibrium rate

Trade unions will not allow wage rates to fall in reaction to market forces, therefore as unemployment was on the increase some years ago unions refused to take wage cuts.

In order to ensure industrial peace the government and the social partners have, over the last 20 years, entered into national wage agreements. All of these resulted in wage increases which were not always directly related to the overall supply of and the demand for labour. Note that the term 'a wage drift' is used to describe any increase in wages granted to employees above the negotiated wage increase for a particular industry.

As part of the above agreements, social welfare benefits have also increased, therefore employers have to offer higher wages to attract people off the dole.

Those people who are in work do not want to see their real wages decreasing, therefore they have sought and received wage increases to compensate for inflation.

Some people have rare labour skills resulting in the supply of that particular form of labour being less than the demand, thus these people can earn very high wages.

✳Wage rates for different forms of labour

So far we have referred to 'the wage rate' implying that there is only one wage rate paid to every worker. This is not the case. We are now going to examine the reasons different workers are paid different wage rates.

1 The supply of and demand for a particular form of labour

If the demand for a particular form of labour is greater than its supply then the competition between employers for the scarce labour will drive up the wage rate earned by that particular form of labour. The reverse applies if the supply is greater than the demand.

2 Different MRPs

Some types of labour have a higher marginal revenue productivity (MRP) than other forms. An employer will not pay a wage higher than the employee's MRP. Thus the higher the MRP the higher the potential wage rate.

3 Different notional MRPs of the labour

Notional MRP is the value which society puts on labour when its actual value cannot be calculated in money terms. How do you calculate the MRP of a road sweeper, a teacher or a nurse? Society sometimes decides the relative value of these workers and wage rates are negotiated accordingly.

4 Training for the job and the cost of that training

Some jobs require a high level of education or training. There can be a high opportunity cost involved in obtaining an education or qualification. In order to encourage a supply of these types of labour, high wages may have to be offered to compensate the people who undertake this education or training, e.g. doctors.

5 Monetary benefits other than pay

Some firms offer non-contributory pension schemes as part of the terms of employment. People working in financial institutions may be offered low interest rates on their mortgage. These terms of employment may result in people willing to accept a lower gross wage as their real income is increased by these benefits.

6 Non-monetary benefits received

Non-monetary benefits received with the job include free travel, free accommodation, long holidays or a car supplied with the job. The same principle applies as to point 5.

7 Working conditions

Generally people working in hazardous or unpleasant conditions seek compensation for these conditions, as few people want to work in these conditions. Thus if the supply of these workers is scarce, then a higher wage rate will have to be offered to increase the supply.

8 Negotiating strength of the worker's trade union

If a worker is a member of a very strong trade union then that union may be able to negotiate a better wage rate for its members than that negotiated by a weaker union.

9 Gender bias

Despite existing legislation a bias still exists in the payment of women in the Irish workforce. Female workers in Ireland earn roughly 80 per cent of that of their male counterparts.

10 Possession of innate talents

Some people possess rare talents and hence may be able to earn very high incomes, i.e. they may earn rent of ability, e.g. sports and pop stars and very efficient organisers.

Factors Determining the Efficiency of Labour

1. **The quality of training and education** received by labour and its ability to put this into practice: The better each of these is the more productive labour will be.
2. **The amount and quality of capital available to labour.** A person can dig out a much bigger area in a day using a JCB than is possible when using a shovel.

3. **Natural ability:** Some people are naturally more talented than others and are hence more productive. These people can often earn rent of ability.

4. **Management expertise:** Some managers can organise their workforce more efficiently than others resulting in a more productive labour force.

5. **Specialisation of labour:** As labour becomes more specialised it can produce more goods at a faster rate and with less wastage of materials.

6. **The living conditions of the labour force:** People living in good conditions and leading a healthy life-style tend to be more productive than those living in poor conditions.

7. **Climatic conditions:** People living and working in moderate climatic conditions tend to be more productive than those living in regions of extreme weather conditions.

The Mobility of Labour

Definitions of the mobility of labour

The **mobility of labour** refers to the willingness of labour to move from one region to another to take up employment (geographical mobility of labour).

Or

It refers to the **ability of labour** to change from one form of employment to another form of employment (occupational mobility of labour).

Restrictions on the mobility of labour

1. **Trade union barriers:** For example, a closed shop policy. This exists when you cannot take up a certain form of employment unless you are a member of a particular trade union and you can only become a member of that union if you are employed in that form of employment.

2. **Lack of knowledge of availability of jobs:** If people are not aware of the existence of employment outside their own geographical region, they are not going to move.

3. **Lack of housing or social facilities:** Few, if any, people are willing to move to an area which does not offer a reasonable standard of accommodation, or which is devoid of social and recreational facilities.

4. **The workforce lacks the skills:** This is the major factor influencing the occupational mobility of labour.

5 **Language or cultural barriers:** Workers are unwilling to move to regions of the world where they feel isolated due to their inability to speak or learn a different language, or to regions whose culture is alien to their own.

6 **Reluctance to leave the home environment:** Many people are very reluctant to leave the area in which they were born and reared, as their entire family and social life is centred there, and they are unwilling to disturb their children's education.

Unemployment

People are termed unemployed only if they are not working, but are actively seeking employment.

Causes and types of unemployment

Frictional unemployment

Frictional unemployment is a situation where people are unemployed on a temporary basis when one industry is declining while another is starting up.

Seasonal unemployment

The demand for some goods and services is a seasonal demand only. Therefore, little or no production takes place outside of that season. Thus the people working in that industry will have no employment for that period of closure. This is very evident in the tourist industry around parts of Ireland.

Structural unemployment

Structural unemployment arises in situations where industries which were major employers have gone into decline and there is no longer any demand for the skills of the former employees.

Institutional unemployment

Institutional unemployment arises when there are obstacles to the mobility of labour or when the incentives to work are decreased.

Disguised unemployment

Some people do not register on the Live Register, but they are available for work. Thus their unemployment is disguised.

Underemployment

Underemployment is when a person is employed just to give him/her an income, but he/she does not add to the total output of the firm, e.g. a son employed on a family farm. The farm may be every bit as productive without the employment of the son. In this situation two people are sharing the one job.

Cyclical unemployment

Cyclical unemployment is a temporary form of unemployment associated with a general fall in the level of demand during a decline in the trade cycle.

Transitional unemployment

Transitional unemployment refers to people who are temporarily unemployed while moving between jobs.

✻A backward bending supply curve of labour

A backward bending supply curve of labour is similar to a normal supply curve of labour, but shows that when the wage rate reaches a very high level the supply of labour decreases, as people prefer an increase in leisure time to an increase in wealth.

Fig 28.4 illustrates this phenomenon. It shows the supply of labour increases as the wage rate increases until the wage rate reaches a very high level, R(h), and then the supply begins to decrease.

Fig 28.4 Backward bending supply curve of labour

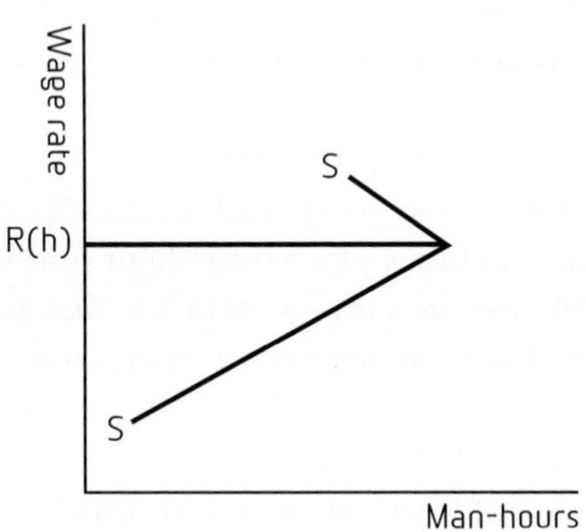

✻Measuring the level of unemployment

The Live Register is a list of all those people who sign a register each week in order to claim some social welfare benefit.

The Quarterly National Household Survey (QNHS) is a survey which sets out to establish the number of people who are not working, but who are actively seeking work. For this reason it gives a more accurate figure for unemployment than the Live Register.

Weaknesses of the Live Register as a measure of unemployment

1. Some people sign on the Live Register only to get the dole and are not actively seeking work. Therefore, they are not unemployed.
2. Some people may be signing on the Live Register and working in the black economy.
3. Part-time workers may sign on for the days they are not working. Therefore, they are not unemployed.

4. Some people sign on only for credits towards their old age pension. Again these people are not unemployed.
5. Some people do not sign on even though they are actively seeking work because they are not entitled to any benefits. These people are unemployed but are not counted as such.

Population Changes

✳Reasons for recent immigration

Increased awareness of employment opportunities in Ireland

The emergence of the 'Celtic Tiger' with its greater job opportunities has attracted immigrant workers. Global communications have made people more aware of the employment opportunities in Ireland.

Some of the multinational companies locating here bring in their own personnel to do specific work. When foreign companies locate in Ireland they often want to continue with a business structure and policy which has been successful for them in their own countries. These companies bring in their own personnel to ensure the successful implementation of these structures.

Membership of the EU

The EU is a relatively prosperous region. Many non-EU nationals seek an improvement in their standard of living and are attracted into the EU. As a member of the EU, Ireland has attracted some of these job seekers.

Ireland's social welfare system

In comparison to some other countries, Ireland offers a caring welfare system which eases the difficulties of relocating here, thus making Ireland an attractive destination.

Lenient immigration controls

The economic downturn in some countries such as Germany and the tighter immigration controls in countries such as the USA and Australia have resulted in Ireland attracting some emigrants who would traditionally have gone to these other countries.

Recruitment by public and private bodies

During the boom period Ireland experienced labour shortages in specific jobs, such as nurses and carpenters. State and private sector agencies sought immigrants to fill these vacancies.

Lower personal tax rates

Personal tax rates have fallen in Ireland, thus attracting people back home who had emigrated in the past due to our previously very high personal taxes.

Better quality of life

People who had emigrated have returned to Ireland to rear their children in what they consider is a better and safer environment.

Humanitarian factors

In the recent past Ireland has welcomed asylum seekers who were forced out of their own countries due to conflicts and wars there.

✳Economic consequences of immigration

Positive consequences

1. Increased demand for goods and services: The level of demand for goods and services will increase as the size of the population increases leading to greater opportunities for businesses.
2. Improved dependency ratio: If immigrants are mainly in the working age group then the dependency ratio will decrease, thus decreasing pressure on government finances.
3. Reduction in labour shortages: Immigrants may fill many of the vacancies which exist in the labour market and help to ease pressure on wage rates.
4. Greater utilisation of services: If the immigrants locate in low-density populated areas services will be more fully utilised in those areas, thus reducing the cost per person using these services.
5. Development of new skills and traditions within society: The economy may benefit from new skills and traditions which the immigrants may bring to the country, helping the society to become more tolerant, efficient and competitive.

Negative consequences

1. Pressure on provision of state services: With an increasing number of immigrants the population will automatically increase, which will put pressure on the government to provide more services for the general population, e.g. health and education.
2. Drain on state finances: The need to provide immigrants with benefits such as temporary housing and social welfare will put extra pressure on government finances.
3. Exploitation of immigrants: If immigrants are not adequately protected they may be forced to live and work in poor conditions and accept low levels of pay. This could oblige the government to implement and oversee a policy that ensures that this exploitation does not occur.
4. Increased dependency ratio: If the immigrants are mainly in the non-working age group the dependency ratio will increase causing a possible rise in taxation.
5. Racism: An increase in immigration may lead to an increase in racism, requiring greater policing resources, which increase government expenditure.

Trends in Employment in Ireland

Let us take a brief look at the changing trends of employment in Ireland. To do this we are going to take some employment statistics over a nine-year period, i.e. from 1998 to 2006 inclusive. This period is sufficiently long to enable us to view the changes that have taken place and observe the pattern of change. The figures are compiled by the Central Statistics Office (CSO) and comply with the standards laid down by the International Labour Organisation (ILO). If we take a look at Table 28.1 some very obvious trends can be detected.

Table 28.1 *Employment and unemployment (ILO) 000s*

Economic Sector	March-May 98	March-May 99	March-May 00	March-May 01	March-May 02	March-May 03	March-May 04	March-May 05	March-May 06
Agriculture, forestry and fishing	136.0	137.3	132.9	122.5	124.0	116.6	117.0	113.7	114.5
Other production industries	302.4	307.7	309.5	318.1	305.0	306.1	300.6	294.2	288.5
Construction	126.1	142.1	166.2	180.0	182.2	191.4	206.0	242.2	262.7
Wholesale and retail trade	211.1	222.5	235.2	247.8	246.8	251.6	260.2	266.9	284.4
Hotels and restaurants	97.8	102.0	108.1	103.8	104.2	114.4	107.8	111.0	116.3
Transport, storage and communication	87.0	96.2	101.3	111.1	111.7	112.1	113.2	118.2	120.7
Financial and other business services	171.1	194.6	210.8	217.1	228.9	227.1	237.0	257.1	267.3
Public administration and defence	70.9	74.5	78.4	81.3	90.6	92.4	89.5	98.2	105.1
Education	93.3	100.6	102.8	103.8	111.3	116.1	117.9	123.1	135.6
Health	113.9	120.3	133.0	144.0	159.3	169.9	177.0	188.0	201.2
Other services	84.5	91.4	93.3	92.4	99.8	95.7	110.0	116.4	120.6
Total in employment	1,494.0	1,589.1	1,671.4	1,721.9	1,763.9	1,793.4	1,836.2	1,929.2	2,017.0
Total unemployed	126.4	96.9	74.5	65.1	77.0	82.1	84.2	85.6	91.4
Total labour force	1,620.4	1,685.9	1,745.9	1,787.0	1,840.9	1,875.5	1,920.3	2,014.8	2,108.3
Not in labour force	1,246.8	1,225.1	1,215.6	1,232.6	1,248.9	1,269.6	1,280.3	1,262.6	1,262.0
Population 15 years and over	2,867.3	2,911.1	2,961.5	3,019.7	3,089.8	3,145.1	3,200.6	3,277.4	3,370.3

Source: *CSO*

Note: The figures in the sectors are given to the nearest single decimal place and may not exactly tally with the total figures.

✳ Analysis of the trends in employment

Agriculture, forestry and fishing

Table 28.1 shows that there has been a decrease in employment of 21,500 in the extractive industries, i.e. agriculture, forestry and fishing. This is due to the increase in the use of capital in these industries, a rationalisation of farm sizes and the changes in the Common Agricultural Policy which was discussed in Chapter 23, The European Union, see p. 243.

Other production industries

While it still represents the biggest single sector of employment, the number of people employed in manufacturing and production has decreased from a peak of 318,100 in 2001 to 288,500, i.e. a loss of 29,600 jobs.

However, at the same time there has been an increase in manufacturing output of almost 28 per cent, which indicates an increase in the rate of productivity per person employed in this sector. This is in line with other developed countries.

But because of the high proportion of UK and American owned companies in this sector, it is vulnerable to fluctuation in the rates of exchange between the euro and sterling and between the euro and the dollar. This re-emphasises the need mentioned in The National Development Plan to develop more indigenous industries.

Construction industry

The most dramatic increase in employment has been in the construction industry, in both absolute and percentage terms. Here, employment has increased by over 136,600, which represents an increase of over 108 per cent. However, there are signs of a slow down in this sector.

Wholesale and retail trade

When employment in the wholesale and retail trade is combined with that in the hotel and restaurant sector, we see that employment here increased by almost 92,000. This reflects the fact that Ireland is increasingly becoming a consumer society. This is also reflected in the growth in the transport, storage and communication industries.

Financial and other business services

The increase of 96,200 in the financial and other business services reflects the growing importance of the banking and insurance businesses in Ireland. The International Financial Services Centre in Dublin alone employs almost 11,000 people and this is expected to increase by 1,000 per annum.

The public administration, education and health sectors

When the public administration, education and health sectors are combined we see that employment here has increased by a massive 163,800. A very high percentage of these employees are employed in public service. This emphasises the importance of the government and other public bodies as employers in Ireland. The increased employment also reflects the increase in government expenditure over this period.

Total in employment

The total number of people in employment has increased from 1,494,000 to 2,017,000, an increase of 523,000.

Total unemployed

The percentage of the labour force unemployed has decreased from 7.8 per cent to 4.3 per cent.

Total labour force

The size of the labour force has increased by almost 488,000, which represents an increase of over 30 per cent.

LEARN THE KEY POINTS

1. Know the definitions of:
   - Labour
   - The labour force
   - Full employment
   - The wage rate
   - The equilibrium wage rate
2. Understand the factors which affect a firm's demand for labour
3. Understand the factors which affect the supply of labour
4. Explain a wage drift
5. Understand the reasons why different categories of workers are paid different wage rates
6. Know the factors affecting the efficiency of labour
7. Understand mobility of labour
8. Explain the restrictions on the mobility of labour

Exam Q&A: See p. 418

Copy questions 1–5 into your answer book and complete each of the sentences by filling in the blank spaces.

1. The labour force is made up of all those people who are ____________ plus those who are ____________ for work at the present ____________.
2. The equilibrium wage rate is the wage rate that brings about an ____________ supply of and ____________ for ____________.
3. A backward bending supply curve of labour indicates that the ____________ of labour will begin to ____________ once a very high ____________ has been reached.
4. The two measures used to ascertain the number of people unemployed are the ____________ and the ____________.
5. Geographical mobility of labour refers to the ____________ of labour to ____________ from ____________ region to ____________ to ____________ employment.
6. Explain the term 'the participation rate' with reference to the labour force.
7. Distinguish between the positive and the negative effect of a change in the wage rate.
8. Distinguish between structural and frictional unemployment.
9. Explain the term 'the notional MRP' of labour.
10. Explain the term 'a wage drift'.
11. What factors may be taken into account when deciding the notional MRP of certain categories of workers? Explain your answer.
12. Explain fully the factors which will influence an employer's demand for labour.
13. Explain fully how a change in the wage rate can affect the supply of labour.
14. With the aid of a diagram, or diagrams, explain why the wage rate will always revert to the equilibrium rate in the long run.
15. Explain fully why some unskilled workers on off-shore oil rigs may be paid a wage rate greater than that of a teacher.
16. Some regions of Ireland are experiencing high levels of unemployment while other regions are suffering a shortage of labour. Outline the factors which may restrict the mobility of labour between these regions.
17. Comment on the changing nature of employment in the Irish economy. A minimum of five points required.
18. How has the recent phenomenon of immigration affected the Irish labour market? Explain your answer.

Chapter 29
Capital and Interest Rates

Capital

Most people associate capital with money. Business people talk of capital as the amount of money they have tied up in their businesses. Banks frequently advise us to invest our capital with them. However, in economics we have a much more specific meaning for capital.

Definitions

- **Capital** is anything made by man that helps to create wealth.

  Or

  Capital is wealth used to create more wealth. The return to capital is called interest.
- **Capital formation** refers to the money spent on capital goods.
- **Capital stock** is the value of capital goods in existence at any given time.
- **Gross capital formation** is the total money spent on capital goods in any given period.
- **Depreciation** is the loss in value of capital goods in any given period.
- **Net capital formation** is the addition to capital stock in any given period.
- **The investment ratio** is gross capital formation as a percentage of GNP.
- **Capital widening** is an increase in the use of capital which leaves the ratio of capital to labour unchanged. This is the increased use of capital throughout an economy or a business. This normally happens during the economic development of a country.
- **Capital deepening** is an increase in the use of capital which increases the ratio of capital to labour. This means making a greater quantity and quality of capital goods available to each unit of labour throughout the economy. This is normally associated with economic growth as distinct from economic development.
- **The marginal efficiency of capital/investment (MEI)** is the extra profit generated by the employment of an extra unit of capital.
- **Social capital** refers to the assets or wealth owned by the community in general, e.g. hospitals, parks and roads. Central or local government usually undertakes expenditure on this form of capital.
- **Private capital** is capital owned by individuals or companies.

Table 29.1 *Capital stock*

Capital stock at 1/1/08 (A)	€1,000,000
Add gross capital formation to 31/12/08	€500,000
Total	**€1,500,000**
Less depreciation	€300,000
Capital stock at 31/12/08 (B)	€1,200,000
Net capital formation: (B) minus (A)	€200,000

Capital stock has increased by €200,000. This is the net capital formation. It is the same as gross capital formation minus depreciation.

Savings

Capital formation requires savings. People must refrain from spending some of their income so that money will be available for investment.

We all earn our income (Y) from the fact that people consume the goods and services that we produce (i.e. from consumption or C) and from the fact that employers who have invested money employ us (i.e. from investment or I).

Thus $Y = C + I$

We all dispose of that same income by spending some of it (i.e. consumption or C) and saving the rest of it (i.e. saving or S).

Thus $Y = C + S$

Therefore $C + I = C + S$

Therefore $I = S$

This means that investment is dependent on savings.

Note: This does not mean that all savings will be invested. It simply means that there must be savings for investment to take place. To encourage people to save, financial institutions offer interest on savings.

✳The reasons why people save

To purchase expensive items in the future

Some products are too expensive to purchase from a weekly or monthly income. The only way some people can afford to purchase these products is to set aside (save) a portion of their income each week or month until they have accumulated the price of the product.

For thrift purposes

Many people deliberately set aside (save) part of their income and restrict their spending in line with a prudent budget. This allows them to avoid wasteful impulse buying.

To earn interest

Most financial institutions offer interest on money saved to encourage saving with them. This acts as an incentive to people to accumulate wealth at a fast rate.

For precautionary purposes

Many people like to set aside (save) money for security purposes, so that if some unforeseen costly event happens they will have the money to meet this cost.

To provide for retirement

Most people are aware that their weekly income will decrease when they retire. Therefore, to prevent any drastic fall in their standard of living people will refrain from consuming part of their income while they are working and thus will have this available to them when they retire. It will supplement their pension. Incidentally, a person's contributions to a pension scheme are a form of saving.

✳ The factors affecting the level of saving

1 The level of income

People on low levels of income may have to spend all of their income to meet the cost of their normal daily needs and wants. Therefore, they cannot save. Conversely, people on high levels of income may have more money than they need to meet the cost of their normal daily wants. Therefore, these people may save. Thus the higher the level of income the greater the potential is for saving.

2 The rate of interest

The opportunity cost of not saving money increases as the rate of interest offered on savings increases. Therefore, (provided income is big enough) people will be enticed to save more as these rates of interest increase.

3 The level of social welfare benefits: pensions

If old age pensions provided by the state are big, there is less incentive for people to save money for their retirement and vice versa. (This is always a dangerous assumption for people to make during their working life, as they have no guarantee that old age pensions will remain big, in real terms, when they retire.)

4 The level of tax on interest on savings

If the level of tax on interest earned increases, e.g. DIRT, this has the same effect as a reduction in the rate of interest and so will discourage savings and vice versa.

5 The rate of inflation

The rate of inflation may result in negative interest rates. If the rate of inflation is greater than the rate of interest, money saved will lose some of its purchasing power. This could discourage saving as people may decide to spend the money while its purchasing power is greatest.

The paradox of thrift

Sometimes, an increase in the marginal propensity to save (MPS) can lead to a decrease in the level of demand in the economy. This in turn can lead to a decrease in the level of income, because fewer people are employed. An increase in the MPS can also lead to a possible decrease in the actual level of savings.

Interest Rates

There are two theories which you must learn concerning interest rates:

1. The loanable funds or classical theory of interest rates.
2. The liquidity preference (Keynesian) theory of interest rates (see p. 358 for more information about Keynes).

✳The classical theory of interest rates

The **loanable funds** or **classical theory of interest rates** states that the rate of interest is determined by the interaction of the supply of and the demand for money.

Here, the supply of money means the amount of money being saved with the financial institutions. The demand for money means the demand for loans from the financial institutions.

This theory states that if the supply of savings (i.e. money or loanable funds) into the financial institutions is not sufficient to meet the demand for loans, then the banks will increase interest rates to attract more savings and vice versa.

Thus the supply curve of money is the normal upward sloping supply curve as shown in Fig 29.1 on p. 315.

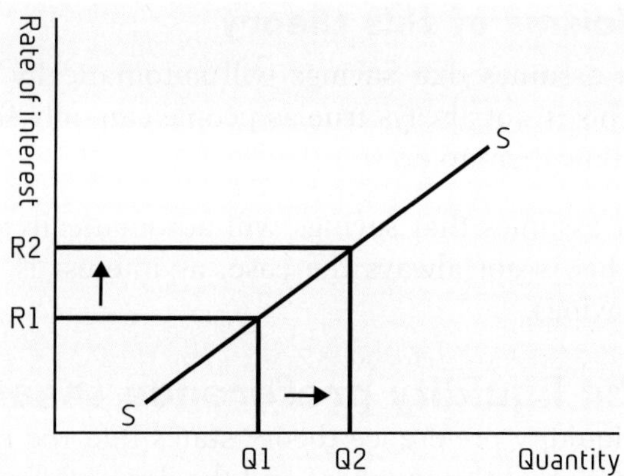

Fig 29.1 Supply curve of money as per the loanable funds theory

The theory states that the demand for loans decreases as the rate of interest increases. This happens because when interest rates increase the cost (or price) of borrowing increases. Therefore, the D curve for money is the normal downward sloping demand curve as shown in Fig 29.2.

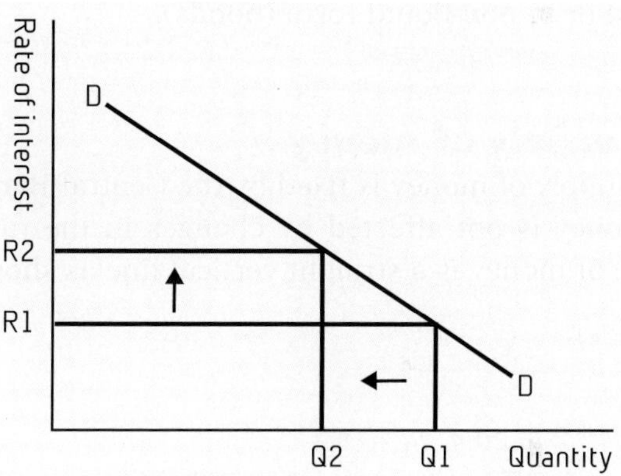

Fig 29.2 Demand curve for money

Thus the rate of interest will settle at the rate that brings about an equal supply of and demand for money, i.e. loanable funds. This happens at the point where the demand and the supply curves intersect as shown in Fig 29.3.

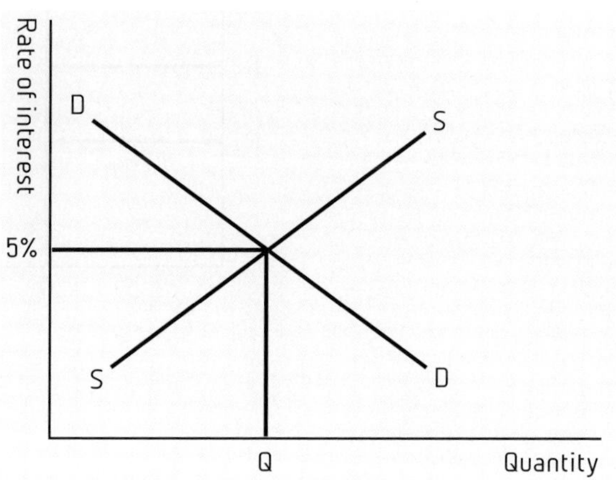

Fig 29.3 Equilibrium rate of interest

Criticisms of this theory

1. It assumes that savings will automatically increase as interest rates increase. This is not always true as people can only save if their income is big enough to allow them to do so.

2. It assumes that savings will automatically decrease as interest rates decrease. This is not always the case, as interest is not the only factor that influences savings.

✳The liquidity preference theory of interest rates

The liquidity preference theory states that the rate of interest is determined by the interaction of the supply of and the demand for money.

In this theory, the supply of money refers to the amount of money in circulation. The demand for money refers to the reasons people want to hold onto money, rather than put it into bonds or tie it up in investments (Keynes referred only to bonds).

Keynes simplified matters by stating that people kept their assets in liquid form (cash) or in non-liquid form (bonds).

The supply of money

The supply of money is fixed by the Central Bank at any given time. Thus the supply of money is not affected by changes in the rate of interest. Therefore, the supply curve of money is a straight vertical line as shown in Fig 29.4.

Fig 29.4 The supply curve of money

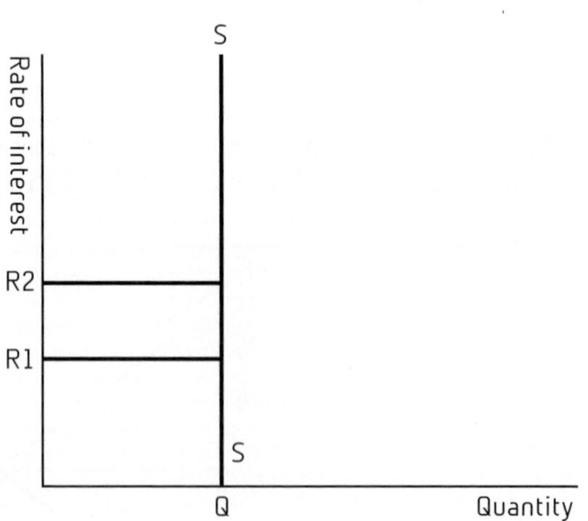

The Demand for Money

People demand money for three reasons:

1. The transactions motive
2. The precautionary motive
3. The speculative motive

✳ The transactions motive

The transactions motive means people want to hold onto money to satisfy their day-to-day needs and wants. The amount held for this purpose is determined by the value of their daily transactions and is not affected by interest rates.

✳ The precautionary motive

The precautionary motive means that people want to hold onto money in case it is needed in an emergency situation. The amount held for this purpose depends on the person's attitude to the future.

A pessimist will hold onto substantial amounts, whereas an optimist will hold very little. The optimist will also be influenced slightly by the rate of interest.

✳ The speculative motive

Keynes used the example of buying bonds in his explanation of the speculative motive. The simplest way to explain this is that people want to hold onto money to have it available for any business opportunity that might arise. These people are motivated by the prospect of making money. Thus as the rate of interest increases, the opportunity cost of holding money increases. Therefore, as interest rates increase less money is held for this purpose.

The overall demand for money will therefore decrease as the rate of interest increases **provided** incomes are firstly sufficient to meet normal needs and wants.

Thus the demand curve for money is the normal downward sloping one as shown on Fig 29.5.

Fig 29.5 The demand curve for money

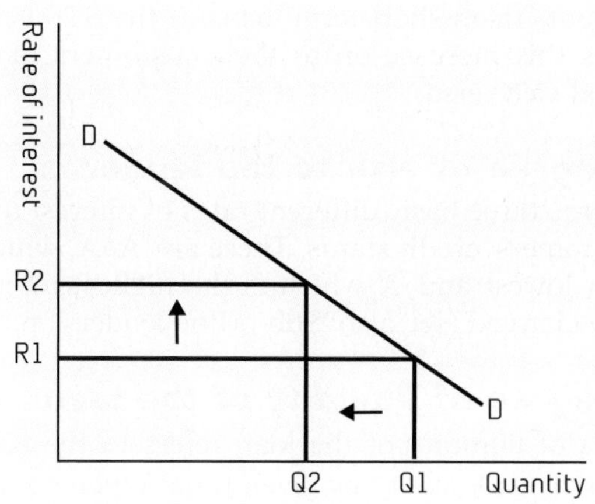

Now superimpose the supply curve of money onto the demand curve for money to establish the equilibrium rate of interest (in this case 10 per cent as shown in Fig 29.6).

Fig 29.6 The equilibrium rate of interest

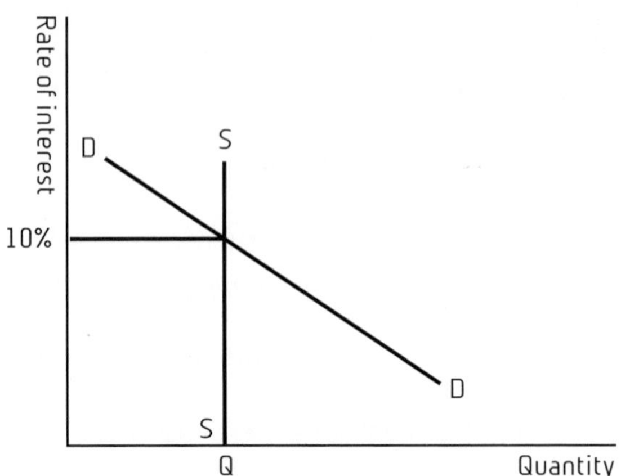

We saw earlier that the supply of money is fixed at any given time by the Central Bank. Thus the only variable is the D for money. Therefore, it is the D for money that determines interest rates at any given time.

✳The factors affecting the rate of interest

The factors below are in addition to the loanable funds theory and the liquidity preference theory.

1 The European Central Bank

The ECB sets the base rate of interest at any given time. This rate is determined by the requirements of the EU economy in general. Any change in this base rate is automatically reflected in the rate charged by all the National Central Banks which are members of the EMU.

2 The short-term facility rate (STF)

The STF is the rate of interest which the Central Bank charges the commercial banks when it grants them short-term loans. If the STF is increased, then the commercial banks pass this increase on to their customers in the form of increased rates of interest and vice versa.

3 The degree of risk to the lender

Banks charge three basic different rates of interest to different customers depending on the customers' credit status. These are 'AAA', which is the lowest rate, 'AA', which is the next lowest and 'A' which is the highest rate. This last rate is the one most commonly charged (see also 'Sub-prime lenders', p. 162).

4 The degree of liquidity of the loan

The degree of liquidity of the loan refers to the relative ease in obtaining instant repayment of the loan at any given time. When somebody obtains a mortgage from a financial institution, the institution holds the deeds of the house and can sell it to obtain any outstanding debt. Because property tends to increase in value there is very little risk attached to the loan, therefore these mortgages tend to carry low rates of interest. On the other hand, unsecured loans tend to carry high rates of interest.

5 The rate of inflation

As the rate of inflation increases, people tend to save less money due to fears of negative interest rates. To overcome this fear banks tend to increase interest rates as inflation increases to encourage a steady flow of savings.

6 The demand for loans in relation to the level of savings

If there is a shortage of funds in the financial institutions relative to the demand for loans, then the laws of supply and demand ensure that interest rates increase and vice versa.

Investment

✳Importance of investment in the economy

- Investment has a multiplier effect on incomes. We have already seen that this means the income created from the investment is greater than the value of the original investment.
- Investment increases the productive capacity of the country, e.g. when new factories are set up more wealth can be produced.
- Investment increases the productive capacity of labour, e.g. a man can dig a much bigger area in a day with a JCB than with his hands.
- Investment increases employment. When investors set up an enterprise they usually employ people to make and distribute their products.
- Investment creates increased government revenue. This revenue will come from the extra PAYE from employees, the extra VAT from the new sales and taxes on profits if the enterprise is successful.

✳The factors affecting the level of investment

1 Entrepreneurs' expectations

Entrepreneurs' expectation about future profits is the most important factor affecting the level of investment. If entrepreneurs expect that profits will be big in the near future then they will invest to take advantage of these profits and vice versa. These expectations are governed by the other factors listed below.

2 The rate of interest

The rate of interest is a cost of production. When interest increases profits decrease, resulting in less investment and vice versa.

3 The cost of capital goods

The purchase of capital goods incurs fixed costs. Like any cost, as these increase profit decreases resulting in less investment and vice versa.

4 Government policy

Governments can encourage investment by creating an atmosphere in the economy which is conducive to investment. (See below, 'Government encouraging investment in the Irish economy'.)

5 The state of technology

As technology improves more goods can be produced at a lower average cost, thus increasing profits leading to more investment.

6 The international economic climate

If the general level of demand and the general level of income abroad are increasing, this will encourage firms to invest in export-oriented industries, thus increasing the level of investment.

7 The domestic economic climate

If the general level of demand and the general level of income in the domestic market are increasing, new firms will be encouraged to set up to meet this domestic demand leading to more investment.

✳Government encouraging investment in the Irish economy

There are various means by which the government can encourage an increased level of investment in the Irish economy.

Grants to firms/taking equity in firms

When a government gives a grant to a firm this reduces the amount of money which this firm must invest in the business, thus increasing the return on the capital which it actually invests. This obviously makes it more attractive to firms to invest in the economy.

In a similar manner, the firm would have to provide less capital if the government took shares in the business, thus reducing the amount of money which the firm must raise.

Reduce company profit taxes

As taxes on company profits are decreased this makes for a better return on capital invested, thus encouraging more investment. The reduction in company profit taxes (corporation profit tax) could result in a situation where normal profits could now be earned, when it was not possible to do so prior to the reduction.

Reduce capital gains tax

Some people set up businesses in order to make a profit on the sale of the business itself after a relatively short period of time. If capital gains taxes (the tax on the profit earned from the sale of assets) are high these people may be reluctant to invest. By lowering these taxes more people will be encouraged to invest.

Improve the infrastructure

It is often said that Ireland has a First World economy and a Third World infrastructure. Poor road and railway systems lead to an expensive and inefficient means of distribution of goods. Additional expenditure by the government on these systems and on our waste disposal system, as well as improving our ports, would act as an incentive to more entrepreneurs to invest in Ireland.

Depreciation to be written off against investments over a short period

Depreciation is the loss in value of assets. It is an expense of running a business. If the price of an asset could be written off over a three-year period instead of a five-year period this would result in less tax being paid on profits during that three-year period. This again would increase profitability and thus attract more investors.

Note: The factors which affect the competitiveness of Irish-based firms on the international market can be relevant to this topic, see p. 279.

LEARN THE KEY POINTS

1. The definition of capital
2. Know the terminology used in conjunction with capital
3. Explain the reasons why people save
4. Understand the factors which affect the level of saving
5. Explain the paradox of thrift
6. Understand the loanable funds (classical) theory of interest rates
7. Understand the liquidity preference (Keynesian) theory of interest rates
8. Explain the factors affecting the rate of interest
9. Explain the factors affecting the level of investment
10. Know how the government can encourage investment
11. Understand the factors affecting the competitiveness of Irish-based industry

Exam Q&A: See p. 422

Copy questions 1–5 into your answer book and complete each of the sentences by filling in the blank spaces.

1 Capital stock is the ____________ of ____________ goods in existence ____________ time.

2 Gross capital formation is the total ____________ spent on ____________ goods in ____________.

3 Depreciation is the ____________.

4 Net capital formation is ____________ less ____________.

5 Two examples of social capital are ____________ and ____________.

6 Distinguish between saving and investing.

7 What is a negative rate of interest?

8 Why is it important to distinguish between gross capital formation and net capital formation in any given year?

9 Distinguish between capital widening and capital deepening.

10 'When there is a substantial increase in interest rates offered by the financial institutions on savings everybody will save more.' Is this a true or false statement? Give reasons for your answer.

11 Explain 'the paradox of thrift'.

12 Keynes identified three motives for holding money. Name and explain each of these motives.

13 How would an increase in the rate of interest affect the amount of money held for each of these motives? Give an explanation of your answers.

14 'The level of investment is determined, mostly, by entrepreneurs' expectations concerning future profits.' Explain the factors which entrepreneurs take into consideration when making their decisions on investment.

15 'Government policies, at any given time, could discourage private investment.' Explain fully any four such policies.

16 Is the liquidity preference theory a full explanation of interest rates? Give reasons for your answer.

Chapter 30
Enterprise and Profit

Enterprise

Most governments in the developed and in the developing world are encouraging the growth of an enterprise culture in their economies. These are economies based on policies which encourage commercial initiative, which are audacious and which require careful management by the investor.

Definition of enterprise

Enterprise is that special form of human activity which organises the other factors of production and undertakes the risk involved in production.

Entrepreneurs

Definition of an entrepreneur

An **entrepreneur** is the person who provides enterprise.

In a small business it is often simple to identify the entrepreneur. It is usually the person who puts up the money to start the business and that person also manages the business. This person is organising the business and is undertaking the risk that the investment in the business may lose.

However, it may be more difficult to recognise the entrepreneur in a very big public limited company. In this situation, the role of the entrepreneur is divided between the risk-takers (the shareholders) and the organisers (the management team).

Whichever way we want to identify entrepreneurs, the essential feature to recognise is that it is those people who provide the initiative and ideas necessary to set up and run a business. It is these people who organise the other factors of production into an effective, productive and, hopefully, profitable unit. The use of the word 'hopefully' indicates that entrepreneurs are taking a risk.

Land lying idle can produce nothing. A machine, capital, is just a lump of metal. Labour is not very productive on its own. Thus entrepreneurs are needed to bring these three factors together to maximise their usage. It is obvious that entrepreneurs are vital to an economy.

Profit

Definition of profit

Profit is the return to enterprise, if the business is successful!

Let us look at the difference between accounting profit and real/true (or economic) profit.

Profit, in the accounting sense, is the difference between total revenue and total explicit costs.

An entrepreneur has to pay all the explicit costs of running the business. However, the entrepreneur also incurs implied costs when running the business (the income he/she has to forego).

Example

In the example below assume implied costs of €60,000.

An economist includes both explicit and implied costs when calculating profit. Thus all costs including normal profit are calculated.

Total revenue	€100,000
Total explicit costs	€60,000
Accounting profit	**€40,000**
Minus implied costs	€60,000
Economic (real) profit	**(€20,000)**

Here, it has **cost** the entrepreneur €20,000 to run the business. If this situation persisted in the long run the business would have to close down.

✳Characteristics of profit

The characteristics of profit are sometimes referred to as the unique characteristics of enterprise.

1. The return to enterprise, profit, is a **residual**, i.e. the payment received by the entrepreneur is that which is left over after the other factors of production have been paid.

2. The entrepreneur is the only factor which can have a **negative return**, i.e. the entrepreneur can lose money. He/she must buy the raw materials, pay the wages, energy costs and overheads. The entrepreneur must hope that the product will

sell in sufficient quantities and at a price which more than covers all of these costs. If the income does not cover the costs then the entrepreneur loses money. The other factors, at worst, may suffer a nil return, e.g. the business may be doing so badly that the owner could not pay any wages.

3 **Profit fluctuates** more than the return to any of the other factors. Labour is usually employed at an agreed wage, which is received each week. Land is usually leased at a fixed rent, which is paid on a regular basis. Because profit is a residual, there can be many periods in a year where no profit is made and other periods when a reasonably good profit is earned.

The uninsurable risks undertaken by entrepreneurs

All business activity is risky and certain events can cause firms to lose money. Some of these risks are common to all firms. An actuary can calculate the probability of the risks occurring and can also calculate the probable financial loss arising from their occurrence. If there are a sufficiently large number of firms sharing the risk and the probability of it occurring is relatively small, then insurance companies will offer insurance cover against these risks. Most firms have no difficulty obtaining insurance against the possibility of a fire damaging their premises or against the possibility of theft of their stock.

However, there are many other risks which all businesses take which will never be insurable because the insurance companies cannot calculate the degree of risk involved. They cannot calculate the potential sum involved in any potential claim, or there is not a sufficiently large number of firms sharing the same risks.

1 **Production takes place in anticipation of consumption.** An entrepreneur relies on market research to indicate what product should be produced. Thus in most cases production takes place in the belief that there is a demand for the good. If the anticipated demand does not materialise then losses will occur. Thus the production of the product was a bad business decision. No insurance company would underwrite this situation. If they did then everybody could set up businesses and the insurance industry would be bankrupt.

2 **The loss of profits caused by sudden increases in the cost of production.** Insurance companies cannot accurately factor this into their calculations; therefore they cannot offer insurance cover for it.

3 **The loss of profit caused by strikes.** Again the insurance companies cannot assess the probability of these occurring and so will not offer protection against them. Do not forget that employers could manipulate workers to go on strike.

4 **The loss of profit caused by changes in consumers' tastes and fashions.** Consumers are human and their tastes can change from time to time. Products that were once fashionable can become unfashionable. It is not always possible to foresee these changes taking place, therefore, no insurance can be offered to cover these situations.

5 **The entry of rival firms coming into the industry**. As more firms enter an industry it is inevitable that some of the original firm's customers will be attracted to the new firms. Thus the original firm's volume of sales will decrease. The extra supply and the extra competition will also drive down the market price, thus decreasing the firm's revenue. This could result in losses for the original firm. No insurance company could possibly give protection for this.

6 **Loss due to the adverse effects of new legislation.** The government may pass legislation requiring new health and safety procedures which are expensive to implement. It may also introduce a new, higher minimum wage rate. These extra costs cannot always be passed onto the consumer; therefore it could result in some marginal firms losing money. As there is no way of predicting these changes in legislation and of knowing their effect on a firm's profit, no insurance company could offer cover for this risk.

7 **Loss caused by the adverse effects of international trade agreements.** From time to time the government enters into international trade agreements with other countries, which hopefully will benefit the overall Irish economy. However, the agreements could have an adverse effect on a small number of firms in Ireland. For example, the government may enter into a bi-lateral agreement with some other country which has a population of 60 million people. While this will open up a new and potentially big market for Ireland's exporters, indigenous firms may suffer as a result of new cheaper imports. The risk of this occurring cannot be calculated.

✳ Importance of entrepreneurs in a free enterprise economy

1 Entrepreneurs organise the other factors of production into productive units. Without enterprise, the other factors would remain idle and there would be no employment.

2 They decide what goods will be produced, and in what quantities they will be produced, at any given time. This is based on their market research and they take the risk of producing these goods. The entrepreneur takes a risk that too many goods may be produced and so he/she will bear the risk inherent in this decision.

3 They set the initial prices at which goods will be sold, in the hope of making a profit. This is usually based on cost price plus a percentage mark-up. The market mechanism then determines the long run price.

4 They invest money into the economy. This increases the productive capacity of the country and also has a multiplier effect on incomes.

5 Entrepreneurs provide an investment outlet for savers. Many individuals do not consume some of their income and are prepared to risk their spare money in somebody else's business, in the hope of getting a better return on it than they would receive from a bank.

✳The importance of profits in a free enterprise economy

1. **Profits encourage risk taking:** It is the prospect of making profit which encourages entrepreneurs to undertake the risks inherent in setting up a business. Without profits no firm would supply goods or services. Thus fewer goods would be available to consumers.
2. **Profits indicate the best use of resources to satisfy consumer demand:** Profits are an indication to entrepreneurs about what goods and services consumers want (demand), and so indicate what areas of investment are the most suitable for the use of scarce resources.
3. **Profits encourage investment:** The prospect of making profit encourages entrepreneurs to invest in ventures. This extra investment increases the productive capacity of the country and the investment also has a multiplier effect on incomes.
4. **Profits provide funds for expansion:** Entrepreneurs may use the profits earned to invest in their existing business, or to expand their existing activities or to diversify into other businesses. Thus they do not have to borrow money at expensive rates of interest or take on extra shareholders.
5. **Profits ensure continuity of production in the long run:** Normal profit is the minimum level of profit required to keep an entrepreneur in production in the long run. If normal profits are not earned, then an entrepreneur will cease operating, hence they are essential to ensure that production continues in the long run.
6. **SNPs reward innovation and encourage cost reduction:** This gets better use of the scarce resources needed to produce goods. Those entrepreneurs who earn SNPs do so because they may be more efficient and because they use innovative ways of producing a product, thus minimising their costs of production. By reducing costs they are minimising, if not eliminating, wastage of resources.
7. **Profits are a source of revenue for the government:** Most profits earned by entrepreneurs are taxed by the government and become a source of revenue for the state. (There are, of course, exceptions to this where the government tries to encourage further investment.) The government can use these taxes to further develop the economy.

✳Level of profit earned by entrepreneurs

All entrepreneurs do not earn the same level of profit: some earn normal profit, some earn supernormal profit and others suffer losses.

The level of profit earned by the entrepreneur depends on:

- The ability of the entrepreneur to organise production in an efficient manner.
- The level of natural ability, i.e. rent of ability.

- The type of industry in which the entrepreneur is operating, e.g. in the long run an entrepreneur will only earn normal profit in perfect and imperfect competition, but could earn supernormal profit in a monopolistic or an oligopolistic market.

✳Reasons for the survival of small and medium-sized firms

Despite the advantages, which large firms gain from the economies of scale, it is still possible for small or medium-sized firms to survive in Ireland's modern economy.

1 Small size of market/scale of operation

The restricted size of the market may not facilitate the operation of large-scale business, e.g. in a rural area a small shop may be viable while a large supermarket may not be.

2 Personal services

Consumers may desire personal attention in the provision of goods or services and a small firm may be the only type of business which can provide this, e.g. a plumber providing repair services to households.

3 Consumer loyalty

A small firm may have built up a reputation over the years in the provision of goods and services to its customers and consumers may respond by their loyalty to that firm, thus making it difficult for other firms to gain a foothold.

4 Desire of citizens to maintain a viable community

Citizens in smaller communities may support local businesses so that the continuity of supply is ensured, thus helping to maintain a viable community. For example, in many areas throughout Ireland communities wish to maintain the existence of 'community' hospitals.

5 Traditional/niche markets

- The type of product or service being supplied might make it more suitable for a small firm, e.g. wedding planners, handmade products and perishable products.
- A small firm may find it easier to locate close to the market, whereas it might be difficult for a larger firm to do so, e.g. roadside sellers of local produce can be flexible in choosing their location.

6 Exclusive nature of the commodity being provided

Heavy goods, which are costly to transport, may be manufactured locally on a small scale to supply nearby markets, e.g. the manufacture of concrete blocks in areas which service local markets.

7 Availability of capital

Small profitable firms may find it very difficult to get the finance to expand their operations and hence the business remains small.

8 Membership of voluntary groups

Some firms producing on a small scale may offset the disadvantage they have in competition with large producers by a joint marketing strategy with other small suppliers, e.g. hotel groups, individually owned grocery shops trading under a shared name such as Spar and Centra.

Note: Students should be acutely aware of the fact that there is a very close relationship between capital and enterprise as entrepreneurs undertake most capital investment. Therefore, when preparing for questions on enterprise, attention should also be given to the factors which influence the level of investment and also to the means by which the government can encourage investment. These are featured in Chapter 29, Capital and Interest Rates.

LEARN THE KEY POINTS

1. The definition of enterprise
2. Understand the difference between accounting profit and true profit
3. Understand the unique characteristics of enterprise
4. Know the uninsurable risks undertaken by enterprise
5. Understand the importance of enterprise and entrepreneurs in a free market economy
6. Understand the importance of profits in a free market economy
7. Explain the different levels of profit earned by entrepreneurs
8. Explain the reasons why small firms can survive in our modern economy

Exam Q&A: See p. 426

Copy questions 1–3 into your answer book and complete each of the sentences by filling in the blank spaces.

1. Enterprise is that special form of __________ which __________ the other factors of production and undertakes the __________ involved in production.
2. Accounting profit is the difference between __________ and __________.
3. Accounting profit minus __________ equals __________ profit.
4. 'Enterprise differs from the other factors of production in a number of ways.' Give a brief explanation of this statement.
5. Distinguish between insurable and uninsurable risks.
6. Identify, with an explanation, the entrepreneur in an enterprise undertaken in a centrally planned economy.
7. Why are entrepreneurs needed in a free enterprise economy? Explain your answer.
8. Explain how the prospect of earning profits encourages efficiency of production.
9. There are a very large number of small and medium sized enterprises in Ireland. How do these enterprises continue to survive even though they do not benefit from the economies of scale? Explain your answer.
10. Ireland needs more indigenous industries. Explain how the government could encourage more native entrepreneurs to establish businesses.

Chapter 31
Population

This chapter is an insight into both global and Irish demographic trends.

There is a great natural temptation, when discussing this type of topic, to throw statistics at a page to highlight points being made. Statistics can be very boring and almost impossible to remember. Therefore, we will endeavour to keep these to a minimum. However, some are necessary.

Demography

Definition of demography

The study of human population is known as **demography**.

A country is **underpopulated** when any increase in the population leads to an increase in the average income per head under given economic resources.

A country has an **optimum** population when its average income per head is at its highest possible level under given economic resources.

Overpopulation exists when an increase in the labour force decreases the average income per head of the population under given economic resources.

The size of a population will change if the birth rate exceeds the death rate or vice versa. This is known as the natural change in the population.

- The birth rate is the number of live births per 1,000 people.
- The death rate is the number of deaths per 1,000 people.

When we make reference to changes in population on a worldwide scale we are referring to the natural change in population.

However, the size of a population of an individual country will also change if the natural change is accompanied by a net change in migration, i.e. if emigration is greater than immigration and vice versa.

Emigration

Emigration is caused by either push forces or pull forces.

✳Push forces

The push forces are those factors that compel people to leave their own country. These factors include a high level of unemployment, low wage rates, lack of promotion opportunities, poor social infrastructure and political reasons.

✳Pull forces

The pull forces are those factors that attract a person to another country. These factors include higher wages, better job experience, greater political stability abroad, a more attractive climate and the desire to broaden one's outlook on the world.

✳Positive and negative effects of emigration

1. A reduction in the level of unemployment. This eases pressure on government finances as expenditure on social welfare decreases.
2. A reduction in the social costs associated with unemployment, e.g. vandalism and crime. If the emigration is of a temporary nature these emigrants may return with improved skills and money to invest in the economy.
3. A smaller domestic market for goods and services decreases investment opportunities and may cause even more unemployment.
4. No return to the government on the money which it spent on educating the emigrants. This is often referred to as 'the brain drain'.
5. An increase in the dependency ratio, as it is usually the people in the 18 to 35 year age group who leave the country, leaving young children and older retired people in the country.
6. A loss to the economy of potential entrepreneurs, as it is usually these enterprising people who are reluctant to wait around for something to improve in a country.
7. Ironically, it may be more difficult to attract more industries into the economy due to the lack of the skilled labour.

World Population

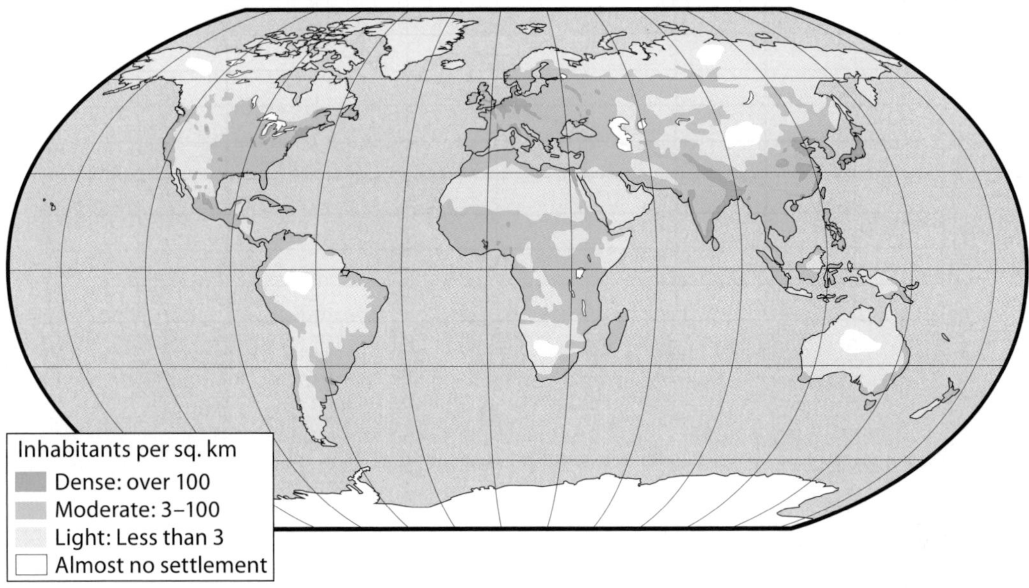

Fig 31.1 Population density of the world per sq. km

According to the US Census Bureau the world population was 6,605,980,890 on 19 July 2007. (For information about population visit *www.census.gov/main.*)

This site also shows that the world population grew from roughly 3 billion in 1960 to 6.6 billion in the year 2000. That is a doubling of the world's population over 40 years and it predicts that it will grow to over 9.5 billion by 2050.

Growth rate in world population

The world population growth rate rose from about 1.5 per cent per year in 1950 to a peak of over 2 per cent in the early 1960s, due to reductions in mortality, see Fig 31.2.

Growth rates thereafter started to decline. This happened because people married at an older age and there was an increasing availability and use of effective contraceptive methods.

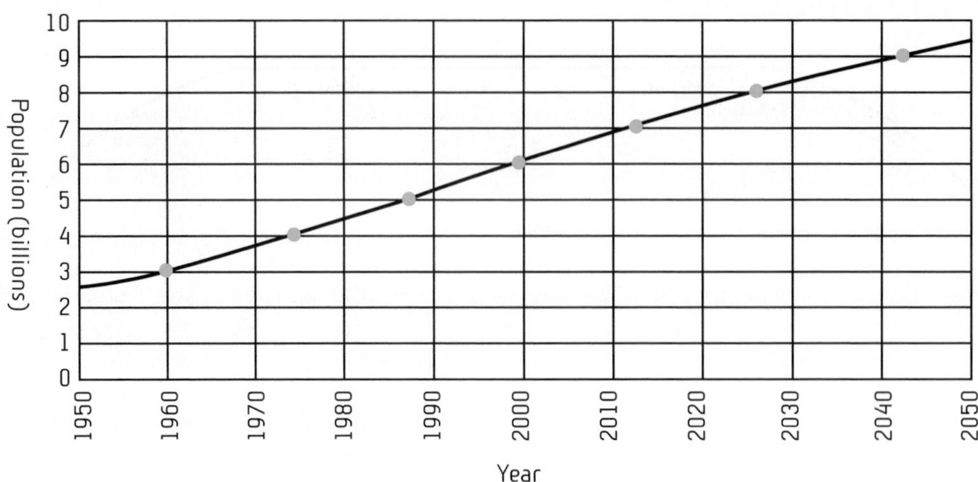

Source: *US Census Bureau, International Data Base, August 2006 version*

Fig 31.2 World population: 1950–2050

Note that changes in population growth have not always been steady. A dip in the growth rate from 1959–1960, for instance, was due to the 'Great Leap Forward' in China. During that time, both natural disasters and decreased agricultural output in the wake of massive social reorganisation caused China's death rate to rise sharply and its fertility rate to fall by almost half (see Fig 31.3).

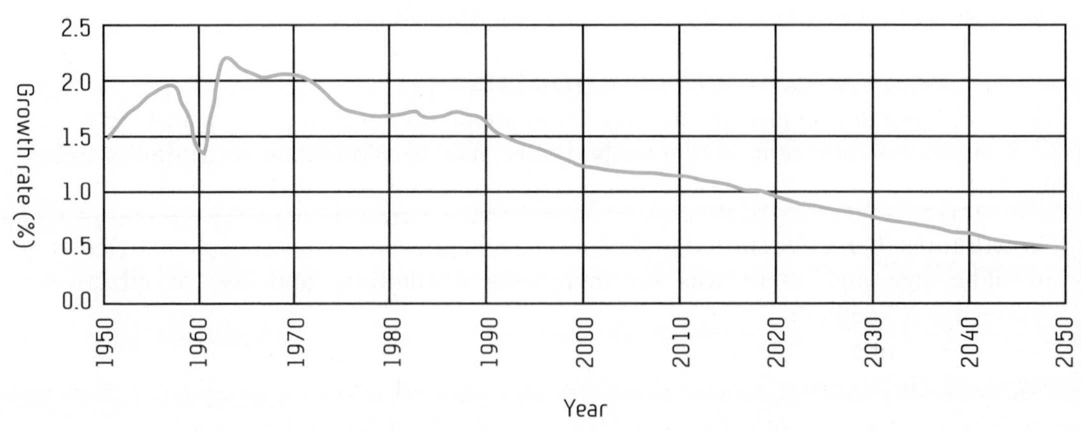

Source: *US Census Bureau, International Data Base, August 2006 version*

Fig 31.3 World population growth rates: 1950–2050

❋Regional distribution of the growth in the world's population 1960–2000

In 1960, 2.1 billion (70 per cent) of the world's 3 billion people lived in the less-developed regions of Africa, Asia and Latin America. By the year 2000 this had grown to 4.8 billion (80 per cent), and 98 per cent of the projected growth of the world population by 2025 will occur in these regions.

Africa

Africa, with an average fertility rate exceeding five children per woman during the entire period has grown the fastest among these regions. There are almost three times as many Africans alive today (767 million) as there were in 1960.

Africa's share of global population is projected to rise to 20 per cent in 2050 (from only 9 per cent in 1960), while Europe's share is projected to decline from 20 per cent to 7 per cent over that same period.

In 1960, Africa had less than half the population of Europe; in 2050, it may be approaching three times as many people.

Asia and Latin America

Asia, by far the most populous region, has more than doubled in size (to over 3.6 billion), as has Latin America and the Caribbean.

North America and Europe

In contrast, the population of North America has grown by only 50 per cent. Europe's population has increased by only 20 per cent and is now roughly stable.

Positive signs for the future

The changing pattern in the distribution of the world's population in itself is not a problem. The major problem is ensuring economic development occurs in these new heavily populated areas.

The United Nations Population Division has shown that a growing number of developing countries have initiated plans in the areas of fertility and mortality reduction. Women are having fewer children than ever before, and population growth has slowed, from 2.4 per cent to 1.3 per cent in the last 30 years.

Problems

The existence of large families, in the recent past, means that there are many more women of childbearing age. Global population is still rising by about 78 million people a year. Half the world's population is under 25 years of age and there are over a billion young people between 15 and 24, the parents of the next generation.

Most population growth is taking place in the world's poorest and least-prepared countries. The fastest growing regions are sub-Saharan Africa, and parts of South Asia and Western Asia. Whether the rate of population growth continues to decline and whether it is accompanied by economic development will depend on the actions taken to improve education, to promote gender equality and to significantly improve access to health services, including reproductive health.

Meanwhile, population growth has slowed or stopped in Europe, North America and Japan. The United States is the only industrial country where large population increases are still projected, largely as the result of immigration. In the twenty-first century, over a billion people are still deprived of basic needs.

Source: *The United States Population Division*

Effects of globalisation

According to the World Bank report, *Global Economic Prospects 2007: Managing the Next Wave of Globalization*, growth in developing countries will have reached a near record 7 per cent in 2006. In 2007 and 2008, the rate of growth will probably decline, but it is still likely to exceed 6 per cent, i.e. more than twice the rate of growth in high-income countries, which is expected to be 2.6 per cent.

The report also predicts that, in the next 25 years, the global economy could expand from $35 trillion in 2005 to $72 trillion in 2030. In the report the author, Richard Newfarmer, states,

> While this outcome represents only a slight acceleration of global growth compared to the past 25 years, it is driven more than ever before by strong performance in developing countries.

François Bourguignon, Chief Economist and Senior Vice President, Development Economics of the World Bank, said,

> The number of people living on less than $1 a day could be cut in half, from 1.1 billion now to 550 million in 2030. However, some regions, notably Africa, are at risk of being left behind. Moreover, income inequality could widen within many countries, compounding current concerns over inequality between countries.

Identifiable requirements

Of the 4.8 billion people in developing countries:

1. Nearly three-fifths lack basic sanitation.
2. Almost a third have no access to clean water.
3. A quarter of people do not have adequate housing.
4. A fifth have no access to modern health services. There is a massive spread of HIV/AIDS.
5. In less-developed regions, a fifth of children do not attend school to the end of primary level.

✳Problems caused by the developed regions of the world

There is escalating pressure on the planet due to increased and wasteful consumption trends, and to the growing numbers of people creating demands for food and water. In addition, the effect of global warming is a growing threat to our ability to sustain our levels of growth. Possible changes, such as the sea level rising and increased storms and floods, could affect billions of people.

Conclusion

The cumulative effects of continuing poverty, gender discrimination, HIV/AIDS, environmental change and shrinking resources for development have the potential to wipe out the benefits of lower birth rates.

Source: *United Nations Population Fund*

The IMF and the Millennium Development Goals

The Millennium Development Goals (MDGs) are a set of development targets agreed by the international community, which centre on halving poverty and improving the welfare of the world's poorest countries by 2015. The IMF contributes to this effort through its advice, technical assistance, and lending to countries. Together with the World Bank, it assesses the progress being made towards achieving the MDGs through an annual Global Monitoring Report.

In September 2000, at the United Nations Millennium Summit, world leaders agreed to eight specific and measurable development goals (the MDGs) to be achieved by 2015:

1. The eradication of extreme poverty and hunger
2. The achieving of universal primary education
3. The promotion of gender equality and the empowering of women
4. The reduction of child mortality
5. The improving of maternal health
6. The combating of HIV/AIDS, malaria and other diseases
7. The ensuring of environmental sustainability
8. The creation of a global partnership for development, with targets for aid, trade, and debt relief

Source: *IMF*

As stated above, the IMF and the World Bank intend to monitor the progress being made towards the achievement of these goals and to implement any new policies which are deemed necessary.

See also: 'The Heavily Indebted Poor Countries (HIPC) Initiative', as outlined in Chapter 24, Economic Development and Growth, see p. 254.

The Irish Scene

Ireland, like all other countries gets the statistical information about its population from the Census Surveys undertaken by the Central Statistics Office (CSO), which are normally undertake twice in every decade. These statistics have very practical uses and the CSO itself lists the following as being the most important.

✳The importance of a census of population

The CSO lists the importance of a census of population as follows:

1. The census gives a comprehensive picture of the social and living conditions of our people. Only a census can provide such complete detail. The census is not, however, an end in itself! Rather the results are essential tools for effective policy, planning and decision-making purposes.
2. Ireland has been conducting Censuses of Population since 1841. This enables us to track developments over a long period with considerable accuracy. The census is therefore a fundamental part of our national heritage and collective knowledge.
3. At national level current population statistics are essential for planning the provision of healthcare, education, employment, etc.

   Regional figures are critical for determining regional policy and for the operation of regional authorities, e.g. regional sections of the HSE and Vocational Education Committees.
4. The greatest strength of the census is the provision of detailed population figures at local level. These help to identify likely demand for schools and hospitals, areas of relatively high unemployment, the best location for new shops, etc.
5. Article 16.2 of the Constitution (Bunreacht na hÉireann) lays down that the total membership of Dáil Éireann depends on the population as measured by the census, i.e. one TD per 20,000 to 30,000 persons. Constituency reviews normally take place once the definitive results of the census have been published.
6. The census is also the only means of accurately measuring the exact extent of migration. By comparing the results of successive censuses, and taking account of the number of births and deaths that have occurred over the same period, we get an accurate measure of net migration (the difference between inward and outward migration). In the three-year period ending April 2005 the CSO estimated that net immigration was approximately 114,800. This represents the difference between 55,800 people who left the country and 170,600 who came into the country. The importance of migration as a component of population change is one of the reasons why censuses are carried out every five years.

Source: *CSO*

Arising from these points let us summarise and state that a census of population in Ireland provides information on the following economic areas which need attention.

1. **Demographic changes:** It provides information on demographic changes both nationally and on a regional basis.

2. **Infrastructural requirements:** It helps the economy plan for future infrastructural requirements.

3. **Planning for the provision of essential services:** It highlights the additional investment required in services such as health and education.

4. **Regional policy:** The government may be prompted to change and develop regional policy if some counties experience depopulation.

5. **Pension planning:** It can highlight the need for the provision of pension funds, both public and private.

6. **Future levels of consumer demand:** Producers can predict more accurately future demand, which reduces the risk of future investment and also ensures that needs and wants can be satisfied.

7. **Labour market:** The data can be used to predict and make provision for future labour requirements.

8. **Profiling of the population:** The population can be profiled by age, gender, nationality, place of residence, marital status, number of children, religion and ethnic backgrounds.

Demographic patterns in Ireland

Relatively recent (the past 200 years) demographic patterns in Ireland are unique in the Western world. Ireland had a population of just over 8 million in 1841, when the first official census was carried out. Of this, over 6.5 million were in what is now the Republic of Ireland.

Now look at Table 31.1 on p. 340 to see the dramatic changes that have taken place since 1841. The highlighted figures indicate that the population almost halved in the 50-year period from 1841 to 1891.

Every Irish student is aware that the biggest cause of this decline in population was The Famine. The Famine was caused by the potato blight during the summer of 1845. It was not unusual to have crops that failed and people thought that it was just an isolated event. However, the potato crop failed for the next four years. The potato was the staple diet for the Irish people at the time and was the only food that was affordable for the masses.

Over the next ten years, over 1 million people died from disease and starvation and 2 million people emigrated.

Table 31.1 The population of Ireland 1841–2006

Year	Persons	Males	Females
1841	**6,528,799**	3,222,485	3,306,314
1851	5,111,557	2,494,478	2,617,079
1861	4,402,111	2,169,042	2,233,069
1871	4,053,187	1,992,468	2,060,719
1881	3,870,020	1,912,438	1,957,582
1891	**3,468,694**	**1,728,601**	**1,740,093**
1901	3,221,823	1,610,085	1,611,738
1911	3,139,688	1,589,509	1,550,179
1926	2,971,992	1,506,889	1,465,103
1936	2,968,420	1,520,454	1,447,966
1946	2,955,107	1,494,877	1,460,230
1951	2,960,593	1,506,597	1,453,996
1956	2,898,264	1,462,928	1,435,336
1961	2,818,341	1,416,549	1,401,792
1966	2,884,002	1,449,032	1,434,970
1971	2,978,248	1,495,760	1,482,488
1979	3,368,217	1,693,272	1,674,945
1981	3,443,405	1,729,354	1,714,051
1986	3,540,643	1,769,690	1,770,953
1991	3,525,719	1,753,418	1,772,301
1996	3,626,087	1,800,232	1,825,855
2002	3,917,203	1,946,164	1,971,039
2006	4,234,925	2,118,209	2,116,716

Source: *CSO*

Simultaneously, the Industrial Revolution in the late eighteenth and nineteenth centuries bypassed most parts of Ireland. This meant that both the push and pull forces ensured that the pattern of emigration would continue. Even after Irish Independence, the twenty-six counties were without any industry and with few natural resources. So the pattern of emigration continued.

✳ Growth of the Irish economy and population

The ending of protectionism in the late 1950s, combined with both foreign direct investment and a marked increase in government investment, heralded a period of unprecedented economic growth and a reversal of the pattern of population decline.

This first period of economic revival continued until the late 1970s. The impact of two very substantial increases in the world price of oil combined with unsustainable deficit financing of government expenditure, led to a sharp setback in Ireland's economic fortunes. By 1987, emigration, unemployment, taxation and government borrowing had all reached excessively high levels.

However, since 1987, there has been both a dramatic and sustained level of growth in the Irish economy. Many studies have attempted to explain this rapid growth and amongst these explanations are:

1. Membership of the European Union
2. Significant subventions (grants) from the European Union
3. Favourable regulatory and investment climate
4. The English language and a lack of cultural barriers
5. Openness to trade
6. Stability of political and legal institutions
7. Social partnership
8. Industry clustering
9. Human resources
10. Education

The cumulative effect of all these factors has been a fall in emigration, the return of people who had previously emigrated and an inflow of labour from other countries. These, accompanied by an increase in the birth rate, have resulted in the increase in population recorded in the 2006 Census.

In its *Preliminary Report on the Census of 2006* the CSO highlights the following points.

1 Highest population since 1861

The population of the state increased by almost 318,000 persons between 2002 and 2006 to reach the highest recorded census level since 1861. The preliminary total for the population enumerated on census night, 23 April 2006, was 4,234,925 persons, compared with 3,917,203 in April 2002, representing an increase of 8.1 per cent in four years or 2 per cent per annum.

2 Migration the dominant factor

On average there were 46,000 more immigrants than emigrants annually over the 2002–2006 period compared with an annual excess of births over deaths of 33,000. The corresponding figures for 1996–2002 were 26,000 and 23,000, respectively.

3 Largest population growth in EU

Looked at from a ten-year perspective, Ireland's population increased at an annual average rate of 1.6 per cent between 1996 and 2006 – the largest population growth rate in the EU. Cyprus (+1.5 per cent) and Luxembourg (+1.2 per cent) were the only other countries to record population growth rates in excess of 1 per cent over this period.

The economic implications of Ireland's increasing population

1. **Larger domestic market:** An increase in the population causes a growth in the demand for goods and services within the country. This may lead to increased opportunities for investment. The increase in production may also allow some firms to benefit from the economies of scale.

2. **Increased pressure on government services:** Most people are aware of the existing pressure on government health and educational resources. A rising population may put further pressure on essential services such as health and education. However, if the growth in population occurs in underpopulated areas services will be more fully utilised.

3. **Increased pressure on the country's infrastructure:** The growing population means pressure is exerted on the infrastructure of the country. While the government has long-term plans to alleviate some of these problems, e.g. Transport 21, there will be short-term problems with transport, communications, waste disposal, housing and social services.

The M1 between Dublin and the border of Northern Ireland has replaced one of the most congested roads in the country

4 **Economic planning:** An increase in population should lead to an increase in planning by both central and local authorities for the future. This will place greater emphasis on the implementation of a successful outcome of The National Development Plan 2007–2013.

5 **Decreased dependency ratio:** Many of the new members of the labour force are young, single immigrants. These increased numbers in the labour force will lower the dependency ratio and lead to increased tax revenues for the state.

6 **Government revenues:** The increase in the size of the labour force and the increase in spending should lead to increased government revenue from both direct and indirect taxes.

7 **Land values:** As population density increases, available land becomes scarce and hence the price of land increases. This will have a significant effect on costs for industry and add to the existing pressure on the price of private housing in the country.

Changing patterns of females in the Irish workforce

The most notable feature of the change in the Irish labour force is the increased participation rate of married females. This is highlighted in Tables 31.2(a), (b) and (c) on p. 344, which show the percentage of the people in each age bracket willing to work in the three identified categories.

In every age group the participation rate is increasing for married females. There are a number of notable reasons for this (no particular order of importance is implied):

1. An increase in the standards of education.
2. An overall increase in the demand for labour which cannot be met by increasing the male participation rate.
3. As the wage rate increases the opportunity cost of not working is continuously increasing.
4. Greater economic pressure to earn more money to pay for mortgages.
5. A changing social attitude towards mothers and their role in society.
6. The individualisation of the income tax system has made a big difference to total family income where both spouses are working.
7. The increases in child allowances and the greater availability of crèche facilities.
8. A greater expectation of a higher standard of living.

Table 31.2(a) Labour force participation rates: males

	Actual %	Actual %	Actual %	Actual %	Forecast %	Forecast %	Forecast %
Age group	1991	1996	2002	2004	2006	2011	2016
25–29	93.1	92.1	91.5	91.9	93.0	93.0	93.0
30–34	94.7	94.8	93.8	93.1	93.0	93.0	93.0
35–39	93.0	93.9	93.8	93.2	93.0	93.0	93.0
40–44	92.2	92.8	92.1	93.0	93.0	93.0	93.0
45–49	90.3	89.7	89.8	91.8	93.0	93.0	93.0
50–54	86.0	84.3	85.4	86.2	88.0	88.5	89.0
55–59	74.9	72.6	75.2	75.5	77.0	78.0	79.0
60–64	55.6	51.8	55.7	54.9	57.0	59.0	61.0
65 +	16.5	15.3	15.1	13.7	16.0	17.0	18.0

Table 31.2(b) Labour force participation rates: married females

	Actual %	Actual %	Actual %	Actual %	Forecast %	Forecast %	Forecast %
Age group	1991	1996	2002	2004	2006	2011	2016
25–29	55.1	66.8	65.7	68.3	69.0	71.0	71.0
30–34	47.2	59.8	65.7	64.4	68.0	71.0	74.0
35–39	40.2	55.4	61.3	62.6	66.0	69.0	74.0
40–44	35.3	49.9	64.0	64.5	68.0	70.0	73.0
45–49	31.5	41.8	61.6	62.3	64.0	69.0	71.0
50–54	26.6	35.2	50.5	56.0	60.0	64.0	67.0
55–59	20.0	26.5	37.2	41.2	43.0	50.0	52.0
60–64	11.7	14.8	21.5	23.7	42.0	28.0	30.0
65 +	2.5	2.6	2.9	2.9	4.0	5.5	6.0

Table 31.2(c) Labour force participation rates: other females

	Actual %	Actual %	Actual %	Actual %	Forecast %	Forecast %	Forecast %
Age group	1991	1996	2002	2004	2006	2011	2016
25–29	86.7	85.3	86.6	83.1	83.0	84.0	85.0
30–34	82.8	83.7	84.8	82.5	83.0	84.0	85.0
35–39	78.8	80.8	80.8	78.0	80.0	82.0	82.0
40–44	73.2	79.7	79.6	76.0	79.0	80.0	81.0
45–49	73.2	78.0	73.4	71.9	73.0	74.0	75.0
50–54	65.5	69.3	66.3	64.3	65.0	66.0	66.0
55–59	55.3	55.3	47.1	63.6	54.0	56.9	58.0
60–64	34.8	35.4	37.7	37.3	38.0	40.0	41.0
65 +	6.6	5.8	4.1	3.8	5.0	6.0	6.0

Source: *CSO*

⁂Evidence of pay differentials

The Programme 2000 (Programme for Government) Working Group commissioned a study by the ESRI to address the following issue: 'Why 25 years after sex discrimination was outlawed, does a gender gap in hourly wages persist?' The ESRI study was completed and their findings published in October 2000.

The 1997 data shows that women earn 84.5 per cent of the average male hourly rate as compared with 80 per cent in 1987 and 82 per cent in 1994. In addition, men are more likely than women to have jobs that include a range of benefits, such as pensions and health insurance, and when account is taken of these benefits the gap between women's and men's average hourly earnings widens to between 16.5 per cent and 17.5 per cent.

Under the current social and economic structure, it is women who typically spend less time in the labour market than men and more time as carers in the home. In 1987, this difference in work life balance accounted for half of the wage gap.

The ESRI study found that about three-quarters of the wage gap is now related to the difference in the labour market experience of women and men, such as women's shorter attachment to the workforce, interruptions in their careers, occupational downgrading on return to work and lower returns to education. The fact that the ESRI study confirms the reasons for this difference does not make the difference acceptable, rather it clarifies the issues that must be addressed in order to bridge the wage gap.

In Ireland, following the publication of the ESRI report, the Irish Congress of Trade Unions negotiated under the PPF (a national wage agreement) that a consultative group on male/female wage differentials be established and that further investigation of the gender pay gap be undertaken, within four specific sectors of the economy,

1. Retail sector
2. IT, electrical and electronics sector
3. Food sector
4. Local government sector

The study described in detail the extent of the pay gap and gender segregation within the four sectors. All four sectors show the existence of a substantial pay gap adversely affecting women, with the retail sector showing a gap of up to 30 per cent.

(Source: Taken from *Report of the Fourth Gender Equality Programme 1999–2004 and Proposal for the Fifth Programme*. Published by ICTU.)

Table 31.3 shows that the narrowing of the pay gap is a slow process.

Table 31.3 *Manufacturing industries: average weekly earnings of industrial workers in each year*

	1998	1999	2000	2001	2002	2003	2004	2005
	€	€	€	€	€	€	€	€
Adult males	428.82	453.04	477.73	512.38	538.38	564.90	588.92	609.91
Adult females	285.36	298.17	324.72	347.32	365.18	393.78	406.83	430.23

Source: *CSO*

Finally, women in Ireland can take comfort from the fact that on average their life expectancy is roughly five years longer than their male counterparts.

LEARN THE KEY POINTS

1. The definition of demography
2. Define an overpopulated economy and an underpopulated economy
3. Define an optimum population
4. Explain natural change in population
5. Explain the positive and negative consequences of emigration
6. Understand world population trends
7. Understand the distribution of the increase in the world's population
8. Know the problems associated with the increase in world population
9. Know the Millennium Development Goals
10. Explain the unique aspects of Ireland's demographic trends
11. Explain the causes of Ireland's recent economic recovery and high rate of growth
12. Understand the economic implications of Ireland's increasing populations
13. Explain the changing patterns of females in the Irish workforce
14. Explain the pay differentials in the Irish economy

Exam Q&A: See p. 430

Copy questions 1–4 into your answer book and complete each of the sentences by filling in the blank spaces.

1 Demography is the study of ____________.

2 A country is overpopulated in the economic sense when an ____________ in population causes a ____________ in the ____________ under ____________.

3 A country is underpopulated in the economic sense when an ____________ in population causes an ____________ in the ____________ under ____________.

4 A natural increase in the size of a population takes place when the ____________ is greater than the ____________.

5 Outline the major causes for concern arising from the increasing size of the world's population.

6 Give a brief explanation of the Millennium Development Goals.

7 Give a brief account of three points concerning the change in Ireland's population which were highlighted in the Census of 2006.

8 Discuss the causes of the increased participation rate of married females in the Irish workforce.

9 What factors have contributed to the gap in the wage rates paid to male and female workers?

10 What effect would a significant downturn in the Irish economy have on the size of Ireland's population? Explain your answer.

Chapter 32
The History of Economic Thought

This chapter deals with the evolution of economic theories and ideas. If we are to understand how we have created our present economies we must understand and appreciate the contributions made by the many individuals and schools of economic thought that have existed through the ages. While we group these individuals under various headings and time periods, you must remember that this is done for convenience purposes only. You may recall that we stated that economic principles are dynamic, as they must change with the prevailing world conditions.

Notes about exam questions

Any questions asked in the exam concerning economists and economic thought expect you to be able to:

1. Know the period in which the economist was writing, i.e. have a good idea of his date of birth and death.
2. The name of a major publication by that economist.
3. Give a summary of the major contributions made by that economist to the development of economic thought, i.e. the main points mentioned in each summary below, where applicable.

Questions on these economists can appear in both Section A questions and as part of Section B questions. When they appear in Section B, they are usually in conjunction with the major topic being tested in that question. For example, Keynes could feature in a question about capital or national income; Ricardo could feature in a question about international trade or economic rent.

The Mercantilists

The mercantilists were writers in the sixteenth and seventeenth century in Europe. The two most famous were Jean Baptiste Colbert and Sir Thomas Mun.

Main ideas

1. It is necessary to have a surplus on the balance of trade to increase the country's wealth. This surplus would bring more gold and silver into the country.
2. To achieve this, exports should be encouraged in any way possible, e.g. subsidies.
3. Goods should be exported at their 'highest value added' level through manufacturing of raw materials.
4. Imports should be discouraged, e.g. by imposing import duties.
5. Imports should be purchased at a base level and then 'worked up' through manufacturing in the domestic market.
6. All exports should be paid for in gold or silver, whereas imports should be traded (bartered) for other goods.
7. They believed in state intervention to aid the economy.

The Physiocrats

The physiocrats were eighteenth century French writers and economists who believed in the rule of nature. The two most famous were Francois Quesnay (1694–1724) and Jacques Turgot (1727–1781) who wrote *Reflections on the Formation and Distribution of Rules*.

Main ideas

1. No state intervention except to uphold the natural law and to protect private property. This is known as *laissez-faire*.
2. Agriculture is the source of all wealth, whereas manufacturing only changes the nature of wealth while trade only changes its ownership.
3. They advocated free international trade.

The Classical Economists

The classical economists were mostly English economists in the eighteenth and nineteenth centuries. These were the first real economists in the modern sense of the word.

Main ideas

1. *Laissez-faire*: The government should intervene in an economy only to raise funds to maintain the legal system, to defend the country and to provide public works, i.e. to build up the infrastructure of the country.
2. The wages fund theory: This stated there was a fixed fund out of which wages can be paid. The wage from this fund would give people a subsistence level of income. If wages increased above this level, the population would rise and bring the average income per person back down to its original real level. The net result of this would be an increase in the cost of production.

3. Wealth comes from production not from trade. They defined productive labour, as that labour which produced goods for sale, or which generated funds for reinvestment.
4. The labour theory of value: The value of a product is equal to the value of the labour involved in its production.
5. The classical theory of interest rates or the loanable funds theory of interest: This states that the rate of interest is determined by the interaction of the supply of and demand for loanable funds. The supply of loanable funds means the amount of money being saved in banks while the demand for them means the demand for loans from the banks.

The main classical economists were: Adam Smith, Thomas Robert Malthus, Jean Baptiste Say, David Ricardo and John Stuart Mill.

Adam Smith

Nationality: Scottish
Dates: 1723–1790
Publication: *An Inquiry into the Nature and Causes of the Wealth of Nations*

Adam Smith

Main ideas

1. Adam Smith advocated the concept of the power of the invisible hand of free enterprise. If each person pursues his/her own individual interests, he/she will benefit society in general. For example, if an individual sets up a business to make as much profit as possible for him/herself, he/she will also create employment for other people.
2. Smith advocated *laissez-faire* (see p. 349).
3. He made a distinction between productive and non-productive labour. Only that form of labour which produced goods for sale, or which generated funds for reinvestment was productive labour. Thus such people as actors, engineers and teachers were classified as non-productive labour.
4. He distinguished between the value in use and the value in exchange of a product (the paradox of value), e.g. water has a very big value in use, but a small value in exchange. It is the opposite with diamonds. (Later explained by the difference between the marginal utility of each product compared to the total utility of each product.)
5. He believed in the labour theory of value (see above).
6. He laid down *The Canons of Taxation*:
   - Equity: Taxes should take account of people's ability to pay the tax.
   - Certainty: People should know what their tax liability is going to be for the

coming year, so that they can set aside money during the year to pay the tax at the end of the year.

- Convenience: The method of paying the tax should be suitable to the taxpayer, not to the government.
- Economy: The cost of administrating the tax should be far less than the income generated by the tax.

7 Smith was the first person to strongly advocate the division of labour (specialisation of labour) to increase production, improve quality and ensure less wastage of raw materials.

Summary of Adam Smith (Scottish)

- Main publication: *The Wealth of Nations*
- The invisible hand of free enterprise
- *Laissez-faire*
- Distinguished between productive and non-productive labour
- Distinguished between value in use and value in exchange
- Labour theory of value
- *The Canons of Taxation*
- The division of labour

Thomas Robert Malthus

Thomas Robert Malthus

Nationality: English
Dates: 1766–1834
Publication: *Essay on the Principle of Population as it Affects the Future Improvement of Society*

Main ideas

1 Thomas Malthus believed that population would grow by a geometric progression, while food supply would only grow by an arithmetic progression. He therefore saw that there would have to be a check on the growth of the population. He identified two types of population checks: preventative and positive checks.

- Preventative checks are those which lower the birth rate.
- Positive checks are those which increase the death rate.

He had little or no faith in the working class successfully practising preventative checks. Also, being a cleric, he did not believe in artificial methods of contraception. Therefore, he advocated that there was a need for occasional positive checks on the growth of the population. Positive checks include war, disease, pestilence and famine.

2 He also advocated the wages fund theory.

3 He is associated with the **paradox of thrift**. This states that if people save consumption decreases, thus leading to an over-production of goods which could not be sold. To overcome this problem he encouraged unproductive expenditure by governments, e.g. the building of parks, in order to put money into circulation to stimulate demand. This was a slight deviation from *laissez-faire*.

Summary of Thomas Malthus (English)

- Main publication: *The Principles of Population*
- Need for checks on the growth of the population
- Preventative checks: lower birth rate
- Positive checks: increase death rate
- The wages fund theory
- The paradox of thrift

✳Jean Baptiste Say

Nationality: French
Dates: 1767–1832
Publication: *Treatise on Political Economy*

Jean Baptiste Say

Main ideas

1 Say's Law: This states that 'supply creates its own demand'. He believed that people worked to supply the goods which they could produce most efficiently, so that they could then exchange their surplus production for money, which they in turn could exchange for goods which they wanted, i.e. demanded. Thus by creating a supply of goods they created a demand for other people's goods. Therefore, the supply of goods created a demand for goods. This concept later became popular with 'the supply-siders'.

2 Say is also credited with the division of the factors of production into four categories: land, labour, capital and enterprise.

Summary of Jean Baptiste Say (French)

- Main publication: *Treatise on Political Economy*
- Say's Law
- Recognition of enterprise as a separate factor of production

✳ David Ricardo

David Ricardo

Nationality: English
Dates: 1772–1823
Publication: *The Principles of Political Economy and Taxation*

Main ideas

1. David Ricardo accepted the wages fund theory.
2. He introduced the concept of **economic rent**. This is any payment to a factor of production above its supply price. Because of the nature of the Napoleonic Wars, food was in scarce supply in continental Europe. Thus it turned to Britain for its food supply. With demand greater than supply, it now became more profitable to supply food in Britain. This meant that less fertile land, which previously had not been used to produce food, was now used for that purpose. However, the more fertile land, which had always been used for food production, was more profitable than the less fertile land. This led to an increase in the demand for this land, thus driving up its rent (price). Landlords were now receiving a price for this land above its original supply price. Ricardo called the amount received above the original supply price **economic rent**.
3. While Ricardo accepted the labour theory of value he realised that this was only a partial explanation of value.
4. He advocated free international trade in a *laissez-faire* society.
5. He developed the law of comparative advantage to explain how countries could benefit from free international trade.

Summary of David Ricardo (English)

- Main publication: *The Principles of Political Economy and Taxation*
- Wages fund theory
- Concept of economic rent
- The labour theory of value was only a partial explanation of value
- Advocated free international trade
- Law of comparative advantage

⁕John Stuart Mill

Nationality: English
Dates: 1806–1873
Publication: *Principles of Political Economy with Some of their Applications to Social Philosophy*

John Stuart Mill

Main ideas

1. John Stuart Mill advocated government intervention in the economy if it improved the welfare of society in general, e.g. he approved of taxation for a more equitable distribution of wealth.
2. He modified the definition of productive labour by stating that certain services could also be classified as being productive, e.g. the work of the government.
3. He rejected the labour theory of value, stating that both demand and supply were equally important in assessing the value of a product.
4. He accepted the wages fund theory. However, he stated that the working class would, in time, become better educated and learn to control population growth.
5. Along with Ricardo he also identified the concept of **economic rent**. However, because economic rent is a surplus above supply price he advocated that it should be taxed as the tax would have no effect on supply.
6. Mill predicted that many industries would become dominated by a small number of big firms due to increasing returns to scale, i.e. if you double the inputs you will more than double the output.
7. To counteract the negotiating powers of these large firms he advocated the establishment of trade unions to represent labour.
8. He was one of the first economists associated with and to write about the law of diminishing returns.
9. Mill stated that the production and distribution of wealth were two independent processes.
   - Production of wealth was determined by the laws of nature and technology.
   - Distribution of wealth was controlled by man.

Because the distribution of wealth was controlled by man he recognised that this could lead to the ownership of wealth being concentrated in the hands of a relatively small number of people. This led him to become disillusioned by the capitalist system and he began to lean towards a mild form of socialism.

Summary of John Stuart Mill (English)

- Main publication: *The Principles of Political Economy*
- Advocated government intervention to improve the welfare of society
- Certain services to be classified as productive
- Both demand and supply were equally important in assessing the value of a product
- Wages fund theory
- Economic rent
- Predicted multinational companies
- Advocated the establishment of trade unions to represent labour
- The production of wealth was determined by the laws of nature and technology while the distribution of wealth was controlled by man

Marxian Economics

Karl Marx

Nationality: German
Dates: 1818–1883
Main publications: *The Communist Manifesto* and *Das Kapital*

Karl Marx

Main ideas

1. Karl Marx stated that the value of a product was equal to the cost of labour necessary to produce the product. Labour was only paid a subsistence level of wages, but was required to work a longer number of hours than was necessary to pay these wages. Therefore, labour was producing surplus value which went as profit for the employers. Marx called this 'the surplus value' of production.

2. This surplus value of production was used by employers to purchase technology, which would reduce the need for labour, thus causing unemployment. This weakened labour's bargaining power when negotiating wage rates thus leading to exploitation of the employed labour force.

3. This would lead to the creation of a two-tiered society, namely 'the proletariat' (working class) and 'the capitalist' classes.

4. The combination of the growing number of unemployed and the exploitation of labour would, Marx predicted, lead to a social revolution where the 'reserve army of the unemployed' would overthrow the 'capitalists' and take control of the factors of production. These factors would then be held in public ownership rather than private ownership.

5 Marx predicted that as technology improved, the production of goods would move towards very large-scale production units in order to get the benefits of the economies of scale. This would lead to the establishment of oligopolistic production of most mass consumption goods.

6 He also predicted that production would become so efficient that producers would, at times, produce more goods than were required by consumers, thus leading to trade cycles.

Summary of Karl Marx (German)

- Main publications: *The Communist Manifesto* and *Das Kapital*
- Labour required to work more hours than necessary to generate the income needed to pay its wages
- Producing a surplus value which was profit for employers
- This profit invested in technology reduced the need for labour, thus creating unemployment
- Leading to a two-tiered society: 'the capitalists' and 'the proletariat'
- Resulting in social revolution where the proletariat would take public ownership of the factors of production
- Predicted the growth of oligopolies
- Forecast the emergence of trade cycles

Criticism of Marx's theory

1 The growth of trade unions has ensured that the working class has not been exploited. However, some people argue that this has only happened in the West, in the Third World workers are still being exploited.

2 His prediction that society would be divided into two classes has proven to be false with the emergence of the middle or professional class.

3 His prediction that the development of technology would lead to mass unemployment has not come true. While technological advances have changed the nature of the production of goods, these advances have also ensured a greater quantity of goods being produced, thus creating more employment in the economy's services sector.

4 Marx's theory on the growth of oligopolies has proven to be correct as has his predictions with regard to trade cycles.

The Neoclassical Economists

The neoclassical economists were writing in the nineteenth and twentieth centuries. They concentrated on microeconomics and the function of the market system and how it allocates the economy's resources. They advocated free enterprise and competition in the market place. The most important of the neoclassical economists was Alfred Marshall.

Alfred Marshall

Nationality: English
Dates: 1842–1924
Main publications: *The Principles of Economics* and *Money, Credit and Commerce*

Alfred Marshall

Main ideas

1. Alfred Marshall was one of the first economists to use econometrics, i.e. the use of maths to illustrate economic theory.
2. He, along with other neoclassical economists, developed the concept of the marginal utility theory of value. However, it was Marshall who first introduced the law of diminishing marginal utility.
3. Marshall's theory of value stated that the value of a good was determined in the short run by its utility and in the long run by its cost of production. Thus he saw both demand and supply playing a role in determining value. He likened both demand and supply to the two blades of scissors intersecting each other.
4. He was the first person to apply the term 'elasticity of demand' to explain the reaction of demand to small changes in prices.
5. It was Marshall who first saw that the return to the factors of production was based on their marginal revenue productivity, i.e. the maximum payment which a factor could receive is equal to the marginal revenue earned by the employment of the last unit of that factor.
6. He introduced the notion of differentiating between the long run and the short run for production purposes. He pointed out that in the short run there was always at least one fixed factor of production, whereas in the long run all factors of production were variable.
7. This also led him to develop the concept of quasi-rent, which he saw as economic rent earned by labour in the short run, which was eliminated in the long run by the increase in the supply of that labour.
8. While Marshall had some sympathy for and understanding of socialist principles he was more in favour of a free enterprise economy with some degree of government regulation. He contended that while the growth of large-scale firms (monopolies and oligopolies) was inevitable in a free enterprise economy that these firms could be controlled by:

- The education of consumers and the spread of consumer information
- The introduction of government controls
- Encouraging the establishment of more small firms
- Ensuring greater honesty and openness in business.

Summary of Alfred Marshall (English)

- Main publication: *The Principles of Economics*
- The law of diminishing marginal utility
- Value is determined by both demand and supply
- Marginal revenue productivity of factors of production
- Distinguished between short run and long run
- Quasi-rent
- Some government regulation in the free enterprise system

John Maynard Keynes

⁂John Maynard Keynes

Nationality: English
Dates: 1883–1946
Main publications: *A Treatise on Money* and *The General Theory of Employment, Interest and Money*

Main ideas

1. John Maynard Keynes advocated that economies could be regulated by government fiscal policy. He advocated budgetary policy as the main economic instrument in the control of the economy.
2. Keynes discovered the multiplier effect, which showed that any injection into the circular flow of income created income greater than the actual size of the injection, e.g. increased government expenditure financed through deficit budgeting. He showed that the income created by an injection was determined by the size of the multiplier, which is that number by which an injection is multiplied to calculate the income created. He showed the formula for the multiplier to be:

$$\frac{1}{1 - MPC + MPM + MPT}$$

3. Keynes developed a theory on interest rates which was different from that of the classical economists. His liquidity preference theory of interest rates stated that the rate of interest settles at the level which brings about an equal supply of and demand for money. In this theory, the supply of money means the amount of money in circulation, while the demand for money means the reasons why people want to hold onto money rather than make it available for investment. He pointed out that the supply of money is fixed at any given time by the Central

Bank, while the demand for money was determined by the amount of money needed for (a) transaction purposes, (b) precautionary purposes and (c) speculative purposes.

4 He did not agree with the concept of *laissez-faire*. He felt that governments, through fiscal policy, could help to control economies. Thus he advocated government intervention to regulate the economy.

5 Savings and investment: The classical economists believed that savings were always equal to investment, as all money saved would be put back into the economy. Keynes disagreed with this theory as savers and investors were two distinct groups of people within the same economy. He stated that savings might be greater than the amount entrepreneurs are willing to invest. If this happened there would be a decline in consumption and the capital stock of the country would be greater than was required to produce this amount being consumed. A low level of consumption thus causes underemployment in the economy.

Summary of John Maynard Keynes (English)

- Main publications: *A Treatise on Money* and *The General Theory of Employment, Interest and Money*
- Advocated fiscal policy as the main method of controlling the economy
- Explained and developed the theory of the multiplier
- Developed the liquidity preference theory of interest rates
- Explained that savings and investment were not always equal to each other

John Kenneth Galbraith

Nationality: Canadian born but spent most of his adult life in the USA
Dates: 1908–2006
Publication: *The Affluent Society*

John Kenneth Galbraith

'One cannot defend production as satisfying wants if that production creates the wants.' This quotation, from *The Affluent Society*, sums up Galbraith's economic philosophy. He felt that too much money was being wasted on frivolous personal consumption, which was driven by the persuasive powers of manufacturers. At the same time, there was very little public capital investment in schools and recreational parks. He thus advocated that the government should increase taxes to restrict the conspicuous consumption and then use that money to provide public capital.

Galbraith also warned of the economic power that large multinational oligopolists could wield by dictating to governments that wished to attract them to locate in their countries. Many of these companies have turnovers far in excess of the GDPs of the smaller countries.

Monetarist Economics

✳Milton Friedman

Nationality: American
Dates: 1912–2006
Main publications: *Inflation, Causes and Consequences* and *A Monetary History of the United States 1867–1960* (co-author Anna Schwartz)

Milton Friedman

1. The monetarists argue that monetary policy rather than fiscal policy should be the main instrument used to control the economy.

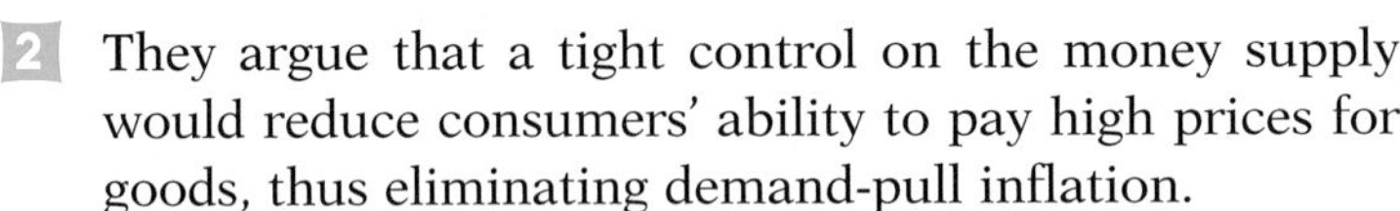

2. They argue that a tight control on the money supply would reduce consumers' ability to pay high prices for goods, thus eliminating demand-pull inflation.
3. They also argue that controlling the money supply also reduces the ability of employers to pay high wages, thus reducing cost-push inflation.
4. The overall reduction in inflation would, they argue, encourage more investment, thus increasing the productive capacity of the country and creating more employment.
5. They accept that the control of inflation has to be a priority over employment in the short run. Therefore, they say that the initial implementation of monetary policy may be accompanied by short-term high unemployment.
6. They advocated a *laissez-faire* style of economy with very little government intervention in economic affairs. The 'free market forces' should be relied on to bring the economy into equilibrium.
7. As a natural consequence of point 6 the monetarists advocate privatisation of all government-owned or controlled business activities.

Summary of monetarism

- Monetary policy reduces both demand-pull and cost-push inflation
- A reduction in inflation encourages investment, thus creating employment
- The control of inflation is a greater short-term objective than the creation of employment
- Advocates *laissez-faire*
- Advocates privatisation

Supply-Siders

Date: Late twentieth century

1 The supply-siders are a group of economists who argue that an economy should be developed by stimulating the supply of goods and services rather than trying to stimulate demand.

2 This can be done by reducing taxes, as this would encourage work and investment, which in turn would increase government revenue.

3 They also advocate deregulation and privatisation in order to encourage competition. This in turn would increase production and reduce prices.

4 The term 'supply-side economics' was coined by the economist Jude Wanniski in 1975 and its usage was enhanced by Arthur Laffer. Supply-side economics is controversial because of its emphasis on the reduction of the higher marginal tax rates which benefits the wealthy. Many critics of the supply-siders feel that the theory is politically rather than economically motivated.

5 The supply-siders used the 'Laffer curve' to show that a reduction in the rate of tax could result in increasing returns to the government.

6 The Laffer curve shows the relationship between tax rates and tax revenue collected by governments.

Fig 32.1 The Laffer curve

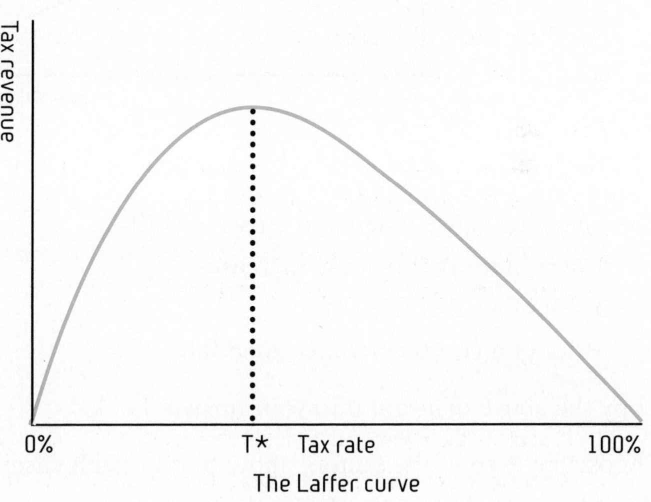

The curve suggests that as taxes increase from low levels, tax revenue collected by the government also increases. It also shows that if tax rates increase above a certain point (T*) it would act as a disincentive to work, thereby reducing tax revenue for the government. Eventually, if tax rates reached 100 per cent then all people would choose not to work, because everything they earned would go to the government.

Chapter 33
Exam Questions and Answers

Chapter 5 Q&A

See pp 27–39

Question 1 Chapter 5

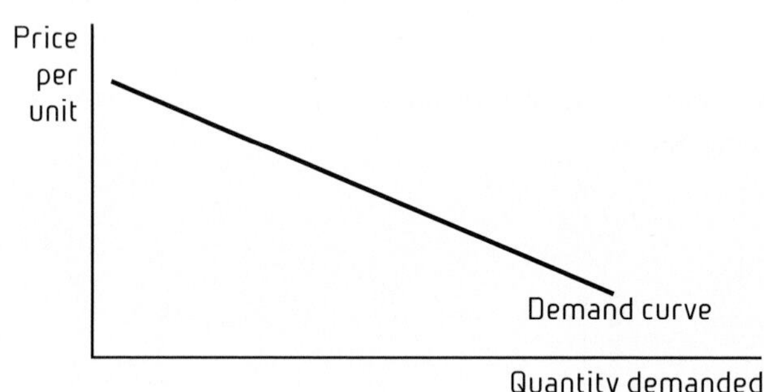

The following cause a demand curve to shift:

(a) Consumers' real income increases

(b) Price of a substitute falls

(c) Price of a complementary good falls

Copy the above diagram into your answer book.

Choose any **two** of the factors above and in **each** case:

(i) Show the shift in the demand curve.

(ii) Explain why the curve has shifted in the direction shown. (20 marks)

(LC Economics, OL, 2000)

Sample Answer 1 Chapter 5

(a) **Consumers' real income increases**

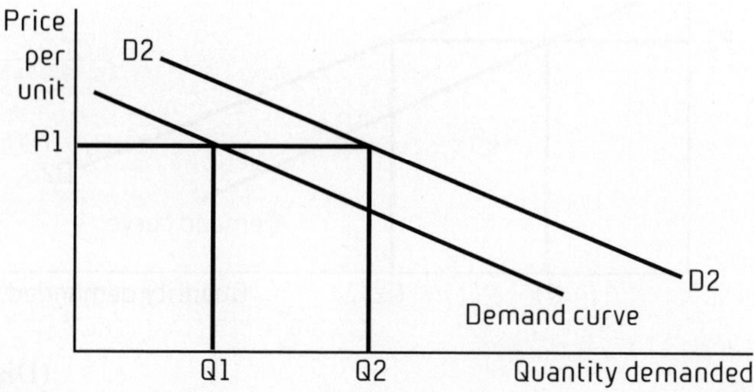

(Diagram 5 marks)

When consumers' real income increases this gives them more purchasing power. Therefore, they will buy more goods at any given market price causing the demand curve to move to the right. (5 marks)

(b) **Price of a substitute good falls**

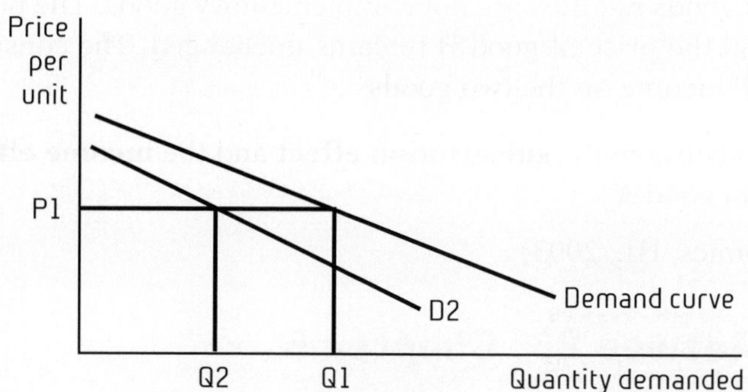

(Diagram 5 marks)

When the price of a substitute good falls many consumers will switch to buying the cheaper good, thus causing a decrease in D for the one whose price has not changed, causing the demand curve to move to the left. (5 marks)

(c) **Price of a complementary good falls**

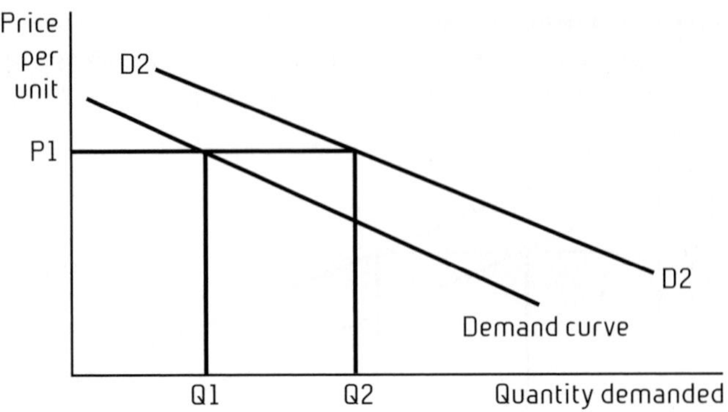

(Diagram 5 marks)

Consumers regard the combined price of two complementary goods as being the price of the transaction. If the price of one of them goes down this makes the price of the transaction cheaper. When price goes down D goes up. Thus the D for the one whose price has not changed will go up, causing the demand curve to move to the right. (5 marks)

Question 2 Chapter 5

A consumer spends all income on two goods, good A and good B. Both goods are normal goods but they are not complementary goods. The price of good A is reduced and the price of good B remains unchanged. The consumer continues to spend all income on the two goods.

Distinguish between the **substitution effect** and the **income effect** of the price reduction in good A. (25 marks)

(LC Economics, HL, 2003)

Sample Answer 2 Chapter 5

Note: While the effect on the demand for good B was not required in this question it is shown here without marks allocated.

Good A

The substitution effect refers to the effect on the demand for a product as a result of a change in the price of that product. The fall in the price of good A makes it relatively cheaper than good B. Therefore, some consumers will switch to the consumption of good A causing an extension in its demand. On the diagram below this causes D to go up from 5 to 8 when the price drops from €5 to €3. (13 marks)

The income effect refers to the effect on the demand for a good arising from a change in the consumer's real income. Normal goods have a positive income effect. The price of good A decreased. Thus real income increased as money income has not changed. As good A is a normal good this will cause an increase in the demand for it. This will cause the D curve to move to the right causing the demand to increase further to 12.

(12 marks)

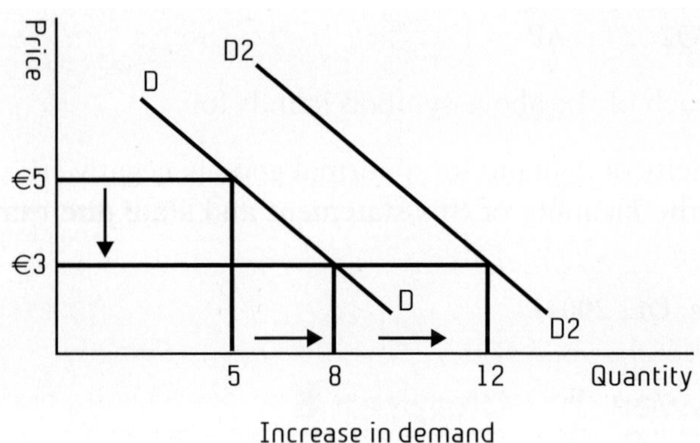

Increase and extension in demand for good A

(If diagram only is given 10 marks)

Good B

The demand for good B will be affected only by the income effect as its price has not changed. The decrease in the price of A has caused an increase in real income. As B is a normal good this will cause an increase in the demand for B.

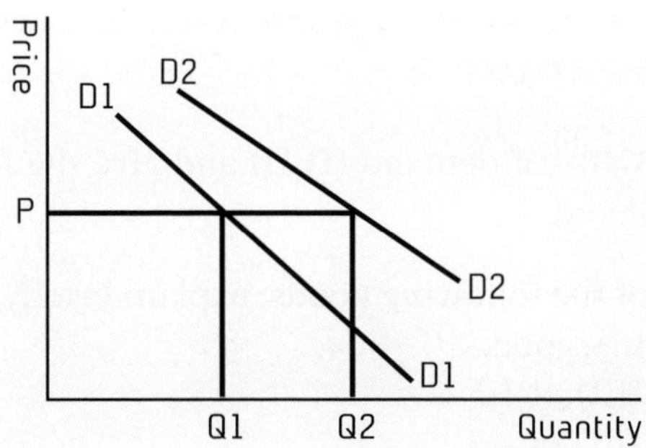

Chapter 6 Q&A

See pp 40–52

Question 1 Chapter 6

(a) The formula for measuring price elasticity of demand is:

$$\frac{P1 + P2}{Q1 + Q2} \times \frac{\Delta Q}{\Delta P}$$

Explain what each of the above symbols stands for.

(b) The price elasticity of demand for a normal good is negative (i.e. it has a minus sign). Explain the meaning of this statement and state **one** example of such a good. (30 marks)

(LC Economics, OL, 2004)

Sample Answer 1 Chapter 6

(a) P1 is the original price of the good; P2 is the new price of the good; Q1 is the original quantity demanded; Q2 is the new quantity demanded; ΔQ is the change in quantity demanded; ΔP is the change in the price of the good.
(3 marks for each symbol)

(b) This means that as the price of the good increases (+ change in P) the demand for it falls (– change in Q). (8 marks)

An example would be mobile telephones. (4 marks)

Question 2 Chapter 6

(a) Define income elasticity of demand (IED) and give the formula by which it is calculated. (20 marks)

(b) In the case of each of the following goods, explain briefly if the good is a normal, an inferior or a luxury good.

- Good A has an IED of 1.5
- Good B has an IED of – 3
- Good C has an IED of 10
- Good D has an IED of 0 (20 marks)

(LC Economics, HL, 1996)

Sample Answer 2 Chapter 6

(a) Income elasticity of demand measures the relationship between a change in income and the resulting change in the demand for a product. (10 marks)

The formula by which it is measured is:

$$\frac{Y1 + Y2}{Q1 + Q2} \times \frac{\Delta Q}{\Delta Y}$$

(10 marks)

(b) A normal good is one which has a positive income effect. Therefore, the income elasticity of demand for normal goods is always positive, as the D for the goods will always change in the same direction as the income change. Applying the formula above, if income increased (i.e. + ΔY) then the quantity demanded will also increase (i.e. + ΔQ). Thus +/+ = a positive number.

Therefore, good A is a normal good. (5 marks)

Good C is also a normal good, but as the IED is extremely big it indicates that a change in income will cause, proportionately, a very large change in demand. Thus good D is also a luxury good. (5 marks)

An inferior good is one which has a negative income effect. Therefore, the income elasticity of demand for inferior goods is always negative, as the D for the goods will always change in the opposite direction to the income change. Applying the formula above, if income increased (i.e. + ΔY) then the quantity demanded will decrease (i.e. – ΔQ). Thus –/+ = a negative number.

Therefore, good B is an inferior good. (5 marks)

While good D has a positive IED this would seem to indicate that it is a normal good. However, when IED = 0 this indicates that the change in income will have no effect on the quantity demanded. These are usually goods which only account for a very tiny fraction of income and are not consumed in very large quantities regardless of the level of income, e.g. salt for domestic consumption. (5 marks)

Chapter 7 Q&A

See pp 53–64

Question 1 Chapter 7

The three diagrams below represent changes in the supply of wheat.

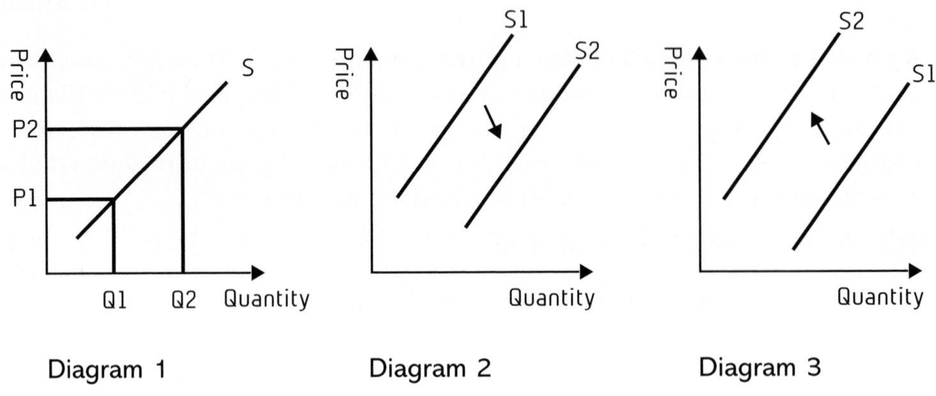

Diagram 1 Diagram 2 Diagram 3

Each of the following developments causes one of the changes shown above:

(i) The cost of wheat seed falls substantially.

(ii) Some workers involved in harvesting the wheat go on strike.

(iii) The selling price of wheat increases.

State which diagram represents each of the three developments listed above, and in each case explain why the supply reacts as illustrated on your chosen diagram.

(25 marks)

(LC Economics, OL, 2003)

Sample Answer 1 Chapter 7

Diagram 1

Diagram 1 shows supply going up as a result of an increase in its market price.

(3 marks)

As the selling price of wheat increases this causes an extension in the supply of wheat, as it is more profitable to supply more wheat at the higher price. This is represented by Diagram 1.

(6 marks)

Diagram 2

Diagram 2 shows an increase in supply. The cost of wheat seed is a cost of production when producing wheat. As the cost of producing a product decreases it becomes more profitable to supply it and attracts more producers into the market. This results in an increase in supply and causes the supply curve to move to the right. (6 marks)

Therefore, Diagram 2 represents the fall in the cost of wheat seed. (2 marks)

Diagram 3
Diagram 3 shows a decrease in supply. If some workers go on strike then less wheat can be harvested making less wheat available for sale. This is a decrease in supply. (6 marks)

A decrease in supply is represented by Diagram 3. (2 marks)

Question 2 Chapter 7

State four factors that affect the supply of a good, other than the price of the good itself, and explain how each factor affects supply. (25 marks)

(LC Economics, HL, 2001)

Sample Answer 2 Chapter 7

(i) The price of other products
(ii) The cost of production
(iii) The state of technology
(iv) The level of taxation (Each point 3 marks)

(i) **Price of other goods**
In this situation the price of other goods refers to other products which the supplier could produce as an alternative to those he is presently producing. A canning factory could relatively easily change from the canning of peas to the canning of sprouts if it became more profitable to do so.

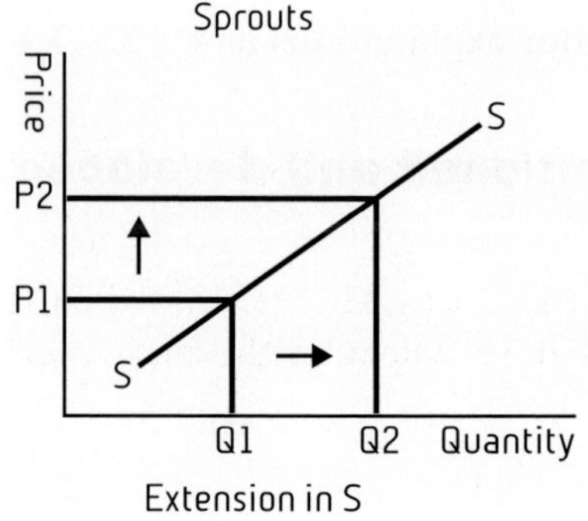

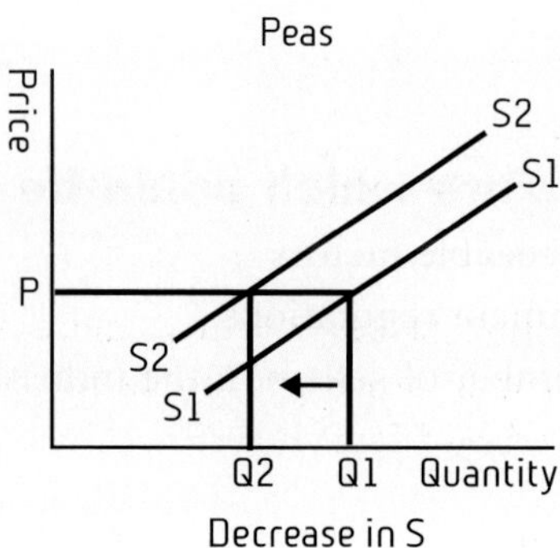

If the firm finds that the price of peas is remaining static and the price of sprouts is increasing to such a degree that it is more profitable to switch its resources to the canning of sprouts then it will cease its production of peas causing the market supply to go down. Hence the supply of peas is decreased as a result of the increase in the price of sprouts.

(ii) **The cost of production**
As the cost of production increases it becomes less profitable to supply goods. Thus some marginal firms will cease production resulting in a decrease in S. Thus an increase in the cost of production causes a decrease in S. Therefore, a decrease in the cost of production would likewise cause an increase in S.

(iii) **The state of technology**
As technology improves more goods can be produced for the same or a lower total cost. Thus the average cost decreases making it more profitable to supply more goods.

Therefore, as technology improves this causes an increase in supply (S).

(iv) **The level of taxation**
As taxes increase it becomes less profitable to supply goods. This happens for two reasons:

1. If the increase in taxation is on corporation profit taxes this results in a lower profit per unit produced and may put marginal firms out of production:

2. If the increase in taxation is an increase in indirect taxation, e.g. VAT, this will increase the market price of the product to the consumer who in turn will reduce his or her consumption. This decrease in consumption may result in the production of the good being unviable for some producers, thus putting them out of business, thereby causing a decrease in supply.

Therefore, an increase in taxation causes a decrease in supply and vice versa.

(Any four explanations at 4 + 3 + 3 + 3 marks)

Other points which could be mentioned and developed

- Unforeseeable factors
- Government regulations
- The number of sellers in the industry

Chapter 9 Q&A

See pp 70–77

Question 1 Chapter 9

(a) A manufacturing firm's costs may be divided into fixed costs and variable costs.

(i) Explain what is meant by both of these types of costs.

(ii) Give **one** example of each of theses costs for a firm. (25 marks)

(b) The following diagram represents the costs of a particular firm in the short run period.

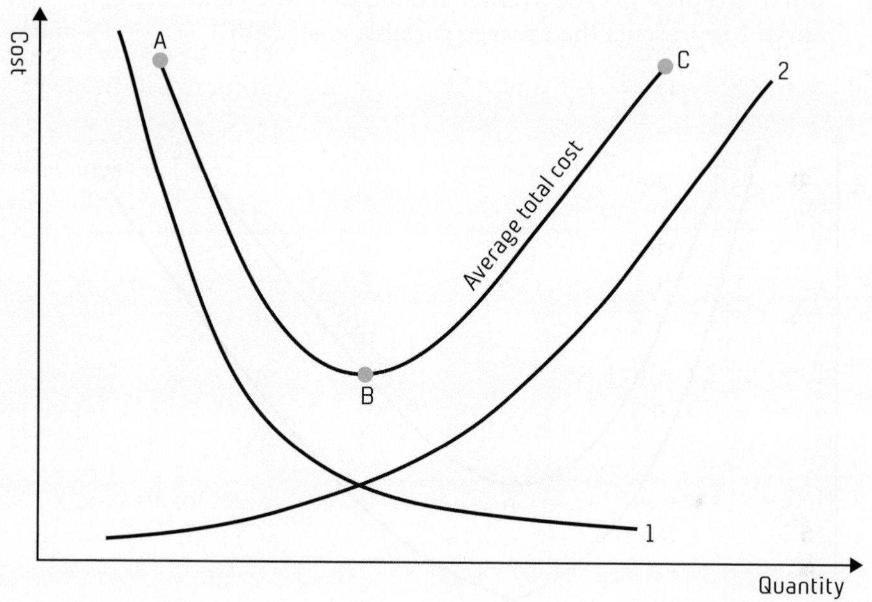

(i) Copy the diagram into your answer book and label each of the curves 1 and 2.

(ii) Explain the reasons for the U-shape of the average total cost curve:

- From point A to point B
- From point B to point C
- The importance of point B (25 marks)

(LC Economics, OL, 1999)

Sample Answer 1 Chapter 9

(a) (i) Fixed costs do not change in the short run as the quantity of goods produced changes. (8 marks)

Variable costs change as the quantity of goods produced changes. (7 marks)

(ii) An example of fixed costs would be the rates paid to the local county council on the buildings. (5 marks)

An example of variable costs would be the cost of raw materials. (5 marks)

(b) (i) Curve 1 represents the average fixed costs (AFC) and curve 2 represents the average variable costs (AVC). (5 marks each)

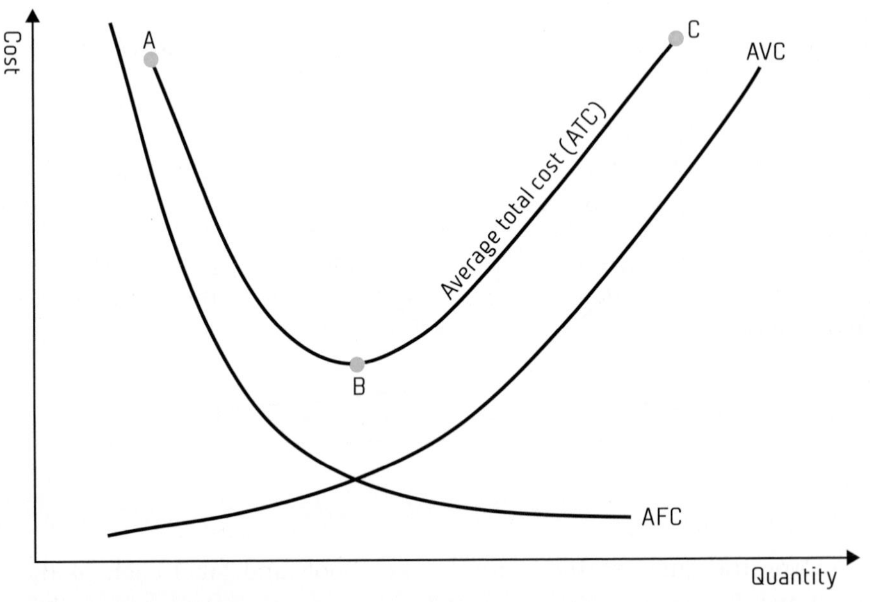

(ii) The U-shaped average total cost curve (ATC) slopes downwards from point A to point B because between these points the effect of the spread of the fixed costs significantly lowers the average total cost. (5 marks)

ATC curve slopes upwards from point B to point C because between these points diminishing returns have set in resulting in an increase in ATC. (5 marks)

Alternative answer for (b)

ATC = AFC + AVC. Between points A and B the fixed costs per item are decreasing at a faster rate than the increase in the variable costs. Therefore, the ATC must decrease. Between points B and C the variable costs are increasing at a faster rate than the decrease in the fixed costs per item. Therefore, the ATC must increase.

Point B is important because it shows the quantity which gives the lowest average cost of production. (5 marks)

Chapter 10 Q&A See pp 78–89

Question 1 Chapter 10

(a) It is generally agreed that the long run average cost curve initially slopes downwards due to economies of scale and then slopes upwards due to diseconomies of scale. These economies and diseconomies can be both internal and external.

(i) Define the underlined terms.

(ii) Distinguish between internal and external economies of scale, giving two examples in each case. (30 marks)

(b) While there can be advantages from producing on a large scale, the majority of firms in Ireland are small. Explain three reasons why small firms survive in the Irish economy. (15 marks)

(LC Economics, HL, 2004)

Sample Answer 1 Chapter 10

(a) (i) Economies of scale are the forces which decrease LRAC as the level of production increases. (4 marks)

Diseconomies of scale are the forces which increase LRAC as the level of production increases. (4 marks)

(ii) Internal economies of scale are the forces within the firm which decrease LRAC as the firm's level of production increases. (3 marks)

Examples are economies of construction and economies of specialisation of labour. (8 marks)

External economies of scale are the forces outside the firm which decrease LRAC as the size of the industry increases. (3 marks)

Examples are specialisation of production within the industry and education and training courses which are more freely available for large industries. (8 marks)

(b) Many small firms survive for the following reasons:

(i) Many small firms offer personal services. (2 marks)

Consumers sometimes like the personal touch and will only deal with small firms where the customer knows all the employees, e.g. solicitors and a local builder. (3 marks)

(ii) Some small firms produce goods which are market-oriented products. (2 marks)

Bulky products with expensive transport costs may be located beside the market and be restricted to one area only, as the cost of long distance deliveries may offset any price advantage. (3 marks)

(iii) Some small firms are members of voluntary groups or are franchise holders. (2 marks)

Many small firms can survive and match the purchasing power of larger firms by operating under these systems, e.g. McDonalds' outlets, Prontaprint and Spar. (3 marks)

Chapter 12 Q&A See pp 95–107

Question 1 Chapter 12

(a) The diagram below represents the long run equilibrium of a firm in a perfectly competitive market.

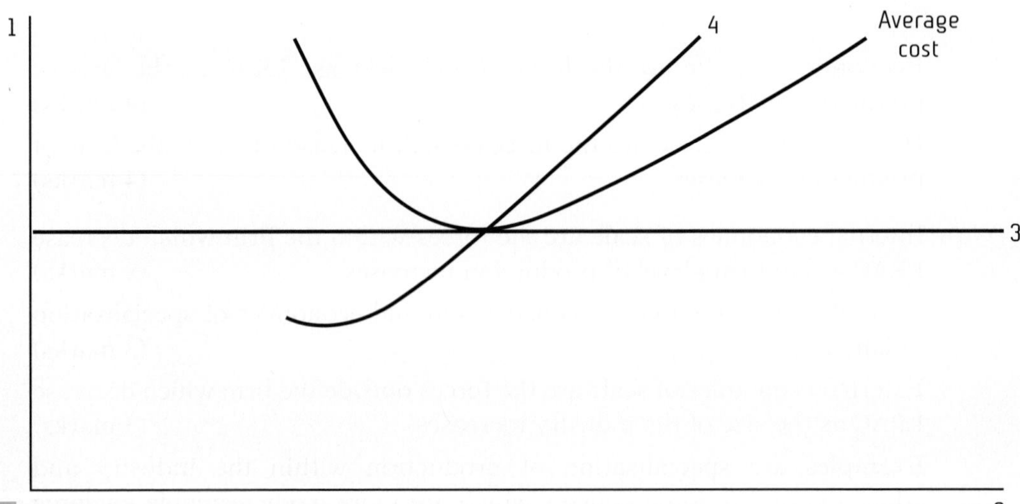

(i) Copy the diagram into your answer book. Clearly label each of the lines numbered 1 to 4.

(ii) Show on your diagram:

- The equilibrium output of the firm (use label Q).
- The average cost of producing this output (use label C).
- The price it will charge for this output (use label P).

(iii) Is the above firm earning normal or supernormal profits? Explain with reference to the diagram on p. 374. (30 marks)

(b) Compare perfect competition and monopoly market structures with respect to the following:

(i) The number of firms in each industry

(ii) The shape of the demand curve of the firm in each structure. (You may use diagrams if you wish.) (20 marks)

(c) A recent trend in Ireland has been towards the privatisation of state-owned companies.

(i) What is meant by the term 'privatisation'?

(ii) Name a major company recently privatised in Ireland.

(iii) State and explain how **any two** of the following may be affected by privatisation.
(1 point required in each case)

- The privatised company
- The consumer of the product or service
- The employees of the privatised companies (25 marks)

(LC Economics, OL, 2000)

Sample Answer 1 Chapter 12

(a) (i) and (ii)

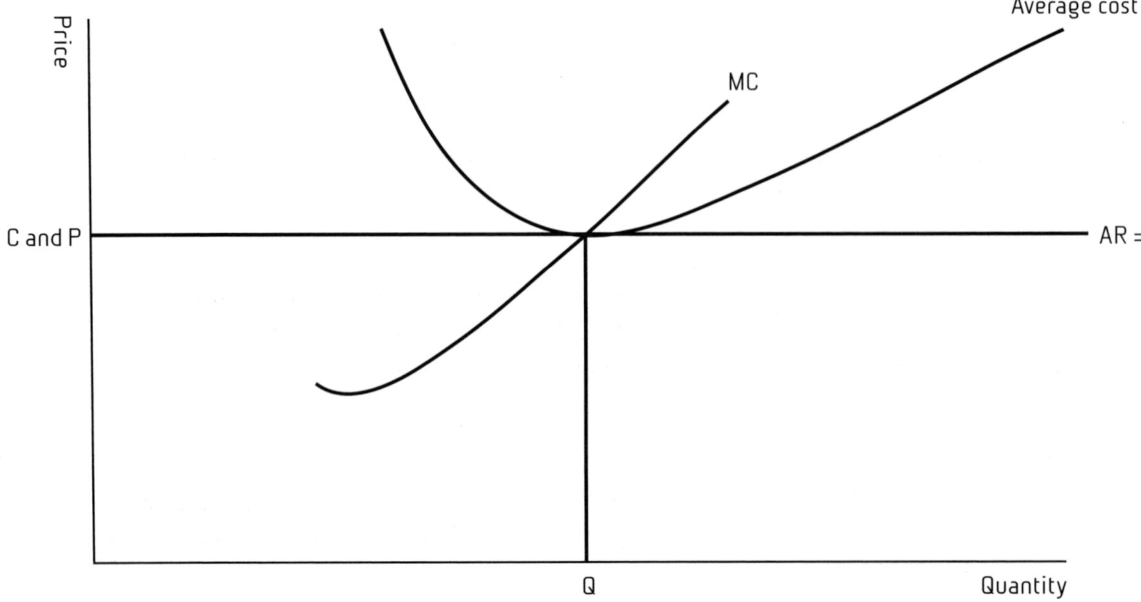

(Lines labelled at 2 marks each + C, P, Q at 4 marks each = 20 marks)

(iii) The firm is earning normal profit (4 marks) because, as shown in the diagram above, the firm's AC = its AR. (6 marks)

(b) In perfect competition there are a large number of firms in the industry while in monopoly there is only one firm in the industry. (12 marks)

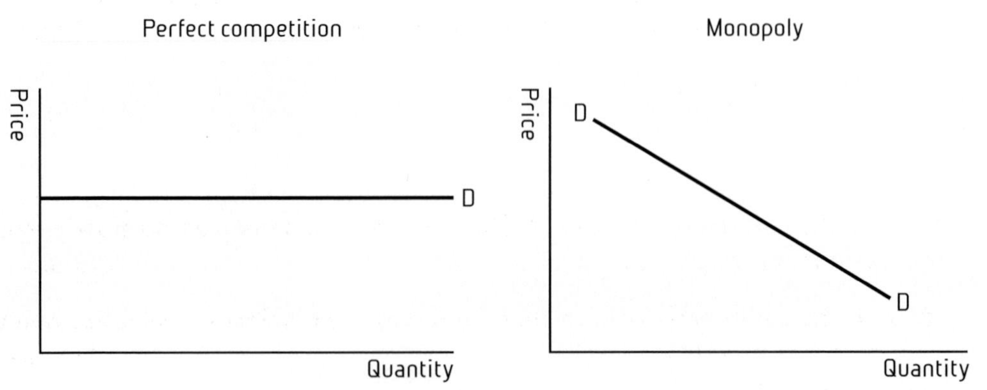

In perfect competition the firm is a price taker, therefore its D or AR curve will be parallel to the quantity axis. The monopolist is the only firm in the industry, therefore it will face a normal downward sloping D or AR curve. (8 marks)

(c) (i) Privatisation means the selling of state-owned assets to the private sector. (7 marks)

(ii) Telecom Éireann was privatised and is now known as Eircom. (4 marks)

(iii) **The privatised company**
It usually benefits by having more finance available to it as it can sell shares to the general public. This will allow the firm to expand and invest in modern technology and become more cost effective.

The consumers of the good or service
Consumers may suffer if the privatised company stopped providing non-profitable services which were previously provided by the state-owned body, e.g. if Dublin Bus were privatised the new company might decide to stop providing a bus service on routes which were unprofitable.

The employees of the privatised company
Employees may be able to negotiate better pay deals by entering into profit sharing schemes or productivity schemes which were not available to them before.

(Any 2 points fully explained at 7 marks each)

Question 2 Chapter 12

(a) Explain the relationship between marginal physical product (MPP) and marginal revenue product if markets are perfectly competitive. State, giving reasons, if you would expect this same relationship to hold if it is a monopolistic market. (30 marks)

(b) Is it better for workers if the firm that employs them is a monopolist or competing in a perfectly competitive market? Explain your answer. (45 marks)

(LC Economics, HL, 1989)

Sample Answer 2 Chapter 12

(a) MPP is the addition to total production caused by the employment of an extra unit of a factor of production. (5 marks)

MRP is the addition to total revenue caused by the employment of an extra unit of a factor of production. (5 marks)

In perfect competition the firm is a price taker, therefore it receives the same price (AR) per unit sold no matter how many units it sells. Therefore, in perfect competition MPP × AR is always equal to MRP.

Qty of labour	Total production	MPP	AR	Total revenue	MRP
1	100	–	€10	€1,000	–
2	120	20	€10	€1,200	€200

Here it can be seen that MPP (20) × AR (€10) = MRP (€200). (10 marks)

This does not happen in monopoly, as the firm must decrease its price if it is to increase its sales. The firm will be getting a smaller price for every unit it sells. Thus in monopoly MPP × AR does not equal MRP.

Qty of labour	Total production	MPP	AR	Total revenue	MRP
1	100	–	€10	€1,000	–
2	120	20	€9	€1,080	€80

Here it can be seen that MPP (20) × AR (€9) > MRP (€80). (10 marks)

Note: In the type of question below you never give a definitive answer where you opt for one form of competition over the other. Give the advantages and/or the disadvantages of each form of competition.

(b) (i) Because there is a greater number of firms in a perfectly competitive industry there is usually a greater number of jobs in this industry as each firm would require its own specialised form of labour, e.g. accountant, supervisor, marketing manager and production manager. In monopoly, the firm may have to employ only one person in each of these positions.

(ii) If one firm closes down in perfect competition it is still possible for the redundant staff to get employment in the same type of industry, as vacancies will always arise in some of the other firms in that industry. If the industry is a monopoly and it closes down then there is no hope of future employment in that industry.

(iii) Because there are many firms in perfect competition employees have more bargaining power when negotiating their wages. In monopoly, there is only one employer, thus reducing the bargaining power of employees.

(iv) Because the monopolist tends to be a large firm there tends to be more opportunities for promotion in this type of firm compared to the small firms in perfect competition.

(v) Because monopolists earn supernormal profits it is more likely that employees could earn economic rent; whereas perfectly competitive firms earn only normal profit, thus it is unlikely that they would pay any economic rent to their employees.

(vi) A monopolist may be less vulnerable to changes in the level of demand in the market. As it is earning SNPs it may be able to afford to decrease P to maintain the same level of sales. A smaller firm earning only NPs may not be able to afford to do so. Therefore, employment may be more secure in monopoly.

(45 marks)

(Any 5 points, with a minimum of 2 points for each side of the debate, at 9 marks each, i.e. 4 marks for mentioning the point plus 5 marks for development.)

Chapter 13 Q&A See pp 108–117

Question 1 Chapter 13

(a) The diagram below represents a **monopoly** firm in equilibrium.

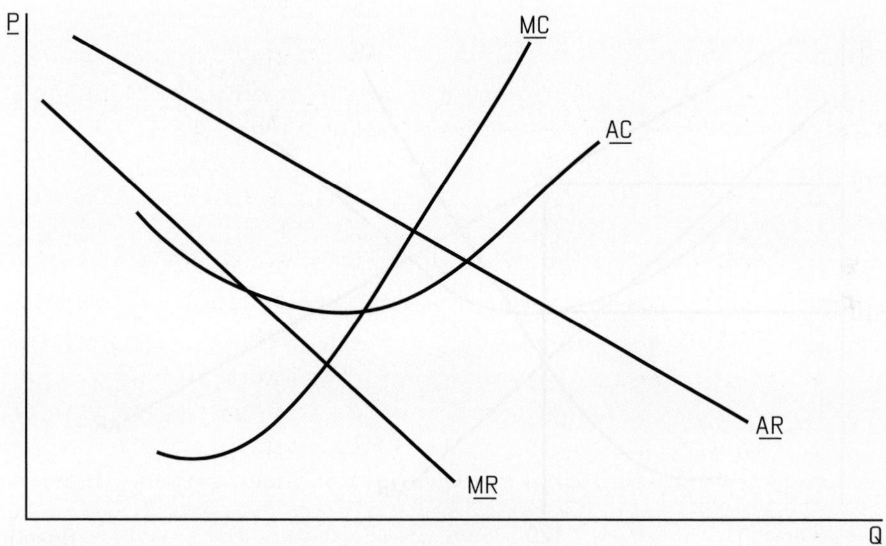

(i) Write out in full each of the six terms underlined on the graph. (12 marks)

(ii) Copy the diagram into your answer book and show on the diagram:
- The output the firm will produce in equilibrium.
- The average cost of producing this output.
- The price the firm will charge for the output produced. (18 marks)

(b) (i) Briefly explain why the monopolist's demand curve (AR) is downward sloping.

(ii) Explain **any two** of the barriers to entry listed below:

- Patents and copyrights
- Economies of scale
- Government regulations (25 marks)

(c) State:

(i) **One** advantage to the employees of a monopoly firm.

(ii) **One** disadvantage to the consumers of a monopoly firm. (20 marks)

(LC Economics, OL, 2001)

Sample Answer 1 Chapter 13

(a) (i) AR = average revenue; MR = marginal revenue; AC = average cost; MC = marginal cost; P = price; Q = quantity. (6 points at 2 marks each)

(ii)

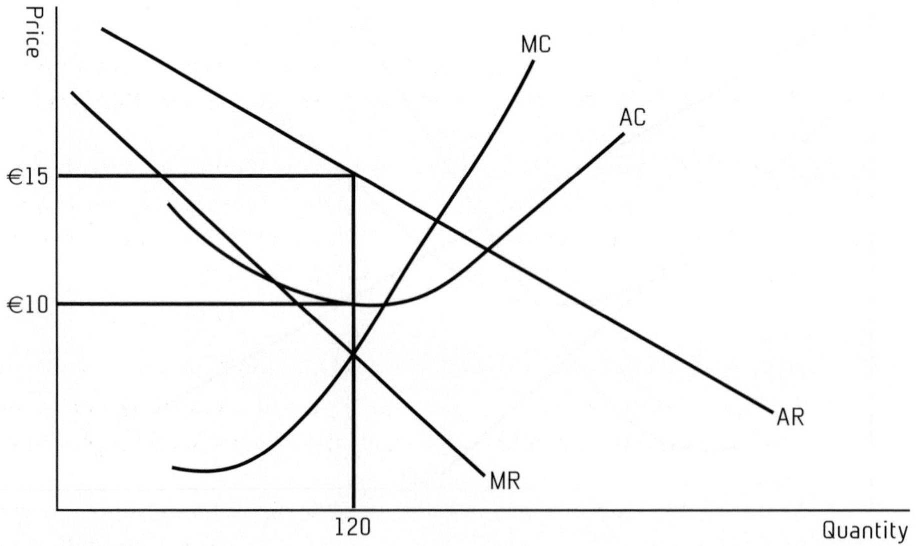

The quantity is where MR = MC to earn maximum profit, i.e. 120.
The AC for 120 is €10.
The price (AR) for 120 is €15. (3 points at 6 marks each)

(b) (i) In monopoly the firm is the industry, as one of the assumptions of monopoly is that there is only one firm in the industry. The demand curve for a normal good is downward sloping, as the firm must decrease price to increase sales. Therefore, the monopolist's demand curve will slope downwards. (9 marks)

(ii) **Patents and copyrights**

The person responsible for the original invention or idea has the sole right to any monetary gain from it.

Economies of scale

The existing firm has a very low average cost of production due to its large-scale production. Any new firm setting up in the industry would not have this low average cost, therefore it could not compete, price wise, with the existing firm.

Government regulations

The government grants the sole right to one firm to supply a good or service.

(Any 2 points explained at 8 marks each)

(c) (i) One advantage to employees of a monopoly firm.

- Employment is more secure as there is no competition in the industry.
- As monopolists earn SNPs the employees are in a better position to negotiate better pay and conditions.
- If a profit sharing system is in operation for employees then they could be in a position to secure substantial gains from their employment.
- In Ireland, many monopolies are state owned, therefore employment tends to be more secure than in the private sector.

(Any 1 point 10 marks)

(ii) One disadvantage to the consumers of a monopoly firm.

- As there is only one firm there is no choice of goods to the consumer.
- A strike in the firm would lead to a total withdrawal of supply from the customers.
- Monopolists earn SNPs which means the consumers are being exploited. (Any 1 point 10 marks)

Question 2 Chapter 13

Describe, with the aid of diagrams in each case, the effect on the equilibrium of a monopolist if there is (a) an increase in its fixed costs, (b) an increase in its variable costs. (55 marks)

Sample Answer 2 Chapter 13

(a) **Effect of increase in fixed costs**

Total cost = Fixed cost + Variable cost

If either fixed costs or variable costs increase then total cost will increase. If total cost increases then AC will also increase. (5 marks)

An increase in fixed costs will therefore cause an increase in AC. Fixed costs have no effect on marginal costs as these depend on changes in production levels. Therefore, the position of the MC curve will not change. (5 marks)

On the diagram below, the original equilibrium was where MC = MR giving a quantity of 100, a price of €8 and SNPs of €5 per item, i.e. AR minus AC1. When the fixed cost increased it caused AC1 to move to AC2. Because MC and MR are still equal to each other at the same point then the quantity will remain at 100, the price will remain at €8. The new AC is €4 so the SNPs will fall to €4 per item, i.e. AR minus AC2. (5 marks)

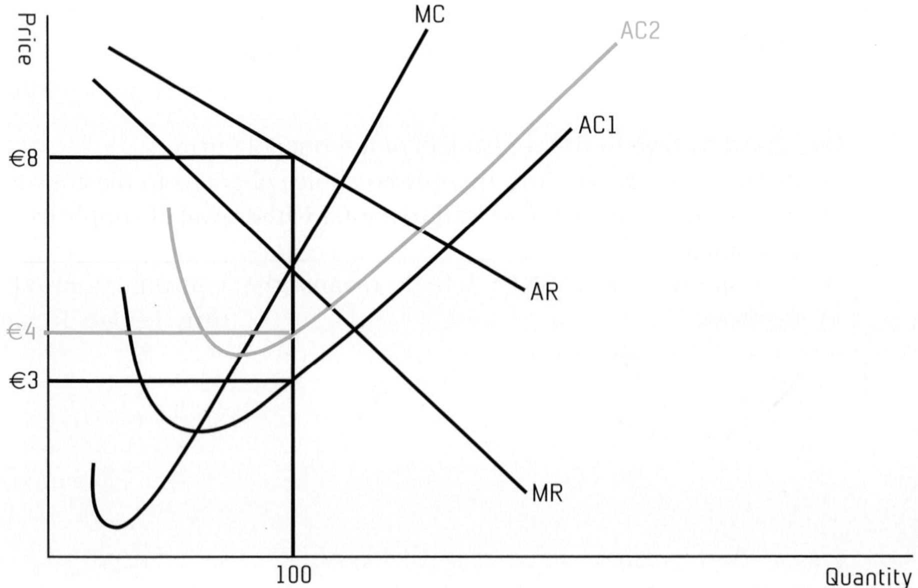

(Diagram 10 marks)

(b) **Effect of increase in variable costs**

Assume the original equilibrium is a price (AR) of €7, a quantity of 100 and SNPs of €4 per unit.

Total cost = Fixed cost + Variable cost

If either fixed or variable costs increase then total cost will increase. (5 marks)

If TC increases then AC will also increase. Thus the position of the average cost curve will move up to AC2 as shown on the diagram below. (5 marks)

When VC increase MC will also increase, as these are the additional costs of producing an extra unit of a good. Thus the position of the marginal cost curve will move up to MC2 as shown on the diagram below. Therefore, when variable costs increase then both AC and MC will increase. (5 marks)

Now MC2 = MR at a different point giving a new decreased quantity of 90 and a new increased price of €8. The new SNPs are now €3 per item. (5 marks)

Note: In this situation the quantity produced always decreases and the price always increases. SNPs can increase, decrease or remain constant depending on the relative changes in AR and AC. If the question dealt with a decrease in FC and VC then reverse the above process.

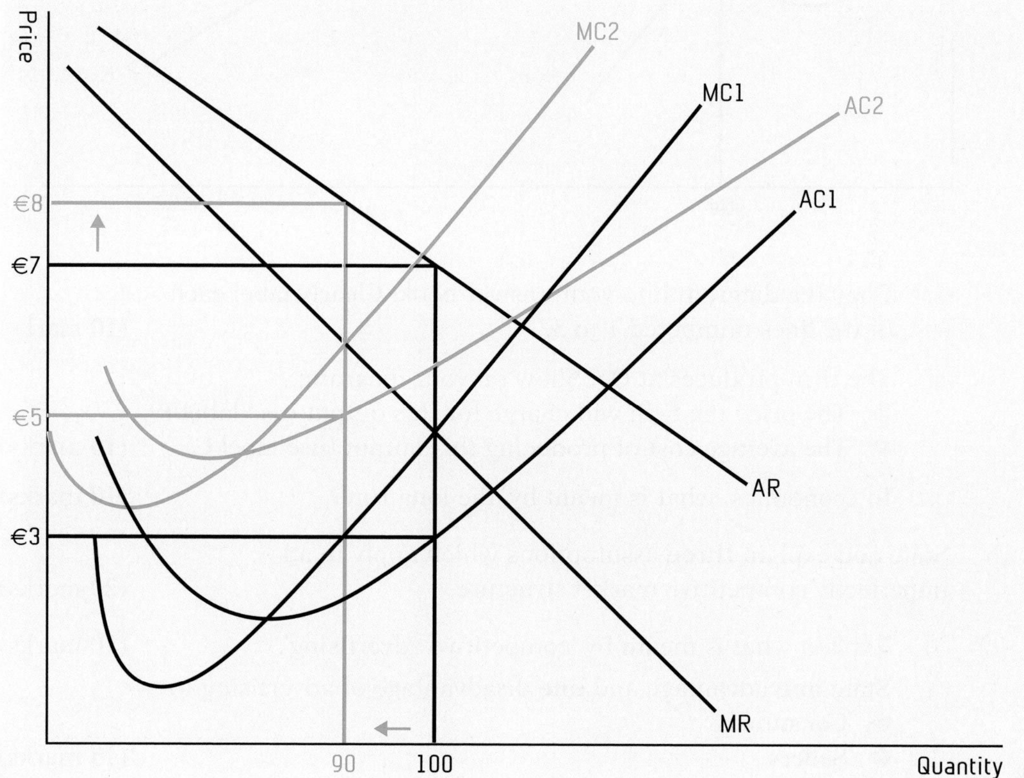

(Diagram 10 marks)

Chapter 15 Q&A See pp 125–130

Question 1 Chapter 15

(a) The diagram below represents the long run equilibrium of a firm in imperfect competition.

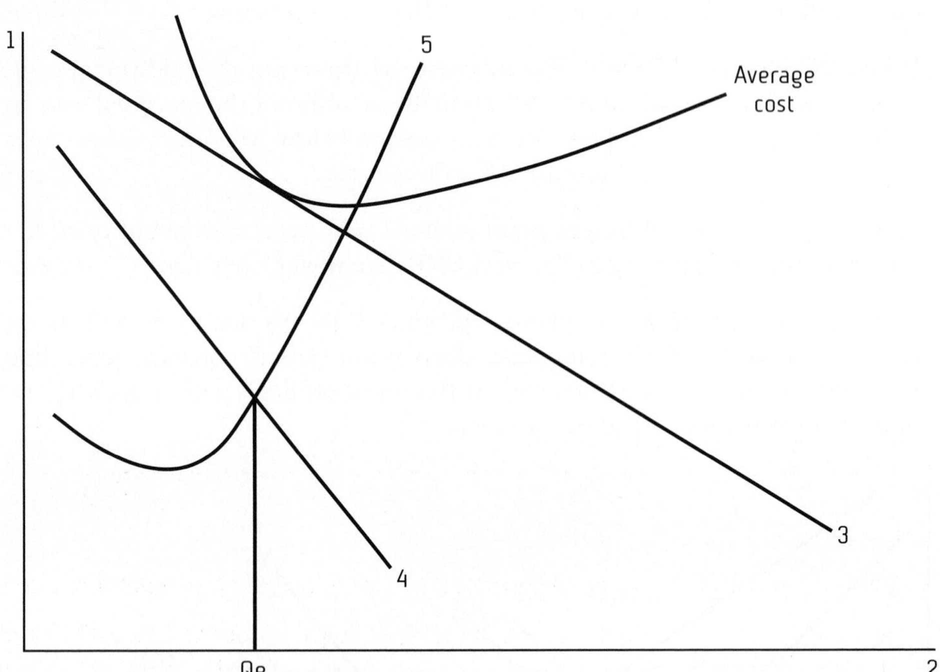

(i) Copy the diagram into your answer book. Clearly label each of the lines numbered 1 to 5. (10 marks)

(ii) The firm produces at Qe. Show on your diagram:

- The price the firm will charge for this output (use label P).
- The average cost of producing this output (use label C). (10 marks)

(iii) In economics, what is meant by 'the long run'? (10 marks)

(b) State and explain **three** assumptions which apply in an imperfectly competitive market structure. (20 marks)

(c) (i) Explain what is meant by 'competitive advertising'. (10 marks)

(ii) State **one** advantage and **one** disadvantage of advertising to:

- Consumers
- Sellers (15 marks)

(LC Economics, OL, 2002)

Sample Answer 1 Chapter 15

(a) (i) and (ii)

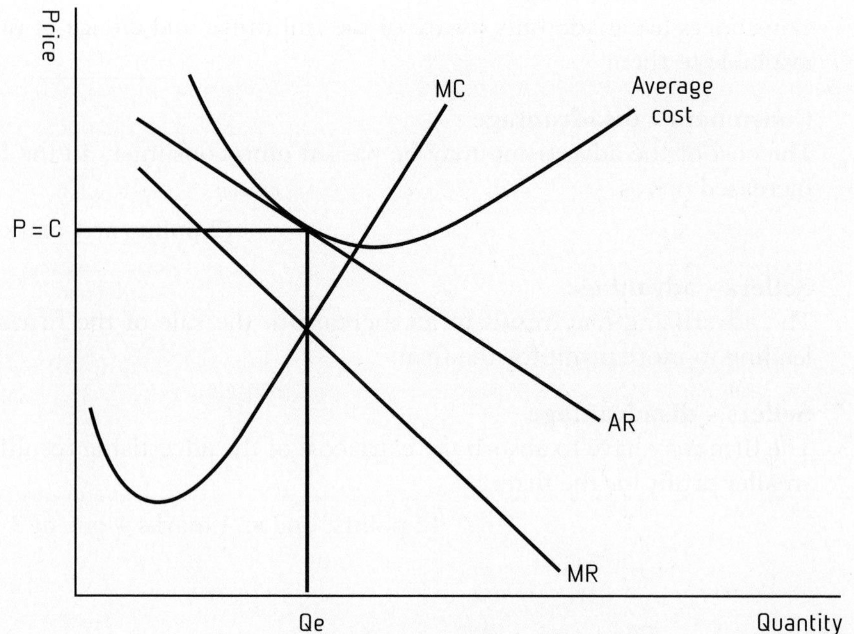

(2 marks per labelled line and 5 marks each for P and C)

(iii) The long run is a period of time long enough so that the quantity of all of the factors of production being used can be changed. (10 marks)

(b) (i) All the firms produce goods which are substitutes for each other. This means that the products produced by the firms in imperfect competition are not homogeneous but are similar to each other and consumers could replace one firm's product with another firm's product to satisfy any one need or want.

(ii) All firms aim to make maximum profit. This indicates that the firms in imperfect competition will produce the output where MR = MC provided MC > MR after that quantity.

(iii) Firms in imperfect competition may have to compete with each other for the factors of production. This means that the firms do not all produce their goods at the same average cost.

(3 marks for each statement + 3 explanations at 4 + 4 + 3 marks each)

(c) (i) Competitive advertising means that each individual firm advertises its own product in an attempt to convince the consumer that the individual firm's product is better than that of other firms in the industry. (10 marks)

(ii) **Consumers – advantage**
Consumers are made fully aware of the full range and choice of products available to them.

Consumers – disadvantage
The cost of the advertising may be passed onto consumers in the form of increased prices.

(2 points at 4 marks each)

Sellers – advantage
The advertising may result in an increase in the sale of the firm's goods leading to more profit for the firm.

Sellers – disadvantage
The firm may have to absorb the extra cost of the advertising resulting in a smaller profit for the firm.

(2 points, one at 4 marks + one at 3 marks)

Question 2 Chapter 15

(a) State and explain the assumptions underlying the theory of imperfect competition. (25 marks)

(b) Draw the demand curve which faces a firm in imperfect competition and justify its shape. (10 marks)

(c) Discuss, with the aid of a clearly labelled diagram, the implications of the assumptions in (a) above, on the equilibrium of the firm in the long run under conditions of imperfect competition. (30 marks)

(d) State **one feature** of this firm in long run equilibrium which would be common to a firm in long run equilibrium under **either** perfect competition **or** monopoly. (10 marks)

(LC Economics, HL, 2001)

Sample Answer 2 Chapter 15

(a) (i) There are many firms in the industry all producing products which are close substitutes for each other.

(ii) There are many buyers in the industry, thus no one buyer by his/her own actions can influence the market price.

(iii) All the firms engage in product differentiation, i.e. firms brand their products to create a distinction between them.

(iv) All firms aim to make maximum profits, i.e. they produce the output where MR = MC.

(v) There is full knowledge of the profit levels being earned in the industry, i.e. all potential investors know whether normal, supernormal or subnormal profits are being earned in that industry.

(vi) There is freedom of entry into and exit from the industry, i.e. there are no barriers preventing firms entering or leaving the industry.

(vii) There can be competition between the firms for the factors of production, i.e. they do not have a perfectly elastic supply of the factors of production.

(5 points named at 3 marks each + 5 explanations at 2 marks each)

(b)

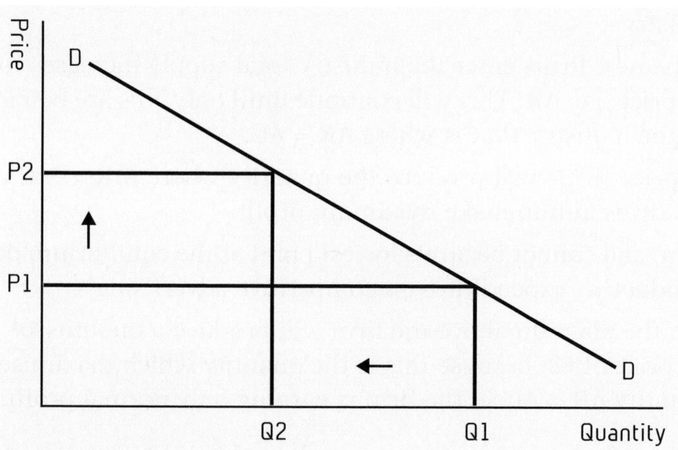

The above demand curve represents the demand curve facing a firm in imperfect competition. In imperfect competition there are many firms producing goods which are substitutes for each other. Thus if a firm increases its price it will lose some of its customers to the firms selling relatively cheaper goods. Therefore, as price increases demand goes down as shown above.

(4 marks for the demand curve + 6 marks for full explanation)

(c)

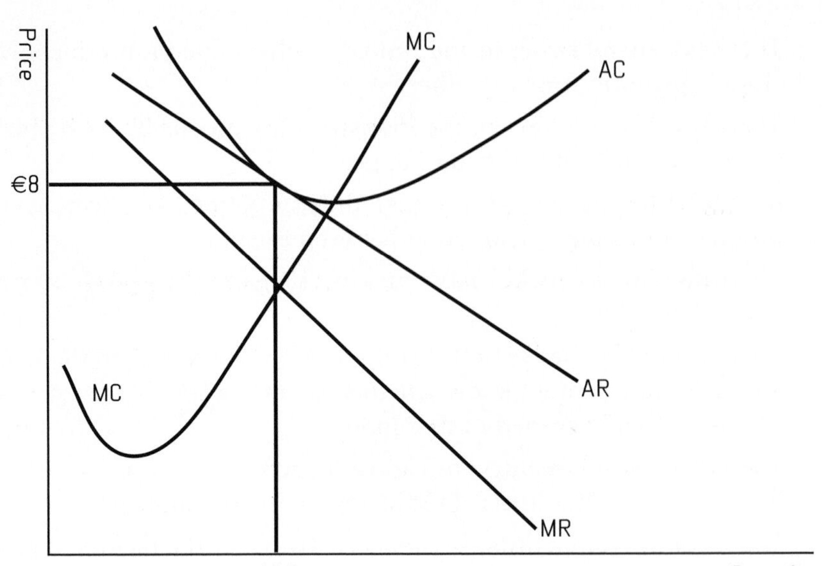

(Diagram 18 marks)

In the short run, firms in imperfect competition may earn SNPs. Because of assumptions (v) and (vi) in (a) above, new firms are attracted by these SNPs into the industry.

When the new firms enter the industry total supply increases forcing down the market price, i.e. AR. This will continue until only NPs are being earned by each firm in the industry, that is where AR = AC.

At this price firms will produce the quantity where MR = MC as it is assumed that the firms aim to make maximum profit.

AC is not, and cannot be, at its lowest point at the equilibrium output due to the 'non-productive' expenditure on competitive advertising.

Thus on the diagram above the firm will produce a quantity of 100 units at the market price of €8, because this is the quantity which maximises profit. Also at this quantity AR = AC so the firm is earning only normal profit. (12 marks)

(d) Firms in perfect competition, monopoly and imperfect competition all produce the **quantity** where MR = MC in order to earn maximum profit.

Or

In imperfect and perfect competition the firms earn only normal profit, i.e. AR = AC at the equilibrium output.

Or

In imperfect competition and monopoly the firms face a downward sloping demand curve, i.e. they must decrease price in order to increase sales.

(Any one feature clearly stated 10 marks)

Chapter 16 Q&A

See pp 131–141

Question 1 Chapter 16

(a) What is meant by an oligopolistic market? Give **two** examples of industries considered oligopolist in Ireland. (20 marks)

(b) (i) Explain with the aid of a diagram the shape of the demand curve of a firm in oligopolistic competition.

(ii) Hence explain what is meant by the term 'rigidity of prices'. (30 marks)

(c) (i) Distinguish between price competition and non-price competition.

(ii) Which form of competition do you consider to be better for the buyer? Give **two** reasons for your answer. (25 marks)

(LC Economics, HL, 1999)

Sample Answer 1 Chapter 16

(a) (i) An oligopolistic market is one in which a small number of very large firms sell products which are close substitutes for each other. (10 marks)

(ii) The petrol distribution and the retail banking industries in Ireland would be two examples of oligopolistic markets. (10 marks)

(b) (i) Because oligopolists interact with each other the firm knows that it faces an inelastic D or AR curve. If it decreases its price, all the other firms will also decrease their prices and there will be very little gain in sales for any of the firms. (5 marks)

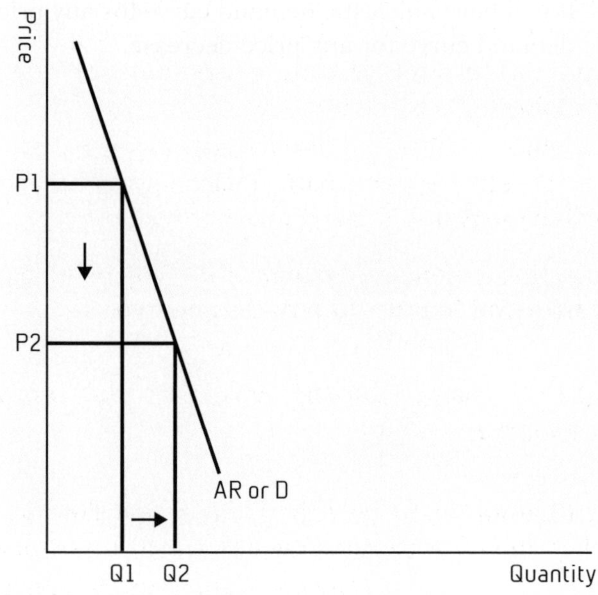

(Diagram 5 marks)

- Likewise, the firm knows that if it increases its price most of its customers will switch to the purchase of one of the cheaper close substitutes available. Therefore, the firm is facing an elastic demand curve for increasing prices. (5 marks)

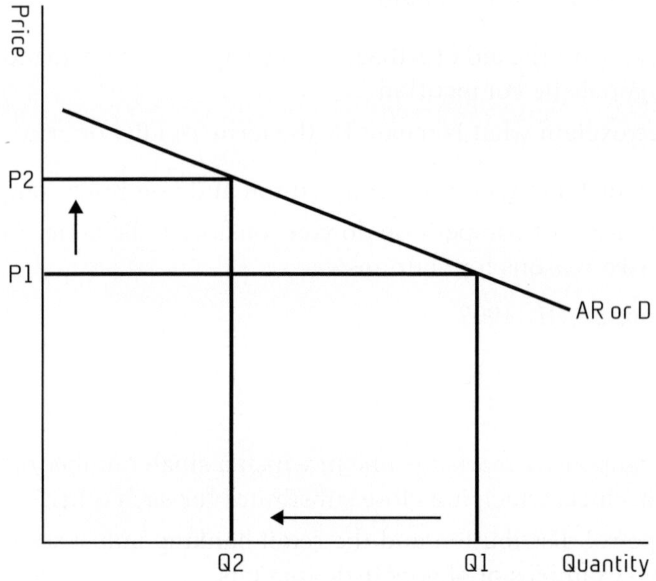

(Diagram 5 marks)

Therefore, once a firm has settled on a price for its product the firm's demand curve is composed of two separate segments of each of these demand curves. It will have an elastic demand curve for any price increase and an inelastic demand curve for any price decrease.

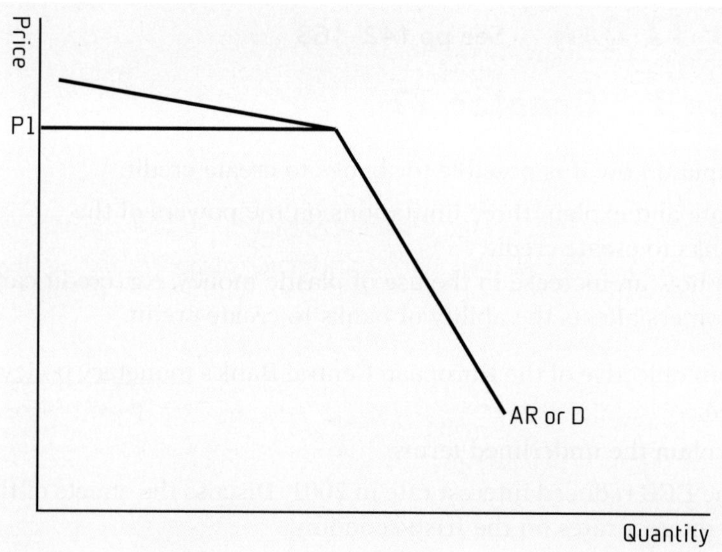

(Diagram 5 marks)

(ii) Once this firm has established the market price of P1 it will be reluctant to change this price, as its total revenue will fall whether it increases or decreases its price. Therefore, the firm will tend to stay with this price, all other things being equal. This reluctance to change price has led to the use of the term 'rigidity of prices'. (5 marks)

(c) (i) Price competition is a situation where firms compete with each other for a bigger share of the market by lowering their prices, whereas non-price competition is where firms compete with each other by offering incentives other than price reductions, e.g. 20 per cent extra at no extra price or 'gifts' being offered with certain purchases.

(5 marks for each description = 10 marks)

(ii) Price competition is better for the consumer.

- Price competition, due to its nature, leads to cheaper prices to the consumer. (8 marks)
- The consumers, frequently, do not need or want the offers under non-price competition. (7 marks)

Chapter 17 Q&A

See pp 142–168

Question 1 Chapter 17

(a) (i) Explain how it is possible for banks to create credit. (18 marks)

(ii) State and explain three limitations on the powers of the banks to create credit. (12 marks)

(b) Explain how an increase in the use of plastic money, e.g. credit cards, by customers affects the ability of banks to create credit. (15 marks)

(c) The main objective of the European Central Bank's monetary policy is to control inflation.

(i) Explain the underlined terms.

(ii) The ECB reduced interest rate in 2001. Discuss the effects of this reduction in interest rates on the Irish economy. (30 marks)

(LC Economics, HL, 2002)

Sample Answer 1 Chapter 17

(a) (i) The primary liquidity ratio (PLR) is the ratio of cash which the banks must hold to claims on the banks.

Assume Mr A lodges €1,000 cash in a bank.

If we assume that the PLR is 1:10 (i.e. 10 per cent) the bank must keep €100 of this in cash. This is 10 per cent of A's claim.

This leaves the bank with €900 cash.

This represents 10 per cent of a loan which the bank could give customer B.

The value of the loan would be €9,000.

Thus the bank has created €9,000 which was not in existence before the €1,000 cash deposit.

The bank has €100 in cash for the PLR for A's deposit and it has €900 in cash for the PLR for B's loan. (18 marks)

(ii) **The PLR**

As customers demand more or less cash at any given time then the Central Bank will change the PLR, thus altering the banks' ability to extend credit. In the example above, if the PLR was changed to 1:5 (i.e. the bank must keep 20 per cent of deposits in cash) then the bank could lend only €4,000.

ECB credit guidelines

From time to time the ECB issues guidelines recommending the level of lending that should be undertaken by banks. This, therefore, could restrict the amount of loans which the banks could extend to their customers.

The availability of cash deposits
As can be seen from the example in (i) above the loan given by the bank not only depends on the PLR but also on the amount of cash deposited. If the deposit above were increased to €2,000 cash then the maximum loan would increased to €18,000.

Note: It is also acceptable to explain any of the powers which the Central Bank has to curtail the banks' lending power.

(3 points at 4 marks each)

(b) As customers increase their use of 'plastic' money then their demand for cash from their bank deposits will decrease. This would allow the banks to decrease their reserve (i.e. the PLR could change from 1:10 to 1:20), thus allowing them to increase their lending. (15 marks)

(c) (i) Monetary policy refers to the policy regarding the amount of money in circulation, interest rates and credit creation.

Inflation refers to the increase in the general level of prices.

(2 definitions at 5 marks each)

(ii) **Borrowing is encouraged.** Borrowing is now cheaper, thus repayments decrease, leaving people with more discretionary income. This could increase demand and thus have an inflationary affect on the economy.

Saving is discouraged. Lower interest rates act as a disincentive to saving, especially if it results in the true rate of interest being a negative rate of interest. This could have an adverse effect on the amount of funds available for investment purposes.

Investment is encouraged. As interest rates decrease, the profitability of investment increases, everything else being equal. This should lead to an increase in the general level of supply and possibly an increase in employment.

Lowers the cost of servicing the national debt. The lower level of interest would reduce the cost of servicing the national debt as less interest has to be repaid on the Eurozone portion of the debt. This could reduce the level of taxation in Ireland, or it could free up money for the government to spend on other sectors of the economy.

Reduces mortgage repayments. This would benefit existing mortgage holders but at the same time it may have an inflationary effect on the price of houses as the demand for them may increase.

(4 points fully explained at 5 marks each.
2 marks each if points are only mentioned)

Question 2 Chapter 17

(a) Money is defined as anything which is accepted in payment of a debt. State two items which are accepted as money in a modern economy. (10 marks)

(b) The four functions of money in an economy are:

(i) It acts as a medium of exchange.

(ii) It acts as a measure of value.

(iii) It acts as a store of wealth.

(iv) It acts as a standard of deferred payment.

Explain what is meant by any two of the above functions. (20 marks)

(c) (i) State any two of the functions of the Central Bank.

(ii) Write brief notes on each of these functions. (30 marks)

(d) Suppose the supply of money in an economy is greater than the supply of goods and services in that economy.

Explain the effects which this might have on either:

(i) The price for goods and services in that economy.

Or

(ii) The amount of goods imported into that economy. (15 marks)

(LC Economics, OL, 1997)

Sample Answer 2 Chapter 17

(a) Cash (notes and coins), credit cards and cheques are accepted as money in a modern economy. (5 marks each for any two of these)

(b) (i) It acts as a medium of exchange.
This means that money is used to allow people to exchange goods freely by accepting money for the goods which they produce and then using that money to buy the goods which they need.

(ii) It acts as a measure of value.
The value of a good is indicated by the amount of money which you must pay for a good. For example, if you pay €10 for good A and €5 for good B this indicates that A is twice as valuable as B.

(iii) It acts as a store of wealth.
When a person saves money he/she is really saving up wealth (a store of goods and services), as the money saved can be exchanged for goods and services at any time in the future.

(iv) It acts as a standard of deferred payment. This means that money allows us to operate an efficient credit system. People can buy goods now and not pay for them until some date in the future. This would be almost impossible under the barter system.

(Any two explanations at 10 marks each)

(c) (i) The Central Bank is the government's bank. The government lodges all its income with the Central Bank and pays out all its expenses on Central Bank cheques. Thus it acts for the government the same way as ordinary banks act for the general public.

(ii) The Central Bank issues the country's currency. The Central Bank is the only institution in the country which can print notes and mint coins for general circulation.

(Two functions named at 5 marks each + 2 explanations at 10 marks each)

(d) (i) If the supply of money in an economy is greater than the supply of goods and services in that economy, this will cause inflation in that economy, i.e. the price of goods in the economy will increase as there is more money than goods available for sale.

(ii) If there is not a sufficient supply of goods available in the economy to match the money supply then people will import the extra goods which they require, causing an increase in imports.

(1 point fully explained at 15 marks)

Chapter 18 Q&A See pp 169–184

Question 1 Chapter 18

(a) The national income of a country is the total of the incomes received by each of the four factors of production in that country in a given year.

(i) Name the **three** ways which are used to calculate national income.

(ii) Give **one** reason why all these three methods are used, instead of one.

(20 marks)

(b) The gross national product of a country at market prices is defined as 'the value of all the goods and services produced in a country valued at the prices paid for them by consumers in the market'.

Explain the effect which each of the following will have on GNP at market prices.

(i) A rise in the level of Value Added Tax

(ii) The payment of food subsidies to Irish producers (20 marks)

(LC Economics, OL, 1998)

Sample Answer 1 Chapter 18

(a) (i) The incomes method, the production method and the expenditure method. (10 marks)

(ii) The three methods are used as a check on each other as all totals should be equal to each other. All three of these should equal each other as all money spent (expenditure) is spent on goods and services which are produced (production) and all incomes are earned from the production of goods and services. (10 marks)

(b) (i) A rise in VAT increases the price which the consumers must pay for the products, therefore it would increase gross national product at market prices. (10 marks)

(ii) When a producer receives a subsidy this is deducted from the selling price of the good, thus the consumer pays less for the good. This decreases the GNP at market prices. (10 marks)

Chapter 19 Q&A See pp 185–199

Question 1 Chapter 19

(a) Explain by means of a diagram the circular flow of income for an open economy and the forces which influence the level of aggregate demand. (25 marks)

(b) The following table shows the level of national income, consumption, investment, exports and imports at the end of Period 1 and Period 2. For the purpose of this question you may ignore the government sector.

	National income	Consumption	Investment	Exports	Imports
Period 1	€4,800	€1,200	€1,100	€1,200	€5,800
Period 2	€5,250	€1,300	€1,200	€1,350	

Calculate the following, showing all your workings:

(i) The level of national income in Period 2

(ii) The marginal propensity to save

(iii) The marginal propensity to import

(iv) The size of the multiplier (20 marks)

(c) Given gross national product at current market prices for the years 1990 and 2000, state and explain the relevance of **four** other pieces of information in assessing changes in the average standard of living between 1990 and 2000. (30 marks)

(LC Economics, HL, 2001)

Sample Answer 1 Chapter 19

(a)

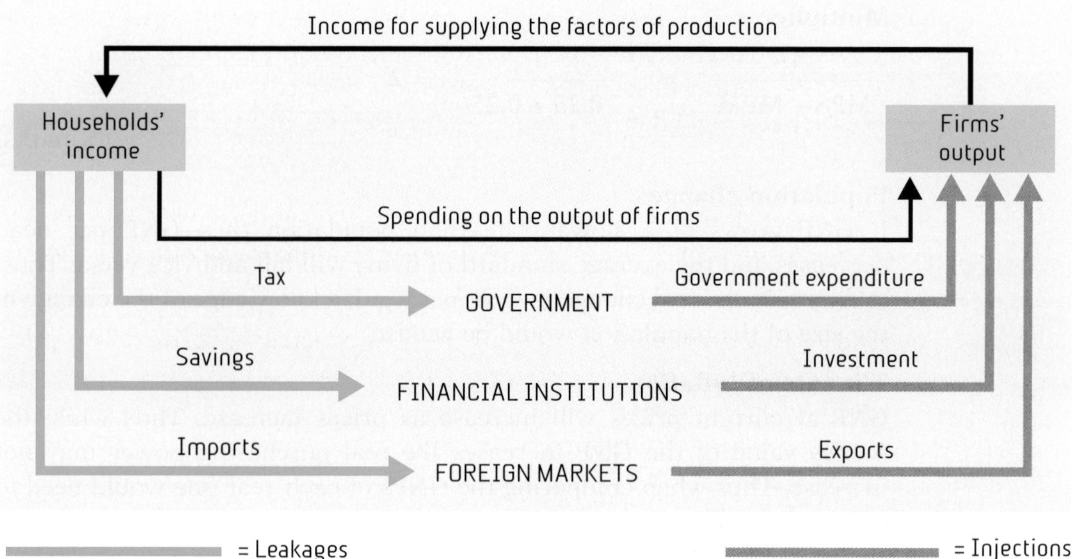

(Identifying the 5 sectors, i.e. household, firm, government, financial institutions and foreign markets at 1 mark each. Identifying the 8 flows at 1 mark each. Identifying the correct direction of each flow at 1 mark each.)

This diagram shows that aggregate demand depends on income earned by supplying the factors of production. However, this demand is decreased by the level of taxation, the level of savings and the amount spent on imports. These are all leakages from the circular flow of income. However, the level of income is increased by any increase in government spending, by investment in the economy and by income earned from abroad from exports. These are all injections into the circular flow of income and increase aggregate demand.

(4 marks)

(b) (i) National income (Y) = C + I + X – M
Therefore Y = €5,250 + €1,300 + €1,200 – €1,350
Thus Y = €7,750 – €1,350, i.e. €6,400 (5 marks)

(ii) The MPS is the fraction or percentage of the last increase in income saved.
Y in Period 2 increased from €5,800 to €6,400, i.e. an increase in income of €600.
C increased from €4,800 to €5,250, i.e. €450. The difference between C and Y = Savings.
Therefore savings in Period 2 = €150
Thus MPS = €150/€600 = 0.25 (5 marks)

(iii) MPM is the fraction or percentage of the last increase in income spent on imports.
Y in Period 2 increased by €600 while imports increased by €150
Therefore MPM = 150/600 = 0.25 (5 marks)

(iv) **Multiplier =**

$$\frac{1}{MPS + MPM} = \frac{1}{0.25 + 0.25} = 2$$

(5 marks)

(c) (i) **Population changes**
If GNP grows at a slower rate than population then GNP per head decreases and the average standard of living will fall and vice versa. Thus, to ascertain the real change in GNP per head, a knowledge of the change in the size of the population would be needed.

(ii) **The rate of inflation**
GNP at current prices will increase as prices increase. Thus while the money value of the GNP increases the real purchasing power may not increase. Thus when comparing the GNPs of each year one would need to adjust these figures for inflation. GNP at constant prices gives a better comparison over any time period.

(iii) **Distribution of GNP**
Sometimes the increase in the GNP is shared by only a very small percentage of the population. Therefore, although the average GNP may have increased, there may be no improvement in the standard of living of the general population.

(iv) **Change in the degree of market orientation**
As an economy grows an increasing amount of activities take place within the market place, thus increasing the money value of GNP. This does not necessarily mean that the standard of living has increased. For example, in 1990 many people may have grown and consumed all of their own vegetables. In 2000 these same people may be buying these vegetables. Thus their standard of living has not increased even though GNP has increased.

Note: Other points which could have been mentioned include:
(i) Changes in quality of goods between 1990 and 2000.
(ii) There may be new goods on the market in 2000 which were not available in 1990 and these are included in the 2000 figures.
(iii) Changes in the level of social welfare.
(iv) Additional social costs; as the economy grows these can have a detrimental effect on the quality of life.
(v) The rates of taxation in the periods being compared, in particular indirect taxes, may not be the same.

(Any 4 points fully explained, 2 at 8 marks each + 2 at 7 marks each)

Chapter 20 Q&A See pp 200–210

Question 1 Chapter 20

(a) Explain what is meant by the term 'inflation'. (15 marks)

(b) What index is used to measure the rate of inflation? (9 marks)

(c) Discuss the effects which a rise in the rate of inflation may have on the following:

(i) People in receipt of social welfare

(ii) Savers

(iii) Borrowers

(iv) Employees (36 marks)

(d) A firm which exports goods from Ireland would favour a lower inflation rate here than that in its exports markets.

In your opinion, why is this so? Answer briefly. (15 marks)

(LC Economics, OL, 1996)

Sample Answer 1 Chapter 20

(a) Inflation means an increase in the general level of prices. (15 marks)

(b) The rate of inflation is measured by the Consumer Price Index. (9 marks)

(c) (i) People in receipt of social welfare benefits normally only receive an increase in these benefits once a year, i.e. at budget time. Thus as prices increase during the year their purchasing power decreases. Therefore, inflation decreases the real income of people on social welfare benefits.

(ii) As prices increase the value of people's savings decreases as the sum saved can buy fewer goods as time goes by, unless the rate of interest is either equal to or greater than the rate of inflation.

(iii) As the rate of inflation increases the real value of money borrowed decreases. For example, if a person borrowed €10,000 for a year and the rate of inflation for that year was 10 per cent then in real terms the value of the debt becomes €9,000 at the end of the year.

(iv) Unless employees receive an increase in money income equal to the rate of inflation their real income decreases during a period of inflation as they would buy fewer goods with their money income as prices increase.

(4 points fully explained at 9 marks each)

(d) If there were a lower inflation rate in Ireland than that in its exports markets, then the price of goods produced in those markets would be increasing at a greater rate than the price of Irish goods. This would make the price of Irish goods relatively cheaper and people in those markets may substitute their domestically produced goods with Irish goods. This would lead to an increase in the volume and value of Irish exports.

- Irish goods become relatively cheaper on foreign markets. (5 marks)
- Irish goods are substituted for the domestically produced goods on foreign markets. (5 marks)
- This leads to an increase in exports. (5 marks)

Question 2 Chapter 20

(a) For a composite (weighted) price index covering the three types of expenditure given in the following table, calculate the index for the current year. The base year value is 100. Show your workings. (20 marks)

Category	% of Income spent on item(s)	Prices of item(s) in base year	Price of item(s) in current year
		€	€
Food	35	8.50	12.75
Clothing and footwear	15	37.50	45.00
Other items	50	20.00	35.00
	100		

(b) Does the Consumer Price Index (CPI) accurately measure changes in the cost of living in Ireland? Explain your answer. (30 marks)

(c) Over the past year the rate of inflation, as measured by the CPI, has fluctuated. Discuss the effects of this development on the Irish economy. (25 marks)

(LC Economics, HL, 2001)

Note: When doing this type of question (a) use the following procedures.

(i) Make a simple price index for each product, i.e. express the current price as a percentage of the price in the base year.

(ii) Multiply the simple price index for each product by its weighting, i.e. the percentage of income spent on it.

(iii) Add together all the answers at (b) to get the CPI for the current year.

Sample Answer 2 Chapter 20

(a) (i) The simple index for food is 12.75/8.50 × 100 = 150

The simple index for clothing and footwear is 45.00/37.50 × 100 = 120

The simple index for other items is 35.00/20.00 × 100 = 175

(3 points at 4 marks each)

(ii) 150 × 35% = 52.50

120 × 15% = 18.00

175 × 50% = 87.50 (3 points at 2 marks each)

(iii) 52.50 + 18.00 + 87.50 = 158

Therefore, the CPI for the current year is 158. (2 marks)

(b) (i) Limited range of products included in the CPI.
Most families spend their income on a very large range of goods. Only twelve categories of goods are included in the CPI comprising roughly 8,000 different goods. There are tens of thousands of different goods on the market at any given time.

(ii) Does not include any new products that have come on the market since the Household Survey.
The Household Survey is carried out once every five years. In the interim between these surveys many new products come onto the market and are widely consumed. These new products are not included in the CPI until the next Household Survey is carried out.

(iii) It overstates the cost of living.
As products included in the CPI increase in price, consumers switch to cheaper substitute goods, thus distorting the weighting given to these products.

(iv) The survey establishes the basket of goods of the 'average' household only. There is no such thing as the 'average' household as the 'average' is merely a mathematical concept. If families do not consume many of the items included in the household basket then the CPI is irrelevant to that family. For example, if a family does not buy cigarettes, alcohol, petrol and meat then the CPI would not accurately reflect their cost of living.

(v) It does not take account of changes in the quality of goods.
Real price increases are often hidden by changes in the quality of the goods being sold. If the average size of a bar of chocolate is reduced by 10 per cent while its price remains unchanged then this really constitutes a hidden price increase.

(vi) It does not make any allowance for differences in rural and urban lifestyles. Many rural dwellers are not affected by the change in price of such goods as potatoes and eggs as they produce these goods themselves for their own consumption. Urban dwellers may spend a relatively large percentage of their income on these goods thus increasing their cost of living.

(vii) It makes no allowance for price increases due to increased indirect taxes. Price increases are often caused by increases in indirect taxes. If the extra taxes are used to provide extra services free of charge to the consumers then their real cost of living has not increased.

(6 points at 5 marks each if fully explained, or 2 marks for each of 6 points named without explanations)

(c) **The effects of inflation**

(i) Because of the higher cost of living, people have reduced purchasing power, which causes a reduction in their standard of living.

(ii) Causes demands for wage increases to compensate for the inflation that, ironically, can further fuel cost-push inflation.

(iii) May cause unemployment if employers who are faced with demands for increased wages and possible loss of markets are forced to reduce costs by reducing their labour force.

(iv) Discourages saving, if there is a negative interest rate, leading to less investment funds being available.

(v) If interest rates are less than the rate of inflation borrowing may increase leading to further demand-pull inflation.

(vi) Adverse effects on the balance of trade:
- Exports become more expensive making them less competitive on the international market.
- Imports become relatively cheaper, thus creating a greater demand for them.

(vii) People on fixed incomes suffer most. These people's real income decreases as inflation increases, e.g. people on fixed pensions.

(viii) Speculation in fixed assets (property) increases, as these tend to increase in value during a period of inflation.

(ix) As a result of (viii) money moves away from investment in wealth creating projects, thus reducing the potential productive capacity of the country.

(x) Rising inflation creates uncertainty in the economy that is unfavourable to investment decisions.

(Any 5 fully explained points at 5 marks each, 2 marks if the point is only mentioned)

Chapter 21 Q&A

See pp 211–226

Question 1 Chapter 21

(a) Taxes can be classified as either direct or indirect.

(i) Explain what is meant by direct and indirect taxes.

(ii) Give two examples of each of these types of taxes. (30 marks)

(b) The four canons (or principles) of taxation are: **equity**, **economy**, **certainty** and **convenience**. Explain briefly and clearly what is meant by each of these canons of taxation. (25 marks)

(LC Economics, OL, 1999)

Sample Answer 1 Chapter 21

(a) (i) A direct tax is a tax on income, while an indirect tax is a tax on a transaction.

(ii) Two examples of direct taxes are PAYE and DIRT. Two examples of indirect taxes are VAT and stamp duties.

(2 definitions + 4 examples at 5 marks each)

(b) Equity means fairness, i.e. the tax should take into account the ability of the taxpayer to pay the tax.

Economy means that the income from the tax should be far greater than the cost of collecting it.

Certainty means that the taxpayer should know at the start of the year what his/her potential tax bill will be at the end of the year so that money can be set aside during the year to pay the tax bill at the end of the year.

Convenience means that the method of collecting the tax should be suited to the taxpayer rather than suited to the government.

(4 points fully explained, i.e. 3 at 6 marks each + one at 7 marks)

Question 2 Chapter 21

(a) In each of the following distinguish between the terms used:

(i) monetary policy and fiscal policy

(ii) progressive taxation and regressive taxation

(iii) tax avoidance and tax evasion. (30 marks)

(b) There has been an increase in government income from taxation in the past year.

(i) Outline **three** reasons for this outcome.

(ii) State **one** revenue opportunity and **one** expenditure opportunity for the government arising from this increased income. Which of these would you consider a priority? Explain your choice. (25 marks)

(c) Explain how an understanding by the Minister for Finance of the concept of price elasticity of demand would help in settling levels of indirect taxation. Use examples to illustrate your answer. (20 marks)

(LC Economics, HL, 2005)

Sample Answer 2 Chapter 21

(a) (i) Monetary policy is policy relating to the money supply, interest rates and credit creation, while fiscal policy is the government's policy regarding taxation and government expenditure.

(ii) A progressive tax is one which takes a higher percentage of income in taxation as taxable income increases, while a regressive tax is one which takes a higher percentage of income from a low income earner than from a high income earner.

(iii) Tax avoidance is the practice of using the tax code to your best possible advantage to reduce your tax liability to the minimum. Tax evasion is the non-payment of taxes due, by either making no tax returns or making false tax returns.

(6 definitions at 5 marks each)

(b) (i) There has been an increase in income tax revenue due to the increase in employment leading to more people paying income taxes.

As average wages are increasing in value in absolute terms, more people are moving into the higher tax bracket and, therefore they are paying more income tax.

There has been an increase in economic growth leading to a higher level of demand for goods and services throughout the economy. This has led to an increase in indirect tax revenue for the government.

(5 marks for any 3 points fully explained)

(ii) The government is presently operating a current budget surplus. An increase in tax revenue gives the government the revenue opportunity of decreasing income taxes or indirect taxes without decreasing its total tax revenue. An expenditure opportunity for the government would be to increase spending on the health or educational services.

The government's priority would probably be to reduce direct taxes as this is politically very advantageous. However, a decrease in indirect taxes would be of benefit to everybody, even the unemployed who would not benefit from the decrease in income taxes.

(Any one revenue opportunity and any one expenditure opportunity at 4 marks each + 2 marks for any stated priority)

(c) The government can raise taxes to either increase its tax revenue or to reduce the demand for certain products.

If the government wants to increase its revenue from the imposition of extra indirect taxes, then these taxes should be levied on goods where price elasticity of demand is inelastic, as the percentage decrease in demand will be less than the percentage increase in the selling price, e.g. petrol.

If the object of increasing a tax on a product is to reduce the demand for that product, then it will only succeed if the price elasticity of demand for that product is elastic, as the increase in price will cause a more than proportionate decrease in demand for the product, e.g. sports cars which have very high CO_2 emissions.

(2 reasons at 5 marks each and 2 examples at 5 marks each)

Chapter 22 Q&A See pp 227–238

Question 1 Chapter 22

(a) (i) One of the government's economic aims is to achieve balanced regional development. Outline **four** possible government policies to achieve this aim.

(ii) 'Policies to achieve balanced regional development may make it more difficult for the government to achieve other economic aims.' Explain this statement, using examples to support your answer. (30 marks)

(LC Economics, HL, 2005)

Sample Answer 1 Chapter 22

(a) (i) Four possible government policies to achieve balanced regional development.

1 Decentralisation
By relocating government departments to local regions there will be an increase in the working population in these areas. There will be a multiplier effect on incomes in these areas, thus aiding economic development in these regional areas.

2 Incentives to attract industry
The government could make some of the under utilised regions more attractive to investors by offering tax relief, subsidies, grants or other incentives to locate there. This would greatly aid economic development in these areas.

3 Investment in the infrastructure in the regions
If investment in the economic and social infrastructure takes place these improvements will make these regions more attractive to work and invest in, and encourage geographical mobility of labour boosting the working population and making such communities viable places to live.

4 The government's Spatial Strategy
The aim of this strategy is to create gateways and hubs throughout the country. These will act as centres for development within the regions, thus improving economic development.

(Any 4 points fully developed at 4 marks each)

(ii) Achieving a balanced regional development will entail an increase in total government expenditure. This conflicts with the government policy of control over public finances, as it may have to borrow to fund this expenditure thus increasing the national debt.

Alternatively, the extra expenditure on regional development may reduce the finances available to increase social welfare benefits nationally, thus adversely affecting the government's policy of achieving an equitable distribution of wealth.

Encouraging people to move to these developing regions will increase the demand for housing in these regions, which may result in an increase in property prices, which is contrary to the government's policy of controlling inflation.

(Explanation of the statement at 4 marks, and 2 points full explained at 5 marks each)

Chapter 23 Q&A See pp 239–253

Question 1 Chapter 23

The enlargement of the European Union (EU) to include many new countries will be economically significant for Ireland.

Outline the main economic opportunities and challenges for the Irish economy following enlargement of the EU. (25 marks)

(LC Economics, HL, 2004)

Sample Answer 1 Chapter 23

Opportunities

1. The population of the EU has increased from 381.65 million prior to June 2004 to 485.12 million on the entry of Romania and Bulgaria in January 2007. This represents an increase in market size of 103.47 million people. Thus Irish firms should be able to gain a share of this market.
2. Irish consumers now have a greater range and choice of goods which can be purchased from these countries, thus improving their standard of living.
3. With the free movement of capital, there are now new investment opportunities for Irish entrepreneurs, which could see their profits increase.
4. With the free movement of labour, Ireland's shortage of labour could be rectified by attracting citizens from these countries to work here. This does not apply to citizens from Romania and Bulgaria. However, people from these two countries can come to Ireland as self-employed people.

Challenges

1. Firms located in these new member states have lower costs of production, in particular lower wage rates. This will make it more attractive for manufacturers to move their production from Ireland to these countries. This could result in a disinvestment in Ireland.
2. Ireland has a very small population and is becoming more and more peripheral from the main centres of population in the EU. This could make Ireland a less attractive place for direct foreign investment, in particular, in terms of foreign investment from non-EU countries.
3. An increased proportion of EU funds will have to be devoted to the development of these new member countries. This will result in fewer funds being made available to Ireland. In fact, Ireland could become a net contributor of funds.

4 The increase in immigration from these new member countries could put extra pressure on our infrastructure, as more houses, schools and medical services will be required to facilitate the immigrants.

(5 points fully developed 5 marks each, with a minimum of 2 points each on opportunities and challenges)

Chapter 24 Q&A See pp 254–268

Question 1 Chapter 24

(a) Define what is meant by the term 'economic development'. (15 marks)

(b) Discuss how economic development in underdeveloped countries might be promoted:

(i) By their own governments

(ii) Assisted by foreign governments. (30 marks)

(c) Outline **three** benefits and **three** costs of economic development to these countries. (30 marks)

(LC Economics, HL, 1999)

Sample Answer 1 Chapter 24

(a) Economic development is the process of increasing average income per head of the population while changing the structure of the economy. (15 marks)

(b) (i) Governments can promote economic development in their own countries in any of the following ways.

1 Provide basic infrastructure

Providing basic infrastructure entails the provision of clean water and basic sanitation facilities as well as the provision of public housing and the development of roads, power supplies and basic communications systems.

2 Promote land and agricultural reform

The government should encourage farmers to diversify production so that they are not totally dependent on one cash crop.

3 Grants/aid

Grants or aid should be given to farmers to increase their production by using more modern production methods. This would release more workers to be available for employment in manufacturing industries.

Ownership of land tends to be in the hands of a small percentage of the population in these countries. The government should devise schemes to spread ownership of land.

4 Improve education standards in the country
Improving education standards in the country should start with a basic literacy and numeracy programme and then as the requirements of the economy change more money should be spent on secondary and third level education.

5 Invest in manufacturing industries (provide capital)
Governments should encourage more enterprise in the economy. They could use borrowings to encourage enterprises (businesses) which could create sustainable jobs.

6 Create stable political environment
Creating a stable political environment entails the elimination of corruption, so that any aid received flows to those to whom it was intended. It would also entail diverting expenditure away from arms spending to more productive expenditure.

7 Curtail population growth
Curtailing population growth could be done through an educational campaign and through the provision of birth control devices. It is easier to increase the average income per head of a small population than that of a large population.

(5 points at 3 marks each)

(ii) Foreign governments can assist in the following ways.

1 Foreign aid programmes
Foreign aid programmes provide the governments of developing countries with money for emergencies, famines, and for more long-term aid to help with the development of the infrastructure, the provision of education, and housing.

2 Restructure the underdeveloped countries' national debts
Most LDCs (least developed countries) have a very high national debt as a percentage of their GDP. If these debts were cancelled, or substantially reduced, then the funds which go to servicing and repaying these debts could be put to more productive use.

3 Enter into trade agreements
Trade agreements should give the LDCs improved access to the markets in the developed countries. This makes it easier for them to export and the foreign currency earned from the exports can then be used to purchase capital goods from abroad.

4 Encourage multinational companies to set up there
Encouraging multinational companies to set up in LDCs would have a triple effect. It would provide the workers with new skills. It would provide much needed jobs. It would provide income tax revenue for the government.

5 Provide technology
The provision of simple technology would increase the productive capacity of the LDCs and result in a higher standard of living.

6 Help promote political stability
Foreign countries could provide peacekeeping troops and reward political stability with more aid.

(5 points at 3 marks each)

(c) (i) Benefits of economic development:

1 Improves the standard of living
Economic development results in more goods being produced and being available to consumers, thus creating a higher standard of living.

2 More employment
Economic development creates extra demand in the economy, which should create more indigenous jobs.

3 More tax revenue for the government
As more jobs are created and as more goods are sold in the economy, more tax revenue is generated for the government and this leads to more services being supplied by government to its citizens.

4 Alleviates poverty
As more people are working less people will be dependent on social welfare, thus allowing the government to provide more social welfare benefits to those who still remain unemployed.

(3 points at 5 marks each)

(ii) Costs of economic development:

1 Harm to the environment
Economic development always entails social costs, such as pollution and damage to the landscape.

2 Migration within the country
Economic development is usually, initially, concentrated in a small number of industrialised regions of the economy. This leads to vast migration to these regions resulting in the depopulation of many rural areas and destroying a traditional way of life.

3 Quality of life may disimprove
Increase in wealth does not guarantee an improvement in the quality of life. Frequently people have to work long hours to increase their income, thus leaving them with very little leisure time. Also the migration into the developing regions cuts people off from their relatives and friends, thus losing their traditional way of life.

4 Unequal distribution of wealth

Benefits of economic development are not always evenly distributed. Economic development is often initiated by individuals and companies. These individuals and companies often increase their profits while still paying low wages. Thus the benefits of the growth are not evenly distributed amongst the general population. Sometimes the rich get richer while the poor remain poor.

(3 points at 5 marks each)

Chapter 25 Q&A

See pp 269–283

Question 1 Chapter 25

(a) The following table illustrates the comparative advantages between countries A and B in the production of food and machinery.

	Commodity Production per person per hour	
Country	Food	Machinery
Country A	16 tonnes	4 units
Country B	32 tonnes	16 units
Total output	48 tonnes	20 units

Country B is more efficient in the production of both goods, but each country could benefit by specialising in the production of one good.

(i) Which good would country A produce? Why? (7 marks)

(ii) Which good would country B produce? Why? (7 marks)

(iii) Calculate the resulting total output, if specialisation took place. (6 marks)

(b) Imports and exports are very important to the Irish economy.

(i) State and explain **two** reasons why imports are important to the Irish economy.

(ii) State and explain **two** reasons why exports are important to the Irish economy. (30 marks)

(c) If Ireland's visible exports are valued at €1,000m and our visible imports are valued at €800m:

(i) Calculate our balance of trade, stating whether it is in surplus or deficit.

(ii) Give **two** examples of invisible exports from Ireland.

(iii) Give **two** examples of invisible imports into Ireland. (25 marks)

(LC Economics, OL, 1999)

Sample Answer 1 Chapter 25

(a) (i) Country A should specialise in food (3 marks), as it is only twice as inefficient in food compared to being four times as inefficient in machinery. (4 marks)

(ii) Country B should specialise in the production of machinery (3 marks), as it is four times more efficient than country A in machinery, while it is only twice as efficient as A in food. (4 marks)

(iii) Assuming constant returns to scale, country A will double its output of food to 32 tonnes and country B will double its output of machines to 32 units. (6 marks)

(b) (i) Imports are important to Ireland because we need to import consumer goods which cannot be made in this country, e.g. cars. We also need to import raw materials, which are required by Irish industry, and which are not available in Ireland. (15 marks)

(ii) Exports are important to Ireland, as we earn foreign currency from our exports to pay for our imports, and a lot of jobs in Ireland are in firms which make goods for the export market only. Without these exports unemployment would be far greater than it is. (15 marks)

(c) (i) The balance of trade is the difference between the value of visible imports and exports. Here this is €200m. (3 marks)

This is a surplus because the value of the exports > the value of the imports. (2 marks)

(ii) Incoming tourism and earnings returned by Irish pop groups from concerts abroad are examples of invisible exports. (5 marks each)

(iii) An Irish firm employing the services of a foreign-based architectural firm and Irish residents going on their holidays abroad are examples of invisible imports. (5 marks each)

Question 2 Chapter 25

(a) The table below illustrates the Law of Comparative Advantage.

Commodity Production per person per hour		
Country	Food	Machinery
Country A	8 tonnes	2 units
Country B	16 tonnes	8 units
Total output	24 tonnes	10 units

(i) State the Law of Comparative Advantage.

(ii) Using the above example, explain why international trade should take place between the above countries.

(iii) Calculate the limits within which the terms of trade would lie for both food and machinery. (25 marks)

(b) (i) Define 'terms of trade' and 'balance of trade'.

(ii) Discuss the effects which an improvement in a country's terms of trade would have on a country's balance of trade. (25 marks)

(c) State and explain **five** possible advantages to the Irish Economy of Ireland's agreement to introduce the euro. (25 marks)

(LC Economics, HL, 2000)

Sample Answer 2 Chapter 25

(a) (i) This law states that, assuming there is free trade, a country should specialise in the production of those goods and services in which it is relatively most efficient (8 marks), and obtain its other requirements through trade. (3 marks)

(ii) Country B has a relative advantage in the production of machinery, i.e. it is twice as efficient in the production of food but four times more efficient in the production of machinery than A. Therefore, according to the Law of Comparative Advantage it should specialise in the production of machinery and obtain its food requirements from country A, which should specialise in the production of food. (6 marks)

(iii) Before any specialisation takes place in country A, 1 tonne of food has the same value as quarter of a machine.

Before any specialisation takes place in country B, 1 tonne of food has the same value as half of a machine. Thus the terms of trade for food would lie between quarter of a machine and half of a machine for 1 tonne of food.

(4 marks)

Before any specialisation takes place in country A, one machine has the same value as 4 tonnes of food.

Before any specialisation takes place in country B, one machine has the same value as 2 tonnes of food. Thus the terms of trade for machinery would lie between 2 tonnes of food and 4 tonnes of food for one machine.

(4 marks)

(b) (i) The terms of trade refer to the relationship between the average price received for 1 unit of exports and the average price paid for 1 unit of imports. It reflects the number of units of imports which can be purchased with a unit of exports.

The balance of trade is the difference between the value of visible exports and visible imports. (10 marks for each definition)

(ii) If a country's terms of trade improve then it is easier for that country to balance its balance of trade, as it would take fewer units of exports to pay for a given number of units of imports.

Or

If a country's terms of trade improved because the price which it receives for a unit of exports has increased, then this could result in fewer exports and less revenue causing a disimprovement in the balance of trade. (This would depend on the price elasticity of demand for the exports.)

Or

If a country's terms of trade improved because the price which it pays for a unit of imports has decreased then this could result in more imports causing a disimprovement in the balance of trade. (This would depend on the price elasticity of demand for the imports.)

(Any one of the above points 5 marks)

(c) (i) Elimination of banking transactions costs when exchanging currencies within the Eurozone. This is especially important to a very open economy. The abolition of these costs would greatly reduce the financial costs involved in international trade for Ireland, as the economy is heavily dependent on importing and exporting.

(ii) Elimination of exchange rate risks in credit trade within the Eurozone. Most international trade is done on credit. It is possible that any profit made on imported goods could be lost in the fall in the value of Ireland's currency when payment for the imports becomes due.

(iii) Elimination of exchange rate risks on borrowings within the Eurozone. This is similar to (ii) but also makes the management of the foreign element of Ireland's national debt easier to plan.

(iv) Should lead to low and fairly uniform rates of interest within the Eurozone. This should happen because to qualify for membership of the Eurozone a country's rate of inflation must be within 2 per cent of the average of the three lowest rates of inflation amongst all members. This is of particular benefit to Irish industrialists.

(v) Greater transparency in pricing in the Eurozone, thus price comparisons in different countries will be made easier. This should lead to greater price competition on the domestic market. The cost of consumer goods should become more competitive in the Eurozone resulting in lower prices to consumers in Ireland.

(Any 5 points at 5 marks each; 2 marks for stating the point and 3 for explaining the point)

Chapter 26 Q&A See pp 284–288

Question 1 Chapter 26

(a) Marginal revenue product (MRP) equals marginal physical product (MPP) multiplied by marginal revenue (MR).

(i) Explain the underlined terms.

(ii) Outline the factors which influence MPP and MRP. (25 marks)

(LC Economics, HL, 2005)

Sample Answer 1 Chapter 26

(a) (i) The marginal revenue product (MRP) of a factor of production is the addition to total revenue (income) caused by employing an extra unit of a factor of production. (2 marks)

The marginal physical product (MPP) of a factor of production is the addition to total production caused by employing an extra unit of a factor of production. (3 marks)

(ii) The factors which influence MPP are:

1 The quality or specialised nature of the factors: If the quality of the factors of production used improves, then they become more efficient and additional output will be produced.

2 The training or education provided for the factors: If the factors of production are trained they become more skilled resulting in increased efficiency and more output.

3 Expertise of the entrepreneur: If the entrepreneur is expert in organising the production unit, then each factor of production will be more productive and work to their maximum efficiency.

4. Law of Diminishing Marginal Returns: As each additional unit of a factor of production is used a point will be reached where the additional output per factor produced will decline.

(Any 2 points fully explained at 5 marks each)

The factors which influence MRP are:

1. The productivity of the factor: Employees may undertake a training course which makes them more efficient. This will result in a greater quantity being produced by each extra unit of labour. When the extra output is sold it will increase the addition to total revenue, i.e. MRP.
2. Increase in the market price of the product: If the market price of the product increases as the extra unit of the factor of production is employed this will automatically increase the addition to revenue, i.e. MRP.
3. The Law of Demand: This law states that a firm can increase its sales (demand) only by decreasing its price. Thus the extra output created by the employment of the extra factor of production must be sold at a lower price causing the addition to total revenue (MRP) to decrease.

(Any 2 points at 5 marks each)

Chapter 27 Q&A See pp 289–295

Question 1 Chapter 27

(a) (i) Define **land** as a factor of production.

(ii) Outline **two** economic characteristics of land.

(iii) Explain the concept of economic rent and illustrate with a relevant example. (30 marks)

(b) The price of residential property has increased in Ireland in recent years. Discuss **four** reasons for this development. (20 marks)

(LC Economics, HL, 2005)

Sample Answer 1 Chapter 27

(a) (i) Land is anything provided by nature which helps to produce wealth.

(6 marks)

(ii) Firstly, land is fixed in supply. This means that mankind cannot increase or decrease its supply. We may be able to change the nature of land but we cannot change its quantity. Secondly, land has no cost of production. Land is a gift of nature, therefore it has not cost mankind anything to bring it into existence. (12 marks)

(iii) Economic rent is any payment for a factor of production above its supply price. An individual may be willing to sell a piece of land for €10,000. This is the supply price. However, due to competition between buyers the seller may receive €25,000. He/she has thus earned an economic rent of €15,000.

(12 marks)

(b) The price of any commodity which is for sale on an open market is determined by the relationship between the supply of and the demand for that commodity. Therefore, residential property would be one of these commodities.

(i) The amount of land zoned for residential property purposes is insufficient to meet the present demand. Thus the scarcity of land has driven up its price, which is then passed on to the buyer of residential properties in the form of increased price of housing.

(ii) The increase in the size of Ireland's population has increased the percentage of the population in the age group which normally constitutes the market for first-time buyers. This has increased the demand for residential property thus driving up its price.

(iii) There has been an increase in incomes in real terms in Ireland in recent years. This, combined with low interest rates, has led to an increase in the demand for second homes or holiday homes. This further increased the overall demand, thus driving up prices.

(iv) Many speculators have been buying up vast tracts of land in the belief that land inflation represents a big return on the money invested. They retain these stocks or banks of land, thus reducing the supply of land available for housing, thereby increasing the price of the remaining land, which is then reflected in the increased price of residential property.

(4 points at 5 marks each)

Chapter 28 Q&A See pp 296–310

Question 1 Chapter 28

(a) State and explain two reasons why different wage rates are paid for different jobs. (20 marks)

(b) Choose any two of the following. State and explain how they influence the supply of labour in an economy:

(i) The level of wages on offer in the economy.

(ii) The normal length of the working week.

(iii) The level of welfare benefits payable to the unemployed.

(iv) The percentage of people in the economy availing of third level education. (20 marks)

(c) Ireland is beginning to experience shortages of labour in certain sectors. In relation to this statement, answer two of the following:

(i) State and explain one reason why such shortages are beginning to occur.

(ii) What is the likely impact of this development on wage levels? Explain your answer.

(iii) State and explain one course of action open to the government to reverse this trend. (19 marks)

(d) How does capital investment in a firm affect labour? (15 marks)

(LC Economics, OL, 2000)

Sample Answer 1 Chapter 28

(a) (i) The length of time spent training for the job and the cost of that training. Some jobs require a high level of education and training. There can be a high opportunity cost obtaining an education or qualification. In order to encourage a supply of these types of labour, high wages may have to be offered to people to encourage them to undertake the study required.

(ii) Monetary benefits other than pay, e.g. non-contributory pension and low interest rate on loans given to employees may result in people accepting a lower gross wage, as their real income is increased by these benefits.

(2 points stated only at 4 marks each +
2 points explained at 6 marks each)

(b) (i) As the level of wages rises, it will cause an increase in the supply of labour as it will attract more people into the economy (immigration) and it will entice some people off the dole.

(ii) The supply of labour is the number of people working multiplied by the number of hours they work. Thus if the normal length of the working week increased this would cause an increase in the supply of labour and vice versa.

(iii) As the level of welfare benefits increase the gap between wages and these benefits decreases. Thus the opportunity cost of not working decreases. This could discourage some people from working, resulting in a decrease in the supply of labour.

(iv) The supply of labour is the number of people working plus the number available for work at any given wage rate. If the percentage of people in the economy availing of third level education increases then the number of people available for work at a given time would decrease. This results in a decrease in the supply of labour, as these people will not be available for work.

(Any 2 points fully explained at 10 marks each)

(c) (i) Production levels are increasing in Ireland in recent years. Many of the firms involved in production require specialised and qualified labour. The supply of the labour needed has not kept pace with the growth in production, resulting in labour shortage.

(ii) The likely impact of this development on wage levels is an increase in the wage rate. The wage rate is the price of labour when D > S price increases. When the D for labour is greater than the supply of it, the wage rate should increase.

(iii) The government could grant more work permits to non-Irish workers to bring the supply up equal to the demand, or it could invest more money in third level education to encourage more people to undertake the education and training required for the available jobs. Thus eventually bringing the supply up equal to the demand.

(3 points fully explained at 6 + 7 + 7 marks)

(d) This question can be answered from two different points of view.
Capital can be considered as a substitute for labour. As firms invest in more capital goods this could result in a reduction in the demand for labour.

Or

Production levels will increase as more capital is used. As production levels increase more labour will be needed in the production and distribution of these goods. This could result in an increase in the demand for labour.

(Either point clearly explained 15 marks)

Question 2 Chapter 28

(a) (i) Name the **two** main sources from which the figures relating to unemployment in the Irish economy are taken.

(ii) State, with reasons, which of these gives the most accurate measurement of Irish unemployment. (20 marks)

(b) (i) Define full employment.

(ii) Outline the major economic consequences of very high employment in the Irish economy at the moment. (30 marks)

(LC Economics, HL, 2002)

Sample Answer 2 Chapter 28

(a) (i) The Live Register and the National Quarterly Household Survey.

(3 marks each)

A person is deemed to be unemployed only if he/she is not working but is actively seeking employment at the current wage rate.

The Live Register is a list (register) of all those people who sign a register each week in order to claim some social welfare benefit.

The Quarterly National Household Survey (QNHS) is a survey which sets out to establish the number of people who are not working but who are actively seeking work at the current wage rate.

(ii) The QNHS is the more accurate measure of Irish unemployment as it counts only people who are seeking employment. (2 marks)

The weaknesses of the Live Register, as a measure of unemployment, are as follows:

1. Some people who sign on the Live Register do so only to get the dole and are not actively seeking work. Therefore, they are not unemployed.
2. Some people may be signing on the Live Register and working in the black economy, thus by definition they are not unemployed.
3. Part-time workers may sign on for the days they are not working. Therefore, they are not unemployed.
4. Some people sign on only for credits towards their old age pension. Again these are not unemployed as they are not seeking employment.
5. Some people do not sign on even though they are actively seeking work because they are not entitled to any benefits. These people are unemployed but are not counted as such. This point allows the Live Register to understate the level of unemployment.

(Any 4 points at 3 marks each)

(b) (i) Full employment means that all those people who are available for work, at the current wage rate, are employed. (10 marks)

(ii)
1. High levels of employment have a double positive effect on the government's finances, i.e. it takes in a higher level of income taxes and it has to pay out a smaller level of social welfare benefits.
2. The general level of spending in the economy is increasing due to the higher level of income from the extra employment. This further increases government revenue from indirect taxes.
3. The extra revenue accruing to the government allows it to increase its expenditure on general services to the economy such as health, education and improved social welfare benefits.
4. When employment increases the average income per head of the population automatically increases. This will improve the general standard of living, as people have more income, causing an increase in the general level of demand.
5. The high level of employment in the economy has created a scarcity of labour in the Irish market. This could have an inflationary effect on the economy, as the scarcity of labour could drive up the wage rate causing cost-push inflation.
6. The adverse effect of point 5 above is that if supply does not grow at the same rate as demand then this could cause demand-pull inflation. This has been seen in the housing market.
7. There is increased pressure on the country's infrastructure. As incomes increase, due to the extra employment, there will be greater pressure put on the usage of roads, telecommunications, waste disposal systems and other forms of infrastructure. This may require increased investment by the government or some private agencies to meet these needs.
8. There may be a deterioration or loss of some services. Sectors of the economy which traditionally paid low wages may find it difficult to attract workers, and the quality of service in these sectors may deteriorate or the services may be discontinued altogether.

(Any 4 points fully developed at 5 marks each)

Chapter 29 Q&A See pp 311–322

Question 1 Chapter 29

(a) (i) Define savings.

(ii) Explain **two** factors which influence the level of savings in an economy.

(iii) State **two** economic effects of increases in the level of savings. (30 marks)

(b) State and explain the advantages of a decrease in interest rates to each of the following:

(i) Borrowers

(ii) Government

(iii) Employers (25 marks)

(LC Economics, OL, 2002)

Sample Answer 1 Chapter 29

(a) (i) Savings mean not spending part of your income. (6 marks)

(ii) The level of income: (3 marks)

People on low levels of income may have to spend all of their income to meet the cost of their normal daily needs and wants. Therefore they cannot save. Conversely people on high levels of income may have more money than they need to meet the cost of their normal daily needs and wants. Therefore these people may save. Thus the higher the level of income the greater the potential is for saving. (3 marks)

The rate of interest: (3 marks)

The opportunity cost of spending money increases as the rate of interest offered on savings increases. Provided incomes are big enough, people will therefore be enticed to save more money as the rates of interest increase. (3 marks)

(iii) Decrease in the level of demand: (3 marks)

As people increase their level of saving they will be spending less money. This will result in a fall in the general level of demand. This could result in the loss of jobs if demand falls too much. This is often referred to as the paradox of thrift. (3 marks)

Greater level of funds available for investors: (3 marks)

Most people save by depositing money with financial institutions. These institutions then lend this money to investors. When this money is invested by entrepreneurs new jobs may be created. Thus when savings increase there is an increase in the funds available to investors. (3 marks)

(b) (i) As interest rates decrease borrowers have to repay less on interest repayments, thus reducing the cost of the loan.

(ii) A decrease in interest rates reduces the cost of servicing the national debt for the government. This in turn could lead to a decrease in the general level of taxation, or the government spending the money on providing more or better services to the general public.

(iii) A reduction in interest rates will reduce the cost of production for employers, as interest repayments are a cost of production. When cost of production decreases profits increase.

(2 points fully explained at 8 marks each + 1 point at 9 marks)

Question 2 Chapter 29

(a) The marginal efficiency of capital is the additional profit earned by an entrepreneur from employing an additional unit of capital.

State and explain why the marginal efficiency of capital may fall. (20 marks)

(b) Explain Keynes's **three** reasons for holding money. Outline **two** main influences on each of these reasons. (30 marks)

(c) Discuss the effects which a rise in interest rates may have on the Irish economy. (25 marks)

(LC Economics, HL, 2000)

Note: When asked a general question, such as (c) above, on the effects of a change in interest rates on the economy always deal with the effect on (i) the consumer/household, (ii) industry, (iii) the government and (iv) the value of the euro.

Sample Answer 2 Chapter 29

(a) The marginal efficiency of capital is calculated by subtracting the MC of capital from the MRP of capital. Therefore, if MRP decreases or MC increases then the marginal efficiency of capital will fall. This could happen in any of the following situations.

(i) If there is an increase in the price of capital goods (MC of capital), while the MPP of capital remained unchanged and the market price of the goods remained unchanged, then the addition to profit must decrease.

(ii) If the rate of interest increased (which is a cost of production), while the MPP of capital remained unchanged and the market price of the goods also remained unchanged, then the addition to profit from the new capital would decrease, as interest is a cost of production.

(iii) If there were a reduction in the market price of the good, then the MRP would decrease, thus reducing the profit from any extra capital employed.

(iv) If there were a decrease in the marginal physical productivity of capital, then the extra output of the additional unit of capital would fall, and if the market price of the good remained unchanged, then the addition to profit would decrease.

(Any 2 points at 10 marks each)

(b) (i) **The transactions motive** (2 marks)
This is the amount of money held for day-to-day expenditure. This can be influenced by any of the following factors: (3 marks)

- The cost of daily transactions: As this increases then the amount of money held to purchase these goods must increase. (2 marks)
- The level of income: As income increases demand for normal goods also increases, therefore the demand for money will also increase. (3 marks)

(ii) **The precautionary motive** (2 marks)
This is the amount of money held for emergency purposes, e.g. illness or house repairs. This can be influenced by any of the following factors: (3 marks)

- People's attitude towards the future: If people are pessimistic about the future, then they may hold a lot of money for this purpose, whereas if they are optimistic then they may hold very little money for this purpose. (2 marks)
- The rate of interest: If the rate of interest increases, then the opportunity cost of holding money also increases, thus discouraging some people from holding money. (3 marks)

(iii) **The speculative motive** (2 marks)
This is the amount of money held, to have available for any profitable investment purpose which may arise in the future. (3 marks)

This can be influenced by any of the following factors:

- The rate of interest: If the rate of interest increases, then the opportunity cost of holding money also increases, thus discouraging people from holding money. (2 marks)
- The market price of shares/bonds: If these increase, then the opportunity cost of holding money also increases, thus discouraging people from holding money. (3 marks)

(c) **Effects on consumers/households**

1. As interest rates increase the cost of repaying loans increases, thus discouraging people from borrowing for consumption purposes, resulting in a decrease in the standard of living.

2. Likewise, mortgage repayments become more expensive, leaving people with less discretionary income, resulting in a lower standard of living.

3. When interest rates increase savings may be encouraged. This could lead to a lower standard of living and a decrease in the general level of demand.

Effects on industry

4. As interest rates increase the marginal efficiency of capital decreases, which could result in a decrease in the level of investment in the economy.

5. If investment is discouraged, then economic growth will decline, resulting in a possible decrease in the level of employment in the economy.

Effects on costs of production

6. Costs of production will increase as overdraft rates and loan rates increase. This will result in possible higher prices and/or a reduction in the numbers employed.

Effects on government

7. Servicing of the national debt will increase, resulting in a higher level of government expenditure. This could result in a higher level of taxation.

8. As consumer expenditure decreases, then the return to government on VAT and other consumer taxes will also decrease. This could result in an increase in the level of direct taxation to compensate for lost revenue.

Revenue received from DIRT

9. With additional savings, the government may receive additional revenue through DIRT.

Effect on value of the euro

10. Rising interest rates may attract mobile money (sometimes called 'hot money') into Ireland, thereby creating a demand for the euro and increasing its value.

(Any 5 points at 5 marks each)

Chapter 30 Q&A See pp 323–330

Question 1 Chapter 30

(a) An entrepreneur requires factors of production to produce commodities. One of these factors of production is 'enterprise'.

(i) Name the other **three** factors of production.

(ii) Explain what is meant by 'enterprise'. (20 marks)

(b) The factor of production enterprise is different from the other factors of production.

State and explain **two** reasons why this is so. (20 marks)

(c) Entrepreneurs are important to the growth of an economy.

(i) State and explain any two reasons why entrepreneurs are so important to the Irish economy.

(ii) State and explain two ways by which the Irish government could encourage more individuals to become entrepreneurs. (35 marks)

(LC Economics, OL, 1998)

Sample Answer 1 Chapter 30

(a) (i) The other factors of production are land, labour and capital.
(3 + 3 + 4 marks)

(ii) Enterprise is that special form of human activity which organises the other factors of production and undertakes the risk involved in production.
(10 marks)

(b) Enterprise is different from the other factors as (i) it is the only factor of production which can lose money, i.e. can have a negative return, and (ii) the return to enterprise fluctuates from week to week or month to month; whereas the other factors have a fixed return, e.g. labour receives an agreed wage each week. (2 fully developed points at 10 marks each)

(c) (i) The reasons why entrepreneurs are important in Ireland:

1. They organise the other factors of production into productive units. Without entrepreneurs very little production would take place in Ireland. Land and capital, as individual factors of production, are inanimate objects and can do nothing on their own. Labour is not very productive without the aid of capital. Thus somebody is required to organise land, labour and capital into a production unit. This is done by the entrepreneur.

2 Entrepreneurs decide what goods will be produced, and in what quantities they will be produced, at any given time. They set up business based on their decision to make products which they hope will make a profit for them. From their market research they decide what products to produce and in what quantity to produce them. Thus at any time whether they are successful or not, it is the entrepreneurs who decide what is produced.

(4 marks for each statement + 5 marks for explanations)

(ii) Ways in which the Irish government could encourage entrepreneurs:

1 Grants to firms/taking equity in firms.
When a government gives a grant to a firm this reduces the amount of money which the entrepreneur must invest in the business, thus increasing the return on the capital which it actually invests. This obviously makes it more attractive to entrepreneurs to invest in the economy. In a similar manner, the firm would have to provide less capital if the government took shares in the business, thus reducing the amount of money which the entrepreneur must raise. This would encourage more entrepreneurs to set up in Ireland.

2 Reduce capital gains tax.
Some entrepreneurs set up businesses in order to make a profit on the sale of the business itself after a relatively short period of time. If capital gains taxes (i.e. the tax on the profit earned from the sale of assets) are high these people may be reluctant to invest. By lowering these taxes more entrepreneurs will be encouraged to invest.

(4 marks for each statement + 1 explanation at 4 marks + 1 explanation at 5 marks)

Question 2 Chapter 30

(a) Define the entrepreneur as a factor of production. (10 marks)

(b) Give two reasons why the factor of production, enterprise, is unique. (10 marks)

(c) What are the non-insurable risks that an entrepreneur faces in business? (20 marks)

(d) Consider the importance of:

(i) Entrepreneurs

(ii) Profits

in a free market economic system. (35 marks)

(LC Economics, HL, 1998)

Sample Answer 2 Chapter 30

(a) The entrepreneur is the individual who organises the other factors of production and who bears the risk involved in production. (10 marks)

(b) (i) The return to enterprise is a residual, i.e. the payment received by the entrepreneur is that which is left over after the other factors of production have been paid. Thus it is not affected by the normal forces of supply and demand. The return to each of the other factors is determined by the forces of supply and demand.

(ii) Enterprise is the only factor that can have a negative return, i.e. it can lose money. The other factors of production could, at the worst, suffer only a nil (zero) return.

(iii) Profit fluctuates more than the return to any of the other factors. Because profit is a residual this can vary greatly from period to period, whereas the return to the other factors is usually a fixed agreed amount.

(Any 2 points explained at 5 marks each)

(c) (i) Production takes place in anticipation of consumption, i.e. in most cases the producer makes goods in the hope that people will purchase them. If the goods are not purchased the producer loses the money that is invested in the production.

(ii) Loss of profits due to sudden increases in the cost of production: Sometimes a producer makes goods on a contract basis. If the cost of production increases after he/she has signed the contract then he/she may suffer a loss on the deal.

(iii) Changes in consumers' tastes and fashions: Fashions can change overnight. If a producer had made a large quantity of a particular product and if fashions (tastes) suddenly changed then he/she would not be able to sell these goods and he/she would have to bear the loss.

(iv) Strikes: If employees go on strike then the manufacturer cannot make any goods. However, he/she will still have to pay the fixed costs thus creating a loss. There is also the added danger that he/she might lose some of his/her customers to other producers.

(v) The entry of new rival firms into the industry: This would have the effect of increasing total supply in the industry, thus bringing down the price of the product. If the firm were earning only normal profit at the previous price then he/she may suffer a loss on the production. The producer may also lose some customers to the new firm.

(vi) Adverse effects of new legislation: From time to time the government brings in new legislation governing terms and conditions of work, e.g. new health and safety regulations, minimum wage rates. These may be costly for the firm to implement and may result in the closure of some marginal firms.

(vii) Adverse effects of international trade agreements: Sometimes governments enter into international trade agreements that are beneficial to the economy in general. However, these agreements do not always suit particular small firms or industries in the domestic market. These agreements may give access to our domestic market to foreign firms. The foreign firms may produce products cheaper than the domestic firms, thus putting them out of business.

(Any 5 points explained at 4 marks each)

(d) (i) The importance of entrepreneurs in a free enterprise economy:

1. They organise the other factors of production into productive units. Without enterprise, the other factors would remain idle and there would be no employment.
2. They decide what goods will be produced, and in what quantities they will be produced, at any given time. This is based on their market research and they take the risk of producing these goods.
3. They set the initial prices at which goods will be sold in the hope of making a profit. This is based on cost price plus a percentage mark-up. The market mechanism determines the long run price.
4. They invest money into the economy. This increases the productive capacity of the country and also has a multiplier effect on incomes.
5. They provide an investment outlet for savers. Many individuals do not consume some of their income and are prepared to risk their spare money in somebody else's business in the hope of getting a better return on it than they would receive from a bank.

(ii) The importance of profits in a free enterprise economy:

1. They encourage risk taking. The possibility of profits encourages people to risk their money in the production of goods which otherwise would not be produced.
2. They encourage the efficient use of resources. If costs are kept down then profits could increase.
3. They encourage investment. This increases the productive capacity of the economy and creates employment.
4. They provide funds for expansion. Most firms retain some of their profits to finance the expansion of the firm.
5. Normal profit, by definition, ensures the continuity of production of goods and services.

(Any 5 points at 7 marks each, i.e. 3 marks for mentioning the point + 4 marks for developing the point. There must be at least 2 points from each list.)

Note: The same answers apply to the questions on enterprise for 1996 and 1994.

Chapter 31 Q&A See pp 331–347

Question 1 Chapter 31

(a) Discuss the economic effects which the recent rise in Ireland's population may have on the Irish economy. (25 marks)

(b) Outline the effects which a rise in the level of unemployment in Ireland may have on:

(i) Government current finances

(ii) The balance of payments (current account)

(iii) Price inflation (20 marks)

(c) Immigration replaced high levels of emigration during the Celtic Tiger period.

(i) Discuss **three** reasons why the trend has changed from emigration to immigration.

(ii) Discuss the economic consequences (positive and negative) for a country experiencing increased immigration. (30 marks)

(LC Economics, HL, 2003)

Sample Answer 1 Chapter 31

(a) (i) **Increased pressure on demand for state services**
As the population increases this automatically creates a greater demand for state services such as housing, medical care and educational services. If the increase in population had not been foreseen by the government it may result in a shortage of supply in these services.

(ii) **Increased pressure on the country's infrastructure**
As the population increases our infrastructure will have to be improved to cater for the extra traffic, waste disposal services, recreational services and communications services which will be required. This will entail extra capital investment by the government.

(iii) **A larger domestic market**
A rising population will automatically create a greater demand for a wide range of goods and services on the domestic market. This will automatically create more investment opportunities and create more employment in the economy. If there is a significant increase in the size of the population it may even lead to some businesses benefiting from the economies of scale.

(iv) **Better utilisation of existing state services**
If the increase in population were centred or located in underpopulated areas of the country then services available in those areas may be more fully utilised (i.e. transport services, schools), thus reducing the cost per person of these services.

(v) **Decreased dependency ratio**
The increase in population may be due to an increase in immigrants who are coming into the country for the sole purpose of taking up employment in sectors of the economy which are experiencing a shortage of labour. In this case, the increased numbers in the labour force would lower the dependency ratio and lead to increased tax revenues for the government.

(vi) **Land/Property values**
As the population density increases, available land and property becomes scarce, thus creating further upward pressure on the price of land and property in this country.

(Any 5 points at 5 marks each)

(b) (i) Effect on government current finances: An increase in unemployment would have an adverse effect on government current finances as revenue from income taxes would decrease and the government would have to increase its expenditure on social welfare payments. (7 marks)

(ii) Effect on the balance of payments, current account: An increase in unemployment would lead to a decrease in the level of national income. The level of imports is directly related to national income, therefore imports should decrease, thus improving the balance on the current account.

(7 marks)

(iii) Effect on price inflation: Income is one of the factors influencing demand in the economy. As unemployment increases, incomes decrease, thus leading to a decrease in demand. This should reduce the level of demand-pull inflation in the economy. (6 marks)

(c) (i) Reasons for emigration to immigration

1. Push-forces, i.e. the lack of employment opportunities, were traditionally the major cause of emigration from Ireland. These forces no longer persist in our economy and so emigration has declined.

2. The boom in the Irish economy since the mid 1990s has resulted in an increased demand for labour. This demand could not be met within our native population, which led to an organised campaign to recruit employees from outside the country, thus leading to immigration.

3. The expansion of the EU gave official access to employment in Ireland to the residents of many other countries who, at the time, were experiencing unemployment or were being paid much lower wages in their own countries.

4. The EU is a relatively wealthy sector of the world's economy. The residents of many non-EU countries want to improve their employment opportunities and are thus attracted to EU countries. Ireland, as a member of the EU, has attracted many of these people.

5 Some of the multinational companies locating here bring in their own personnel to do specific work. When foreign companies locate in Ireland they often want to continue with a business structure and policy which has been successful for them in their own countries. These companies bring in their own personnel to ensure the successful implementation of these structures.

(Any 3 points at 5 + 5 + 4 marks each)

(ii) Positive and negative consequences for a country experiencing increased immigration.

Positive consequences

1 Reduces labour shortages: Immigrants may fill those vacancies which exist in the labour market which allow businesses to expand and also helps to ease any upward pressure on wage rates.

2 Increased demand for goods and services: The level of demand for goods and services will increase in the country, thus creating more investment opportunities and creating more employment.

3 If immigrants are mainly in employment in the country, then they will increase government revenue through their income taxes and the indirect taxes gained from their spending on goods and services.

Negative consequences

4 If the immigrants are not in employment, then the government will have to pay out extra money on all forms of social welfare payments. This will cause a drain on government finances.

5 With an increasing number of immigrants there is pressure on the government to make extra services such as educational and health services available to immigrants.

6 The economy may suffer extra social costs arising from racism, and extra problems arising from exploitation of the immigrant population.

(4 points at 4 marks each. There must be 2 positive points and 2 negative points mentioned.)

Glossary

This is not an exhaustive list of all terms used in economics at Leaving Certificate level. However, it does cover the most common words and phrases used at this level.

accelerator principle States that as demand continues to grow it will eventually cause a more than proportionate increase in investment.

accommodating transactions Transactions on the capital section of the balance of payments that make it balance in the accounting sense. It usually means changes in the value of the external reserves.

ad valorem tax An indirect tax that takes a certain percentage of the price of the good, e.g. VAT.

aggregate demand Total demand in an economy that is made up of consumption plus investment plus government current expenditure plus exports minus imports.
Or

aggregate demand $Y = C + I + G + X - M$

arbitrage Buying a commodity (usually a currency) in one market and selling it immediately in another market to exploit variations in prices in the two markets.

asset Anything owned by, or owed to, an individual or firm.

autonomous consumption The level of consumption that is not dependent on income. Even if a person has no income he/she must still buy food, etc. and may have to use up his/her savings to do so, or the person may have to borrow to do so.

average cost (AC) Total cost divided by quantity produced.

average fixed cost (AFC) Fixed cost divided by quantity produced.

average propensity to consume (APC) The percentage of total income spent on consumer goods.

average revenue (AR) Total revenue divided by quantity sold.

average variable cost (AVC) Variable cost divided by quantity produced.

balance of autonomous transactions (on the balance of payments) The balance on the current account plus inflows of long-term capital.

balance of payments A record of a country's international economic transactions over a year. It is divided into (a) the balance of trade, (b) the balance on the current account and (c) the balance on the capital account.

balance of trade The difference between the value of visible exports and visible imports.

balance on the capital account A balance that shows the inflow and outflow of capital funds during the year.

balance on the current account The difference between the value of total exports and total imports + or – net factor income with the rest of the world + or – net current transfers.

barter The exchange of one good for another good without the use of money.

benefit/cost analysis A comparison between the total costs and the total benefits of capital projects. The demand for projects combined with a limited budget means that the government must undertake such an analysis to get the optimum use of its budget.

benefit in kind (income) Any non-money income earned, e.g. car supplied to an employee, non-contributory pension and reduced interest rate on loans.

benefit in kind (social services) Goods or services that the state provides directly to the recipient, e.g. butter or fuel vouchers. It is a form of income in kind.

bi-lateral trade When a country carries on most of its trade with only one other country.

birth rate The number of live births per 1,000 of the population per annum.

black economy The unregistered productive sector of the economy. It does not pay taxes and its production is not included in the national income accounts.

black hole in the economy The non-documented inflow or outflow of funds from the economy. Officially it is called 'the net residual' or 'errors and omissions'. It is the difference between the actual change in the value of external reserves and the change in the value of these that should have happened according to the official balance of payments figures.

break-even point A point on the consumption function curve where the value of consumption is equal to the value of disposable income.

broad money supply The total cash outstanding plus balances in current accounts in licensed banks and all other balances in licensed banks, plus borrowings from other credit institutions, less interbank balances (*see also* **money supply**).

budget The planned income and expenditure of an organisation or country.

built in (automatic) stabilisers Changes in government expenditure and tax revenue which occur without any change in government policy as national income changes. As national income increases tax revenue automatically increases. This has the effect of dampening inflation in the economy and also providing the government with the extra funds needed to finance its current expenditure.

business (trade) cycle Refers to the periods of growth and recession experienced by economies. The classical stages are: the trough, followed by the recovery, followed by the boom, followed by the peak, followed by the recession, followed by the depression, followed by the trough, etc.

Canons of Taxation Guidelines set down by Adam Smith for the operation of a tax system: equity, convenience, certainty and economy of taxation.

capital Anything man-made that is used to create wealth, e.g. delivery vans, factories, machines and computers used in businesses.

capital acquisition tax A tax levied on gifts and inheritances, over certain values, received by individuals.

capital expenditure Spending on capital goods.

capital formation *see* **capital expenditure**

capital gains tax A tax levied on the profit earned from the sale of an asset.

capital taxes Taxes levied on the stock of wealth owned by an individual or organisation. The two main ones are: (a) capital gains tax, a tax on the profits from the sale of assets, (b) capital acquisition tax, a tax on gifts received or on inheritances.

cartel An agreement between firms in the same industry to implement common strategies, thus allowing them to act as a monopoly.

cash ratio The ratio of cash that the banks must hold to claims on the banks.

centrally planned economies or **command economies** Economies where all economic decisions are taken by the central authorities, e.g. by the government.

commercial banks *see* **retail banks**

common market An agreement between countries to (a) abolish all duties on goods moving between them, known as a free trade area, (b) impose common external tariffs and (c) to allow free movement of the factors of production between the countries.

complementary goods Two or more different goods that must be purchased together to satisfy any one need or want, e.g. cups and saucers.

conspicuous consumption A situation where some people purchase goods simply to display their wealth because the goods bought are expensive. This only happens over a given price range.

constant tax price index (CTPI) The CPI (see below) when the level of indirect tax is kept constant, i.e. any increases in indirect taxes are not included in the price of goods after the base year.

consumer price index (CPI) An index compiled by the CSO to measure changes in the general level of prices since a base year.

consumer surplus The difference between the market price of a good and the higher price the consumer would pay rather than do without the good.

consumption function curve A graph that shows the different amounts spent at different income levels.

cost/effectiveness analysis This is done when there are alternative methods of achieving an aim in order to ascertain which method gives the best return on money invested.

cost of production Any payment that must be made to ensure that production of a good or service continues.

cost push inflation Describes a general increase in the price levels in a country caused by an increase in the cost of production.

cross elasticity of demand Measures the relationship between the change in price of one good and the resulting change in demand for another good. Its formula is:

$$\frac{P(A)1 + P(A)2}{Q(B)1 + Q(B)2} \times \frac{\Delta Q(B)}{\Delta P(A)}$$

current budget A statement of the government's planned current income and current expenditure for the coming year. It can be a balanced budget, a deficit budget or a surplus budget.

current budget deficit Occurs when planned current expenditure is greater than planned current income.

current budget surplus Occurs when planned current income is greater than planned current expenditure.

current expenditure The day-to-day expenditure involved in running a business, government or household. The expenditure is usually repeated at least once a year.

customs duties Taxes levied on imports.

deadweight debt Borrowed money which when spent adds nothing to the revenue of the government, i.e. it is not self-financing.

death rate The number of deaths per 1,000 of the population per annum.

deflation A decrease in the general level of prices. It happens when the general level of demand < the general level of supply.

demand (D) The number of units of a product that consumers are willing to buy at any given market price at any given time.

demand curve A graph showing the demand for a product.

demand deposit account A bank account where no notice of withdrawal has to be given.

demand pull inflation Occurs when the general level of demand in an economy is greater than the general level of supply, resulting in an increase in the general level of prices.

demand schedule A table showing the demand for a product at any given market price at any given time.

demography The study of human populations, including their size, growth, density and distribution, as well as statistics regarding birth, marriage, disease and death.

depreciation The loss in value of capital goods.

derived demand This exists when a product is not purchased for its own direct utility, but for the additional utility that it adds to another product, e.g. the demand for bricks is derived from the demand for houses.

devaluation Occurs when a country reduces the exchange rate of its currency against the currencies on the international market.

 direct taxes Taxes levied on income, e.g. PAYE and DIRT.

discretionary income The part of disposable income that a person has left after paying all essential bills. The person is then free to spend this income on anything he/she chooses.

diseconomies of scale Forces that increase the average cost of a firm as the firm gets bigger. These can be internal or external.

disguised unemployment Many people who are available for work do not register on the Live Register as they are not entitled to any social welfare benefits, but they are unemployed. Underemployed people are also included in this category of unemployment.

disposable income The amount of a person's income available for spending. It is usually the person's income after statutory deductions.

dissaving When consumers either go into debt or use up some of their past savings for consumption purposes.

dumping Occurs when goods are sold on a foreign market at a price lower than that on the domestic market in order to sell off excess production without lowering the price on the domestic market.

earnings drift *see* **wages drift**

economic development The process of increasing average income per head in an economy while changing the structure of the economy. It usually entails moving from a mainly agricultural and rural economy to an industrial and urban economy.

economic dualism Occurs in less developed countries when the majority of the population earns a subsistence level of income (or even less), but at the same time there is one sector of the economy that is flourishing and is of great benefit to only a small number of people.

economic goods Any goods or services that people are willing to pay for, i.e. they can command a price.

economic growth The process of increasing average income per head of the population without changing the structure of the economy.

economic planning A process of the government consulting with the social partners in order to set targets for the immediate future on a range of economic issues, e.g. the National Development Plan and Towards 2016.

economics An inexact social science that studies human behaviour in relation to aims and scarce means that have alternative uses.

effective incidence of a tax *see* **incidence of a tax**

embargo A ban on exports to, or imports from, a specified country. It can also be a ban on the exporting or importing of a particular product.

enterprise A special form of human activity that organises the other factors of production and undertakes the risk involved in production.

enterprise economy *see* **free market**

equilibrium The situation from which there is no tendency to change. It is the ideal situation under a given set of circumstances.

exchange risk The risk undertaken by an importer who buys on credit, and a borrower who borrows from abroad. The amount they owe will increase if there is a devaluation of their currency.

exchequer balance The difference between total government expenditure (both current and capital) and total government revenue.

exchequer borrowing requirement (EBR) The amount of money the government borrows in any one year to finance its current and capital expenditure. It is the old term used to describe a deficit on the exchequer balance.

exports Any goods or services supplied by residents of a country which when sold to another country result in an inflow of money.

external diseconomies of scale Factors outside of the firm that increase its AC as the size of the industry increases.

external economies of scale Factors outside of the firm that decrease its AC as the size of the industry increases.

favourable balance of trade (surplus on the balance of trade) Occurs when the value of visible exports is greater than the value of visible imports.

favourable terms of trade The price received for a unit of exports is greater than the price paid for a unit of imports.

fiat currency *see* **token money**

fiduciary issue *see* **token money**

fiscal drag Occurs during a period of buoyancy in an economy and means that while government income (from taxation) is greater than planned its expenditure remains at the planned level.

fiscal policy The government's policy on expenditure and taxation.

fixed costs Costs that do not vary as the level of production varies in the short run.

fixed supply Occurs when a fixed quantity of goods available for sale must be sold, regardless of market price, e.g. vegetables brought to a central market on a daily basis.

free market An economy where all economic decisions are made by individual households and firms with no government intervention.

free trade area An agreement between countries to abolish tariffs on goods coming from their respective countries.

frictional unemployment This is a situation where people are unemployed on a temporary basis when one industry is declining while another is starting up.

full employment All those who are willing to work at existing wage levels are employed.

funding (as a role of the Central Bank) The Central Bank forces the commercial banks to exchange short-term government bonds for long-term government loans. It is an attempt to reduce the commercial banks' credit creating ability.

funk money Money that is continuously moved from country to country to avail of the highest interest rates at any given time.

general government balance (GGB) This is total income minus expenditure of all arms of government, i.e. central government, local authorities, Vocational Education Committees and non-commercial state sponsored bodies.

general government debt The cumulative gross debt of the local government sector, the non-commercial state sponsored bodies and most of the national debt. It excludes central government liabilities to institutions classified within the general government sector; these are included in the national debt.

Giffen good An inferior good that experiences increased demand when the price rises and decreased demand when the price falls, e.g. rice and potatoes for people on very low incomes.

Gresham's Law States that bad money drives good money out of circulation.

gross capital expenditure/formation The total value of expenditure on capital goods in an economy in a year.

gross domestic product (GDP) The total value of all goods and services produced in the country before depreciation is deducted.

gross national product (GNP) GDP + or – net factor income with the rest of the world.

high street banks *see* **retail banks**

homogeneous goods Identical goods produced by different producers. It applies to goods produced under conditions of perfect competition.

imports Any goods or services purchased by the residents of a country that cause money to leave that country.

imposition of a tax The person or company on whom a tax is levied, e.g. excise duties on petrol are levied on the petrol companies.

incidence of a tax Refers to the person on whom the burden of the tax falls, e.g. the imposition (see above) of excise duties on petrol is on the petrol companies, but they pass this on in the form of increased prices to the consumers, thus the effective incidence of the tax is on the consumers of petrol.

income Earnings at any given time, i.e. it is a flow of wealth.

income effect The effect that a change in income has on the demand for a product. It is positive for normal goods and negative for inferior goods. A positive effect means that income and demand change in the same direction, whereas a negative effect means that they change in opposite directions.

income elasticity of demand (YED) Measures the relationship between a change in income and the resulting change in demand, the formula for it is:

$$\frac{Y1 + Y2}{Q1 + Q2} \times \frac{\Delta Q}{\Delta Y}$$

income in kind Any income that is not in the form of money, e.g. use of a company car.

indicative planning Any voluntary plan entered into by the social partners to ensure maximum growth for the various sectors of the economy in a national context, e.g. Towards 2016.

indirect taxes Taxes levied on transactions, e.g. VAT and stamp duties.

infant industries New industries in a country which have not yet grown big enough to gain the benefits of the economies of scale.

inferior good A good whose positive substitution effect outweighs its negative income effect, e.g. monochrome TVs.

inflation Describes a general increase in price levels in an economy.

injections Any transactions that increase the size of the circular flow of income. The three main ones are: investments, exports and increased government expenditure.

institutional unemployment Unemployment caused by barriers to the mobility of labour, e.g. closed–shop practices, lack of schools in the areas where there are jobs available, or lack of suitable housing in these areas.

interest rate The return to capital or the income earned from deposits with a financial institution.

internal diseconomies of scale Factors within the firm which increase its AC as the size of the firm increases.

internal economies of scale Factors within the firm which decrease its AC as the size of the firm increases.

investment Expenditure on capital goods.

invisible exports Services supplied by residents of a country, which when sold to non-residents, cause money to come into the country.

invisible imports Services supplied to residents of a country by non-residents, which cause money to leave the country.

iron law of wages *see* **subsistence theory of wages**

joint demand *see* **complementary goods**

joint supply A situation where the production of one good automatically leads to the production of another good, e.g. mutton and wool, beef and hides.

kinked demand curve The demand curve associated with the Sweezy model of oligopoly. It shows demand being elastic for increasing prices and inelastic for decreasing prices.

labour Any human effort that helps to create wealth.

labour force The people who are in work and who are available for work at the current wage rate.

labour force survey Shows the number of people who are unemployed and who are actively seeking employment.

labour theory of value States that the value of an object is equal to the quantity of labour which it can command for itself. Adam Smith, who was one of the classical economists, first put forward this theory.

Laffer curve A graph devised by Arthur Laffer to show that little revenue would be gained by the government from a tax rate which is either too high or too low. There is an equilibrium rate between the two which maximises revenue for the government and encourages maximum effort from the suppliers of the factors of production.

laissez-faire An economic policy advocating that there should be little or no government intervention in the economy.

land Anything supplied by nature which helps to create wealth. It has two distinct characteristics: (a) it is fixed in supply and (b) it has no cost of production.

law of absolute advantage States that countries will trade with each other and benefit from the trade so long as each of the countries has an absolute advantage in one of the goods being traded. An absolute advantage exists when it takes less of the resources of one country to produce a unit of a product than it does of the other country's resources.

law of comparative advantage States that countries will trade with each other and gain from the trade so long as there is some relative difference in the efficiency of both countries in the production of the goods being traded.

law of diminishing (marginal) returns States that as additional units of a variable factor of production are used in conjunction with a fixed factor then at some stage the average output per factor employed will decrease.

law of diminishing marginal utility States that as a consumer consumes extra units of a good then at some stage the marginal utility derived from the consumption of the good will begin to decrease.

law of equi-marginal returns States that a consumer will be in equilibrium when he/she spends his/her income in such a way that the ratio of marginal utility to price is the same for all goods which he/she purchases.

leakages Any transactions that reduce the size of the circular flow of income, the main ones are taxes and imports.

legal tender The amount of an official currency which a creditor must accept in payment of a debt.

lender of last resort Describes the Central Bank when it lends cash to the commercial banks when there is a run on cash at the banks.

limit pricing An agreement between firms in an oligopoly market to set a relatively low price for their products which would make it unprofitable for new firms to enter the market. This can be done because the existing firms in the industry are already gaining from the economies of scale.

liquid asset Any asset which can be turned into cash quickly, e.g. government bonds.

liquidity preference The reasons why people want to hold onto their money rather than make it available for investment.

liquidity preference theory of interest States that the rate of interest is determined by the interaction of the supply of and the demand for money, where the supply of money is the amount in circulation and is fixed by the Central Bank. The demand for money is the reason people want to be in a liquid position.

Live Register A list of people under the age of 65 who are able and willing to work but who cannot find employment. They register at their local employment exchange for social welfare benefits.

long run A period of time sufficiently long so that all of the factors of production can be varied in quantity.

long run equilibrium of a firm (a) MR = MC to earn maximum profits, (b) AR is at least = AC to earn normal profits.

luxury goods Normal goods that have a high price elasticity of demand, i.e. they are very responsive to a change in their price, e.g. elective airflights.

macroeconomics Deals with broad aggregates within economic systems and the interaction between these aggregates. It deals with topics such as employment levels, national income, money supply, inflation and international trade.

marginal cost (MC) The addition to total cost brought about by the production of an extra unit of a product.

marginal efficiency of capital/investment (MEC or MEI) The addition to total profit brought about by the employment of an extra unit of capital.

marginal physical product (MPP) The addition to total production brought about by the employment of an extra unit of a factor of production.

marginal productivity theory of wages A firm will employ the quantity of labour at which the wage rate is equal to the marginal revenue productivity of labour.

marginal propensity to consume (MPC) The tendency to spend a percentage of the last increase in income on consumer goods.

marginal propensity to import (MPM) The tendency to spend a percentage of the last increase in income on imports.

marginal propensity to save (MPS) The tendency to save a percentage of the last increase in income.

marginal revenue (MR) The addition to total revenue brought about by the sale of an extra unit of a product.

marginal revenue product (MRP) The addition to total revenue brought about by the employment of an extra unit of a factor of production.

marginal utility (MU) The addition to total utility brought about by the consumption of an extra unit of a product.

Marshall-Lerner condition States that a devaluation of a country's currency will improve a country's balance of payments only if the sum of the price elasticities of demand for the country's exports and imports is greater than one.

merit goods/needs/wants Goods which society deems should be available to everybody at some minimum quantity, regardless of their income. These would include food, clothing, shelter, education and medical services.

microeconomics Deals with individual units in economics and the interaction between them, e.g. the individual consumer, the individual household and the individual firm. It deals with supply and demand showing how many goods will be produced and consumed at given market prices at given times.

mixed economy An economy where economic decisions are made partly by the government and partly by the market mechanism.

monetarism An economic theory that states that the size of the money supply determines the level of economic activity.

monetary policy The policy that controls the amount of money in circulation, interest rates and credit creation. It is determined by the ECB and implemented by the Central Banks.

money Anything that is accepted by the vast majority of people in exchange for goods and services.

money supply Traditionally, money supply refers to the amount of money in circulation. It is divided into two sub-divisions.

M1: The **narrow money supply** is the currency in circulation (outstanding) plus balances in current accounts in all licensed banks in the state.

M3: The **broad money supply** is M1 plus all other balances in licensed banks plus borrowings from other credit institutions, less interbank balances.

In more recent times we tend to identify three categories of money supply.

(Narrow) M1	(Broad) M 3 = M 2 +
Currency outstanding and overnight deposits	Repurchase agreements
(Intermediate) M2 = M1 +	Debt securities up to 2 years' maturity
Deposits with an agreed maturity up to 2 years	Money market funds/units
Deposits redeemable at notice up to 3 months	
Post office savings, bank deposits	

monopoly An industry in which there is only one producer of the product.

monopsony A situation where there is only one buyer in the industry.

multilateral trade When one country trades with many other countries and no significant percentage of its exports or its imports go to or come from any one other country.

multiplier The number by which an injection into the circular flow of income is multiplied in order to calculate the income created by the injection. The full formula for the multiplier is:

$$\frac{1}{1 - MPC + MPM + MPT}$$

national debt The total amount of money borrowed by central government and not repaid to date, less liquid assets available for the redemption of these debts at the same time.

national income The total amount of income earned by residents of a country who supply the factors of production in any given period. It is usually measured annually.

nationalisation The process of a national government acquiring the ownership of a private business or industry.

National Treasury Management Agency A body that manages the national debt, the National Pension Reserve Fund and other funds on behalf of the government.

near money Money lent for a very short period of time and repayable on demand. Credit cards and charge cards are also regarded as near money.

needs The basic requirements necessary to preserve life, i.e. basic food, clothing and shelter.

negative interest rate Occurs when the nominal rate of interest is less than the rate of inflation.

net factor income The term used in national income to describe the difference between income repatriated by Irish factors working abroad and income repatriated by foreign factors working in Ireland. It can be a negative or a positive figure.

neutral budget A budget that has neither an inflationary nor a deflationary effect on the economy.

nominal interest rate The rate of interest quoted by financial institutions.

non-price competition A situation where competitors in a market do not compete with each other by altering their prices but by emphasising product differentiation, e.g. (a) 'New Improved Brand', (b) giving better guarantees with their product and (c) sales promotions gimmicks.

normal goods Goods which have both a positive substitution effect and a positive income effect.

normal profit (NP) The minimum level of profit needed to keep an entrepreneur in production in the long run.

official external reserves A country's official holdings (under the control of the Central Bank) of foreign currencies, gold and other reserves such as SDRs with the International Monetary Fund.

oligopoly An industry in which there are only a very small number of very large firms, e.g. the commercial banking industry in Ireland.

open market operations Describe the Central Bank's buying and selling of bonds on the Stock Exchange when it is trying to influence the credit creating capacity of the banks.

opportunity cost Describes the alternative that you forego when you make a purchase. It arises from the fact that we have limited incomes and cannot satisfy all of our needs and wants.

optimum population When a country's average income per head is at its highest possible level under given economic resources.

overpopulation Describes when an increase in the labour force decreases the average income per head of the population under given economic resources.

paradox of thrift Sometimes, when there is an increase in the MPS this leads to a decrease in the level of demand, which leads to a decrease in the level of income and a decrease in the actual level of savings.

paradox of value Some goods have a high value in use but a low exchange value;

whereas other goods have a low value in use but a high exchange value. This is explained by the difference in their marginal utilities.

participation rate Describes the percentage of the active population who are either employed or available for work at any given wage rate.

Philips curve A graph showing the relationship between the level of unemployment and the rate of inflation.

price competition Competitors in a market compete with each other by trying to undercut each other's prices.

price discrimination When a firm charges two or more different prices for the same product on two or more different markets and the difference in price has nothing to do with any difference in cost in the markets.

price elasticity of demand (PED) Measures the relationship between a change in the price and the resulting change in demand for a product. Its formula is:

$$\frac{P1 + P2}{Q1 + Q2} \times \frac{\Delta Q}{\Delta P}$$

price indices *see* **consumer price index**

price leadership Refers to a situation in oligopoly where the dominant firm acts as a monopolist and sets a price which will earn it maximum profit. All other firms in the industry then accept this price.

price taker A firm that cannot determine its own price. The price that the firm receives for its product is determined by the interaction of the total supply of and total demand for that product in the industry.

primary liquidity ratio (PLR) *see* **cash ratio**

primary sector The sector of the economy that provides unprocessed food and industrial raw materials, i.e. farming, fishing, forestry and mining.

principle of equi-marginal utility *see* **law of equi-marginal returns**

private cost The direct cost to an individual or firm using a product.

privatisation The sale or transfer of public sector services or assets to the private sector.

production possibility curve (PPC) A graph that shows the different quantities of two goods that an economy could produce with limited productive resources. Points along the curve describe the trade-off between the two goods. The curve shows that increasing the production of one good reduces production of the other good.

progressive tax A tax that takes a higher proportion of income as taxable income increases, e.g. PAYE.

proportional tax A tax that takes a constant rate of tax from income as income rises.

purchasing power parity (PPP) theory States that in a free market, the rate of exchange of a currency will settle at the point where its internal and external purchasing powers are equal.

quasi-rent Any short-run economic rent earned by a factor of production. It happens because there is a temporary shortage of that factor, i.e. $D > S$.

quota A limit put on the number of units of a product that can be imported.

rate of exchange of a currency The price of one currency in terms of another currency.

rationing Imposing a limit on the number of units of a good that may be purchased by any individual, so that scarce commodities are divided out fairly among consumers, thus preventing any increase in the price of these goods.

real income The purchasing power of money income.

real interest rate The difference between the nominal interest rate and the rate of inflation. This can be either positive or negative.

rediscount rate This was the rate of interest that the Central Bank charged the commercial banks when it discounted first-class bills of exchange for the banks. This practice no longer continues.

regressive tax A tax that takes a higher percentage of income from the lower income earners than from the higher income earners, e.g. VAT.

rent of ability An economic rent that can continue to be earned in the long run. It usually applies to an entrepreneur who has exceptional business acumen and who cannot be easily replaced.

residual unemployment People who for medical reasons cannot work, and those people who just do not want to work.

retail banks Banks that operate extensive branch networks and deal directly with the general public. They publish interest rates and charges.

revaluation A country increasing the rate of exchange of its currency against other currencies.

revenue buoyancy A situation where the actual tax revenue in a year is significantly greater than that outlined in the current budget for that year.

rolled over debt The substitution of an old debt for a new one, e.g. if the government owes €1m to A it can borrow €1m from B to pay A.

sale and repurchase agreement Under this type of agreement the Central Bank offers to purchase the commercial banks' stock (or part of its stock) of government securities and to sell them back after an agreed period of time.

saving Describes not spending part of income.

Say's Law States that supply creates its own demand.

seasonal unemployment Some industries operate full scale only at certain times of the year. For the rest of the year the employees in this industry are seasonally unemployed.

secondary liquidity ratio (SLR) The ratio of liquid assets (usually government bonds) held by the banks to claims on the banks.

secondary sector The sector of the economy that processes the output of the primary sector and manufactures finished goods.

short run (SR) A period of time sufficiently short so that at least one of the factors of production being used is fixed in quantity.

short run equilibrium of a firm (a) MR = MC to either maximise profits or minimise losses and (b) AR must at least = AVC to cover its variable costs.

short-term facility rate (STF) The rate of interest that the Central Bank charges the commercial banks when they borrow cash from it for a very short period of time.

sight deposit account *see* **demand deposit account**

social costs The cost that society pays for the existence of a product, e.g. pollution and loss of a park in order to build a factory.

special deposits Deposits of cash that the commercial banks must give to the Central Bank. It is one of the Central Bank's means of restricting the credit creating ability of the commercial banks.

specific tax A tax levied on a good at a fixed amount irrespective of the price of the good, e.g. a €1 tax on a gallon of petrol irrespective of the price of a gallon of petrol.

stock appreciation Occurs when the value of capital stock increases.

structural unemployment Caused by the decline of a particular industry and when the skills acquired in this industry are no longer required elsewhere making it very difficult for the redundant workers to obtain employment anywhere else.

subsidies A direct payment to a producer from the government to keep down the market price of the product.

subsistence theory of wages States that wages will always remain at subsistence level. If wages increased above this level, workers would have bigger families, thus increasing the supply of labour, thereby causing wages to decrease. On the other hand, if wages went below the subsistence level workers could not afford to have as many children, thus creating a scarcity of labour and driving the wage rate back up again. This theory is associated with the classical economists.

substitute goods Two or more different goods that can be substituted for each other to satisfy any one need or want.

substitution effect The effect on demand of a change in the price of a product while real income remains unchanged.

supernormal profit (SNP) Profit that is above normal profit. It is a form of economic rent.

supplementary deposits *see* **special deposits**

supply (S) The number of units of a good made available for sale at any given market price at any given time.

supply curve A graph showing the relationship between market price and the quantity of a good made available for sale at any given time.

supply price of a factor of production The minimum payment that must be made to a factor of production to bring that factor into existence and to maintain it in employment.

supply schedule A table showing the supply of a good at any given market price at any given time.

tariffs Taxes on imports, usually charged as a percentage of the cost of the good.

tax wedge The difference between the cost to the employer of employing a person and that person's after-tax pay.

terms of trade The relationship between the price of a unit of exports and the price of a unit of imports.

Or

The number of units of imports that can be purchased with the money received from one unit of exports. The formula is:

$$\frac{\text{Index of Export Prices}}{\text{Index of Import Prices}} \times \frac{100}{1}$$

If the answer > 100 then the terms of trade are favourable, and they are unfavourable if the answer < 100.

tertiary sector The sector of the economy that deals with the distribution of finished goods and the provision of services.

time deposit account A bank account where notice of withdrawal must be given.

token money A form of money whose exchange value is greater than its intrinsic value.

trade cycle *see* **business cycle**

trade protection Refers to the measures adopted by a country to reduce imports.

transfer cost The minimum payment that must be made to transfer a factor of production from one industry to another.

transfer earnings The income that a factor of production could earn if it was transferred to its best alternative employment.

transfer payments Taxes levied on one person's income being given as income to another person, e.g. social welfare payments.

transitional unemployment People who are temporarily unemployed while moving between jobs.

true interest rate *see* **real interest rate**

underpopulation A country is underpopulated when an increase in the population leads to an increase in the average income per head under given economic resources.

utility The benefit or satisfaction derived from the consumption of a good.

variable costs (VC) Costs that change as the level of production changes, e.g. electricity and transport charges.

variable exchange rate The rate of exchange of a currency being determined by its supply and demand on a daily basis.

wage drift When the market wage rate is greater than the negotiated wage rate, or when the actual wage rate is greater than the official wage rate.

wage rate The price of one hour's labour.

wages fund theory *see* **subsistence theory of wages**

wages gap *see* **wage drift**

wealth A stock of goods and services.

Index